War in the Desert

By the same author:

ALPINE ELITE

AUSTRO-HUNGARIAN INFANTRY, 1914–18

GERMANY'S ELITE PANZER FORCE: GROSSDEUTSCHLAND

PANZER: ARMOURED FORCE OF THE THIRD REICH

PANZER ARMY AFRICA

PANZER GRENADIERS

THE KILLING GROUND

WAR ON THE EASTERN FRONT

With Matthew Cooper:

HITLER'S ELITE: LEIBSTANDARTE SS ADOLF HITLER

James Lucas

War in the Desert

The Eighth Army at El Alamein

ARMS AND ARMOUR PRESS

London — Melbourne

Published in Great Britain in 1982 by
Arms and Armour Press, Lionel Leventhal Limited,
2—6 Hampstead High Street, London NW3 1QQ
and at
4—12 Tattersalls Lane, Melbourne,
Victoria 3000, Australia

British Library Cataloguing in Publication Data
Lucas, James
War in the Desert
1. al'Alamayn, Battle of, 1942   I. Title
940.54'23   D766.9
ISBN 0-85368-549-5

The Eighth Army badge, .303 ammunition clip
and 'V' cigarettes on the jacket of this book were kindly
provided by the Imperial War Museum. Photograph
by Michael Dyer Associates.

Typeset by Typesetters (Birmingham) Limited.
Printed and bound in Great Britain at
The Pitman Press, Bath.

CONTENTS

MAPS AND DIAGRAMS

DEDICATION

The scene in which this book is set is a desert area of North Africa, a vast and mostly arid waste that covers nearly a thousand miles between the River Nile and the city of Tripoli. In all that inhospitable region, one area is set apart. It is a narrow strip of Egyptian territory between El Alamein, a wayside railway station some sixty miles to the west of Alexandria, and a native track some ten miles to the west, the Trigh Sidi Abd el Rahman. This unremarkable spot is the field of the Battle of El Alamein, fought out during the last weeks of October and the first weeks of November in the year 1942. That victory, won by principally British arms, was as important as the great contemporary struggle at Stalingrad. The triumph at El Alamein set in train a series of British and, later, Allied military victories that vanquished the Germans in Western Europe, just as the Red Army's victory on the Volga was the decisive battle that halted and flung back the German march to the east.

In these pages will be found accounts of the battle recalled chiefly by men in the lowest echelons of the British Army — the ordinary soldiers — for it is my intention as far as possible to let them recount the fighting in their own words. In some cases, it will be necessary to place their stories within the wider picture, and I shall then draw upon regimental or divisional records. This is because the fighting soldier's view of battle is limited. The attacking infantryman sees only the narrow strip of land over which he is advancing. His concentration is upon the ground he is crossing — for he is aware that death lurks on or in that ground — and the knowledge reduces the focus of his attention to the immediate and the close at hand. The tank driver sees little through the battle slit of his machine: swirling sand and the ground directly ahead limit his horizon. The tank gunner sees only the target framed in his sights. The ordinary artilleryman's world is the pit in which his gun rests, a world of fuze setting, of aiming and of violent explosions. The world of the mine-lifting Sapper is even more confined: it is restricted to the area around or below the mine that his detector or bayonet has located. Such men as these did not see the detailed general staff maps upon which both armies were set out in tidy chinagraph and upon whose surfaces the trained eye could see the swing of battle. Not for those at the bottom of the military hierarchy was there a full knowledge of plans whose unfolding would send them off on their several dangerous tasks. There were Orders Groups, of course. These were pre-battle briefings at which junior officers tried to explain the commander's intention and describe to their men the way in which it was intended that the battle should develop. But such O Groups did little, if anything, to enlighten the ordinary soldiers, excellent though the intention was. What does the composition of an army corps mean to a soldier whose military world is contained within the compass of a rifle company, a tank squadron, an artillery battery or the field company of Engineers in which he is serving?

This, then, is the war of the ordinary man, not that of politicians or generals, nor even of brigade or of battalion commanders, but of the fighting soldiers themselves. Some had spent years in 'the blue', as veterans called the vast and open spaces of the desert, crossing and recrossing the same ground in one offensive after another. At the end of each bewildering operation, they were left wondering what had been achieved for all their effort, and they questioned whether final victory would ever come. The Battle of El Alamein demonstrated that it would. The preparations made in the months before the offensive opened, the plan that was designed and the flexible battle fought to carry out that plan, all combined to produce the victory for which they longed and to which they had contributed.

It is by deliberate choice that most of those whose exploits fill these pages are soldiers. This is not to deny nor to diminish the vital part the navies and air forces played in the war; but I have chosen to stress the army's role and to include chiefly the stories and the actions of those fighting men who saw and fought their opponents on the ground.

All the events portrayed in this book happened forty years ago. The world has changed, and certain features of the Western Desert have also changed. The countries of Egypt and Libya are more prosperous now, and their peoples are more self-confident. Recent travellers report that the flies are gone, for now there are no rotting bodies or decaying food on which they can feed. The wrecks of guns and tanks that once littered the battlefield have vanished; only the hidden menace of the mines remains, and one day they too will have been cleared. It is all so different. And yet one thing remains constant: the desert is much as it always was. Out in 'the blue', away from the big cities, to stand alone brings back the memory of the desert's unbelievable quiet. The eye sees again the half-remembered vistas, the wide horizons, blue sky and baking sun. The landscape of the desert is usually a harsh one, but it is also one that can produce scenes of almost inexpressible beauty. A former soldier who goes out into the desert at night relives a past that is four decades dead. As one sits wrapped in the echoing silence of a desert night, a star shooting across the sky will take the mind back to other nights of youth and of danger, and eyes seek once more signal flares rising and falling in the dark night sky. Ears strain, almost by instinct, to hear again the rumble of distant guns or the clatter of tank tracks. And one remembers with deep emotion the comradeship of those with whom one shared great experiences.

DEDICATION

The men who served in the desert went on to other campaigns. The veteran quartet of 1st and 7th Armoured, 50th Tyne Tees and 51st Highland Divisions took part in the fighting for Sicily before going on to the liberation of Europe. The New Zealanders and the Indians were locked in battle throughout the length of the Italian peninsula, and won particular distinction in the battle for Monte Cassino. The 9th Australian went to war against the Japanese in New Guinea. The French, the Greeks and the other Allied and Imperial troops, all fought on until victory was won. For the Axis troops, after El Alamein there was only defeat. For the Panzerarmee, the end came when its units were forced to surrender in Tunisia. Very few German or Italian troops escaped from Africa to fight another day.

So many men. So many experiences. Those who survived the battles are scattered world-wide. Most will still remember the Battle of El Alamein, even though for some the memories may be bitter. Many consider the victory they won at El Alamein to be one of the great events of their lives, and recall the days with deep emotion. Michael Lee, once a platoon commander in the Northumberland Fusiliers, in reply to the question, 'Were they good days for you?', typifies the feelings of the many. His answer was, 'Oh yes. Happy days with my men. . . . I have always longed to meet them again. Where are all the Geordie men I loved and commanded, now?'

It is to the memory of such comradeship that I dedicate this book.

James Lucas, London, 1982.

ACKNOWLEDGMENTS

The idea of this book, the Battle of El Alamein from the view point of the ordinary soldier, was that of my dear friends Tonie and Valmai Holt. Because of the pressure of work connected with their successful battlefield tour company, they felt themselves unable to complete the work and passed to me the results of their early research. I built upon that foundation and then added details that I gained from interviews and correspondence with former soldiers in the United Kingdom, the Dominions and Europe. In addition to those comrades who had filled in and returned the questionnaires sent out by the Holts, there were many old soldiers who gave me details that have enabled me to complete the story.

No book is the product of a single person, and this one, more than any other I have written, is really the work of those comrades to whom I have already made mention — those former combatants who have recalled for me and given me leave to use their memories of the war in Africa. Some of their stories have been included verbatim; from others only a striking paragraph or a single telling sentence has been taken and woven into the narrative; and still others have had their words rewritten and included as part of one of the general accounts of action found in the text. In addition to the personal memories, I have drawn upon unpublished material in the form of unit war diaries as well as Army newspapers, and battalion, regimental or divisional histories.

My grateful thanks go to the officers of the several archives at home and abroad whose records were consulted. Particularly, I should mention my colleagues in the Department of Printed Books and the Department of Documents of the Imperial War Museum; and Messrs Charman, Clout and Reed. To illustrate the book, I have drawn heavily upon the archive of the Department of Photographs of the Imperial War Museum, the help of whose officers — my colleagues Mrs Bell, Messrs Hine, Pavey, Williams and Willis — is acknowledged here. To my wife Traude, whose encouragement sustained me in the months of writing, re-writing and reading the typescript, goes my love; as it does to my daughter, Barbara Shaw, who typed the book. I am also indebted to those who carried out research for me, particularly to my eldest grandson, Simon Shaw; and not least to my publishers and friends, Lionel Leventhal and his splendid staff, of whom David Gibbons, as editor of this book, was my closest collaborator. To them all go my sincere thanks for the help they so willingly gave, without which there would have been no book.

James Lucas, London, 1982.

1.

OFFENSIVE AND COUNTEROFFENSIVE
OPERATIONS FROM JUNE 1940 TO JUNE 1942

On 10 June 1940, war came to the African continent when Benito Mussolini, the Fascist dictator, declared that a state of hostilities existed between Italy and the Western Allies, France and Great Britain. The war situation at that time was a critical one for Britain. In the first six months of 1940, Germany had subjugated most of Western Europe. In a swift assault, she had defeated both Denmark and Norway. Even before military operations in that theatre had been completed, Hitler had begun a new war in the west and had fallen upon Holland, Belgium and France, overrunning the Low Countries in less than a week. There then followed a fast campaign during which the French Army was defeated and the British Expeditionary Force was forced to evacuate the Continent. In the dying stages of the fighting in the west, the Italian dictator, believing the Allies to be powerless, ordered the army in his Libyan colony to take the initiative and to attack Egypt. The Second World War, which had begun in Europe and now seemed to be dying down in that continent, had broken out in a new place. From June 1940 to May 1943, powerful military forces fought across the Western Desert of Libya and Egypt, that shallow crescent of Arab countries that lies on the southern shore of the Mediterranean between the 12th and 30th degrees of longitude east and constitutes, in the main, a bleak, empty and inhospitable waste.

At this point, before the fighting starts, it is perhaps appropriate to ask why three European nations fought in those Arab countries. For what did they battle so hard and pour out so much effort, such vast amounts of materials, into the campaigns? Surely, it could not have been merely for possession of a million square miles of sand?

THE BONE OF CONTENTION

To begin with, the importance of the Mediterranean in the unfolding of the Second World War must be understood, for that great inland sea binds together three continents: Europe, Africa and Asia. During the Second World War, no other area of the globe was of such strategic importance — it was the epicentre of a world-wide conflict. It follows then, that whoever dominated the Mediterranean controlled to a great extent the movement and supply of armies both in the eastern Mediterranean as well as in the Middle East.

Italy had conquered Libya before the First World War, and had added it to her older African possessions of Somaliland and Eritrea. In the years of Mussolini's dictatorship, from 1923 onwards, intense colonization had taken place in the Libyan possessions: Italian farmers were settled and towns of neat, whitewashed houses were planted along a narrow coastal strip of land, the only fertile soil in all the 400,000 square miles of territory.

Britain, not herself a Mediterranean nation, had by tradition been deeply involved in maintaining the balance of power in that area. Her strategy in time of war had always been a maritime one, relying principally upon the blockade of her enemies on the mainland of Europe. In earlier centuries those enemies had been France and Spain, and to contain them in the western Mediterranean the Royal Navy had occupied strategic bases in and around Gibraltar and as far east as the island of Malta. When the Suez Canal had been opened, the scope of Imperial defence had needed to be widened, for there were now two gateways to the Mediterranean. Britain already held the western one, Gibraltar. To dominate the eastern one, Britain signed a treaty under which she was permitted to establish and to maintain military and naval bases in Egypt. From those bases during the First World War the British Army under Allenby mounted a campaign against the Turks, the result of which was the destruction of the Ottoman Empire. British influence in the area expanded to cover not only the Canal's western approach, Egypt, but also its eastern approach, Palestine. During the locust years of peace, the 1920s and 1930s, the British Army as a whole was run down. Forces in the overseas garrisons suffered the most severe cuts. Nevertheless, commanders in the Middle East, although working on a hand-to-mouth basis, trained their men well, and were able to form the British troops in Egypt into a highly professional force, familiar with the desert, experienced in its many moods and trained to use it as an ally. Years before the outbreak of the Second World War, military expeditions tested the 'going' in the southern sand seas. Royal Engineer cartographers produced maps of such detail and accuracy that, during the desert campaigns, they were highly prized booty by the Germans, who had otherwise to rely upon the inaccurate and often fanciful information given in the maps issued by the Italian Comando Supremo.

One problem to be faced by both Britain and Italy, in the event of a war between them, was the reinforcement and supply of armies in Egypt and Libya, for neither was native to Africa. Supplies of men and equipment for their garrisons in those territories could only come from the mother country and, to assure the flow of supplies, control of the seas and of the air would be decisive. In the case of Great Britain, convoys to her armies in Egypt would have to run the gauntlet of enemy ships and aircraft operating in the Mediterranean. The alternative to forcing the passage was to pass convoys around the Cape of Good Hope. The Italian supply routes were not long, and could in theory be protected by Italy's huge navy and strong air force for the whole of the voyage between Sicily and the port of Tripoli. The Italians would, however, be facing the Royal Navy, a weapon of tremendous power; a force that would wage an aggressive war against the enemy convoys.

The third European power concerned with the fighting in Libya and Egypt was Germany. The Germans were neither native to the Mediterranean nor had they Imperial routes to protect. There were a number of reasons for their involvement. They were drawn in initially to rescue the Italians, who were in danger of being driven out of Africa. This was the German short-term objective. In the middle-term, Nazi strategy aimed at the destruction of British influence in the southern Mediterranean, and to help them achieve this they had in Libya a ready-made base. Some German writers have ascribed a third aim, a long-term one — the global strategy plan of a link-up with the Japanese. This concept anticipated a German pincer thrusting along the line of the northern Mediterranean, isolating Turkey and driving through Iraq. While this northern arm was striking for the oilfields of the Middle East, a second, southern, one from Libya would smash the British in Egypt and turn northwards through Palestine to meet the Iraq pincer. These two arms would then be joined by a third, which would come driving down through southern Russia and the Caucasus. The Germans envisaged that their armies in the Middle East, combined in a solid 'panzer' block, would then advance towards India, encountering in their march the forces of Imperial Japan driving westwards through India. A pair of arms, the one German and the second Japanese, would thus encircle the world.... It is hard to believe that such a grandiose scheme was ever taken seriously by the German Supreme Command.

These, then, were the protagonists. Great Britain saw victory in the Western Desert as a sealing of the blockade along the southern Mediterranean and as a stepping-stone to an eventual re-entry into Europe. Germany, too, saw the region as a stepping-stone to other, wider objectives. Italy alone was less concerned with global grand strategy: all she wanted was to hold her African Empire and, if possible, to enlarge it by the easy conquest of Egypt. It was the misfortune of Libya and Egypt for this clash of arms between the European nations to take place on their lands, across a hot and desolate desert wilderness that General von Ravenstein was to describe as 'a tactician's paradise but a quartermaster's hell'.

THE 'BENGHAZI STAKES'

The British Army's Middle East Command, against which Mussolini was preparing to march, had in peacetime embraced the territories of Egypt, Sudan, Palestine, Cyprus and Transjordan. That already vast

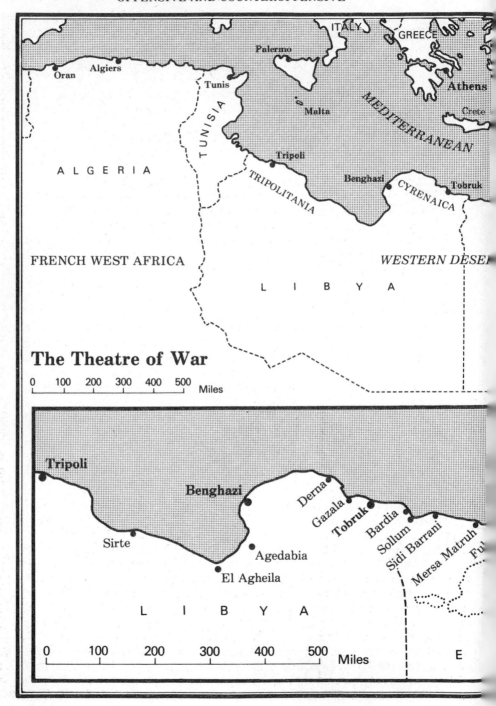

The Theatre of War

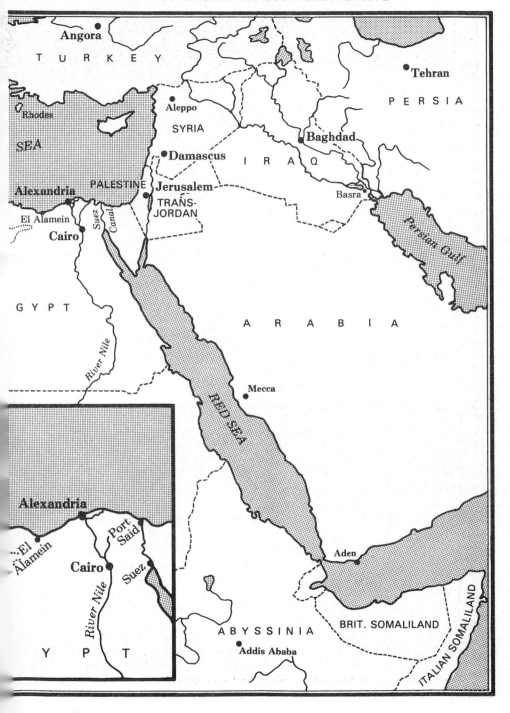

region was enlarged, following the outbreak of the Second World War, to include Aden, British Somaliland and the Persian Gulf. The whole was the responsibility of a single officer, the Commander-in-Chief, Middle East, who in 1940 was General Sir Archibald Wavell. From the countries over which he had control, he could deploy troops to meet an enemy threat from any direction: from the north, through Russia into Iraq and Iran; from the north-west, out of Turkey; or from the south flank, coming up out of Arabia. In June 1940, that enemy was Italy and the direction of her attack would be upon the troops holding the western flank, North Africa.

Following the Italian declaration of war, there were border clashes in which British tank and armoured car detachments showed their superiority and so dominated the Fascists that they were quiescent for months. Elsewhere in Africa, Italy had had some successes against the British, however. Between the colonies of Eritrea and Somaliland lay British Somaliland. Subjected to overwhelming attacks from her more powerful neighbours, the tiny British garrison withdrew. The Italians were jubilant and anticipated a rapid advance upon other British possessions in Africa. Fired with wild enthusiasm, Mussolini ordered Marshal Graziani, the Italian Commander-in-Chief in Libya, to strike across the Egyptian frontier and capture Alexandria. Graziani was well aware of the parlous state of his units and protested vigorously to Mussolini and to the Comando Supremo in Rome. He argued and prevaricated, refusing to move until the armadas of tanks that he had been promised had been delivered — but all in vain. He was still waiting for the arrival of the armour when the impatient Mussolini finally issued a direct order. The Army in Libya was to undertake the operation during September.

On the 13th of that month, the advance guard left Fort Capuzzo and led the mass of the army across the barbed-wire fence that marked the Egyptian/Libyan border. Within a week, the host had foot-marched 60 miles into Egypt and had taken the small town of Sidi Barrani. The 'glorious advance' of Graziani's army then halted, far earlier than the British Command had anticipated. Italian engineers proceeded to construct a fan of seven military camps, within whose perimeters the bulk of the Fascist forces lay inactive, in the role of an army of occupation, for over three months. Meanwhile, the British commander-in-chief had allowed the Italians to undertake their slow, hesitant and fearful advance, much to the annoyance of Winston Churchill, who wanted victories from his generals and neither retreats nor excuses for inaction. Instead, Wavell watched and waited until the enemy was complacent and less watchful. Then he struck.

On 6 December, while the hesitant hosts of Graziani still rested in the deserts of Egypt, they were surprised by Wavell's 'Thirty Thousand'. The victory for which Churchill longed was in train. An offensive planned as a five-day operation generated its own momentum. In a series of rapid blows, it drove the Italians out of

Egypt, across the width of Libya and very nearly out of Tripolitania. Had that occurred, then the war in North Africa might well have ended in the spring of 1941. Wavell's highly efficient British force, well led and confident, had destroyed the brave but badly-led Italian Tenth Army, a host more than ten times its size. In his counterstroke, Wavell had advanced his men more than 500 miles in ten weeks, mostly across trackless desert. During that short period of time, the British Cyrenaica Force, as it was known, had taken 130,000 prisoners, including seven generals — and this for a loss of less than 2,000 in killed and wounded. Ahead of Wavell lay the opportunity, once his losses had been made good and his outworn material had been replaced, to destroy the Italian Empire in Africa. But this was not to be his prize. Political decisions made in London called for the army in the Western Desert to be used in another theatre: Wavell, in obedience to those orders, removed the veteran divisions of his Command and sent them to Greece.

The defeat of Graziani's army caused Hitler to reconsider plans that the German Army High Command (OKH) had prepared to destroy British influence in the Mediterranean theatre of operations. One proposal was the despatch of a support group to underpin the Italian forces in Libya, and in view of the situation there the German leader gave orders that German forces be despatched. Italian morale was immediately raised by the reinforcement. It was not the mere addition of numbers, but the fact that experienced and battle-hardened German soldiers would take the field alongside the Italians.

When Erwin Rommel, the commander of the Afrika Korps, arrived in Tripoli, the Italians had been all but totally defeated. Within a few months, he had so firmly set his mark upon the Axis conduct of the campaign in Africa that he ceased to be the subordinate of the Libyan High Command. Rommel came to the desert with instructions to conduct an 'offensive defence', to act as a blocking force around Sirte. He had other ideas. On 31 March 1941, some six weeks after disembarking in Tripoli, he began offensive operations against the British. The speed of his assault was bewildering, and most of the ground that Wavell had captured from the Italians was retaken. Only the port of Tobruk held out against every attempt by the Axis forces to capture it. The German offensive halted at Halfaya Pass to regroup and to reprovision.

On 15 May, a British limited offensive, Operation 'Brevity', opened. This was aimed at gaining jump-off points for a later and much bigger offensive that would smash the German armour and raise the siege of Tobruk. Initially, the assault met with success, but then occurred the first real contest between the impetuous, cavalry-minded British armoured regiments in their under-gunned machines and German defences based on a line of 88mm guns. Not only did the German pieces outrange the armament of the British vehicles, but the 88s had the greater accuracy because they fired from a stable platform and not from a moving one, and the velocity of their shells tore apart the thin armour of the British tanks. A different type of war had come to the desert. In 1940, armoured cars had raided the Italians with light cavalry panache. But tactics that had obtained against the Fascists failed when applied by British tank crews to the Germans and their accurate, rapid-firing, anti-tank guns. At the end of a few days of battle, the outcome had been decided: Operation 'Brevity' had not succeeded.

Goaded by the Prime Minister into another premature action, Wavell launched Operation 'Battleaxe' on 15 June 1941. The plan was to hold German attention at Halfaya Pass with one column while others were sent in against Sollum, Fort Capuzzo and the German base at Sidi Azeiz. Rommel was condemned to inaction because of his supply problem, and was content to let the British armour immolate itself on his dug-in guns. Then, when the attackers had been weakened sufficiently, he unleashed part of his panzer force upon the dispersed British formations. Operation 'Battleaxe' died. The attempt by Eighth Army to raise the siege of Tobruk had failed, and most of the vehicles that had been sent to the desert with such high hopes of victory lay shattered and ruined. Churchill lost faith in Wavell — indeed, it is doubtful whether he had ever liked the taciturn, intellectual soldier who wrote poetry. For his part, Wavell considered that the Prime Minister's military career, beginning at Omdurman and ending with a short spell in the trenches of the Western Front, did not allow him to understand the unusual problems of fighting a battle in so singular a terrain as the desert. Wavell was replaced as Commander-in-Chief, Middle East, by Auchinleck, an Indian Army general who inspired confidence in Churchill.

From June to November 1941, there was a lull in the desert fighting. No major offensive was undertaken by either side. In this period of relative peace, both sides made ready for future battles and built up their strength. To Eighth Army there returned those divisions that had been victoriously campaigning against the Italians in Ethiopia, Eritrea and Somaliland. With this new strength, together with that of the new infantry divisions fresh from the United Kingdom, there was hope of being able to launch a successful attack to destroy the Axis armour and raise the siege of Tobruk. On the other side of no man's land, the newly-named 'Panzer Group Africa', consisting of three veteran divisions of the Afrika Korps, backed by equally veteran units of the Italian Army, trained and prepared for action.

It was the British who struck first. On 18 November, Eighth Army opened Operation 'Crusader'. The intent was the same as in 'Battleaxe' and the outcome was initially the same: however, 'Crusader' was a battle of attrition, and one in which the Axis forces finally came off worst. In the face of continuing British pressure, Rommel withdrew to El Agheila. Tobruk was relieved, but Eighth Army was overstretched and it needed urgent reinforcement.

On the world stage, a fresh crisis for the Allied powers had meanwhile arisen. In the Far East, the Japanese had opened a new war and, in a series of rapid blows, had overrun Burma and parts of Malaya; now they were threatening India. To counter that menace, convoys of British troops despatched from the United Kingdom to reinforce the army in Egypt were diverted to the Far East. Equipment intended for Eighth Army was being sent to Burma or was being convoyed to Russia to support the Red Army, which was battling at the gates of Moscow. From the Prime Minister's viewpoint in London, Eighth Army had given its opponents a hard knock in the 'Crusader' battles, and was in the dominant position; the desert army could do without the promised men and supplies, for these were needed more urgently in other theatres. Churchill's rationale was that Rommel had been forced to withdraw: therefore, Eighth Army must be winning.

Judging by losses alone, it would certainly seem that the Axis forces had been defeated. But this was a false conclusion. There were factors other than the casualty lists to be considered, among which was the temporary loss of British naval and air superiority in the Mediterranean. As a result of the Japanese entering the War, squadrons of British aircraft had been diverted to the Far East. By a strange turn of fate, it was precisely at the time when RAF strength in the Middle East had been reduced that that of the Luftwaffe was increased. This had occurred as a result of the transfer of squadrons from the Eastern Front, where the severity of the Russian winter had forced a scaling down of air operations. Concurrent with the loss of air superiority was the sudden reduction in British naval strength. Attacks by Italian frogmen and by U-boats reduced the number of the Royal Navy's major units in the Mediterranean, and then the Australian cruiser in those waters (HMAS *Sydney*) was withdrawn to serve in the Dominion's defence. During this period of crisis, naval superiority passed temporarily into enemy hands. Axis shipping was able to pass freely between Sicily and the ports of Libya and to reinforce the armies there on a massive scale. One convoy, for example, brought in 45 Panzer IVs, and other groups of ships conveyed a further 55 tanks as well as a great number of other types of armoured fighting vehicles, together with supplies of fuel. With this reinforcement, Rommel resolved to regain the initiative by mounting a short, sharp offensive. The intention was to destroy Eighth Army's armour and relieve the isolated Axis garrisons in Bardia and in the Halfaya/Sollum areas.

The offensive opened on 19 January 1942, under the cover of a blinding sandstorm and in a security blackout so tight that neither Rommel's superiors in Libya, nor the Comando Supremo in Rome, nor yet the German High Command were aware of his intentions. The German commander's panzer columns raced into action, and in a series of battles shattered the British armour in just under a week. Then German reconnaissance columns probed deep into the desert spaces.

Benghazi fell on the 28th, and by the second week of February the Axis forces had reached what was to become known as the Gazala Line.

From the middle of February, there was once again a period of relative calm. Both armies were extended along a line running inland from the coast and into the desert. Between them lay extensive and well laid out minefields, which were continuously improved and strengthened. A great number of the devices in the British fields had been taken from the Tobruk defences. That port now lay so far behind the British front-line that its defences were allowed to run down. The opinion held was that Tobruk was not endangered, and that its minefields could be better employed elsewhere. And so the armies in the Gazala position lay behind their gardens of death, as each prepared to take up the struggle once more.

THE 'GAZALA GALLOP'

In the late spring of 1942, the fortunes of the Axis powers were rising to a climacteric. The German Army held in subjection most of Europe between the Atlantic coast of France and the banks of the River Don in Russia. On the high seas, U-boat packs, enjoying the fruits of new technology, were sinking Allied ships in alarming numbers. In the Far East, the Japanese were driving out the Americans and British from their overseas possessions and seemed set to rule the Pacific. In Africa too, it was clear that the German-Italian armies were preparing themselves for a new offensive. On every front, democracy stood at bay.

It was certainly a situation to worry Auchinleck, the Commander-in-Chief, Middle East. In a memorandum to the Middle East Defence Committee, he warned that the Axis were gaining command of the seas in the eastern Mediterranean, and that the Allies could do nothing to prevent this. He advised the Committee that the British forces were preparing for an offensive against Rommel, but stressed that strategically it could have no effect upon the fighting in the other and principal theatres of operations, Russia and the Far East. In response to a bombardment of telegrams from Churchill, Auchinleck gave it as his intention to attack the Axis forces during the dark period of June. This ambition remained unfulfilled.

On 26 May, Rommel pre-empted the planned British offensive with a massive operation of his own. It opened with a feint attack in the north carried out by a predominantly Italian force, XXI Corps, supported by German troops. This was intended to hold British attention while the Italian XX Motorized Corps together with the Afrika Korps made the main effort in the south. The plan was for the advance to be made in bright moonlight and at a controlled speed, along the front of the British minefields and defended localities known as 'boxes'. At a point some miles south of Bir Hakim, the southernmost 'box' of the British line, the armoured strike-force would halt and reorganize, ready to enter into the next phase of the offensive. This was then to drive around the Bir Hakim 'box', thereby outflanking the British line, and drive northwards along the back of the British minefields and 'boxes' towards the sea. En route, they would engage and destroy the British armoured divisions. The open right flank of Rommel's force would be covered by the 90th Light Division.

The first part of the Axis plan succeeded brilliantly. The mass of over 5,000 vehicles drove by compass bearing and arrived at their rendezvous point at dawn. The advance northwards began, but then there came a disruption to the plan. Axis intelligence sources had not noted the presence of another 'box' south of Bir Hakim and the left wing formations of Panzerarmee struck this. The garrison of the 'box', the Indian 3rd Motor Brigade, held off the attacks of the Ariete Division and of two battalions of the 21st Panzer Division for nearly an hour, but then a strong attack by the 5th Panzer Regiment rolled over the under-armed Indian infantry. The Ariete then came up against the garrison of Bir Hakim, a force of Free French units, which halted the Italian unit's advance. As a result, during the afternoon of 27 May, there arose a crisis for the Germans. The forces that were to sweep along the line of British 'boxes' had encountered two new weapons; Grant tanks and 6pdr anti-tank guns. The combination of a reliable and well armed tank and a powerful anti-tank gun slowed the Panzerarmee advance. The manoeuvring forced upon the German and Italian units in an effort to fight down the opposition used up their petrol, and there were no supplies coming through. The garrison at Bir Hakim and British tank detachments had intercepted and destroyed the German 'soft-skin' vehicle columns. The attack was being starved to death.

Short of fuel and ammunition, the German and Italian divisions regrouped and withdrew towards the British minefields, which they then began to gap from both sides. The intention was to push corridors through the British fields and thereby shorten the journey the supply columns would have to make. To British eyes at that time, it seemed as if Rommel's forces were surrounded and in a hopeless situation. The German commander, on the other hand, saw his troops as being in a 'bridgehead', out of which they would burst when supplies came through. Once he had captured Bir Hakim and forced a breach in the Gazala Line, then his forces would have torn the British defences wide open. From such a position, he would then resume the northward advance and go on to destroy the British armoured formations.

Along corridors cleared in the British minefields, columns of lorries carrying supplies began to reach the panzers; Rommel could now enter upon the next stage of his plan. As a first move, he needed to take out a British 'box' that lay midway between Gazala and Bir Hakim. This was garrisoned by the 150th Brigade of the 50th Tyne Tees Division.

The 150th was destroyed after days of fighting an isolated and unsupported battle. Scattered British armour was launched in piecemeal attacks, but failed to dislodge the panzer forces. Then Rommel turned southwards, and the full force of the Axis attacks fell upon Bir Hakim. There, the French position rapidly became hopeless, and on 10 June they were ordered to withdraw. The reduction of Bir Hakim assured a firm supply line to Rommel's forces, and he then sent a panzer column northwards while his other units attacked the Gazala Line 'boxes' in turn. During its advance, the column heading northwards overrolled the headquarters of the 7th Armoured Division, thereby leaving this experienced tank division of Eighth Army without leadership at the height of the battle. Only days later, the German column was in position near El Adem and was threatening Tobruk.

12 June 1942 was a day of disaster for Eighth Army. The two German panzer divisions, acting in concert, smashed the British armoured reserve, and at the end of the day Eighth Army could muster only seventy 'runners', while the German and Italian armoured divisions had between them more than 160 machines. Two days later, faced with the prospect of utter defeat, Ritchie, commander of Eighth Army, ordered a withdrawal from the Gazala Line. The positions that Eighth Army was supposed to hold, as directed by Auchinleck to Ritchie, were west of Tobruk; but the Eighth Army commander had

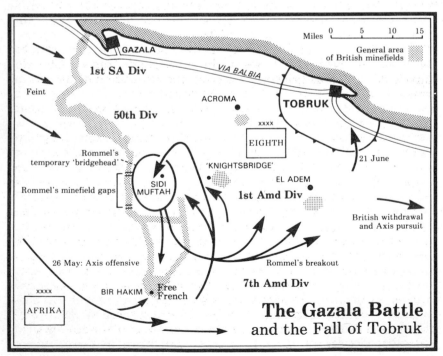

The Gazala Battle and the Fall of Tobruk

ordered a retreat to the line of the Egyptian frontier, and it was to there that the British and Allied units streamed — not always in orderly and disciplined columns. El Adem, the key to Tobruk, fell on 16 June; one day later, the last remnants of the British armoured force were flung back near Sidi Rezegh.

Now, with no threat to his flank, Rommel advanced upon Tobruk. That town had become a symbol of British resistance, and it was to destroy that symbol that the German-Italian army opened upon the town the full fury of their might. The Luftwaffe deployed its aircraft on a massive scale. Nearly 600 sorties were made on 20 June, the first day of battle. A crushing aerial bombardment and the employment of every available gun in the Axis forces covered the attack of the panzer and infantry formations. This went in across minefields that no longer held mines, for these had been removed to thicken the Gazala Line. The German main effort was made against the point of the town's defences that were known to be weak. In an explosion of fire and movement, the Afrika Korps drove through the shattered defences and forced the surrender of the town on 21 June. Rommel was jubilant. Among the stores that fell into his hands were 1,400 tons of petrol, 2,000 lorries and 5,000 tons of food. If the panzer units could maintain the advance, and if supplies could be brought into Tobruk, then there was no need, as he saw it, for Panzerarmee to halt along the line of the Egyptian frontier. Those had been his orders: he was to halt at the frontier while other Axis forces assaulted and captured Malta. But in Rommel's eyes there was now no longer any need for the Malta enterprise — his men had captured Tobruk.

To British strategists, Tobruk had little real significance, but politicians of both sides saw it in propaganda terms. Churchill considered its fall as grievous, affecting the reputation of the British armies. Hitler made Rommel a field marshal for his victory and, not to be outdone, Mussolini promoted to the same rank his senior commanders, Cavallero and Bastico.

Meanwhile, 'up the blue' and east of Tobruk, men were still fighting and dying as British units stood and carried out rearguard actions, seeking to hold back the onrushing panzers, or flung themselves, their weapons and their vehicles into defiant counterattacks. Alarmed at Ritchie's failure to control the battle, Auchinleck took over command of Eighth Army. He had wanted the army to withdraw only a short distance, but realised that it would be unwise to confuse his commanders and their men with conflicting orders. He allowed the main body of his army to head eastwards, and placed rearguards in front of Mersah Matruh. Churchill promised him 300 Sherman tanks, for it was armour the army needed. But the Shermans did not arrive straight away, and in reply to more insistent messages from Churchill, demanding action, Auchinleck pointed out that Eighth Army was trying to train a force and to use it on the battlefield at one and the same time. He then went on to explain that infantry masses were no use without guns and tanks, and that infantry could not win battles in the desert so long as the enemy had superiority in armour. It was unpalatable to the Prime Minister, who saw in them a lack of will to attack and, therefore, a valid reason to replace the Commander-in-Chief, Middle East, with a more dynamic man. . . .

It was not in Rommel's nature to allow an opponent to escape to fight another day. His Order of the Day, issued after the fall of Tobruk read, 'We have taken in all over 45,000 prisoners and destroyed or captured more than 1,000 armoured fighting vehicles and nearly 400 guns. During the long and hard struggle . . . you have dealt the enemy blow after blow. Now for the complete destruction of the enemy. During the days to come I shall call upon you for one more great effort to bring us to this final goal.' He urged his troops on and they responded, carrying out his orders however demanding, for they knew that Rommel spared no one − least of all himself.

Inspired by their seemingly-tireless commander, the German troops fought on and on, with the mirages of Cairo and Alexandria to spur them. They advanced 100 miles on 24 June, and their reconnaissance battalions were by that date well inside Egypt. Two days later, in a fresh burst of energy, the Afrika Korps burst through a ten-mile gap at Mersah Matruh between X Corps and the 1st Armoured and the New Zealand Divisions and began to roll them up. Entries in war diaries of the period reflect chaos. From Eighth Army Headquarters, orders went out that, in effect, authorized each corps commander to act as he saw fit in the best interests of his own formation. The result was an almost total lack of co-operation between the individual corps and also between them and Army Command. There were a great number of small and isolated actions carried out in which groups of outnumbered soldiers fought desperately to gain time. In such battles the 1st Armoured and the New Zealand Divisions lost heavily. On 29 June the port of Mersah Matruh, some 140 miles east of Tobruk, fell to the Germans. There seemed to be nothing between the panzer spearheads and the Suez Canal except groups of fleeing British troops.

1 July 1942 is a date and a day that has acquired the cynical name 'Ash Wednesday'. Alarmed by the storming approach of the enemy, British official bodies, the Embassy and General Headquarters in particular, began to burn confidential files. Clouds of smoke carried black paper ash up into the Cairo air, and rumours spread among the native population that the British were preparing to leave. Major units of the Royal Navy steamed out of the base at Alexandria, and the Army began to prepare for street fighting in the principal cities. C. P. Wyborn, at that time a Wren Writer (a female clerk in the Royal Navy), was working in the old Egyptian Royal Palace at Ras el Tin when the first news of the Gazala battle came in and it seemed as if the rout of Eighth Army was complete. 'A short spell of intensive bombing eventually led to the decision to declare Alexandria an 'open city', and the withdrawal of all service personnel began. This had been

anticipated and preparations begun for such a contingency. The particular job of the group of which I was a member was to ensure that three copies of all the highly-secret reports and records were made and packed in 'coffins' (the naval term for the chests provided for this purpose), and to destroy originals and any extra copies that might exist. This took some considerable time . . . we had seen everything packed and sealed . . . we had no idea what lay in store for us . . . nor, apparently had anyone else. We were conveyed to the railway station and loaded into a train made up of cattle trucks.

'At Ismailia an emergency base had been set up . . . we continued our journey to the SS Princess Kathleen anchored some distance offshore. This was to be our home for some weeks and an uncomfortable one it proved to be . . . the ship was alive with enormous cockroaches. . . . The heat and humidity were intense, washing facilities primitive and very inadequate, and altogether conditions were pretty grim. Morale was reasonably high however, and discipline was kept up with morning parades each day when we were expected to present ourselves for inspection in as smart a condition as possible. Air raids were frequent as the enemy attempted to bomb the oil refineries at Suez, and watching the flares and anti-aircraft fire became our nightly entertainment. . . . When we returned to Alexandria it was heartening to see how much our presence was welcomed by the few remaining service personnel in the city. . . . It was also amusing to see how the local population had anticipated the defeat of the Allies. Formerly, from every store and window looked down the features of the Allied leaders, Churchill, Roosevelt, Stalin and Chiang Kai-Shek. These were now replaced by pictures of Hitler, Goebbels, Goering, Mussolini and their minions, although the local people seemed rather confused at the continued absence of the Germans and Italians and the prevalence of British uniforms.'

Contingency plans had indeed been drawn up for the complete evacuation of Egypt and for Eighth Army to divide and withdraw — one part of it up the Nile and the other into Palestine. The civilians who stood to lose most if the Germans occupied Egypt made their own arrangements, and choked the exits from Cairo and Alexandria with masses of cars and lorries. A run on Barclay's Bank in Cairo resulted in the paying out of a million pounds in cash in one day. There were many Egyptians, however, who looked forward with keen anticipation to a British defeat, and who expressed their feelings in small but obvious ways. The number of incidents rose where well educated natives replied to questions put to them in English by spitting at the enquirer. There was a general hatred of foreigners, of the French and British, which mounted as the situation grew more tense.

The 'Gazala Gallop' had cost Eighth Army 50,000 men, and the front-line units were reduced to almost nothing. But it was upon those men that the might of Panzerarmee's next blow would fall. Doggedly and determinedly, the fighting units stood to arms.

2.

STALEMATE

FROM JULY TO SEPTEMBER 1942

By the end of June 1942, the men of the Panzerarmee believed they could smell the heady perfume of victory. The British were defeated! Except, that is, for a remnant or two who were holding some positions at an obscure railway station called El Alamein and those other British who, scattered by the fury of Rommel's offensive, were streaming eastwards towards the Nile, hoping to escape the pursuing panzers. The momentum of the Gazala battle might be sufficient to take the German armour to the very gates of Alexandria. Corporal Kingston of a British Signals detachment, quartered in a vermin-ridden wooden hut in a camp near Mena, was certainly aware of the danger: 'We knew there was a flap on. Convoys of trucks carrying all manner of things passed down the road out of the desert and towards Cairo. The Sappers had built auxiliary bridges across the Nile. We thought they were erected to speed the flow of vehicles across the river so that they could take up positions on the other side. Rommel and his men were really only just up the road. A couple of hours drive away, about the distance from London to Brighton. And it didn't seem that we could stop him. According to reports, we had lost most of our guns, nearly all our tanks, and the PBI was being rounded up en masse somewhere near Gazala. The 50 Div had taken a pasting. Tobruk had fallen. It was a rotten period.

'Yet with all that, with the enemy only a couple of hours' drive away, life in the Mena hotels still carried on as if there was no threat, no danger. The 'Cairo Canaries' as we called the staff officers at headquarters, didn't seem to care that a determined panzer colonel might soon be driving past at the head of a column of Nazi tanks. The Canaries sat there drinking their iced drinks, dancing, chatting to the ladies and to the rich gyppos who came out to Mena to escape the heat of Cairo. I reckon that most of the wogs wanted the Germans to win. Certainly the student mobs did, and hundreds of them used to demonstrate in the streets of Cairo, shouting slogans and clapping their hands. Lots of Jews left Cairo about that time, taking tickets into Palestine. The roads out of Cairo were choked with cars. There were masses of people at the railway stations all trying to get away and leave the city. All frightened by the rumours that these were the last trains which would leave the city. There were Greeks, Jews, French and the indefinables: I suppose these were Armenians. According to the SIB officers, they had passports for every country in the world.

They were all trying to buy tickets for Aleppo, Turkey or East Africa.

'I saw ambulance convoys coming back from the desert and also troop carriers full of wounded. The men in the open 3-tonners were nearly all asleep. They looked shagged out. All of us in my unit (we were a link station) wondered if we would be ordered to pull back across the river or whether the Army had forgotten all about us. Whenever we heard armour we thought it might be a column of Mark IVs coming down the road. If we saw armoured cars we all thought it might be Eighth Army rearguard coming by to tell us that they were the last vehicles and that the next ones we would see would be those of 21st Panzer. Of course, it didn't happen like that, and the fear that we had been forgotten soon went when orders came for us to move up the blue. New divisions were coming from Blighty, and 51st Highland, which had just come out, needed to become acclimatized. They were to take over our camp. The bugs in the Mena barracks would soon make the Jocks realize that Egypt was a land of blood suckers — animal and human.'

The British were beaten! Axis propaganda machines poured out a flood of praise upon their victorious troops and eagerly anticipated the final thrust that would take Rommel and his men to the Nile. Mussolini flew to Libya, heavily escorted by fighter aircraft, and prepared to lead a victory march through the principal cities of Egypt mounted on a magnificent stallion.

The British, however, were not beaten. It may well have been considered by other people that they had been defeated. The soldiers of Eighth Army did not realize this. Puzzled they were at the rapidity with which they had had to withdraw. Baffled they were. But defeated they were not. An Egyptian, a member of the Nationalist Wafd Party, is reported to have watched the columns of the desert army pouring down the western road towards Alexandria in the days following the battle at Gazala. German radio stations had told of the British defeats in the desert, facts that had been admitted by the BBC. The Egyptian civilian, a graduate, a politician and a highly intelligent man, believed the German stories of a routed army fleeing for its life, and he had gone out to see and to rejoice in the ruin of the occupation force of his country. He had gone out to see the shattered British stream in panic towards the Nile. He was disillusioned. It was certainly true that columns of military transport choked the roads. But those columns passed him at correct speed and at regulation distances. There was some confusion with artillery batteries mixed in with armoured cars and motorized infantry, but this was not the undisciplined mob he had expected to see. The dust-covered soldiers sitting in the backs of the lorries did not look panic-stricken — they looked bored. From some vehicles came raucous singing, and when a column halted there was a scramble as men flung themselves from the lorries. But this was not so that they could rush blindly into the desert in fear: they wanted to get a fire going. Within minutes of halting, there was a brew-up going at the side of nearly every vehicle. The British were taking tea. Some of this so-called panic-stricken rabble even began to kick a football. It was clear that the British were too mad to realize that they had been defeated. The Egyptian academic returned home a sad man. The British had only suffered a setback.

THE BATTLEFIELD

In his book *Nine Rivers from Jordan*, Denis Johnston, at that time a BBC reporter, described El Alamein in these words: 'We got out of our trucks and turned off to the left at a crossroads. Presently, we drew up by the empty sidings. There was a sort of goods yard and a compound surrounded by barbed-wire on a line of crazy poles. Behind the station buildings stood a row of shattered shacks with their doors hanging open. The whole place was littered with empty barrels and broken crates, and everywhere the brickwork was chipped and pock-marked by machine-gun bullets. Where the road crosses the metals stood a signal, its arm inappropriately set at "safety". The entire neighbourhood seemed to be completely deserted and, as I mounted the platform, I read on the front of the building the name of the place, "ALAMEIN". A small railway station set in the midst of some hundreds of miles of nothing whatever; that is all there is at Alamein.'*

The battlefield was not big. At its narrowest, there were barely ten miles between the British forward defence lines and the Rahman track in the German rear. The battlefield from north to south was about forty miles wide as the crow flies. In the north, Eighth Army's line touched the sea, ran through salt marshes and then entered a two-mile wide strip of land through which ran the parallel lines of the main road and the railway track. Farther inland was the limestone plateau upon whose gritty surface most of the fighting in the October offensive took place.

Rising out of the desert there were pieces of high ground that afforded good observation, and both sides sought to seize those and to incorporate them into their defensive complexes. The British held the high ground around El Alamein station and two low hills, Tel el Eisa and Tel el Mukhkhad. Thereby they dominated the ground towards the German held Miteiriya Ridge and Kidney Ridge, its northern extension. That high ground ran on a generally north-south line and thus formed a barrier to any advance by Eighth Army. To the southeast of Miteiriya and some twelve miles inland was the long and narrow length of Ruweisat Ridge, running on an east-west line. The extreme western end of Ruweisat was in Axis hands, but Indian troops of XXX Corps held the remainder of the feature. To the south of

* Verschoyle [Deutsch], London, 1953.

Ruweisat lay Alam Nayil Ridge and to the east of that Alam el Halfa Ridge. Both these pieces of ground were held by Eighth Army, and both ran in an east-west direction.

The course of the fighting between the end of August and October was to be dominated by two battles: that of Alam el Halfa, a German offensive, and Operation 'Lightfoot', Montgomery's Alamein. In both operations the key to victory lay in the possession of certain ridges. For the Germans in their attack, the need to gain either Ruweisat or Alam el Halfa Ridges was paramount, for these dominated the central and the southern parts of the battlefield. For the Eighth Army's forthcoming offensive, the vital ground was Miteiriya Ridge and its extensions in the northern sector of Panzerarmee's front. The seizure of those high points would allow Eighth Army to dominate the ground up to a native track, the Abd el Rahman trigh. The principal Axis minefields and defences lay in front of the Rahman track; once across it and the Battle of El Alamein was as good as won, for behind it lay open desert. Victory in the Battle of Alam el Halfa and in the Battles of El Alamein depended very largely upon these low outcrops of rock, unknown until battle gave them immortality.

Surprising though it might appear, the selection of El Alamein as the place at which the British Army would stand at bay to face the Axis assaults after Gazala was not an accidental choice of ground. The position was well chosen: a narrow front with flanks that could not be turned, set upon high ground that afforded good observation over that open plain across which the attacking Panzerarmee would have to come. Auchinleck had observed at a pre-war map exercise in the United Kingdom that the El Alamein position was the barrier to any direct assault coming from the west, and he had added to its strength during his time as Commander-in-Chief, Middle East, by ordering additional fortifications to be prepared.

There had been no defences at all until Graziani's army began its advance upon Alexandria in 1940, but then a start was made at preparing the ground and erecting the first positions. When Wavell's offensive destroyed the Italian army, the threat to Egypt seemed to have receded and the pace of construction slowed. This was to be the pattern of events over the next years. Any enemy drive towards Alexandria resulted in intensive defence activity; once the danger had lapsed, the effort was reduced. In April 1941, the 50th TT Division was set to work, and existing positions were improved and increased in number. In the autumn of that year, the pace of work was once again increased, this time using other units. The result of this new flurry of activity was the construction of three large defended localities along a line running from El Alamein station to the Quattara Depression. The first and largest of these defensive areas was intended to hold an infantry division and was sited around El Alamein station to defend the coast road, the railway track and the water supply. The other two, the Deir el Quattara and the Jebel Kerag, both natural defensive positions and both located in the south of the line, were each intended to hold a brigade group and were sited to defend the approaches to the ridges of Ruweisat and Alam el Halfa.

Late in 1941, pillboxes were constructed in the El Alamein line to hold anti-tank guns. Observation posts were established and trench lines laid out. The ground around each of the three positions was extensively and thoroughly enclosed with barbed-wire and simple belts of mines. There were even elementary anti-tank ditches dug in the limestone rock, but in the event these proved to have little practical value. Included in the defensive works and set underground were hospitals, store rooms and headquarters complexes. Each of the defensive areas had piped water, drawn from large underground reservoirs constructed in the immediate area of the El Alamein railway station and pumped through a pipeline from the River Nile, nearly 60 miles away. The dependence of the army upon the single coast road to supply the growing number of divisions was an intolerable situation that was resolved by laying out desert tracks giving access to the battlefield zone. These were specially routed to avoid the worst 'going', but where this had to be crossed, a Sommerfeld track, a wide wire mesh, was laid upon the loose desert surface to give grip to lorry tyres. One important length of such track was laid from Mena, a suburb of Cairo, to join with 'Barrel' track, which led from the Nile into the forward defence zone at El Alamein.

The forward defensive positions had been laid out and prepared, but Eighth Army Command was aware of the need for a defence in depth, so defensive works, chiefly concrete pillboxes and field fortifications were constructed at several places along the line of the Nile and of the Suez Canal. Thus, along the Canal, the Nile and along the western edge of the Delta, there stretched a long-stop line of defences that backed those already finished or under construction in the principal defence line at El Alamein. And, to support the army in the forthcoming operations, eleven new desert landing strips were constructed.

In addition to the semi-permanent defensive works, there was another less obvious and more flexible type of barrier — the minefield. The mine, and particularly the anti-tank mine, exerted a tremendous influence upon the course of operations in the desert. By a skilful siting of fields, an enemy attack could be channelled into predictable routes of approach or his advance halted completely. Mines permitted a commander to hold a great length of front with a minimum of troops. At the time of the first battles in Libya, none of the major armies had appreciated that mine warfare was an operational skill to be mastered, or that it had strategic as well as tactical capabilities. Once that appreciation had been made, both sides acted quickly and laid out large numbers of devices, often incorporating existing enemy fields into their own defensive complexes.

Newly-laid fields overlaid, crossed or intersected older ones, so that the Western Desert, particularly the area west of El Alamein, became

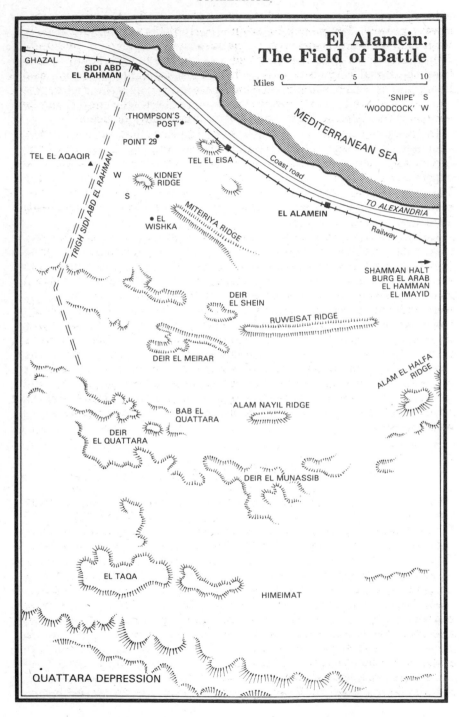

El Alamein:
The Field of Battle

a deadly maze to be traversed in the fearful knowledge that danger was always present. The precise location of early fields was seldom known, for it had not been the practice of the minelaying Sappers to distribute field traces to the other arms of service. In the British Army it had been the Royal Engineers alone who were responsible for laying and lifting mines, and this knowledge had been closely guarded; but now it was to be shared among infantrymen and others who might, in the course of the fighting, have to lay or lift the deadly devices.

In the first years of the desert campaign there had been a critical shortage of British official anti-tank mines, and the Army had been forced to issue contracts to local light-engineering companies to supply mines of a pattern known as the EPI (Egyptian Pattern Mark I). This was a highly unstable device, dangerous when being laid and even more so when being lifted, for its gelignite filling sweated in the heat. That sweat was nitroglycerin.

In those days of crisis, when the Royal Engineers depended largely upon local supplies of mines, these were laid very sparingly in small 'boxes' around fortified positions, or placed in strips across tracks and areas of good 'going'. When supplies improved and standard pattern British mines were received in large numbers, then the narrow strips were widened to become belts and the ground between 'boxes' thickly sown. An area of 'boxes' linked by dense concentrations of mines was known as a 'marsh'. The British positions at El Alamein were eventually to be covered by three large 'marshes' extending from the coast to the Taqa plateau, behind which other 'marshes' were set out on sensitive sectors of the front or across routes of easy access. Behind its belts of mines and protected by its concreted defences, Eighth Army would meet Panzerarmee's onslaught on a battleground of its own choosing.

THE FIRST BATTLE OF EL ALAMEIN

As it turned out, the momentum of Rommel's headlong advance from Gazala was insufficient to allow the panzers to crash through the El Alamein defences, and Rommel's attempts at forcing the narrow defile between the Mediterranean and the Quattara Depression were halted. The first of these attempts came in during the afternoon of 30 June when, after a 40-mile drive through the burning day, Rommel's forces bumped against the outposts of the El Alamein line. They cannot really have been called a force, for on that day the Afrika Korps mustered only 55 tanks. But Rommel was impatient to push on. He knew that the British must not be given time to recover, or they would improve their defences and stiffen their resistance. Yet the German leader also knew that he had driven his men hard. The Germans and the Italians had been through five weeks of almost continuous battle, and had long passed the limits of human endurance. Nevertheless, he had to ask them for one further effort if he was to 'bounce' the British positions.

Obsessed with the need to press on, Rommel spent too little time in reconnaissance and paid the price. When his advance re-opened at 03.00 hours on 1 July, the 15th Panzer Division crashed into an infantry brigade holding strong and prepared defences at Deir el Shein. The presence of British troops in that place had not been reported, and the Indian regiments — new to battle — held off the 15th and then the 21st Panzer assaults and delaying the Axis advance for almost a whole day. During the fighting, British armour arrived in the area and chased 15th Panzer from the field. In its sector, 90th Light Division had done no better: the divisional 'sitrep' that evening reported that its movement forward had been halted and that its infantry was digging-in. 1 July had been a disastrous day for the Panzerarmee and there had been heavy losses, particularly among the panzer regiments. The daily strength return reported that the Afrika Korps had only 37 'runners'. Rommel's attempt to pass the Afrika Korps and the 90th Light Division round the southern defences of the El Alamein line had failed.

A resumption of the attack on the following day brought no better result. The 90th Light made no ground at all and was subjected to aerial bombardment by the 'Party Day Rally' Mitchells, eighteen aircraft that flew across the skies in perfect formation and bombed with frightening precision. A counterattack against the 21st Panzer Divisions launched by the 4th Armoured Brigade forced the Germans back along Ruweisat Ridge. By evening, the strength of the Afrika Korps had shrunk to 26 tanks.

Both on the 2nd and then on 3 July, German infantry and armour supported by the Stukas, the Black Hussars of the air, pounded the British positions. Time after time the grenadiers and the panzers drove in; time after time they were held and then driven back, for it was clear that now the British had recovered and were prepared to wait for the attack to roll in upon them. Then, from their prepared defences and holding their fire until point blank range, they destroyed the Axis assaults. The main effort made by Panzerarmee on that day was south of Ruweisat Ridge, and the panzer attacks chiefly against the 1st Armoured Division were fought to a standstill. The German line, for all the effort that had been made, had reached a point only nine miles east of the Deir el Shein. British counterattacks came in, and the New Zealanders in one spirited advance succeeded in overrunning parts of the Italian Ariete Division before going on to drive back elements of the Brescia Division from its positions at the western end of the El Meirar Depression.

The strength returns sent in by the Afrika Korps on the evening of 3 July indicate the fierceness of the fighting and how determined had been the resistance by Eighth Army. The strength of each German division in the Afrika Korps had sunk to about 1,500 men, with the

Italian formations in even worse shape: Ariete, for example, had only five tanks and two guns. There comes a time when all the sacrifices and efforts are pointless, and the wise commander who sees that point arriving calls off the attacks and regroups. Rommel told OKH that the offensive was being broken off, and in this acceptance of the fact that the Panzerarmee was unable to crash the El Alamein line came, perhaps, the realization that time had run out for him. Rommel's frontal assaults against Eighth Army in the El Alamein positions had failed. The British were entrenched and resolute. The defences they were holding were the last naturally strong ones before the Nile, and they were determined to hold them.

With the Axis halted temporarily, it was the turn of the British to launch their attacks, and these came in at the Deir el Shein sector, seeking to crumble the Axis resistance. Throughout that hot July there was a series of attacks and counterattacks aimed at fixing the front, each side striving to establish a strong tactical position. The first of that series of operations was made on 4 July when the 15th Panzer was pushed back along Ruweisat Ridge. The determined attack by Eighth Army seemed likely to capture all the high ground, but the advance died in the fire of dug-in 50mms and 88s and repeated Stuka dive-bombing raids. The British advance halted, but the intention of the offensive had been realized in that most of the ridge had passed into British hands: only the extreme western edge was still held by the Germans. The awareness that, for the moment, he had lost the initiative must soon have come to Rommel, for on 5 July he ordered the laying of minefields and began the layout of defensive positions.

On 10 July, the Australians, posted in the coastal sector, launched a determined assault that not only smashed the Italian Sabratha Division but captured from the Italians the Tel el Eisa hill. Reacting to pressure in the most sensitive part of his battle line, Rommel brought northwards the 21st Panzer Division to block any further British advance in the coastal sector. With the German armour now drawn off, attacks were launched against the Italian Pavia and Brescia Divisions holding the central sector. On Ruweisat Ridge, the 21st Panzer reappeared and fought for three days to regain the high ground. While that fighting was raging, the Australians struck again and beat the Trieste Division, capturing 800 men. Once again the strength returns show how desperate was the situation facing the Panzerarmee. More than two-thirds of its infantry force, one-third of its field guns and more than a half of the anti-tank guns had been lost. On 21 July the Afrika Korps had only 42 tanks, although there were nearly 100 undergoing repair; the Italians had 50. In Eighth Army the 1st Armoured Division had over 170 machines ready for action, and in the 23rd Armoured Brigade, which had arrived recently, there were a further 150.

Then occurred a mistake that shows how easily the fortune of battle can turn. Auchinleck re-opened his offensive on 21 July along

Ruweisat Ridge, hoping to smash the Afrika Korps and to expel the German forces from the high ground they held. The fighting for the feature was as bitter as ever, and in a night battle the New Zealanders lost nearly 700 men. Early in the morning of 22 July, the 23rd Armoured Brigade, ten days out from England but at full strength, was ordered forward. Its armoured regiments roared past the New Zealand flank and blundered into a minefield. There the tanks halted, and while they stood immobile they were shot to pieces by the panzers and the accompanying anti-tank guns — 93 British vehicles were lost in three hours. The Eighth Army returns show that it had lost a total of 131 machines, that is about 40 percent of its strength as well as 2,000 infantry on that single day. That day of disaster was followed on 26 July by another one for Eighth Army. In blinding sandstorms, British infantry assaults that had gained their objectives were thrown back by Panzerarmee. 1,000 men were lost to Eighth Army on that black day, and the reason for the defeat was that the armour had, once again, blundered into another minefield.

At the end of July, and with the realization that his troops were exhausted and could do no more, General Auchinleck called off the battle. Eighth Army had achieved so much. The disaster at Gazala had forced them to withdraw nearly 200 miles, and at the end of that retreat they had not only stood at bay to meet the Panzerarmee onrush but had then gone over to the offensive. In the blazing heat of summer, they had driven the Germans and the Italians from much of Ruweisat Ridge. Now the soldiers were exhausted. But so too were the Axis troops. By unspoken consent, the pace of operations faded away and then stopped altogether. Both sides began to build up their forces for the offensive that each intended to mount. Axis pressure on Malta drew off some British strength and allowed convoys of supplies to reach Rommel's forces. Newer types of Panzer III and IV with stronger armour and a more powerful gun had arrived, together with a new division of infantry, the 164th, taken from occupation duties in the eastern Mediterranean, and the Ramcke Parachute Brigade. Reinforcements for the Italian corps also poured in, and these included the Folgore Parachute Division, a first-rate unit that was credited in British intelligence summaries as being the equal of any standard German division.

The First Battle of El Alamein had ended, but on the British side plans were already maturing for a resumption of the offensive. In the light of the biographies and autobiographies of the famous that have been produced, and in the claims made concerning Eighth Army's intentions, from a report prepared by Auchinleck's Chief of Staff at that time, provides some interesting reading. An extract is reproduced opposite. As early as 27 July, the weaknesses of Eighth Army appear to have been known, a forecast of Axis intentions had been made, and the decisive sector on which the future great Battle of El Alamein would be fought had all been predicted.

27th July 1942
An Appreciation of the Situation in the Western Desert:

EL ALAMEIN

Factors

Strength
The Axis is unlikely to secure a decisive majority over Eighth Army, since the Germans would have an inferiority of infantry of about three brigade groups and a superiority in armour of possible 40 percent. It would seem, therefore, that . . . they are hardly strong enough to attempt the conquest of the Delta except as a gamble and under very strong air cover . . . any offensive action would have to be 80 percent German.

Training
None of the formations in Eighth Army is now sufficiently well trained for offensive operations. The Army badly needs either a reinforcement of well trained formations or a quiet period in which to train.

Time and Space
Had the enemy the available resources, Italy and Germany are both nearer to El Alamein than is anywhere in the United Kingdom. The enemy should, therefore, be able to reinforce quicker than we. On the other hand, apart from distant Benghazi, he has only two serviceable sea ports, Tobruk and . . . Matruh. He is faced with long road hauls and a sea passage vulnerable to air-raid and submarine attack. This affects the build up of reserves for an offensive. We are nearer to our bases. Our limitation is the rate that men and materials can reach Egypt from overseas. His limit is the rate at which it can reach his troops when it arrives. This indicates the necessity of blocking Tobruk and Matruh and attacking his road communications and shipping.

Russian Front
The operations of Eighth Army are linked to the fate of Russia. Should the Axis penetrate the Caucasus, Eighth Army might be reduced to the lowest margin to provide reinforcements for the new front. Moreover, an Axis success in Russia would release air and land forces and equipment for the reinforcement of the Western Desert.

Tactical Techniques and Future Organization
We have to prepare to fight a modern defensive battle in the area of El Alamein—Hamman. The troops detailed for this must be trained and exercised so as to get the maximum value from the ground and from the prepared positions. Eventually we will have to renew the offensive, and this will probably mean a break through the enemy positions about El Alamein. The newly trained infantry and armoured divisions must be trained for this battle and for the pursuit. . . .

'MONTY'

During the time that Auchinleck had been changing the military situation in the Western Desert by his skilful employment of troops and his tactical ability, political crises at home had brought Winston Churchill and General Brooke, the Chief of the Imperial General Staff, to Egypt to see for themselves why Eighth Army seemed to lack the ability to beat the Axis forces. The Prime Minister and his party arrived in Cairo on 3 August, and two days later went forward to Auchinleck's headquarters where he shared the primitive living conditions of his fighting soldiers. Churchill was unimpressed by this Spartan behaviour just as he was unimpressed with the reasons why troops fresh out from the United Kingdom could not be rushed from the troopships into the front-line. The date of 15 September, which Auchinleck gave as the earliest on which a successful operation against Rommel could be undertaken, was rejected by Churchill, who needed victories (or at least the prospect of them) to impress Stalin whom he was soon to meet. If Auchinleck could not produce the victories then he would have to make way for a commander who could. General Gott, who was the first choice as Eighth Army commander, was killed in an aircraft on 7 August and the next choice, Bernard Law Montgomery, was sent for. General Sir Harold Alexander became Commander-in-Chief, Middle East.

How did the ordinary soldier view Churchill, the British war leader, and Montgomery, his choice as leader of Eighth Army? There were many who respected and honoured both men as the 'saviours' of their country and of Eighth Army, but a great number were opposed to them — and for a great and surprising variety of reasons. R. P. Hill of the RASC was annoyed at a Montgomery Battle Order that contained the phrase 'knock them for six'. 'We thought', commented Hill, 'that we had had a cricketer posted to us.' One aspect of Montgomery's methods that annoyed not only Driver Hill, as he then was, but also a great many others was the Eighth Army commander's ability to isolate himself. 'He would shut himself up in his caravan from 6pm to 6am. Rommel wouldn't have.'

Auchinleck, on the other hand, is seen in retrospect with sympathy and compassion. Veterans of the campaign, particularly those who had then been in the desert for a year or more, still remember Auchinleck's soldierly qualities. To those who had been out in the desert even longer, Wavell was the finest general. His had been the greatest victories. The first had been won against odds of more than ten to one, and it had been a crushing defeat for the Italians. The long experienced soldiers compared Wavell against Montgomery and the latter compared badly.

The question of whether Auchinleck or Montgomery produced the plan that defeated Rommel's next offensive was not one considered by the ordinary soldiers. The new commander made himself known to the men under him and, within a few weeks of taking over, Montgomery had become known by reputation if not by sight. Unlike the warriors who had preceded him, Montgomery appreciated the value of publicity and the fact that most men wanted to belong to a winning team. He was determined to make Eighth Army a winning team to which all his soldiers would take pride in belonging. He produced that feeling and it endures today, more than four decades removed from the desert battles.

Knowing the strength of his army, being aware of the assurance of supplies and with impeccable intelligence information, Montgomery could feel confident. Through the highly secret 'Ultra' sources — a fount of Intelligence so secret that knowledge of it has only recently been revealed — the Eighth Army commander knew almost as soon as the Axis politicians in Rome and Berlin of the plans that Rommel was making. And Montgomery knew even before Rommel did, so fast and accurate was the British intercept and decoding service, of instructions that Rommel received from his masters. Thus, Montgomery was in the fortunate situation for a commander of knowing what his enemy intended. He knew that the German leader proposed to take the initiative towards the end of August, and he knew the plan that would be followed. Yet the British leader was a cautious man. He was keenly aware that even with the superiority in men and equipment that would soon be his, and even with a foreknowledge of the enemy's plans, the battle might still be lost. The secrets of 'Ultra' had been given to former commanders of Eighth Army; they too had had assured supplies; and yet they had failed. Montgomery was determined that he would win, and resolved that he would achieve victory by not asking too much of his troops at any one time. He would restore confidence to his troops by winning a successful battle in which it would be demonstrated that Rommel *had* been beaten once and could be beaten again. He knew that his own army was at that time too weak to undertake an offensive against the Panzerarmee, and determined that the imminent German offensive should provide the object lesson.

THE BATTLE OF ALAM EL HALFA

For his part, Rommel knew that his proposed attack was a gamble, but one that had to be taken. It would be his last chance: with every passing week, Eighth Army was growing stronger.

If he were to succeed in gaining his objective, the city of Alexandria, he would first have to defeat Eighth Army holding its positions in both defence lines — the principal one at El Alamein and the secondary one on the Nile. The only way in which he could accomplish that would be to renew the frontal assault that he had already broken off as too costly. There was no alternative. The flanks of the El Alamein position

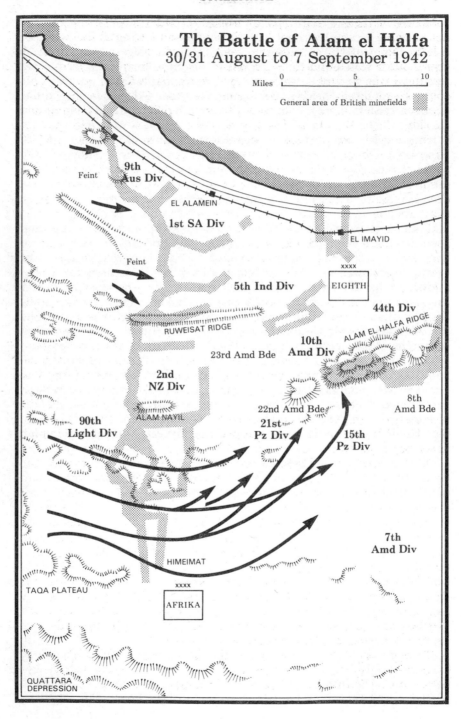

The Battle of Alam el Halfa
30/31 August to 7 September 1942

Miles 0 .... 5 10

General area of British minefields

9th Aus Div

Feint

EL ALAMEIN

1st SA Div

EL IMAYID

Feint

5th Ind Div

XXXX EIGHTH

44th Div

ALAM EL HALFA RIDGE

RUWEISAT RIDGE

23rd Amd Bde

10th Amd Div

2nd NZ Div

22nd Amd Bde

8th Amd Bde

ALAM NAYIL

90th Light Div

21st Pz Div

15th Pz Div

7th Amd Div

HIMEIMAT

TAQA PLATEAU

XXXX AFRIKA

QUATTARA DEPRESSION

could not be turned, and to pass through the Quattara Depression was not possible — Rommel had actually sent a group to establish whether a large body of heavy military vehicles could force a way through there, but it was found to be impassable even to loaded camels. What remained was to find some weak spot in the British line where a gap could be made and exploited. There was one. It was in the south, between the left flank of the New Zealand Division at Alam Nayil and the edge of the Quattara. The gap was twelve miles wide and was not strongly held, but it was frequently patrolled by vehicles of 7th Armoured Division. Rommel's obvious move, once he had passed through that gap, would be to seize the dominant high ground and to use it as a springboard from which to drive northwards and get behind the great mass of Eighth Army standing firm in the defences of the El Alamein line.

His plan was therefore to take the great mass of Panzerarmee and to pass it quickly eastwards through the gap, between the Bab el Quattara and the high ground around El Taqa. At El Hamman the advancing formations were to halt and then face left: the whole of the attacking German/Italian line would then be facing northwards. From that halt line, the Axis divisions would drive northwards, taking the Eighth Army from the rear, cutting off the British units and destroying them piecemeal. It was to be a repetition of the great left hook that had brought victory at Gazala only three months before.

The offensive was to open at 23.00 hours on 30 August, and at 06.00 hours on the following morning the northward drive would begin. The two German reconnaissance groups that were to form the outside flank had only seven hours in which to penetrate the British minefields and to advance along the thrust line to El Hamman. So it was essential that the British minefields be gapped quickly. Indeed, the whole plan depended upon this.

There would be difficulties connected with the execution of the battle plan. Each division needed space in which to manoeuvre — so much space that the units forming the outside wing of the northward wheel, and which would have the longest distance to travel, would need to cover 30 miles in their easterly advance before they reached El Hamman and swung left. One tactical feature was important to both sides. This was Alam el Halfa Ridge. If the Germans could bypass it quickly to the east, then they would have a clear run to the places on which they intended to meet and destroy the British armour. If Montgomery could hold Rommel from the Ridge then the battle was his, for the German commander would not dare to move eastwards towards the Nile so long as the undefeated Eighth Army was in a position to sever his lines of communication.

Montgomery held Alam el Halfa Ridge with the 44th Home Counties Division, a formation that had arrived only a short time before in the Middle East. Part of his armour, the 22nd Brigade, he placed on the western edge of the Ridge; and farther to the west was the 'box', held by the New Zealand Division and the 132nd British Brigade, at Alam Nayil. This New Zealand 'box' was to be the strong 'shoulder' of the British line. To the south and to the east were the regiments of the 7th Armoured Division, which would withdraw in the face of the Axis advance and thereby entice Rommel's forces into a three-sided trap. From each side of the trap, fire would be poured upon the German and Italian troops as they advanced northwards. Montgomery stressed that his armour would be controlled, and not loosed to fight uncoordinated actions. The panzer forces must be allowed to beat themselves against a wall of British tanks and anti-tank guns. The armour of the 22nd Brigade was to be supported by dug-in anti-tank guns and by field artillery.

An armoured attack switched rapidly backwards and forwards across a battlefield in the hope of finding a weak spot in the enemy front is an operation that can only be carried out if the attacking army has uninterrupted supplies. The Panzerarmee was in no such situation. The two panzer divisions of the Afrika Korps were down to petrol supplies that gave each tank less than a hundred miles of mobility. The promises to supply fuel had not been fully carried out because the ships were being sunk at sea. It was only upon Kesselring's assurance of air-lifted supplies that Rommel launched the Second Battle of El Alamein — a battle better known to the British as the Battle of Alam el Halfa.

During the night of 30/31 August, Panzerarmee attacked, only to find that the minefields through which they had been ordered to pass in a matter of hours were denser and deeper than had been supposed. Their gapping attempts did not go forward without opposition, and there were terrible losses to the predominantly Italian teams. As day dawned on 31 August, the Panzerarmee was still struggling to bring itself out of the British minefields instead of approaching El Hamman, the point at which the great northwards wheel should have begun. German losses had been severe and included General von Bismarck, the commander of the 21st Panzer Division, who had been killed, and General Nehring, commander of the Afrika Korps, who had been wounded. Faced with this failure of his plan, Rommel's initial reaction was to abort the offensive; but instead, influenced by General Bayerlein, his Chief of Staff, he reduced slightly the extent of his left wheel so that its main weight would fall upon the western end of the Alam el Halfa Ridge. This was precisely what the British commander had hoped and prepared for. When the panzer advance was resumed, it was six hours late.

The 15th Panzer Division opened its attack at 13.00 hours and this was followed an hour later by that of the 21st Panzer Division. But the direction in which the panzer regiments moved was taking them away from the British prepared defences, and the tanks of the outpost line were ordered to show themselves so as to entice the panzers to charge. This was a tactic which Rommel had often used against the British armour — and now Eighth Army was using it against him. The German regiments took the bait and turned to engage the British vehicles and anti-tank guns forming a decoy line ahead of the 22nd Armoured Brigade.

'The CLY were out there, and when the Germans engaged them there were the last knockings of a Khamseen that had been blowing all day. The German tanks came out of that dirty khaki curtain and within a couple of minutes, or so it seemed, the CLY was shattered.' The whole of 22nd Brigade suffered terrible losses, but they were most severe among the squadrons of the County of London Yeomanry in their Grant tanks. Because of the design of those machines with the main gun mounted low in the hull, the tank's superstructure projected above any crest behind which it was trying to take a 'hull down' position. The Panzer IV with the new and powerful 75mm gun exploited that defect, and one after another the Grants blew up or burst into flames. They were fuelled by high-octane fuel, and when this ignited the resulting explosion gave the crews no chance to escape. All through that day the smoke clouds of burning Grants rose in the sky. With the CLY effectively disposed of, or so the panzer crews thought, the machines of the 21st Panzer rolled forward, seemingly impervious to the shells that the Rifle Brigade anti-tank gunners were firing at them. Only the timely intervention of the Royal Tank Regiment forced back the Germans from Alam el Halfa Ridge, and only the onset of darkness stopped the 15th Panzer Division from outflanking the British 22nd Armoured Brigade. During the night, aircraft of the Royal Air Force, supported now by squadrons of the United States Air Force, bombed the concentrations of Panzerarmee vehicles. There was no respite for the Germans and the Italians.

At first light on 1 September, the 15th Panzer Division was sent in again to work round the 22nd Brigade's eastern flank, but the attacks had as little success as had those of the 21st Panzer Division on the previous day. The battle continued throughout this day and the next, with air operations playing an increasingly important part. The Luftwaffe in Africa was reinforced by squadrons brought in from Crete. Dive-bombing raids by Ju 87s had always been a feature of desert life, but during the Battle of Alam el Halfa they reached a peak.

Attacked from three sides, it soon became clear to the commander of Panzerarmee that the offensive had failed and that the only solution was to break off the battle and to withdraw. Despite opposition from Kesselring, Rommel gave the necessary orders, and the force that had advanced with such high hopes began to pull back. Now was the time for Eighth Army to spring the trap and cut off the Axis forces. To carry out this operation, the New Zealand Division with its attached British 132nd Brigade was ordered to mount the only set-piece infantry attack of the whole operation. This would push southwards to the Munassib Depression and seal the British minefields behind Panzerarmee, trapping the Axis force in front of Alam el Halfa Ridge.

The advance did not go according to plan. A diversionary attack by the New Zealand 6th Brigade alerted the German defenders, so that when the two battalions of the Queen's Own went in they struck fierce opposition and the leading companies suffered heavy casualties. The weakened battalions could not maintain the advance, for they were silhouetted against the burning vehicles of their unit transport. Neither could the platoons dig into the rocky surface of the desert. The West Kents lay illuminated by the burning lorries and by flares dropped by Luftwaffe aircraft on open ground swept by enemy fire. The battalions were pulled back to a ridge some distance to the north of the Munassib Depression, and there they were reorganized. The attempt to block Rommel's retreat had failed, and both battalions had lost heavily — the 4th Battalion, Kents, for example, had suffered 250 casualties. The feeling among the survivors of the 132nd Brigade was that they had been sent into a suicide attack.

The Second Battle of El Alamein, the Battle of Alam el Halfa, was dying away. It had been a British victory, one which demonstrated that firm control of a battle was all important to its successful outcome. It was a tidy little battle that had gone as planned.

There was no follow-up of the retreating Panzerarmee. Montgomery did not consider that his troops were sufficiently well trained to undertake such an operation. The Germans and Italians pulled back under continual assault from the squadrons of the Allied air forces. The last major offensive the Axis was to undertake in the Western Desert had ended. Panzerarmee had advanced its front a little, and now held the British 'January' and 'February' minefields; these were absorbed into the existing enemy defensive systems that ran along their front from just west of El Alamein down to the Quattara Depression. The Germans and Italians also retained certain pieces of high ground from which they could observe movement in the British lines. In actual losses, the Axis casualties were 3,000 to Eighth Army's 2,000 men; in terms of equipment, each side lost about 38 armoured fighting vehicles; the Axis lost 33 guns; the British rather more. Losses in aircraft were about even, just under 100 machines each.

The intention behind Rommel's drive had been to bring the Panzerarmee to the Nile. In this he had failed. On the British side there had been the short-term objective of halting that thrust and in the medium term to build up the morale of Eighth Army so that it could achieve the long-term objective, to smash Panzerarmee in the battle that Montgomery was planning — the Third Battle of El Alamein.

THE NEW BROOM

Not long after the guns of the 7th Armoured Division had fired the last harrying shots at the retreating enemy forces, Montgomery began the task of preparing Eighth Army for the next step in his campaign to defeat Rommel. He was aware that the morale of his soldiers would rise as a result of the victory — albeit a defensive one — that had been gained at Alam el Halfa. But he needed more than that. He had to conduct and win an aggressive battle. The question uppermost in his mind was whether his army was capable of fighting the type of battle he had begun to plan. From personal visits to his men, it was clear to Montgomery that the army was brave but baffled. The soldiers had fought well in past battles, but they had not gained the prizes their efforts should have brought them. He found they could not understand why the British Army was not winning the desert war.

Among the conclusions that Montgomery drew from studying earlier offensives in the desert, and from his own handling of the Alam el Halfa battle, were that his courageous but confused soldiers needed to be retrained. Until that training had been undergone, the arms of service could not be totally effective in their own roles, nor able to use their special skills in collaboration with the other branches of the army. The friction between the men of the various arms of service had developed in certain cases into mistrust and hostility: relations between infantry and armour were notoriously bad, and the feelings between infantry and Gunners far from harmonious. The great problem was not to retrain the soldiers in how to handle their weapons or in the execution of some tactical problem, but how to bring them together and to make the various arms of service work as a team. There was a need for officers and men to rethink their attitudes and to overcome their prejudices. It was, perhaps, the greatest of Montgomery's many achievements that he took the disparate forces under his command and welded them into a whole whose members, eventually, did not see themselves as cavalry, as Gunners or as infantry, but as men of Eighth Army, equal partners in battle. Under Montgomery, Eighth Army was to become a host of warriors dedicated to beating their opponents quickly, efficiently and, if necessary, ruthlessly.

Nobody would be unaffected by the new broom that had arrived in the person of the new army commander, and his first directives were to achieve the removal of a great number of officers. General Headquarters in Cairo had expanded from the small group of staff officers who served Wavell in 1940 into a mass of military bureaucrats. Being located in comfortable Cairo, few officers at GHQ knew of the privations that were being suffered only a lorry ride away and, in the opinion of the great mass of the army, they cared even less. What did those officers, known to all as the 'Cairo Canaries', as 'Groppi's Light Horse' or as 'The Gabardine Swine', care that water was rationed to a couple of pints per day 'up the blue'? How could they, with cheap and abundant supplies of alcohol, understand the conditions endured by men whose ration of beer was, perhaps, a bottle every month? Life in Cairo went on very much as it had done in peacetime, with siestas after lunch, short working hours and long meal breaks.

The arrival of the puritan-minded general who ordered physical training for all ranks threw a great number of officers into despair. The seeming dependence of Eighth Army HQ upon a mass of exquisite young liaison officers was shown to be false, and ceased abruptly once Montgomery had settled in. The number of those fashionable but unproductive soldiers was reduced. They were either posted to active service units or were sent home (a fate that produced from James McNally of 68th Medium Regiment, the wry comment, 'There was no chance of *our* being sacked.') The social life of Cairo suffered under the moral outlook of the new commander: for a great many people, it had suddenly ceased to be a cheery war.

'The blue'. Long vistas, an unending wasteland of sand and grit. **Above:** American tanks that were issued to Eighth Army in the early fighting were unsuitable as battle tanks but did fulfil a role as patrol or reconnaissance vehicles. This very early photograph shows Stuart I tanks in open formation. **Left:** The windscreen of this Jeep is in the standard position, laid flat so that the sun's rays reflecting from it should not betray the vehicle's position.

Sand, shale, grit, rock — the desert surface was all of these. **Above:** This photograph shows very well the surface of a trigh with the ruts in the track. The faster the movement across this kind of terrain the greater the cloud. Indeed, any movement threw up clouds of dust. **Right:** The true face of the desert over which the fighting took place. It is not sand, but small rock and greyish grit.

Underground shelters of any type were taken over by the troops as refuges from the bombing. **Left:** This dried out well was ideal and served as the company office for an infantry battalion. A well in the desert is not a small circular hole in the earth but a wide and deep excavation, often going down one hundred feet or more. **Below:** An example of how catacombs could be turned into a battalion headquarters.

The road forward for some; the end of the road for others.
Above: The main road between the Delta and the forward area, looking eastwards. The signs include not only location boards but also warn drivers to obey Military Police traffic instructions. **Right:** British infantry inspecting a captured German Schmeisser machine-pistol. Both men are carrying ammunition pouches, small pack, belt, bayonet, and personal weapon, but neither has a water bottle which suggests that the photograph is posed.

3.

'THE BLUE'

'The blue' was by common definition a right bastard. It may have been a paradise for tacticians, but it was a harsh and ruthless tyrant, who punished the ignorant, the stupid and the weak with frightful suffering. It was a foretaste of Hell for those who lived in it. Europeans killed there died in a region that, although alien to their backgrounds, had become a sort of homeland to them as it had been to the Arabs for thousands of years. The native population saw with unemotional eyes the great variety of foreign soldiers passing across the territory: British, Italian, German, French; white, black, brown; Christian, Jew, Hindu, Muslim, polytheist or just simply atheist; all at one time or another served in 'the blue'. To each army, the impartial natives sold the few things they had to offer. A unit's laager for the night might seem to have been placed in the middle of a completely empty strip of desert. Within minutes, there would be Arabs around the perimeter holding in their hands the undersized products of their scruffy hens. Bargains would be struck — cigarettes or dried tea for eggs — and each party would do its best to cheat the other. It was the practice of the British to use tea once, then dry it out and use it for barter. The Arabs would hope to steal the goods proffered by the soldiers and run off into the desert without surrendering their own goods. The poorest of the poor, the Arabs and the ordinary soldiers, each was seeking to defraud the other.

What was it like to be 'up the blue'? Usually, an indescribable misery. To many soldiers, it was completely beyond belief that so much fighting should take place for so many acres of nothing. It was a hostile environment and one from which every feature that could make for ease of living was absent. There was little water, and there were no restaurants to supplement the boring, inevitable rations; no bars, no cinemas, no comfort and no sex. Instead, there were flies, fleas and sickness and a great deal of danger. This did not come from natural fauna. There were some scorpions and a few snakes, but not enough to become a feature of everyday life. Inland from the coast, there were no birds and almost no vegetation but camel thorn. In one unit, there was on one occasion excited comment when a group of drivers sent out to a collection point reported that they had seen. . . a tree. The dangers of the desert came from the enemy dive-bombers and artillery bombard-ments, from panzer thrusts or infantry assaults, and all those things were in addition to the miseries of the *normal* desert life. Yes, life 'up the blue' was a bastard. Noisy, comfortless, frightening and dangerous.

It is a belief, widely held but quite erroneous, that the whole of the desert territory of Libya and Egypt is one huge expanse of golden sand dunes — the name 'Western Desert' might seem to support that belief. In the deep south of both countries, there are indeed stretches of such terrain, but the surface over which fighting took place is grit, a dirty-grey/brownish crust, the product of centuries of erosion of the limestone rock that covers much of the area.

Extending a short way inland from the Mediterranean shore there is a narrow, fertile and intensively cultivated plain, behind which rises an escarpment of limestone cliffs ('djebel' in Arabic). The distance inland at which these cliffs begin varies, and at some points (particularly at Sollum) they rise sheer out of the sea. The steep gradients and crumbling surfaces of the djebel make them impassable at some places to anything but tracked vehicles and, in some parts of the region, even they could not negotiate the wadi-scored surfaces. Extending inland from the djebel and sloping gently southwards is a limestone plateau the surface of which is dotted with rocks and stones. Wind and weather have scoured the plateau surface and produced a layer of the grit that varies between a few inches and several feet thick. Amongst the soft limestone are areas of harder rock which have withstood erosion, and these areas stand above the plateau surface forming low ridges and small hills. These, although usually less than 300 feet above the surrounding surface, form natural observation points, and during the fighting possession of them was vital. Other patches of the limestone surfaces are softer, and upon these the scouring action of the wind-borne sand has worked to produce depressions ('deir' in Arabic) of varying sizes. Smaller ones provided ready-built defensive positions, while the bigger ones were natural obstacles. The biggest and best known of the larger deir was the Quattara, a depression thousands of square miles in area, whose salt-marsh bottom is 400 feet below sea level and whose walls are steep, high cliffs. The Quattara was impassable, and it formed a flank that could not be turned.

Farther south, as the plateau subsides, the terrain takes on more and more the traditional image of the desert, with great rolling dunes of sand. On such a surface, 'going' was poor to impassable, and vehicles moved only with difficulty. The sand seas, which begin some 50 miles inland from the coast, forbad the movement of armies along the deep southern flank except for specially equipped and outfitted units, such as the Long Range Desert Group and the Special Air Service, which had their bases there and were able to cross the hostile and trackless wastes with little difficulty. The presence of the two natural barriers — the Mediterranean Sea in the north and the sand seas in the south — hemmed the armies into a lateral battleground of great depth but of little width. The battleground of Libya and Egypt was less than 70 miles wide but was over a thousand miles long. (As examples of the great distances between the inhabited localities, it was more than 300 miles from the capital city of Tripoli to Buerat on the eastern border of the province of Tripolitania; to El Agheila on the south-western edge of Cyrenaica it was 470 miles; Benghazi was 650 miles distant, and the Egyptian border was over 980 miles away.)

To nourish the armies, there was only one all-weather main road in Libya, the Via Balbia. Following the coast from Tripoli to Sollum, it linked the coastal towns of Libya (there being no important inland settlements). Of these coastal towns, only three (Tripoli, Benghazi and Tobruk) had harbours capable of unloading by merchant ships. The Via Balbia and the ports were vital to the movement of supplies.

The Via Balbia ran east-west, and the only other routes along which movement could take place were the native tracks ('trigh' in Arabic). These tracks usually connect waterholes or wells ('bir' in Arabic) and are nothing but desert paths, caravan routes, hardened by the passage of human feet or camel pad. The trigh is remembered by one German soldier as 'a track, as straight as a ruler, but nothing more than a used path. The surface was perhaps a hundred metres wide, but driving along it was slow because of the likelihood of running off the beaten path and into the loose desert. We had to make frequent halts to clear sand from the air filter. That sand is not hard and white, but a fine powdery dust, reddish yellow in colour. Driving along the trigh one was always accompanied by a dust cloud thrown up by the movement of the wheels — irrespective of the speed — and that cloud hung marking the vehicle's position. To drive behind another vehicle meant always driving through a sort of fog; but one made up of sand which penetrated everything — mouth, eyes, clothing, weapons and the motor itself. Conditions were dreadful.'

The trigh are not roads, and their surfaces crumbled under the movement of heavy lorries and tanks. Deep ruts were created and, to avoid these spring-shattering channels, drivers took to using the trigh edges, thus widening the original track. In winter, the infrequent but heavy rains formed the dust surface into mud that held wheeled transport fast.

Where two or more trigh cross, there is usually to be found a landmark such as the tomb of some local Muslim saint (which the word 'Sidi' in place-names indicates); in an otherwise trackless and featureless region, such junctions were vital points of reference. Indeed, so important were they to the course of an offensive that they were frequently garrisoned or at least regularly patrolled. And, as points of reference known to all, they were also used as advanced supply depots. To fight in the desert was like fighting at sea. Movement was made with minimal landmarks, and one's position was reckoned by the use of compass bearings and speedometers. There were certain features, of which trigonometrical points were the most usual, and many of these had been erected in peacetime to aid cartographers. The positions of other reference points were based upon these. 'It was in the early days quite astonishing to see a place-name marked on a map', recalls one veteran, 'and then to drive up to it by correct and faultless navigation only to find that it was neither a town nor even a collection of native huts but simply a cairn of stones with perhaps a salt-water well and a few bushes or camel thorn.'

The desert is arid, hot by day and cold by night, and without cover. The surface into which one dug a slit trench might turn out to cover hard rock about two feet down, or it could be firm sand into which a position could be dug without much effort. It could also be a hard and bare section of stone into which no deep trench could be dug. In such cases, the only protection against bullets and shell splinters was a low wall of stones and rock — a sangar — inside whose circumference the time was passed, cramped and uncomfortable.

From May to October, the climate is sub-tropical with a dry, searing heat during the greater part of the day — propaganda photographs of the Afrika Korps show men frying eggs on the metal parts of an armoured fighting vehicle. Temperatures rise steadily from about 10 in the morning until about 5 in the afternoon by which time the intense heat slowly gives way to a refreshing coolness as the sun sinks. After dark it turns cold, and by October the contrast between the heat of the day and the coolness of the night was sufficient to require the wearing of greatcoats. During the winter, heavy rains cause floodwater to pour down the wadis and cover the land. This water is rapidly absorbed, but the surface of the desert remains wet and slippery with a sticky mud. Although sandstorms ('Khamseen' in Arabic) can blow at any time, they are more frequent in the spring, when the wind direction changes from north to south-west, bringing with it an immediate high rise in temperatures. At such times, the air becomes thick and clammy, breathing is difficult and visibility reduced. Most of the soldiers who served in the desert remember with particular bitterness the sand-storms and the flies: both had a relentless quality that could bring the European soldier to a point of deep depression.

On the other hand, few could forget the great beauty of the desert, particularly of the beautiful dawns and the spectacular sunsets. The desert night and the luminosity of the stars also featured highly in correspondents' answers and the intense darkness of a starless night was also stressed. The darkness was so deep that to leave one's slit trench or tent to go to the latrines was an adventure not undertaken without having first taken a compass bearing. The rank and file who had no compasses used the simple device of a peg banged into the ground and a length of cord, which was paid out until the latrine was reached; the cord guided one back in the dark. Those who may find it unbelievable that direction can be lost so easily should remember that there was no light and nothing by which to orientate oneself. A slit trench was so small that it could easily be missed.

It may also seem unnecessarily fussy that, with a desert area of hundreds of square miles in which to carry out natural functions, the

British Army should have insisted upon the strict hygiene precautions which so many former soldiers recalled. The desert rose was not, so far as the men of Eighth Army were aware, a wind-blown carving of silicate that the scouring effect of sand had formed into a flower. Rather it was a hole dug in the desert into which a bottomless empty petrol tin was buried vertically and upon which was set another petrol tin at an angle. These were urinals; and they were chlorided frequently. In most static areas, the latrine proper was a hessian screen stretched on poles surrounding a deep trench. Depending upon the ability of the unit's pioneer section, the seating arrangement was quite sturdy. In less mobile units, semi-permanent latrines were erected: a box seating arrangement with three or four holes. The whole thing was placed over a latrine trench. Obviously, the farther forward one went, the more primitive was the arrangement, and holes dug in the sand were often the latrines of the infantrymen. Wherever possible, thorough precautions were taken to ensure the hygienic state of the latrines. In countries remarkable for the number and variety of fly-borne diseases, the most strenuous efforts had to be made to keep the plague down, and the supervision and control of latrines was one such measure. Dysentery has decimated more than one campaigning army, and the fact that in Eighth Army the number of such cases was low was due to the strictly enforced regulations instituted by the Army's hygiene sections.

Flies were horrible. They settled on anything and everything — the sight of bodies of soldiers crawling with maggots and black with the effect of decay and of the sun was common. A former member of 50th Division's Provost Company, A. W. Evans, remembers vividly one effect of the sun upon the dead. 'After the German retreat at Alamein we advanced through minefields, following up. I was on duty all day on the Italian side of the minefields to direct the Brigade's vehicles to their allotted direction . . . they would come back for me. A few yards from where I was standing there was a depression in which there were several bodies hastily covered with sand, here and there a leg or arm protruding and part of a machine-gun barrel also sticking up. I was idly watching these as the last of the vehicles passed, and was waiting to be picked up. My opposite number was on the British side of the minefields some distance away, also waiting. It had been very hot, around 100° I should think, but now the sun was beginning to set and it was getting colder. I put on my greatcoat, although I had been wearing shorts and khaki shirt all day, when I noticed the arm that was sticking out of the sand with its fingers outstretched. As I looked I saw the fingers slowly close to a clenched position. I felt my hair bristle as I was certain the poor fellow must be dead underneath the sand, for the hand was already turning black. I felt very relieved when I suddenly remembered the sharp difference in temperature that was causing this contraction. However, I was glad when our relief truck arrived and picked me up.'

Unlike the Axis armies, Eighth Army was not verminous. The war diaries of the 90th Light and 21st Panzer Division both recorded numerous instances of lice infestation among troops in the forward areas, and the British Field Hygiene Sections reported on the verminous condition of many Italian prisoners of war. That Eighth Army was less affected by the pests was probably due to the liberal use of AL63, an effective anti-louse powder, or to the fact that units in the forward zones were rotated more frequently than were Axis troops. It is always easier to remain clean when one has had opportunities for washing uninterrupted by shell and machine-gun fire.

To launder clothes was no problem for units stationed near the sea or in towns. Those farther inland who had access to petrol could dhoby their KD (khaki drill) in that fuel and then hang them to dry in the sun. The remainder laid out their KD, sometimes scrubbed with sand, on the desert's dusty face and hoped that the purging action of the sun would bleach out the dry sweat and evidences of wear. The desert army was no place for prudes. While clothing was drying in the sun, its wearer would usually wander about dressed in boots and cap. Groups of bathers seen from a distance seemed to be wearing white bathing trunks until at closer range the white trunks were discovered to be the less tanned naked lower torsos contrasting vividly with the deep sunburnt bodies, faces and legs.

The opportunity to wash as thoroughly as in sea bathing or at some bir came infrequently, and for much of the time the body was covered with a layer of germ-laden desert dust. Slight abrasions infected by that dust turned quickly into ulcers, and most men suffered at some time from those weeping, unsightly but not very painful open abscesses. There were, at that time, no drugs to cure the affliction of desert sores: penicillin came in much later, or was perhaps reserved for more serious wounds, while sulpha drugs did not come to Africa until the American units landed as part of the Allied army in Algeria. The standard treatment for desert sores was Gentian violet, a blue dye with slight antiseptic qualities which was liberally applied to affected parts. Its efficacy was questionable — certainly it did not heal the sores from which I suffered. Major Michael Lee, formerly of the Northumberland Fusiliers and a time-serving soldier very aware of the prevalence of skin diseases in the Orient, disinfected with Milton the water in which he washed and shaved. He is convinced that this simple precaution kept him free from desert sores.

Life 'up the blue' was simple. 'Stand to' in fighting units was just before dawn, that time of the dying night when the enemy assault was most likely to come in. There was work of some sort to do throughout the day until evening 'stand to', and then dark came with onrushing suddenness. Soon it was pitch dark and one turned in. Very few had the opportunity to illuminate their tents or bivouacs, and black-out precautions were strict, absurdly so in view of the well illuminated chief towns of Egypt, above which hung at night a corona of light.

In the vacuum of time, it was easy to forget individual days, and one realized it was Sunday only when (if one was out of the Line) the padre celebrated Holy Communion. In units behind the lines, the days of the week were more easily brought to mind. In one RASC detachment, the former Corporal Eyre and his comrades recalled evenings back home by selecting their best KD or battledress and then, washed, shaved and as immaculate as it was possible to be, they would sit around, smoking, chatting and reading. Gentlemen always dress for dinner, and even in the deserts of North Africa the tradition was maintained by the other ranks of this RASC unit.

What did one read? There was little. Books that had been brought from the United Kingdom or others bought while on leave. The Army's newspapers seldom reached down to the level of rifle companies or their equivalent, and news was generally circulated by word of mouth, that unreliable vehicle for the transmission of truth: indeed, few veterans of the desert war can recall reading an Army newspaper and even smaller is the number who enjoyed the shows presented by ENSA.

The cynical belief is still maintained that the artistes of ENSA came out to Egypt more to enjoy the luxuries and the sun of the Middle East and less to entertain the fighting men. There was one story, probably apocryphal but indicative of the attitude of the soldiers who spread it, that ENSA artistes who had come to the Middle East applied for and received their Africa Star ribbon before it was ever on issue to the Army. Very few soldiers had any sort of entertainment other than the divisional concert party. These were, usually, well produced revue-type entertainments, lacking only real girls in the dancing roles.

There were no women 'up the blue'. Perhaps, without being ungallant, I should qualify that statement by adding that there were no *available* women. There were nursing sisters and the ladies who ran the mobile tea canteens of the Salvation Army and the Church Army, but there were no girls with whom one could talk or flirt. And, there being no women, there was no sexual outlet. Most of the desert soldiers were unmarried, and probably the greater number of those were without sexual experience. The Army, working on the assumption that 'what you've never had you'll never miss', that if there are no women about one's mind does not dwell on them; and, finally, that a body physically exhausted with hard work does not seek sexual release, ensured that the number of women in 'the blue' were few and inaccessible, and that the troops were kept fully occupied. For single men, the idea that 'what you've never had you'll never miss' may have applied, but for married men abstinence must have been unbearable. Certain pressures kept them chaste. Homosexual activities were both a military offence and morally repugnant to most soldiers. The only relief was masturbation; silently, at night and followed by feelings of guilt, remorse and shame.

To be billeted, or to stay for a few days, in one of the larger towns of Libya was to relive half-forgotten ways of life. There were shops, cafés and women. One correspondent, who prefers to be unnamed, recalled: 'During the Crusader battle I had been wounded, slightly, but enough when added to desert sores and other things to be evacuated through the CCS to a base hospital set up in Benghazi. Remember, this was in December 1941. I had been up the blue since the very early days and had had no leave at all — except for a 48-hour pass after a course down near Geneifa where I had managed to get to Ismailia.

'You can't imagine how exciting it was for me when I got out of the hospital and into town — yes, even a little town like Benghazi. Just to walk on pavements again. I was like a kid. There were shops and people, not just soldiers and not just Arabs, but Italians, men and women. Mind you, mostly they would have nothing to do with us, but just to see women again was enough. Until those days in Benghazi it hadn't really struck me how much we give up when we go off to war. Our Konner (food) was always the same. No little luxuries, and there was never any time off. No rest, no relaxation. Never enough water and never — well, almost never — any beer and, of course, no women. Up the line, we never had time to think about sex, and in the so-called rest areas we had to be careful with the bints who were out in the dunes. They were all Arab girls, and if you caught a packet your pay was stopped and all allowances home as well. So the family at home not only suffered financially, but were told why they were suffering. VD was considered to be a SIW (self inflicted wound) and most men were scared of catching a dose. So we went without or relieved ourselves.

'I got lucky in Benghazi. There was an Eyetie family near a café I went to, one of the few that were not out of bounds. The old Mama asked if I'd like her to do my washing in exchange for food. I flogged a little Beretta pistol to an RASC storeman in a ration point and collected a handful of tins every day. I'll not forget how that family liked bully. After a couple of days, the married daughter and I got together. We didn't go all the way. She wouldn't because she was recently widowed — I think that was the reason, and I wouldn't because of the wife back home. But we pleased each other. Of course, all I wanted to know was that women were still in the world. All she wanted was to have a man's shoulder to cry on, a man to cook for and to fuss over. We were both lonely in our own way. So I had a family in the desert and I spent quite a bit of time there in that café. There was a canteen in Benghazi, the Red Shield, I think — the Sally Army. They didn't have much, but the chance to sit down and have a cup of tea was novel. The weather they said was terrible, rainy, cold and miserable, but for me just to see wet pavements again was a breath of home. I got RTUd (returned to unit) after ten days and caught a lift back up the big tarmac road. My mob was dead lucky to be moving back as a complete unit when Rommel put in his attack at the end of January 1942. We got into our allocated positions in time and intact. From what I heard, a lot of the tank mobs and their infantry escorts panicked and ran. The

Indian regiments which stood fast copped a packet. I was told that for days groups of blokes would come in, marching out of the blue and into our lines. One lot told us that the Germans had told them they had no time to take prisoners, as the panzers were all set to drive on Alex, and that soon the whole Eighth Army would be in the bag.'

The problem of sex in an all male society, and the moral standards of the old Army, provide an interesting contrast with the moral climate of today. An officer in the Eighth Army reflects on the way things were: 'Sex life? There isn't any out here in the desert. The nearest women are back in Alex unless there is a field hospital back towards Anriyah. But it often goes through my mind up here in the desert where life is monastic . . . wholly a man's world, a soldier's world . . . must have been like this in those Beau Geste stories. Fort Zinderneuf and all that! One looks back to evenings in Cairo or Alexandria — the parties, the dances, the sitting out among the palm fronds in the foyer drinking. Or there was the occasional visit to Mary's House or the 'Garden of Flowers', so called (Jardin des Fleurs), Greek and French girls mostly. But that is all in the past. I notice that friends and buddies in the sections sleep together, two sharing a bed, and one wonders whether they satisfy each other's need in this way — mutual masturbation or whatever. One does have homosexual feelings sometimes up here — they are all such marvellous chaps to soldier with, so patient and humorous, but one cannot entertain the idea; it would be monstrous — the sixth commandment and all that — and Father used to say that that kind of thing was a kind of lunacy, to couple with one's own sex. So it is better to burn, as St. Paul said, and one's mind does not harp on the theme. Then its a good thing that when we go bathing in the sea all are naked, there are no trunks or things like that; it is healthier and more natural. Rather like the old adverts for Pears soap in the 20s, a lot of naked schoolboys frolicking about in an English stream. So one leaves it to wet dreams and sometimes masturbation. About every ten days I feel the urge, but I remind myself that food is the primitive instinct; one must feed; one does not need sex. You can live without it; priests do, so why not we also? And then there is the daily duty which keeps one busy on other things, and sex is not a man's whole world as they say. So an army can exist in the field without it and has to.

'And now? Thinking back to that period in the light of the present world of sexual liberation and of homosexuality between consenting adults, would it have made any difference then if that had been the legal situation? No. For the Army, things would have been the same as they are for the services even yet. To be the patient or the agent in such an affair was, and is, illegal and liable to court-martial action. And then one was older than the men one commanded and to have taken such an advantage was unfair, unjust and corrupting more than any hard porn literature. No, it was best as it was: A joke. If someone said you were homo, then you replied 'Who with?' and there the matter was ended. How was it, I wonder, in the armies in other theatres. They used to say that in India, when Lady Roberts persuaded Lord Roberts to close the brothels, the VD figures went up and homosexuality was rife. It was best not to think too much about it and that way worked out for the best, too.'

What did one do in the pauses − those leaden hours when the sun struck down, when flies crawled over bodies and faces, congregating around the corners of the mouth or attacking the eyes, searching for moisture? Those hours and days when there was no real action, just waiting. One wrote letters or received mail. This came at more or less regular intervals, but woe to the soldier wounded or sick. His mail would follow him, arriving always too late to catch him as he progressed from battalion to hospital, to convalescent depot, through reinforcement camp and transit camp back to his battalion. Weeks after his return, letters would be delivered bringing news months old.

The most efficient method of writing home was to use an airgraph. These were over-large sheets of paper on which one wrote in larger-than-usual handwriting. The airgraphs were then microfilmed at base, so that millions could be sent in a single aircraft-load. When the film was received in the United Kingdom, the negatives were developed and printed to an 8-inch by 6-inch image, enclosed in a window envelope and posted. It was a typical piece of Army organization − well thought out, flawlessly executed, simple and quick to operate. All mail home was subject to censorship, but once a month there was an issue of a 'green envelope'. The letter contained in a green envelope was not subject to censorship at unit level; one could write of personal matters without one's own officers learning of them; but it might be intercepted and censored at base. The letter in a green envelope placed a soldier on his honour not to reveal information of a military nature. How often (or indeed whether at all) that trust was betrayed cannot be known, but there were often times of personal crisis when one longed for more than one green envelope. One correspondent, formerly Corporal Eyre of the RASC, recalled an NCO who overcame the shortage by employing a local Italian printer to produce a thousand forgeries.

Among the chief memories of our correspondents are the songs that had been sung in the United Kingdom and which had accompanied the troops overseas. Vera Lynn is the singer most remembered as well as a certain lady, unknown by name to most who heard her, but remembered as the 'Lady in White', who sang to the troopships that arrived at or departed from Durban. At whatever time of the day or night the convoy came in or sailed away, the Lady in White would be there singing through her megaphone. The men who sailed in the convoys that went around the Cape, recall with affectionate memory that lady and the welcome they received from the people of South Africa. The song *Lili Marlene* is not often mentioned, for to hear Lala Andersen sing that song required a wireless set and the only ones were official sets with earphones.

Nostalgia played an important part in the lives of the soldiers fighting overseas and especially of those men in units that suffered high casualty rates. The memory of home and the need to be loyal to it and to its attitudes were powerful emotional ties. Inevitably, there were those who, for whatever reason, were not able to follow or adapt to the accepted codes of behaviour. Such men usually deserted — joined 'Trotter's Union', a euphemism employed in some battalions. Nor was it only the rank and file who did that. Numerous officer deserters could be met in Cairo, impeccably dressed scroungers who would approach a newcomer to the desert and ask for a cigarette or a loan of money, always because their wallet had been stolen by Arab pickpockets. The well-disciplined greenhorn would respond immediately, glad to have been of service to an officer. Eventually, he would learn of the existence of the military demi-monde of outcasts. Other ranks in the big cities had little chance of hiding themselves: the military police were far too vigilant. Even in the desert itself, those who deserted and disguised themselves as Arabs could be picked out because of their Western habits. They would always try to brush away from their faces the flies that crawled over them; the Arabs, in contrast, made no attempt to keep the flies away. Officer prisoners, stripped of their rank after courts martial had sentenced them, were confined in a detention camp near Geneifa in the Canal Zone and were subjected to exceptionally harsh treatment by the 'screws' who ran the camp. The treatment seemed aimed at humiliating the prisoners rather than retraining them to take a useful part in the War. The senseless tasks of the detention camps, which included polishing rusted tin cans or piling up pyramids of cannonballs, were certainly penal but hardly productive.

The crimes for which one could be sentenced to detention camps were trivial by civilian standards, and serious crime was rare. Rape and murder were almost unknown; desertion and disobedience to orders were the two principal crimes that filled the camps and, of course, stealing or looting. In the poverty-stricken Italian colonies, there was little if anything to take, although German reports talk of a wave of terror and looting suffered by the Italian colonists in Libya at the hands of Australian troops in Benghazi. Looting was really a matter of interpretation. To troops in the Line, an abandoned tank was a sort of steel oasis wherein might be found water, food, cigarettes, possibly NAAFI/EFI supplies and even changes of clothing. To the simple fighting soldier this was a sort of bonus. Eighth Army commanders viewed it in a different light. A memorandum laid down that the looting of captured material, or even of material of one's own side abandoned in the desert, was a penal offence, and that offenders were to be reported in order that disciplinary action could be taken against them. The memorandum concluded with the remark that the threat of disciplinary action had been insufficient to maintain discipline in such matters.

The hysteria regarding discipline expressed by the higher echelons of the Army were not always shared by regimental officers. Justly renowned is the commanding officer of one British infantry battalion whose unit, having suffered severe losses, was returned to Egypt. His men relaxed in Cairo after the strain of battle, but many fell foul of the provost marshal's policemen and were 'crimed' for minor infringements of dress regulations. On the CO's table at battalion headquarters the 252s (the Army's charge sheets) piled up. Angered at the attitude of base 'wallahs' toward the fighting men of his battalion, the colonel retaliated in the only way he could and recorded on every 252, in the section reserved for 'punishment awarded', the single terse and uncompromising word: 'Beheaded'.

However much the fighting soldiers may have disliked or even despised the provost in the big cities, there is nothing but unqualified praise for the divisional military policemen, particularly those who directed traffic through minefield gaps, immaculately turned out, with the aplomb and precision of a British 'bobby' in peacetime. The job they did under the heaviest fire deserves the praise that is bestowed upon them by Corporal Eyre. 'Looking back on the breakthrough after the battle, I remember how my feelings towards the MPs changed. Before Alamein, I used to think of them as officious and bullying, but when I saw those Redcaps standing in the middle of the minefields directing traffic through I realized what a tough job they had been doing.'

That was life 'up the blue'. Rarely was leave granted to the fighting soldiers, and short were the periods grudgingly allowed. To be wounded and to be convalescent was for most the sole opportunity to see something of the big towns of Egypt. Those places were an experience. Even to soldiers born and bred in the teeming cities of Britain, the noise, the bustle and above all the smells of the Egyptian towns were bewildering and irritating after the silence and isolation of the desert. One saw once-familiar things as trams and shops through new eyes, and one questioned social conditions that had once been accepted in the United Kingdom. The poverty and the degradation suffered by the 'fellahin' were in stark contrast to the elegant, pomaded men and especially to the exquisite ladies who, tightly corseted, with breasts projecting like melons, bejewelled and perfumed, sat for hour after hour over coffee cups, speaking French with staccato Arabic delivery.

Contrary to most people's belief, it was not the first ambition of the ordinary soldier on leave to find a sexual outlet. Most were too frightened of VD to risk intercourse with a casual girl picked up somewhere. In addition, the emphasis on continence and the social pressures to conform to contemporary, British, rigid standards of sexual morality kept most chaste. One boasted, of course, of conquests made. But many, perhaps most, of the sexual exploits were the products of the imagination of men who still thought that sex was something that mothers and fathers did. In any case, 'Monty' (rumour having saddled the Spartan general with the blame) had closed the brothel area of the Birka in Cairo and Sister Street in Alexandria. The licensed premises which peacetime soldiers remembered with advantages, and in whose small rooms it was said that generations of soldiers had spent their pay and their energies, had been shut. So one could risk the out-of-bounds area and its associated dangers of the pox or a knifing — or one could go without. Most did just that.

On the infrequent — no, rare — occasions when a short period of leave was granted and one had reached, let us say, the city of Cairo, one booked in at a leave hotel such as the Salvation Army's establishment near the Ezbekiah Gardens. The first demand was for a bath. The sheer, hedonistic luxury of washing in clean water, hot water, as much water as one wanted, was the first and greatest luxury. 'Up the blue', water was hoarded like a miser's gold, but in the big towns it could be squandered, wasted, poured away without thought. And yet, I wonder if even today those who served in the desert ever waste water, remembering how precious it once was?

After bathing and changing, there was tea to be enjoyed . . . cups of it, sweet and not tasting of chlorine or petrol. Tea and the chance to relax, knowing that no call would come to stand to, take post, stand guard, or mount a picquet, to lay mines or go out on patrol. One had time to oneself.

A quick shufti at a map showed the relationship of the principal streets to Cairo Main Station and of that place to the Salvation Army hostel. Then it was time to move out, somewhat hesitantly, into the masses of people who crammed the pavements. To those of us raised in a land where modest and decorous voices were the norm, the raucous pavement noises were shattering. It seemed that among the Egyptians quite ordinary conversations were conducted as a sort of shouting match, with voices rising in pitch, vehemence and delivery as the telling point was made.

Cairo was rich in military canteens, and the food in most was good. Almost any dish could be obtained, and the idea of a breakfast consisting of fresh pineapple followed by a brace of roast pigeon and bacon was, perhaps, unusual, but not excessively so. To most of those fresh from the desert, the demand was for egg and chips and still more egg and chips — a reaction to the absence of eggs in the desert and to the inability of battalion cooks to fry chips.

For entertainment there were cinemas. The principal ones showed films with Arabic subtitles. These ran as a continuous roll of symbols at the side of the screen when English-language films were being shown. One cinema, remembered by most of those who went to Cairo, had a sliding roof that was drawn back at night so that one sat in cool, star-lit darkness. Performances ended with the playing of the Egyptian national anthem, which the soldiers sang to words so bawdy that, thankfully, they were not understood by the Egyptian patrons

61

who would surely have taken exception to the slanderous remarks made about the Egyptian royal family.

As an alternative to the cinemas, there were the oddly administered clubs serving the ordinary soldiers. To those who went to Cairo, the names 'Pam Pam' or 'Sweet Melody' will bring back memories. Such clubs were probably a compromise thought up by the Army Command who, aware that soldiers might want to find a sexual outlet, and knowing that the Birka where such relief might have been obtained had been declared out of bounds, hoped that the mere presence of the girls in the clubs might be sufficient. There were girls in the clubs; but what girls! They were not Arab, nor were they French. They were probably Coptic Christians who were saving the commission they earned for use as a dowry. The unsuspecting soldier going into a club would suddenly find that a dark and buxom girl had snatched his hat and was seated at a table. When he approached the table to demand the return of his headgear, there would be an imperious clap of the girl's dark hands. A waiter would appear carrying glasses of coloured water, misnamed 'cherry brandy', and the unlucky soldier was poorer by ten ackers (about two days' pay for a British private soldier). Each time the girl clapped, the bearer came with his little glasses. Those girls could drink glass after glass at a very fast rate, and a month's pay could vanish in ten minutes down the plump throats of girls who gave a hint of a promise of sex in the display of a bit of cleavage, but gave nothing else. They were probably all virgins.

Alcohol was consumed in the clubs, but only by the soldiery: girls were not allowed to sit at a table on which there was alcohol. The only stuff available was beer, Stella beer, a lager type of brew, which to men raised on Burton Bitter was an insipid beverage. Properly tanked up on Stella — such a feat was possible, but it needed to be worked at — one sat back to enjoy a sort of cabaret, which was a feature of the early evening. I remember one poor, frightened girl of about fourteen vainly trying to continue her version of a Scottish dance to a background of fighting and swearing from a hostile audience. The band that supplied music throughout the evening was secured behind a chicken-wire fence, a primitive but effective device that kept it safe from the empty bottles which started to fly about towards nine in the evening. It was at about that hour that shuffling waiters dexterously swung chairs and tables away from the soldiers using them. This was not an attempt on the part of the management to provide a space for general dancing. Rather was it an attempt by that same management to prevent the furniture from being smashed into baton-sized pieces and used by battling groups of soldiers. There was always a fight. Who fought whom varied almost from minute to minute: at times, it would be British versus Kiwis, Scots versus English, infantry versus Gunners. Alliances were fickle things, and many fought for the sheer joy of it.

Such were the simple pleasures of the common soldiers. Those sophisticates who yearned for better things than sweaty evenings in the Pam Pam might go to Groppi's for ice cream and cakes. Groppi's was incredible, with food under glass, the rooms cool and probably air-conditioned. It was a haven of elegance and luxury in a city whose main tone was filth and misery. The common soldiery were not, however, encouraged to go to Groppi's. The finer places and pleasures were very much kept for commissioned ranks.

There were probably some soldiers who visited the pyramids or the museums of Cairo while on leave, but these men must have been a minority. This was neither indifference to culture nor ignorance of it on the part of the mass. Rather it was a question of priorities. Coming into a town after months or even years in military discomfort and masculine isolation left one hungry for those things that had once been familiar. Carpets on the floor, soft beds, tea in bed, baths and food. The time spent enjoying those left little time to spend looking at lots of stones that were thousands of years old.

Suddenly the time had run out. It was all over. The leave had come to an end . . . the Jewish Serviceman's Club with its schnitzels overflowing the plate and its crumbly cheesecake . . . the Victory Club . . . the Kiwi Club . . . all that was in the past. Ahead lay the black road running, seemingly endless, through the empty, grey-yellow landscape towards the Front. There was still a long way to drive, and there was no need yet to look out for the signs that located the battalion, so one lay back and remembered the Arab boot-blacks with their brushes filled with liquid blacking, the kiosk nearly opposite Shepheard's hotel that sold dirty books, the shops crammed with expensive consumer goods. One remembered the officer deserters, who slept (so it was said) in garages and cadged cigarettes from private soldiers who still respected men with pips on their shoulders. Oh yes, and one remembered the letters that should have been written and never were.

Within half an hour of leaving Cairo by truck, the signs began to appear along the side of the road. Another 30 minutes, and boards with the divisional markers were thick everywhere along the verges. Less familiar boards belonging to unusual units came and went, and then suddenly there was the 'Div' sign with our battalion's number painted on it. There over the dunes was home: not the half-remembered one of dreams and aching longing, but the present one, one that might bring death and privation, but one that also gave companionship and loyalty. Even before the dunes were crossed and the battalion area came into sight, you knew you were home. In the hot afternoon, a bugle would sound. The notes of the regimental call . . . and then, perhaps, the urgent demand for the orderly sergeant. The regimental call brought one back to reality. Cairo was a dream far away down that long, black road. Here was home. And it was good to be back.

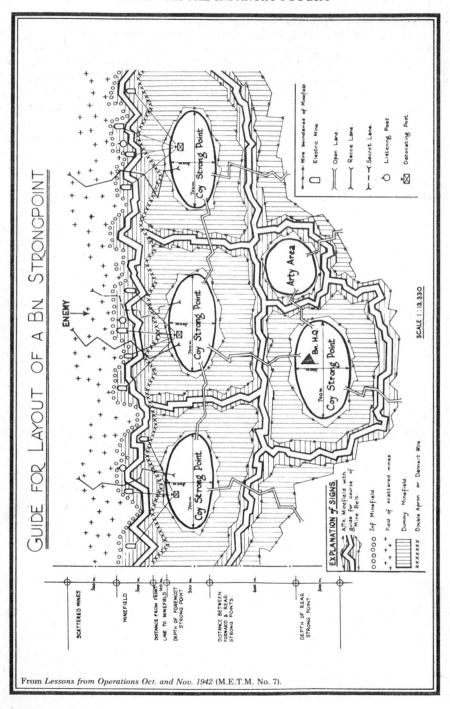

GUIDE FOR LAYOUT OF A BN. STRONGPOINT

ENEMY

Coy Strong Point

Coy Strong Point

Coy Strong Point

Coy Strong Point

Arty Area

Bn. H.Q.

700 m.

SCALE 1 : 13,330

EXPLANATION of SIGNS.

	A.Tk. Minefield with guide for course of Mine Belt.
ooooo	Inf Minefield
+ + +	Field of scattered mines
	Dummy Minefield
xxxxxxx	Double Apron or Dannert Wire

··I·· Wire boundaries of Minefield

☐ Electric Mine.
) (Open Lane.
))((Recce Lane.
)—Y—(Secret Lane.
⊙ Listening Post.
⊠ Detonating Post.

SCATTERED MINES
300 m.
MINEFIELD
300 m.
DISTANCE FROM FRONT LINE TO MINEFIELD 900 m.
DEPTH OF FOREMOST STRONG POINT 300 m.
DISTANCE BETWEEN FORWARD & REAR STRONG POINTS. 600 m.
DEPTH OF REAR STRONG POINT. 300 m.

From *Lessons from Operations Oct. and Nov. 1942* (M.E.T.M. No. 7).

4.

THE WAR THE INFANTRY FOUGHT

Like so many of his principal subordinates in Eighth Army, Montgomery had fought as a front-line infantryman in the First World War. Like them, he had known the heart-rending, shattering experience of going up to the Line with a battalion at full strength and of bringing it out of action reduced to a cadre, its men having been flung away in futile attacks. For in war the heaviest burden of battle always falls upon the foot soldier. Infantrymen are the nomads of the battlefield. They have no homes, as have the men of the tank regiments, the transport columns or even the artillery. The soldiers of each of those arms of service has a fixed place of abode, which, even if it is a vehicle, wheeled or tracked, is nevertheless a base, a home in which extra food, extra water, bed rolls and certain little luxuries can be carried. The infantryman porters what he needs; and his needs are simple ones. Water, food, ammunition and, perhaps, a change of socks — sufficient to cover the basic needs of a warrior in battle. He has no room for luxuries or for unnecessary items.

For the Battle of El Alamein, he would have been dressed in the same type of thick battledress that he had worn in the United Kingdom with an overcoat to keep out the bitter cold of the late October nights in the desert; these, leather boots (which soon took on a patina of greyish/yellow grease) and a steel helmet constituted the basic uniform. The webbing equipment he wore was as simple and as unelaborate as the uniform. A waist belt carried two long straps that passed over the shoulders and helped to support two oblong pouches, one on either side of the belt buckle. The belt carried a bayonet on the soldier's left side, a flat, cloth-covered water bottle on his right and a two-piece entrenching tool in a webbing cover fixed on the belt, at the back of the body. Set high up between the shoulders was a small webbing pack. This held a two-piece mess tin, a groundsheet or anti-gas cape, socks, and a holdall containing soap, toothbrush, flannel, razor, and needles and thread. A few tins of corned beef, some dry biscuits and, now and again, cans of stew or some other part of the Army's composite ration filled the pack. An enamelled one-pint mug dangled from the back of the small pack. The oblong pouches on the front of the body each contained three loaded magazines for the Bren gun. With those, a couple of linen bandoliers, each holding 50 rounds of rifle ammunition, and a few cast-iron hand grenades, the British infantryman was ready for war.

There were, of course, variations in the amount of ammunition or equipment, as there were in the establishment and armament of units at various times during the war. Weapons proven to be useless — such as the 2-inch mortar and the Boys anti-tank rifle — were replaced.

THE INFANTRY UNIT

The lowest tactical group in the infantry was the Section. At full strength, this was a corporal and nine men. The Corporal was armed with a machine-pistol, usually a Thompson submachine-gun. When the infantry section was marching, the second man in the single file was the Bren gunner. His task of serving the 26-pound, light machine-gun was shared by the third man in the file, although everybody in the section took turns at carrying the weapon. Then came three riflemen whose principal task it was to protect the Bren gun or to act as gunners should the need arise. Two bomb throwers and a lance corporal completed the section file. Three such sections, together with a small headquarters group of a lieutenant, a runner and a signaller, constituted a Platoon. A sergeant was the second in command, and there were times when officer casualties were so high that sergeants took over and led platoons. A Rifle Company was made up of three platoons, commanded by a major with a captain as second in command. They, plus a company sergeant major, stretcher bearers, signallers and runners, were banded into a headquarters group.

Four companies and a specialist or headquarters company formed a Battalion. Within the battalion headquarters company was a platoon of men who fired cast-iron, 10-pound bombs from a number of 3-inch mortars — the battalion's field artillery. By the time of El Alamein, each battalion also had a number of anti-tank guns to counter the sudden attacks by German armour. A platoon of Bren gun carriers, small, tracked vehicles used for reconnaissance and to porter supplies, formed the battalion's armoured detachment. The men of the motor transport platoon drove a number of wheeled vehicles, 3-ton and 15-cwt lorries as well as platoon utility trucks, light vans about the size of a large car. These vehicles constituted the battalion's transport column, and included for each company a 3-ton truck to carry all the remainder of the clothing and effects of its soldiers. Each battalion also had a medical group, the regimental aid post. An officer of the Royal Army Medical Corps, sometimes with one or two men of his own corps and aided by men of the battalion's band who had been trained as stretcher bearers, tended the sick and wounded. A communications network between battalion headquarters and its rifle companies was maintained by a few men of the Royal Corps of Signals augmented by specially trained infantrymen. There was also a pioneer platoon and then an administrative group — cooks, clerks, regimental police and the battalion chaplain.

This tiny, self-contained world numbering at full strength just over one thousand men was divided into three echelons. The rifle companies, the mortars and the anti-tank detachments were the 'F' (fighting) Echelon. Behind them (how far behind depended upon the tactical situation) was 'A' (administrative) Echelon, the battalion's ammunition distribution point, controlled by the regimental sergeant major. Farther back still was 'B' Echelon, where the cooks prepared the food and into which came supplies and ammunition for 'A' Echelon, sent forward from the next highest unit in the infantry military chain, the Brigade. This 'B' Echelon fed 'A' Echelon, which then passed supplies to battalion headquarters and from that group to the fan of rifle companies holding the battle line. The full strength of a battalion was seldom put into action at any one time. Conscious of the heavy casualties that usually befell the infantry, a proportion of officers, senior non-commissioned officers and experienced soldiers from the companies was withdrawn before each attack. Those men left out of battle (LOBs) were intended to form the nucleus around which a battalion, shattered by losses, could be reformed.

Small infantry units have the power by themselves to win only tactical successes, and by the time in which this book is set infantry section tactics had been formalized into a battle drill. Those simple routines were designed to enable a section, for example, to take out an enemy machine-gun position. More elaborate platoon drills were evolved to capture or destroy enemy strongpoints. Larger objectives were the target of company and battalion drills. The basic infantry task was to seize and consolidate its grip upon ground held by the enemy. To accomplish this, the infantrymen had to close with the foe and to destroy him. Excepting the Russian front, it was seldom in the Second World War that masses of infantrymen of either side confronted each other in hand-to-hand combat. The infantry battlefield was empty until the men of an attacking force rose up out of the slit trenches in which they had been sheltering, and moved, usually at a marching pace, towards those defences in which were concealed the forces of the enemy. If the assault were successful, the enemy abandoned his trenches and a number of small figures would be seen running, at some distance, through the desert. Should the attack fail, then the assaulting troops, seen by the defenders as scattered groups of men trudging forward, would withdraw, regroup and come forward again — and again — and again.

Very few men of a rifle company would know either what the objective was or when they had reached it. They might be told that the battalion's task was to seize a certain point or to reach a particular area. To the simple soldiers, who lacked maps or compasses by which to orientate themselves, one place in the desert looked very much like any other. The attack would begin, and to reach the objective the infantry would move forward, stolidly and unflinching (unless enemy fire forced them to carry out some tactical manoeuvre) until a sight of the enemy gave them the opportunity to fire their weapons, or until the officer halted their advance with the information that they had gained the objective.

It all sounds so simple, so uncomplicated and so basic. But to reach that objective the infantry, those nomads, had to walk through barrages of enemy artillery that crashed down in an effort to deter them. They walked through curtains of enemy machine-gun and rifle fire. Frequently, they advanced towards their objectives across those gardens of death, uncleared enemy minefields; and, when they had reached the undistinguished map reference that was their target, they would have to hold it against the enemy's infantry and armoured counterattacks until the time came for them to begin a fresh assault to drive the enemy from his new defensive position. All that they did, and they did it on a pint of water each day, a tin of bully beef and some biscuits, on packets of terrible 'V' cigarettes and possibly stew and tea at night. And they were the lowest paid men in the Army, for it was not held to be skilful or worthy of reward to be an infantryman.

A DAY IN THE LIFE . . .

'Two nights ago we moved into our positions, relieving another mob that had held the line for eight days. The first part of the approach march was made by lorry to a point about ten miles from divisional headquarters, and then it was a foot march across the desert. The night was pitch dark with low cloud and no stars. Stars gave some light; surprising when one thinks of how far away they are and how small they seem to be, but star shine is sufficient to give little light. The night we took over there was no light at all, and our officers marched by compass bearing. The ground in that sector was made up of small pieces of almost triangular rock, and as the move was made by night we could not see what was underfoot, so that several men twisted their ankles.

'During the march there were the usual, unexplained and annoying delays. The column would suddenly halt and we would stand waiting in the darkness. The most frightening rumours flew up and down the column. That the Jerries had broken through, that there were tanks ahead, that we were crossing a minefield, that we were marching straight into enemy lines — the usual remarks which can so easily destroy morale. The explanation for one halt turned out to be that the guide who had come to lead us into his unit lines was late. When our man arrived he led us at a brisk pace along a white tape to some place where we sat down to eat a meal which had been brought up. We were in dead ground about two miles behind the front-line. Battalion set up its main headquarters there. Battle headquarters or TAC HQ was set up less than a mile behind the forward line. We had two companies in the Line. Mine was one.

'The guide for our company then led us forward up a fairly steep incline. This was made of a sort of loose shale, and we slipped about without gaining a real foothold. We scrambled up the slope cursing and blinding our way towards the top. We were halted just below the crest. The guide had told our company commander that Jerry usually sent over a barrage about that time of night. We were late in reaching the rendezvous and should have relieved the platoons in the line by that time. The guide had said that the little Jerry infantry gun usually fired a dozen or more rounds to catch ration parties coming up and over the crest. So our major had halted us on the reverse slope and below the crest.

'The guide was right. There was a light whirring sound and then a series of quick flashes and mild explosions along the ridge. Nobody was hurt. We waited for a while and then moved over the crest downhill and onto the level ground. We took over the mob's positions, and then our officer came round to see that we were settled in. My slit trench was on the left of the platoon line, about twenty yards from the slit of the right hand man of the platoon on our flank. I was by myself. I didn't like being alone. Not that I was frightened of the dark, but because when there's two to a slit one can sleep even when both were supposed to be on sentry. It was stupid to do this and really risky, but we were all so terribly tired.

'During the night our platoon sergeant came round and ordered us to 'stand to'. It was still dark, but dawn comes very quickly to the desert. Not much more than five or so minutes separates total darkness from clear light, although the sun takes another hour to come up over the horizon. In that pre-dawn half light, Jerry often made his attacks, coming out of the darkness at us. So did we, and another favourite time for assaults to go in was last light, just before night set in. There was no attack that morning. Less than an hour after "stand to", we were "stood down" and cleaned our weapons, equipment and smoked. We were all waiting for the first brew to be given out. It had come forward during the last hours before dawn. We were then put on half alert — that is, one man in two was ready for immediate action. Jerry was away over the low crest some way in front of us. We were in dead ground and could not be seen, so it was all right to move about in the open. There was always a risk that one of his "long-range snipers" (the artillery) might open up, but it was a chance that one had to take.

'There was a sudden flurry of shells — ours going over to smother him. This served to keep Jerry's head down while our ration parties came over the crest. There were two more porters than normal; they were carrying water so that we could use what was left in our bottles for washing and shaving, with perhaps a half cup left over for a brew-up later in the morning. Washing was perhaps the most primitive thing in the desert. Four of us would each give half a mug of water, and then we would toss for the first go. By the time the fourth man had had his wash and shave there wasn't much water left, but any that was over would be kept and either left for later in the day or one of us would have an all-over wash. This usually used up the two pints of water. Teeth were cleaned in a little drop of fresh water in a mug; some used a mouthful of tea, although some men brushed "dry" so as not to waste water.

'Sentry duty was the main task of the day, and aircraft spotting was most important. The Messerschmitts that roared low over the desert to machine-gun troops on the ground usually did little harm, for they had passed over us before they could take proper aim. The fighters caused no damage, quite different to the Ju 87 dive-bombers, which were alarmingly accurate.

'After breakfast we waited for tiffin or lunch; cheese or bully and biscuits and a brew-up. If we had the water we had our own brews. We liked the German Esbit cookers; little stoves fuelled with cubes of solidified alcohol. These gave off no smoke, no fumes and were efficient. The British Army was said to have "Tommy Cookers", but, apart from the time on an exercise in Scotland before we came overseas, I was never issued with a Tommy cooker for the whole of the War. When we could get hold of a drop of petrol, we would make a "Benghazi". This was a simple stove fuelled by petrol. A small round tin, a cigarette tin for example, was excellent. It would have a couple of ventilation holes punched around the rim and then the tin would be half filled with sand. A drop of petrol was poured in and a mess tin of water was placed on top. The petrol was lit and a couple of minutes later there was boiling water. Somehow we all carried supplies of tea, sugar and dried or tinned milk. The tea always had the taste of chlorine and some of it was also slightly salt. Those of us who had been boy scouts put a matchstick in the water to take out the taste of petrol, but the taste of chlorination was always there.

'Our guns fired concentrations at intervals to disguise the activity that was going on in our lines, like the arrival of the ration parties. For the evening meal the QM would send up M & V stew, corned beef fritters or something else that was basic and tasty. "Compo" rations did not come in until quite late in the fighting, so that it would be true to say that we fought on bully and biscuits. Breakfast was bacon, usually, and for tiffin, cheese. Bread we seldom had, and never in the Line, and it was always biscuits. There was an awful jam that we got from Palestine "Melon and Lemon". It was tasteless, and these days whenever I see Polycell it reminds me of that terrible jam.'

Patrols were another of the daily, or more usually nightly, duties. There were three main types. A standing patrol guarded some point in no man's land that it was decided would have to be denied to the enemy — a minefield gap, for example. The composition and number of men of a standing patrol varied: eight men and a sergeant was usual. The patrol would reach its designated area after dark and would occupy the objective until just before first light. It would withdraw to the Line and be back in the company's positions before 'stand to'.

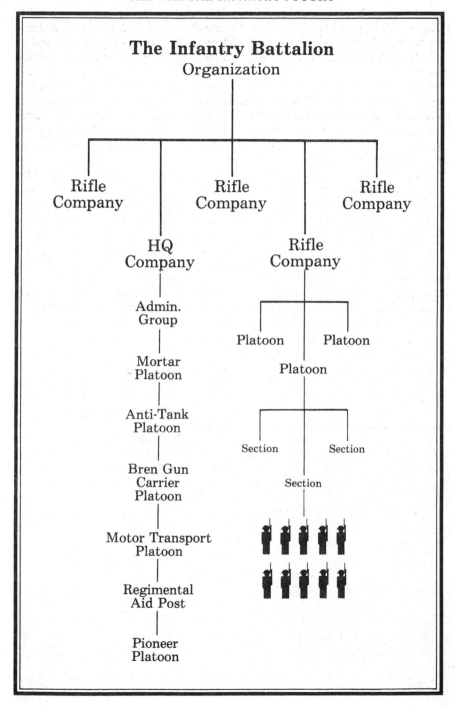

The Infantry Battalion
Organization

Rifle Company   Rifle Company   Rifle Company

HQ Company   Rifle Company

Admin. Group

Mortar Platoon

Anti-Tank Platoon

Bren Gun Carrier Platoon

Motor Transport Platoon

Regimental Aid Post

Pioneer Platoon

Platoon   Platoon

Platoon

Section   Section

Section

Reconnaissance patrols went out to gain information on the enemy's positions or movements, to check the ground in front of battalion or to carry out any one of a number of miscellaneous intelligence tasks that were required to gain a total picture of the opposing force. The duties of these first two types of patrol did not, normally, demand that they should seek out the enemy: that was the task of the fighting patrol. It was the often-repeated demand of British senior officers that the British front-line should extend forward to the German wire. The Army was urged to 'dominate no man's land' and to achieve this by aggressive patrolling. For this sole purpose, heavily-armed fighting patrols were sent out to kill the enemy. The strength of such a group varied according to the circumstances, but 30 men was not unusual.

Patrols were usually sent out by night, although daytime groups did operate. During the late afternoon, the patrol members were gathered to be told of the task ahead of them. They would then return to their slit trenches to sleep or rest. There would be an early meal followed by a check on weapons. Conscious of possible casualties, all letters or papers identifying the unit would be left behind.

As swiftly as a cloak thrown across the sky, it would be dark. All along the forward defence lines small groups of men, on both sides of no man's land, would rise out of the trenches and set out into a night of uncertainty, danger and possible death. The standing patrol, having approached to within a few hundred yards of the objective it had to guard, would be halted while a corporal and a couple of men went forward to check that the slit trenches were not occupied by aggressive panzergrenadiers or belligerent Bersaglieri, that the slits had not been booby-trapped and that the area was clear of the enemy. The patrol would move in, the sentries would be posted and the times of relief given to them. Half the patrol would then settle down in the rocky sandy, uncomfortable slit trench. One man in two stayed awake, peering out, freezing cold, into the dark and mysterious night.

'The stars come out. They are sufficient to lighten the darkness, but in that light mysterious shadows are born and seem to move backwards and forwards across the face of the desert. Are those patches of darkness shadows, or are they groups of the enemy moving into the assault? Ears are strained to catch the faintest noise. Was that the scrape of a rifle on stone? Did that shadow move again? Oh Christ! Nobody wants to make a fool of himself by challenging a shadow — yet if it is no shadow then the Jerries are now within grenade-throwing distance. The desert in the early hours of the night and especially in rocky areas is full of mysterious sound. Rocks, expanded by the sun, cool, contract and groan or crackle gently. Night and nerves magnify these sounds into the racking gasps of an approaching enemy or the crunch of his boots moving over the bare rocks.'

Sometimes during the night, far away there would be vague noises, perhaps footsteps, faintly heard. A report to the corporal might bring back the officer's reassurance that it was a British fighting patrol going about its work.

'There's a sudden sound behind — good God, have they got behind me? The corporal's reassuring north-country tones come out of the night: "Wake your oppo up, it's time for him to do his stag." Relief — blessed relief. The mate sharing the trench is woken. It is his turn to stand up and keep watch, yours to crouch shivering on the rocky bottom of the slit, to cover the head and face and body with a blanket, and under its cover to light a cigarette and relish that first warming, relaxing puff. For the next two hours you can lie there, in the cramped and sandy grave, luxuriating in being relieved from the responsibility of being the sentry on duty.' On guard, the two hours of duty seemed to pass so slowly; the two hours of sleep rushed past in seconds. Very few had a watch. The sergeant had a service issue pocket watch and officers usually wore wrist watches, but the rank and file depended on the sergeant's timekeeping.

Fighting patrols were really frightening. First of all was the knowledge that the patrol's whole purpose was to look for battle. On either a standing or recce patrol, one prudently hid if an enemy force came along, but on a fighting patrol every effort was made to ambush and to destroy the enemy. 'In one daytime patrol (pre-Alamein but still indicative of the type of action) we had searched through a small collection of ruined houses in an isolated, destroyed and burnt-out settlement just off the Via Balbia. An Italian patrol was spotted and we hid behind the walls and the piles of rubble that had once been little whitewashed houses. Our sergeant waited until the whole Italian group was passing our front, then he stood up and shot their officer with his Tommy gun. The Italian officer was the last man in the line, and I remember that he held a peeled orange in his hand. Those heavy, 45-calibre bullets smashed his head. It was sickening. The sergeant got four others in that first sweeping burst of his gun. The remaining members of the Italian patrol ran off, but we caught most of them. Some were wearing a sort of soft red fez with a very long blue tassle.

'Then there was the time we struck at a German patrol. It was another daytime stunt. We pinned them down, but they fired off flares and within minutes we were being bombarded. Under cover of their barrage, they attacked us. They must have had a reinforcement group close to hand, for when the attack came in there was a lot more of them in the assault than we had fired on in the beginning. They came on in rushes. Contrary to popular belief, the desert is not flat so that there is always dead ground. A group of Jerries would run out and then flop down into some hollow. There would be bursts of fire from their Spandaus and another battle group would make a quick dash. Soon we were under pressure and had to leapfrog back towards our own lines. It was very frightening to hear the Spandaus at close range and to see the bullets tearing up the ground. Jerry hand grenades could be flung some distance, but they had only blast effect. Their mortars were deadly, and they brought them into action so quickly that it was unbelievable.

'Recce patrols were messy affairs if we had to go through the pockets of some poor devil who had been killed and had been left lying out on the sand for a couple of days. People talk about rigor mortis, but after a day or two the limbs were flexible again and indeed, after a week or so, a quick pull on an arm or leg would detach it from the torso. Two day old corpses were already fly blown and stinking. There was no dignity in death, only masses of flies and maggots, black swollen flesh and the body seeming to move, either because of the gases within it or else the thousands of maggots at work. We had to take documents, identity discs, shoulder straps, anything of intelligence value. Pushing or pulling those frightening dead men to reach their pockets was sickening. Of course, we couldn't wash our hands — one rubbed them in sand — sometimes we rubbed them practically raw if it had been a particularly disgusting day.

'The flies were horrible. When we disturbed them they would rise from the corpse in an incandescent cloud and would settle on us, walking on our living flesh with feet that had only seconds before been resting on the blackening horror at our feet.

'To sum it up, patrols were a real bastard. It was usual that an all-night patrol excused one from duty for up to six hours afterwards, depending on how strong the platoon was. If we had had a pasting and there were not so many men left, then a few hours rest was all that we could get. The fewer the number of men in the line the more often guard came round and the more often we were out on patrol. Twice a week was an average.'

You can say, then, that life in the line was a long march in, boring guard duties, poor food, little water, bombardments, patrols and the possibility of being killed at almost any time of the day and night, until that happy evening finally came when the unit was relieved. Then there was the long march back to 'B' Echelon and back to formal parades, haircuts, weapon training and sleep. The first parade — roll call — when a unit came out of the line was always emotional, particularly if the battalion had suffered heavy casualties. On that first parade, the company would stand as if at full strength, each man in his usual place, and the gaps in the files demonstrated how severe had been the fighting. In front of the company, the sergeant major would call the roll. When no voice answered to the name, a dialogue would begin to determine whether the absent soldier had been killed, wounded or was missing. Who had seen him fall? Where had he fallen? Had it been checked that he was dead? The dreadful catechism would continue.

This was the time when, if no reinforcements to the battalion were coming up, that platoon or companies would be broken up or amalgamated and new loyalties and friendships formed. Friendships in the infantry had the strength of the biblical love shared by David and

Jonathan, but such friendships were often as brief as the life span of a butterfly. The comradeship of the battlefield is a strange and terrible thing, and because of its precarious nature it makes bonds which link the survivors of the fighting more closely than brothers, for decade after decade of peacetime. It is that loyalty which most soldiers miss in peacetime.

THE INFANTRY ATTACK

The planned and organized set-piece infantry attack could be a beautifully produced and orchestrated affair. That there were some attacks which did not have a high degree of planning or involve the complete co-operation of all arms, or that there were even assaults mounted without any support (and, seemingly, without any plan) is perfectly true; but they are not dealt with here.

In the early days of shortages and make-do, attack and defence were frequently ad-hoc, but it is of late 1942 that we speak. For the British, supplies of arms and, above all, men were coming into the desert in far greater numbers than they had before, and these reinforcements gave Eighth Army qualitative and quantitative superiority. Thus, immediately before El Alamein and always thereafter, attacks were set-piece and well planned affairs.

The object of an infantry attack would be to wrest territory from the enemy. That the enemy would normally resist this operation with every type of weapon he could muster is self-evident. It was the task of the infantryman, whether he was carried into battle as a lorry-borne rifleman or walked in on his feet, to occupy and to hold ground. Only he could do this. Tanks might roar and rattle, encircling, cutting through territory in wide, scythe-like operations, but once the armour had ridden by, the area reverted to being enemy territory once again and remained so until the infantry captured and held it. Armour unsupported by infantry did not have the capacity to dominate a whole area; nor was artillery alone able to hold ground. Shells could not permanently deter a force determined to occupy a piece of ground, nor could a barrage, however devastating its ferocity or however long its duration, altogether crush the determined infantryman. Once the barrage stopped, then from out of the shattered earth a dusty, dishevelled and battered infantryman would rise, place the butt of a light machine-gun into his shoulder and, with controlled bursts of fire, engage the advancing enemy.

First, last and always it was the foot soldiers: in the British service, men of the line regiments who pitted themselves against a storm of bullets and shrapnel to carry out the most basic of all military operations — to attack, to seize and to hold the enemy's territory.

One of the two favourite times for attack was before first light, an assault coming out of the darkness to overrun the enemy and capture his positions before the light of day exposed the attacking troops to machine-gun and artillery fire. The other time was at last light, an approach march in the evening and then, as the light vanished quickly from the sky, to open the attack and to complete this in the dark against a demoralized enemy. Often, night assaults were made at the time of a waxing moon so that the attacking infantry had some light. Later during the war in continental Europe, the use of searchlight beams reflected from low clouds produced the same effect.

Let us follow the fortunes of an assault made at last light. Where possible the assaulting troops were rested, and we join the riflemen of an infantry company late in the afternoon in positions some half a mile behind their own front-line. During the morning, the Colonel's O (Orders) Group — officers and senior NCOs — have gone into the forward defence zone and studied the ground over which the companies will advance that evening. Compass bearings have been taken, topographical features noted and the terrain conditions studied before the O Group's return to Battalion TAC HQ, in the vicinity of which the companies that are to make the assault are carrying out their final preparations.

At TAC HQ, tasks vital to the success of the forthcoming attack are being undertaken. As a liaison between the infantry and the artillery batteries, which are to lay before the attackers in their advance a barrage of high-explosives, is the Forward Observation Officer (FOO) and his signallers. This small group of artillerymen often accompanied the battalion when it made a major attack. The FOO directed the fire of the distant gun batteries onto targets invisible to the gunners sweating at their pieces. It was vital that there was the closest liaison between the infantry officers and the FOO. The accuracy of the gunners, the speed with which targets could be engaged, a controlling of the pace of the advance or a speeding up of the lifts of the creeping barrage — all these were points that often determined the success of an operation.

'Sometime after tiffin there is the stomach-turning call "NCOs to Platoon O Group!" and the private soldiers watch the small knot of men gathered round the lieutenant as he explains the plan of the attack. The corporals return and brief their sections. "We're doing a two-company stunt. We're on the right, "D" Company on the left. The objective is the Jerry first line on Point 36. We go in at last light with a barrage. Just before dark we'll get behind the crest there, which "B" and "C" Companies are holding. The form-up position (FUP) will be just below the crest on the reverse slope, and the start line will be on the forward slope. We've got about four hours to go. The water truck will be here soon. Bottles will be filled, hard tack issued. Two tins of bully, two packets of biscuits. We may be out a couple of days before relief.

'There'll be a brew-up and a meal at five. Two grenades per man. Bren mags filled. The CSM will issue extra bangoliers of ammo. Some of it will be tracer, some armour-piercing. Keep these separate from the ordinary rounds. The officer will take the parade before we move off. Hand in papers, letters and anything else to the LOBs. Now clean weapons and try to get some kip in.

'The desert afternoon, even in autumn, is very hot, and the men lie sweating, scratching, trying to rest. Some actually do sleep, but for the great majority the pre-battle feeling, an amalgam of excitement and fear, prevents it.

'The water truck comes forward and the flat bottles are filled with warm water, saline and heavily chlorinated. Poor stuff, but every drop is cherished for God alone knows when they'll get a refill. The company storeman, the QM and the CSM pass quickly from slit trench to slit trench, handing out corned beef and biscuits, cotton bandoliers of rifle ammunition and the heavy Mills hand grenades. A long time after they passed comes one of the LOBs with the small boxes of sensitive fuzes for the bombs. The base plug of the little iron casing is unscrewed, and delicately a curved tube — the detonator — is taken out of the protective box and placed in the body of the Mills bomb. With the base plug refitted the lethal thing is ready. The removal of a split pin will release a control lever and cause the grenade to explode within seconds.

'The sun passes overhead and shines behind the enemy lines. It is now about four in the afternoon. There is the sound of a lorry: the ration truck with the evening meal is coming up. It is the usual Machonachies meat and vegetable stew. Few feel like eating, but all do. It might be the last hot meal for days.' There were some units that did not give their men a meal before an attack for fear of complications in the event of a stomach wound.

'The tea is hot, strong and sweet. There is enough for two mugs each. The soldiers sit about savouring the luxury of a second cup, smoking and chatting. There is a slow build-up of tension. Mentally, the warriors are preparing themselves for the coming battle. Increased amounts of adrenalin are being released into the bloodstream, improving senses already razor keen. The soldiers become aware that their reflexes are quicker and their movements more decisive. The primitive hunting instincts are being re-awakened. Eyesight is sharper, the better to spot a quarry. Hearing becomes more sensitive, ready to catch the smallest sound of the pursued. Smells are suddenly overpowering: the urine smell of men and of their unwashed bodies; the lingering stink of petrol, heavy on the air even though the ration trucks have long since driven away; and the sweet smell of rifle oil on the bolt. Even the desert smells, a sort of hot, dry, sour smell of dust long undisturbed.

"Get dressed!" The decisive stage of the pre-battle preparation. The waist belt still hangs loose with the pouches swinging. The belt is fastened and the small pack is swung into position between the shoulders. Buckle tongues clip into the receivers on the top of the pouches. A final check. Water bottle? Shake it. Full. OK. Bayonet. Entrenching tool? Pick up the cotton, khaki-coloured bandolier and drape it across the body from right shoulder to left hip. Two grenades, one in each of the battledress blouse's breast pockets, and then the rifle with its breech still covered in the canvas hood to protect it from the pervading dust. Steel helmet on, strap at the back of the head.

"Fall in!" We wander across to where the sergeant is standing. There is a sudden infection of yawns. We are all suddenly and mysteriously tired. It is as if the mind, conscious of the demands that will be made during the coming battle, is slowing down the body's physical actions so as to store energy for the struggle. "Any letters or papers?" The sergeant questions and hands the small packets we give him to one of the lucky buggers who have been left out of this fight. "Right, here comes the officer. Platoon, 'shun!" and we stand still. The lieutenant looks so young; too young to have the burden of looking after us on his shoulders, but that's what he's got his pip for. "I won't pretend it'll be easy. Jerry will do his utmost to stop us, but we're going in two companies strong. Keep going. No stopping for the wounded and don't walk too fast. The artillery is laying a creeping barrage ahead of us, and we don't want to walk into it. Good luck, lads. Right: standing load!"

'We throw our rifles forward, flip open the bolt and insert ten rounds. There is a slight resistance as the top bullet is pushed forward, and then there is the fat, satisfying sound as the brass case fits snugly into the breech. There is one up the spout now. Safety catch on. We sling our rifles onto our shoulders.

"Right, Corporal, lead on!" Our small file, five paces between each man, joins the other sections, and we all, the whole company in single file, move towards the sun, which is no longer the hot and glowing monster of early afternoon but a benevolent parent, warm and gentle. We are walking into the setting sun, and the dust thrown up by our column's marching feet hangs shining in the air like a golden veil. The figures at the head of the column are almost swallowed from sight by the dust, and those about twenty paces in front of me seem to be enveloped in a cloud of gold.

'By the side of the track there's a small group of figures. The CO, the RSM, some men from HQ company and our own LOBs. This is no time for ribald chat nor for formalities, but our lieutenant salutes the commanding officer and I wonder whether through his mind has flashed, as it has through mine, the gladiator's valediction, "Hail! We who are about to die salute you."

'Far away behind us there is a series of popping sounds, and seconds later shells from our 25pdr batteries whirr over our heads to explode in smothered 'crumps' somewhere on Jerry. All the artillery batteries of the division are stonking the length of his line in front of us. This is to bewilder him and to hide the point at which our two-company attack will go in. The guns have been giving Jerry a pasting at intervals throughout the day. Perhaps the barrage may bluff him into not realizing that behind the shells we shall be coming.

'We walk for about half an hour. There are stops when the Jerries lay down a counter-fire. This is a standard procedure. They fire on pre-selected points behind our line. One of those points is the crossing of two narrow tracks: some heavy stuff has fallen there. The ground begins to rise, and it is clear that we are near our battalion's forward defence zone. Just below the crest we halt and spread out in a long extended line on the reverse slope of the small ridge. This is the forming-up line. How long we are likely to remain there we don't know, so some men lie down resting uncomfortably on the rocky ground, propped up by their small packs. There is little talking; no noise except the barrage. Time for a quick smoke. Hands still automatically cupped round the lighted match, even though we are out of sight of the enemy and it is still not dark. It is nearly twilight. The red ball of the sun is almost gone from the sky, but as usual there is a truly beautiful sunset. Sunrise is equally spectacular. The sudden thought, will I see tomorrow's dawn, is rejected. Too morbid. We'll have casualties, and if I have to go I wouldn't mind a quick bullet. But if my time is not up, dear God, to be blinded or castrated. . . .

"On your feet!" We stand up. The western sky is a blend of pastel shades, among them eau-de-Nil. If only the Nile really had that colour. Flamingo pink and Madonna blue predominate. "Let's go!" The company, extended in a single line across nearly half a mile of desert, covers the last few paces to reach the crest, and like a thin black wave crosses it. Just below the crest on the forward slope — that is the side of the ridge facing the enemy — are located the daytime look-out positions of the men from our front-line companies. The ground is shale and rocky so that their slit trenches are quite shallow and they have had to pile up pieces of rock and large stones to form sangars behind which they shelter. I don't like sangars. I prefer to be dug-in. The rocks and stones making a sangar fragment so easily that a single bullet strike can fling off half a dozen razor-sharp rock fragments to wound or blind. Dug-in I feel safe against almost anything; in a sanger I'm visible and vulnerable.

'We are accompanied as we cross the crest by the remainder of the front-line company. At dark each night, the platoons move from the reverse slope and take up position on the forward slope. Not only do they form there a defensive line with a good field of fire but now, if our attack fails and Jerry counterattacks, then they will form a long-stop defence.

'Just below the crest on the forward slope, we pass through the sangars held by men who have been stuck in them all day without being able to move. The soldiers look at us with tired, emotionless eyes. There's nothing to say. It's all been said before. The extended line halts. The company commander and our lieutenant check their watches. While we wait I look around me. Small patches of red light glow and die as the shells from our barrage crash onto the enemy line. There is a sustained, red glare away to our right; a burning vehicle, perhaps. The stars are shining brightly in the dark sky behind us. In the not-quite-dark sky before us, they are still pale.

"Forward!" The attack is under way. Without drama or histrionics, the infantry line moves. Knees are bent so as to adjust to the gradient of the hill. Now only a mile or so separates us from the little djebel that is our objective. I suddenly remember that the breech cover is still on my rifle, I feel down the stock, undo the brass studs and put the thick canvas hood inside my battledress blouse. Our rifles are still slung; they won't be needed just yet.

'There is a sudden, lower whirring in the air and about 150 yards ahead of our extended line there are twinkling points of fire. For a second or two there is doubt. Is this Jerry's counter-fire? But then comes the reassurance: it is the start of our own creeping barrage. The shells fly over. "Crash", and each explosion lights up the darkness a little. The lights go out suddenly as the Gunners increase the range. Then the line of lights sparkles again — like will-o'-the-wisp, beckoning us on.

'The sounds of the creeping barrage and of the stonk being laid on the enemy's position intermingle and are indistinguishable. They are a single, loud drumming, a crashing and banging that fills the night to the exclusion of everything else. So loud is the noise of the barrage that the flight of shells of the German counter-barrage when they come in are unheard until a loud and very near "crump, crump, crump" and the buzzing sound of shrapnel tells us that we are under fire. The counter-barrage is indiscriminate. Jerry is firing blindly, pasting an area and hoping to hit us without knowing what damage he is doing — indeed, if he is doing any at all. "Stretcher bearer!" Yes, someone must have been hit.

'There's a sustained "crash, crack, crack" just to my left, and tracer shells from our 40mm anti-aircraft guns fly fast and low over our line. The AA guns are being used in a ground role, firing tracer direct onto the objective to keep us in the right direction. They will fire long bursts at regular intervals throughout the attack. We begin to close in towards each other — against all orders, but a natural instinct. We close in until we can sense the nearness of our comrades. Ahead of us, Verey lights rise from where Jerry is. Green and red signals hang and burn like Roman candles in the sky.

'While we've been advancing, the moon, just under half full, has risen, and its pale light gives some illumination. The shell fire and the dust this has raised have reduced visibility. It's like walking through mist, the sort of light autumn mist one gets back home, only not a damp, moist fog but a dry and dusty one.

'There is a sudden furious sparkling of lights to the right — mortar bombs, and they're falling on a very narrow sector. It's a Jerry mortar-bomb barrage falling on a gap in his minefield. He's stonking the gap to catch us if we bunch-up — as he thinks we will — to pass through the minefield lane. The Sappers have told us that this field is not sown with AP mines, but is laid with anti-tank Teller mines. We all hope that they are right. In any case it's too late to worry, for we know that about 200 yards ahead up the slope we are climbing must be our objective.

'There is a lot of tracer flying about now. Our AA guns are pointing us to the target, and there is an almost continuous stream like cherry-coloured wire above our heads from Jerry's Spandaus. They're either firing on a fixed line into some point way behind us because they think that we're farther back than we really are, or we could be in dead ground. Our guns are bombarding Jerry's rear area now to keep his reserves from coming forward.

'The line halts. There's a whispered conference. There are about six Spandaus firing on our platoon front. Each of our sections will take out a couple. This is a game we've played before and we deploy, working forward, crouched and moving swiftly. As we get near our first Spandau, we are met with bursts from Schmeisser machine-pistols and the flat "crack" of German hand grenades. Crouching low, we swing higher up the slope moving from rock to rock. There are several very loud bangs — Mills bombs — away on our left. Then a few more. We've got a dead-keen corporal in the platoon who usually takes off his equipment so as to give his throwing arm more freedom when he goes out bombing. He is doing well tonight. The Spandau fire has slackened. The Jerries we're up against are probably getting rattled. They know that some of our lads are behind them now, bombing their way along the sangar line. I know what is going through their minds: when will the Tommies get to us? Our Bren gunner stands up to fire from the hip, but a burst from a Schmeisser cuts him down. This lot of panzergrenadiers are not demoralized yet. Some more of their grenades burst around us. One of our bombers creeps up, passes me and lies down on his left side. From a small linen sack of bombs, he takes one and flings it.

"Down!" he shouts. There is a loud explosion. "Down!" He's thrown a second bomb. The Schmeisser fires defiantly. "Down!" Again the loud detonation, and then silence. . . .

'The number two on the Bren and the corporal stand and fire at the German sangar. No reply from that one, but there is from another a bit higher up the slope. There is a very long burst as the Spandau gunner traverses along the place where we are lying. It is surprising how flat you can get if you try. Two Mills bombs burst on the crest above us. A fire breaks out. Grenades explode. Some of them are Jerry rifle grenades — their soft explosions are quite distinctive. The Bren gun seems slow and old and tired when compared to the ripping-cloth, hysterical sound of the Spandau, but it's a good and reliable gun. I've taken over now as Bren gunner. Both our numbers one and two have been hit; the number one is dead.

'The tracer stream coming from the Spandau dominating us suddenly flies into the dark sky and then stops. A bomb has obviously got the gunner. There is no more firing coming at us. The officer blows his whistle and we move uphill. Suddenly he stops us. This is it. We're on the objective. It's been a cakewalk this time. All we have to do now is to dig and to consolidate our hold on the position. Oh yes, and a recce patrol to sweep our front. Jerry will bombard us in a minute or two. His Verey lights fire desperately into the sky. He's probably calling down a barrage upon us, and behind the incoming shit there'll be an assault group of panzergrenadiers. Let's hope they leave their tanks behind. I don't feel like dodging a panzer tonight. We're on the objective. It's been a doddle. Our company lost fourteen men: three dead, eleven wounded, one of them very seriously. Like I said, this time it was a cakewalk; its not always so easy. There are times when it's really dead dodgy.'

INTENSIVE TRAINING

During the forthcoming battle, it would be the task of the infantry to do all this yet again. The infantry battalions would be the first to cross the unknown and secret dangers of no man's land, defying in the dust-obscured moonlight the machine-guns of the enemy's outpost line. Then, calmly facing the prospect of death or mutilation from sudden explosion, they would march across Panzerarmee's main minefields, encountering in their slow-paced advance greater and more furious opposition from defensive artillery barrages, mortars and heavy concentrations of machine-guns, all working in concert to halt them.

Montgomery would have to husband very carefully the few, the very few infantry battalions of his army so that not a single man was wasted. Not only were they vital to the operation that he was presently planning, but as battle-hardened veterans they would spearhead future offensives in other theatres of war. If he were to prevent the lives of his soldiers from being wasted, then the army commander would have to plan his battle carefully, leaving nothing to chance. He would also train them hard, for he knew that sweat in training saves blood on the battlefield. He would give them every possible help and encouragement to ensure the success of that training, for in the battle plan that he was working out everything depended upon the infantry and had to be related to them, certainly for the early stages of the offensive. It would be the task of the infantry, covered by a creeping barrage, to clear the enemy and thus allow the minelifting Sappers to open paths out of which the armour could debouch and fight the decisive battle.

One of the means employed in training the infantry for the forth-coming battle was to send them into mock assaults across ground similar to that over which their battalions would be attacking during

Operation 'Lightfoot' — the codename for the offensive. In that way the terrain would be familiar to them. The sham attacks were rehearsed repeatedly in daylight. At first, platoons practised taking out enemy gun pits and small defended positions. Then followed exercises at company and then at battalion level. Detachments from infantry battalions freshly arrived from the United Kingdom, who were therefore unbroken to battle, were attached on a temporary basis to other units in the front-line, in order to gain experience of active service conditions. The new boys were shown how to patrol, how to handle mines, how to read the noises of the night and how to adapt themselves to the primitive conditions of desert life. Training for the infantry units was so intensive that battalions out of the line were spared the futile guard duties, parades and picquets that were the usual routine of a formation resting after battle. Unnecessary duties were cut to a minimum in order to allow field training to be undertaken.

The emphasis then turned onto carrying out night attacks — operations in which the British excelled and the Germans did not. What was striven for in those latter stages of training was fluency in the difficult task of linking infantry and armour at night. That difficult task of marrying together two units with different concepts of battle was vital to the course of the offensive. It was rehearsed over and over again, until a stage was reached where liaison and co-operation had become second nature to both parties.

The daylight manoeuvres were monitored by officers with stop-watches, who regulated the speed at which the infantry advanced. This was increased or reduced in order to keep pace with the artillery's creeping barrage. This was another important consideration. If the infantry advanced too quickly, then they would walk into their own barrage and suffer unnecessary casualties. If they were too slow, then German and Italian soldiers who had recovered from the fury of the bombardment would have time to man their machine-guns and meet the British infantry lines with a hurricane of fire. Then again, undefeated enemy strongpoints might slow the advance so much that the infantry would lose the protection of the barrage. To avoid such disasters, the assault battalions would be accompanied by artillery officers whose task it would be to report back any obstruction. These officers could halt the barrage or even recall it to bombard some particularly obstinate enemy position. It was the task of the guns to lift the infantry onto their objectives and to maintain them there by destroying the Panzerarmee's counterattacks. The drills and procedures to ensure those aims were practised, rehearsed and rehearsed again, by day as well as by night.

To ensure that battalions attacked their given objectives, accurate navigation would be needed during the opening phases of the battle. This was one of the most difficult tasks that faced a commander: to know at any given time the exact location or position of his battalion.

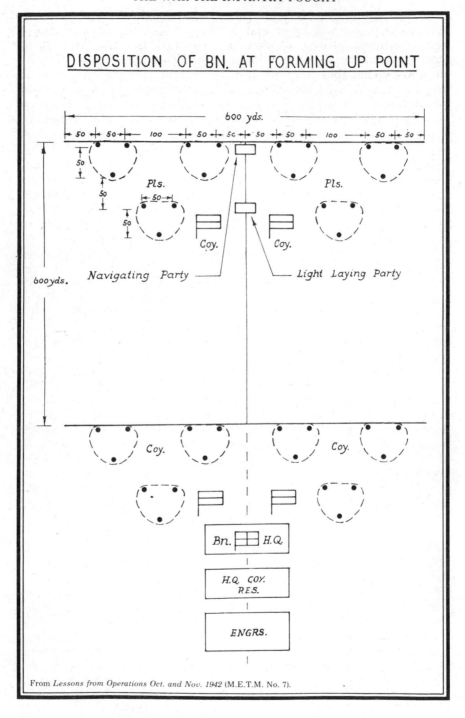

DISPOSITION OF BN. AT FORMING UP POINT

Even by day it was difficult to fix one's position in the almost featureless desert. At night and during a battle in which visibility would be impaired by explosions and churned up dust, the task of accurate location was almost impossible. Yet it was important that units knew that they were moving in the right direction and how far they had advanced. A simple but effective means was to be employed to determine when the infantry companies were on their objectives. The distance to the objective would be measured in paces. Officers or senior NCOs were to move with the advancing lines and count aloud the number of paces that had been marched. These 'pacers' would march in pairs, and the reason for that duplication is obvious: there would be death in any number of guises on that battlefield and the casualties would be certain to include some pacers. If one were hit, the survivor would co-opt another infantry NCO as his number two, and then that pair would march on together.

To point direction in a situation where a compass bearing might be read inaccurately, flights of tracer shells from Bofors guns were to be fired onto the objectives and a pair of searchlights would illuminate the sky to give a constant bearing point. At intervals during the infantry advance, the line would halt while the pacers checked the compass bearings, calculated the paces still to be marched and then led the line forward again. During those short pauses, and so that the infantry did not lose the barrage, the guns would continue to bombard the same area, 'marking time' until the infantry moved off again.

Throughout the last half of September and during the first weeks of October, infantry training continued, reaching a climax with simulated attacks in brigade strength across the familiar ground of the company and battalion exercises. These were the final dress rehearsals, and it was during these final manoeuvres that any loose ends were tied. Then the training and the exercises tailed off and most units rested, with only route marches and physical training to keep the men at the peak of fitness.

Now, only time separated the unblooded warriors from their testing and the veterans from that terse order that they had heard so often: 'The Company will advance. . . .' Now, all the battalions were prepared and ready. Ahead lay something dramatic, but as yet there were no details, for Montgomery had not yet disclosed them to his commanders. This he was to do a week or so before the opening of Operation 'Lightfoot'. They and their men would then know what was expected of them. The soldiers could already guess, however, that what they had prepared, trained and were now waiting for would be hard and dangerous. And while they waited those who were able bathed in the Mediterranean, while those who were in positions deeper inland sweated in slit trenches and dug-outs eating their unchanging diet and drinking their brackish tea.

5.

THE WAR IN ARMOUR

Those who fought in tanks saw themselves very much as an elite; latter-day knights in armour, and therefore socially far above the footslogging plebs. Between the infantry and the armour there was mistrust — almost a mutual hatred. The infantry despised the armour for continually leaving the battlefield at times of acute crisis. The tank men accused the infantry of demanding armoured support whenever it felt itself threatened. Little was done, before El Alamein, to explain to the tank troops the fears and feeling of defencelessness of the foot soldiers when under attack by German tanks, just as nobody had bothered to explain to the infantry the weaknesses of armour and the frequent need of its machines to withdraw from the battlefield to refuel and to re-ammunition. Neither arm of service understood the needs of the other, and nobody had bothered to tell them what those needs were.

There were three types of tank men: there were regiments that had once been line cavalry; others that had once been yeomanry; and the men of the battalions of the Royal Tank Regiment. The attitude of the recently converted cavalry to the 'mechanics' of the RTR was condescending, and this was much resented. However, whether they were 'swish' regular cavalry, exclusive yeomanry regiments or Royal Tank Regiment, the tanks were the same for all, as were the battles. It was the approach to the fighting that differed.

In the desert, British armour had always shown up poorly against the German panzer force, and it is important that the causes for this lack of success are understood. The most basic reasons were that the British vehicles were under-gunned and under-armoured; in simple terms, British tanks could be killed before they could hit the enemy. For example, the fast but mechanically unreliable Crusader had 33mm of armour on the front hull plates. The gun on the German Panzer III, the 50mm with capped shot, could penetrate 41mm of armour at 1,000 yards. The Crusader mounted a 2pdr gun that could penetrate 40mm of armour at 1,000 yards, but the thickness of face-hardened armour on a German Pz.Kpfw. III was 50cm. Some tanks other than the Crusader did have thicker armour, but these types were slower in speed and all were armed with the little 2pdr gun as main armament. Not until the Grant and then the Sherman came into service were British tank men able to engage the enemy on equal terms. Another defect in the British armament was that the 2pdr fired only solid, uncapped shot. This was

87

essential when fighting against another tank, but it meant that such targets as enemy infantry, anti-tank guns and soft-skinned vehicles could not be affected except by a direct hit. The German guns fired both armour-piercing shot and high-explosive shells, as did the tank gun on the Grant and the Sherman.

There was a continual race in the desert war between the need to thicken a vehicle's armour and the ability of the gun to penetrate the plates. The 2pdr in the British Crusader was replaced by the 6pdr, which came into service shortly before El Alamein and could kill German AFVs at 1,500 yards range. Then, too, the 75mm gun that was fitted in the Grants and Shermans could destroy the German machines at quite long ranges. On the German side, the short 5cm anti-tank gun was replaced by a long one and the short 75mm in the Panzer IV by a long 75mm; but only a few Panzer IVs at El Alamein were fitted with this gun. There was also another piece of ordnance that was, arguably, the most deadly of all the anti-tank guns in action at that time. This was the '88' — the 8.8cm German flak gun. When employed in a ground role it was deadly, and its muzzle velocity was sufficient to propel a 20-pound shell across 2,000 yards and through 83mm of armour plate. But it was also very vulnerable, far more so than the low-slung 50mm guns and Russian 76.2mm guns which were then coming into use in German hands.

The other reason for the poor showing of British armour before El Alamein was in the matter of tactics. The British cavalryman, who had been recently converted to fight in a tank, still retained the spirit of the 'arme blanche' and sought to destroy his enemy by closing with him and engaging in single combat. To the German panzer commanders in general and to Rommel (the exponent par excellence of the blitzkrieg tactic) in particular, the proper role for tanks was not to engage in duels: enemy armour was to be destroyed by the anti-tank artillery, and particularly the 50mms and 88s. The panzers were to create and spread confusion in the enemy's 'soft' rear areas. There were, of course, occasions when it was necessary for German armoured fighting vehicles to take part in tank versus tank combat, but when they did so, their advantages of thicker defensive armour and heavier guns came into full effect. Before El Alamein, the usual sequence of a meeting between British and German tanks was that the British tank line would sweep down in a charge only to have its vehicles destroyed before they could take effective action. The desert would be littered with the knocked-out or burnt-out wrecks of gallant but futile cavalry-type attacks. Montgomery was an infantryman and viewed tanks with the eye of a foot soldier. Nevertheless he, of all the commanders who led Eighth Army, understood the secret of armoured warfare — that tanks must be used in mass and should not be squandered against enemy tanks unless this situation were absolutely unavoidable.

From a review of past armoured battles, one fact was obvious to him: British tanks had been mishandled. Much of the fault lay in the attitude of the tank men, whose approach had proved a recipe for disaster. Time and again, British units had seen groups of panzers and had charged them — only to find that the enemy vehicles had been a bait, behind which lay ambush lines of anti-tank guns upon which the British armour had been impaled and destroyed. Montgomery was determined that the old ideas had to go. The days of tank regiments charging about the desert moving unsupported into the attack were over. Actions such as those had been costly in men and machines. They could be afforded no longer. The new army commander was determined that from now on the armour would be tight-reined. His plan for the Battle of El Alamein foresaw a battle of attrition, but he was determined that, when Panzerarmee broke, Eighth Army would still have sufficient armour in hand to complete the task of destroying its opponents. To ensure this he was determined to keep in his hands the decision of when and where the armour should be put in. He would not delegate that authority, and upon that point he was inflexible: the control would rest with him alone.

His plans had their opponents, of course. There were the tank men who thought in terms of 'blitzkrieg' and armoured assault, and who did not take well to the idea of an infantryman telling them their business. But events were to prove him right. Under him the armour would form a mass to be used as a solid block, so that wherever he placed it the British tank force would be superior to any grouping that Panzerarmee could muster. With numbers in his favour and with the new improved tank guns, the armour must prevail so long as its superiority was not dissipated in 'penny-packet' attacks.

The tank men had to learn, to train and to absorb new ideas and to accept new methods. It was with the commanders of the armour that Montgomery had the greatest trouble. The senior commanders realized that the destruction of the armoured force would leave Egypt defenceless, and they were prepared to temporize rather than risk total loss. Montgomery's optimism could not at first infect them — they had seen it all before. But gradually from squadron level there was an awareness of a new spirit animating Eighth Army. The realization grew that this time there was planning for a purpose, and training to fight a decisive battle. The desire to win grew in the tank men. They, too, looked forward with confidence to the new offensive, for they had the new Shermans, they had learned to use the Grants successfully and they were going into battle with up-gunned Crusaders. This time they would take on the panzers and beat them.

THE TANK CREW

A tank gave one mobility, and those who had wheels or tracks could carry all sorts of simple luxuries denied to the foot soldier, who carried his world on his back. It was customary in armoured units (and the yeomanry were particularly notorious in this respect) for officers to take lorries into Alexandria or Cairo and to buy additional foods and luxury goods for use 'up the blue'. As a justification for their action, it might be claimed that from the front-lines at El Alamein to these cities was a scant two or three hours drive, so that the officers were not absent from their units for very long. Nevertheless, it was bad for the morale of the army as a whole to know that some units could be favoured in that way, and the practice was forbidden before the Battle of El Alamein.

As a result of the purchases made by the squadron officers, most tanks went into action with food, drink and equipment other than that supplied by the Army. Thermos flasks, canvas 'chatti' water bottles, tinned fruit, tinned sausages, sleeping bags and primus stoves were bought by crews out of a fund to which each contributed according to his means. These simple things helped to ease the Spartan life 'up the blue' — according to the cavalry, there was very little virtue in being uncomfortable just for the sake of it. . . .

The Crusader tank had a crew of four or five men: commander, driver, co-driver, turret gunner and wireless operator/gun loader. The troop commander was usually a junior officer (sometimes a sergeant) and the other two troop tanks were commanded by sergeants or corporals. Those officers who had survived the bloody battles of 1941 and early 1942 were leading squadrons or even regiments, teaching and training the new units fresh out from the United Kingdom in the details that would enable them to fight their tanks with confident assurance in the forthcoming battles.

The commander guided his vehicle to a point at which the gunner could fire the main armament and destroy the enemy, and he had also to conform to orders from his superior officers that came to him via the wireless, 'netted-in' to the regimental or squadron frequency for that day. The commander could fight his tank with hatches closed. If he did, then his range of vision was limited to what he could see through the cupola periscope, so it was more usual for him to stand in the turret with his head and shoulders projecting through the cupola. More than that and his body was vulnerable to enemy fire, but at least such a stance did give him an all round view and 'lifted' his crew psychologically, for it showed that their officer was not afraid. One tank commander remembers: 'Before one charge, the enemy was thought to be only a transport column; but as we poured down the stony slope and prepared to open fire we could see that the trucks had been merely a screen and that behind them, squatting evilly on the sand, was a group of 88s. How naked I felt as the solid-shot projectiles swished and cracked about my head. Some shot fell short to hit the ground and to split up into large shining fragments. These caught the sunlight as they flew, and it was hard to believe that the pretty, harmless-looking points of light had the power to decapitate me.'

The driver sat in his cramped compartment. His feet rested on the accelerator and brake pedals, and in his hands were thick steering sticks. For the machine to change direction it was necessary to pull on a lever. That action varied the track speed, and a quick revving of the engine produced the power to spin the machine, turning it in its own radius. The driver's only view was ahead, and he looked through a narrow slit in the hull plates filled with a four-inch thick piece of armoured glass or through periscopes. In some tanks, his nearest companion was the co-driver who fired a machine-gun and brewed the tea.

Closely confined within the vehicle's turret was the gunner. A loader fed the weapon with shells and also served as a wireless operator, receiving and acknowledging the orders that came through on the set. To load the 2pdr, he brought a round up to the gun breech; the rim of the projectile tripped two levers on the breech as he pushed in the shot, and this closed the breech. He then tapped the gunner on the elbow to indicate that the weapon was loaded. He could see through a periscope, but usually he was only aware of the fury of the battle when near misses rocked the machine or a direct hit penetrated.

The gunner looking through the telescopic lens of his sight saw the cross-hairs of a graticule, which in battle would be aligned on an enemy target. There was a sort of yoke fitted with a strap, which fastened around the layer's left shoulder and bound him tightly to the gun. A simple movement of his shoulder, thrust into a crutch, raised or depressed the gun. To traverse the gun the whole turret was rotated, and this was achieved by electricity or hydraulics under the control of the gunner turning a spade grip. While one hand traversed the gun, the gunner's shoulder raised or depressed the weapon, his free hand hovering between the trigger handles of the Besa machine-gun and the trigger of the 2pdr cannon as he waited for the commander to indicate the target that had been selected and the weapon with which it was to be engaged.

In this little world, the patience of the hunter, the high-spirited skill of the good point-to-point rider and the ferocity of a wild beast decided whether, at the end of the day, the crew sat drinking tea in a bivvy alongside their vehicle, or whether they were a statistic in the day's sad total of casualties. The men of a crew formed a single unit whose members had to be compatible and whose trust in each other was absolute: not only did they fight in the closest proximity, but also ate and slept by the side of their vehicle, usually under one tarpaulin. Eccentric personal habits or odd behaviour were, therefore, not encouraged.

Three or four tanks formed a troop, four troops (plus a squadron HQ of three tanks) a squadron, and three squadrons a regiment. A regiment at full strength could expect to field a battle line of 61 armoured fighting vehicles. That line was backed up by a number of soft-skinned lorries, on which were carried fuel and ammunition as well as the fitters to keep the fighting squadrons and their crews supplied

while they were in action. This second group was the 'A' Echelon,
behind which was 'B' Echelon, where the tankless crews, cooks, clerks
and other LOBs stayed.

FIGHTING IN ARMOUR

The day in a fighting troop in close laager began with 'stand to' and
dispersal just before dawn followed by the first brew-up of the day. If
the unit were not called to action, the forenoon was spent in vehicle,
wireless and weapon maintenance. Lunch — the almost inevitable
bully and biscuits — was followed by more checks on the vehicle,
replenishment of spent stores from the 'A' Echelon trucks, by training
and by exercises in tactics, signals procedures and in any one of the
myriad tasks that were vital to the running of the tank.

A troop in action was one stripped for battle. At first light a sentry
roused the crews, whose sleep that night might have been only two or
three hours. After a brew-up the crew would mount their tanks, each
crew member wrapped in his own thoughts of what the day might
bring. Then from the centre of the regimental laager, where the
commanding officer's tank was positioned, a high whine of the electric
starting motor would signal 'make ready', and then came the engine's
roar as it sprang into life.

Five minutes later, following the CO's lead, the whole desert was
throbbing with the noise of the regiment's vehicles preparing for
battle. The colonel's tank, its pennant flying, led the column as it
drove out of the eastern dawn and into a west still not yet lightened,
and grey with the dying night. The armour was 'driving to contact' —
the preparation to battle.

At a command, the regiment, in a single file, divided itself into three
squadron columns; thus deployed, it sent out patrols to locate the
enemy. Into the CO's earphones crackled messages on the brigade net,
pinpointing the location and strength of the enemy's force. The enemy
had to be found, and in the desert finding one's way was no easy thing.
By day, there was the primitive but reliable sun compass, fitted to
most vehicles and more reliable than the magnetic prismatic compass
because it was unaffected by metal, while the speedometer also helped
to calculate distances travelled. To supplement those devices, the
Army had set up white-painted barrels alongside the tracks. Each
barrel bore a number and its position was marked on maps. It was,
however, still very easy to be lost in an area almost totally devoid of
landmarks, and the most usual reason for two units failing to meet as
planned was the failure of one or both to read a map correctly or to
navigate accurately.

After each action it was the custom of British armour to withdraw
from the battlefield, forcing the commander, already exhausted from
the strain of combat, to take up the additional burden of searching for

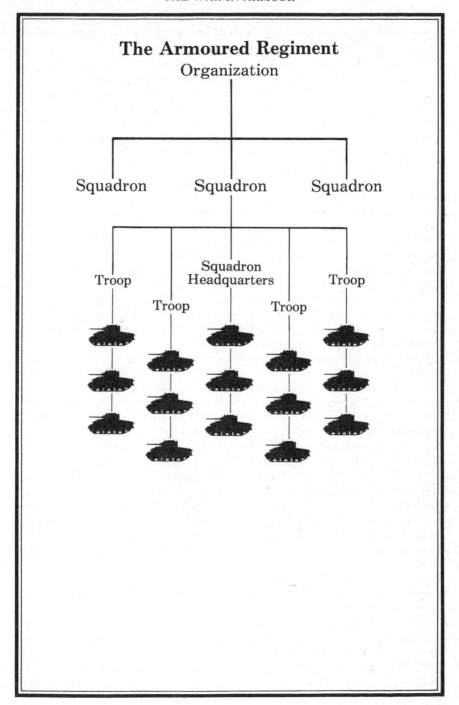

The Armoured Regiment
Organization

Squadron   Squadron   Squadron

Troop   Squadron   Troop
Headquarters

Troop   Troop

regimental laager. Then, after refuelling and rearming, with only a few hours sleep, the British driver was faced with the need to drive back again to the battlefield in the morning. It was an exercise that wasted both time and fuel — a direct contrast to the German tactic of remaining on the field. Not only were German crews, and particularly drivers, spared the strain of the journey, but in the case of immobile or damaged tanks the German recovery teams could collaborate with the vehicle crew to turn a vehicle into a 'runner' again. (Here was another contrast: the recovery teams of the Royal Electrical and Mechanical Engineers worked at best by torchlight or by inspection lamps hidden under tarpaulins. The panzer repair men worked in the open desert and often under floodlight. They were thus able to repair and to hand over repaired vehicles to the crews without delay.)

A tank commander of the time takes up the story: 'Ahead of our regiment lay a djebel, a low ridge of dun-coloured sandstone, dully reflecting the sun that shone upon it. It was still early in the day, and the sun had not yet reached the fierce heat of early afternoon. There was still time to think idly and to listen in the earphones to the Signals traffic that was passing. Then comes the crackling message that orders the squadrons into battle formation. The ground is familiar. It is yesterday's battlefield, and we are passing through a graveyard of our fallen comrades. The tanks leave behind them as they race forward a plume of sand, which hangs above them like a plume in the immobile air, betraying to any watching enemy the speed and strength of our movement.

'Scattered across the sand over which we fought so hard yesterday — was it really only yesterday? — are the steel tombs of our comrades and our enemies. Three of ours, a whole troop caught by an 88, lie smashed. Smoke is still seeping from one of them, but their crews are safe, all except for two men, both drivers. The battle has moved westwards and northwards. Yesterday it was on our side of the escarpment; today it is on Jerry's side, and we hold the high ground.

'The driver increases speed to bring the tank climbing through the loose stones of the ridge. Each of the vehicles of our squadron is visible as they race up the slope, but the rest of the regiment is hidden in the dust cloud that accompanies our every movement. We are nearing the enemy, heralding our coming not with clouds of glory but with clouds of dust.

'Below the djebel crest we are halted for fresh orders. There might be a half hour's wait. There is time for a brew. The gunner/co-driver jumps down onto the floor of the desert, unhitches the flimsy, half fills it with sand and soaks it with petrol, lights the mixture and places a dixy over the flames. This may be the last brew for hours. It may well be the last brew today. If for any reason the engine's cooling system leaked it would be the crew's drinking water that would have to fill the leaking radiator. The moving tank and its gun are the important things. Fuel for the engine and ammo for the guns. Water for the crew is a very low consideration. The crew are not the masters but the servants of the machine. In deep and appreciative silence we drink the brew. The CO and the squadron commanders have gone forward on a recce. From the Signals messages, the situation forward of us is not a healthy one. Even from a reverse slope position we can see the black smoke that tells of fires, but we do not hear the guns very clearly. They are just a rumble of sound. This is not really surprising, for we all are deafened from the roar of the engines and are still suffering from the noises of yesterday's battle.

'O Group is called. I'm wanted. The squadron commander briefs us on the targets and on the approach route. The enemy panzer force seems to be hard pressed, and our wireless intercepts tell us that he has asked for his 'A' Echelon to come forward. It will be our task to intercept and to destroy the soft-skinned convoy before it can refuel or resupply the panzer regiment.

'Into the turret. The familiar smell of hot engine oil and sweat. Earphones on and then comes the metallic voice ordering us forward. "Driver advance!" I order, and we traverse the slope in first gear, climbing slowly until we reach the djebel crest. We cross. Christ Almighty! Below on the plain there is an almost unbelievable confusion spread out for miles and miles. Most of the area is covered by black clouds of smoke at whose bases I can see dull, cherry coloured flames. These are probably burning tanks, but too far away to see whether they are ours or theirs. To the right there are sudden, quick flashes and within seconds the crash of explosions; loud enough to be heard above the engine's roar. Tall columns of erupting sand show that we are under fire.

'We move looking for a good hull-down position. Our target is not yet in sight. There is another crackling instruction, and we head off on a long detour, skirting the places where fighting seems to be most heavily concentrated. The battlefield forms on two sides a natural, if shallow, arena. There is the escarpment down which we have just driven and then, running at about right-angles to that and about six miles away, a lower ridge on which we have been ordered to concentrate.

'The midday heat is oppressive and airless. The sky is becoming dull and vaguely copper coloured. Even the flies have vanished. It is a Khamseen blowing and straight into our faces. The world is suddenly blotted out in an oven heat, and millions of stinging sand granules drive red-hot needles through my flimsy khaki drill shirt. In such close proximity to the enemy it would be foolish to close the hatch and to wait out the storm. Just as well. Our target, the convoy of lorries, has been sighted — sighted in these conditions?

'The squadron commander asks for confirmation. The Khamseen is blowing itself out, comes the answer; the enemy lorries are halted, below us in the bowl of the amphitheatre. The wireless message to move comes through. "Driver advance!" Blindly, and riding almost by instinct, we slowly descend the escarpment. In the dark, hot atmosphere of the Khamseen, the driver has the task of moving the heavy vehicle downhill without shaking the crew too violently. As it is, we are thrown from side to side, and it is clear that we have several times dipped into infantry slit trenches. The sky lightens so quickly it is almost beyond belief. One second it is a dirty murky oven; the next a clear and sunny afternoon. In that clear sunshine I can see the soft-skinned vehicles below. They are still out of range and we increase speed to close with them. It is difficult at that range to pick out details. The surface of the desert is shimmering, and in the heat haze the dark vehicles seem tall and quiver and tremble.

'The enemy must have seen us, for the lorries break formation, make a sharp left turn and head away into the desert in line abreast. Soon they are hidden in the cloud of dust that each throws up as we, bouncing and rocking, reach the flat ground. Full ahead, and on either side of me the other tanks of the squadron pour forward like a wave. Out of the dust cloud there suddenly looms an Italian tank, which opens fire with a machine-gun on the squadron commander's machine. Then, as the dust swirls, we see a whole group of them. The squadron commander gives us our targets, and I relay the orders to my crew. "Driver halt!" [In those days one halted the vehicle to fire the main armament. It could be fired on the move, but with little hope of accuracy. It was better to halt and take proper aim.] "2pdr, traverse left . . . more . . . more. . . .600 [yards]. Steady. On. Hornet, fire!" There is a deafening crack, surprisingly loud from such a slim gun, and the enemy machine, which even the Italians call the 'mobile coffin' suddenly slews round and halts. Nobody gets out. "Driver advance" and we move towards our dead victim. There is a sudden and terrible crash and our tank sways wildly. A cloud of dust and a strong stink of cordite comes up through the hatch. "Driver advance!" and we move forward again. In reply to my questions, we seem to have suffered no damage. The main armament is certainly working and the tank is running well. But we have been hit quite hard by something, almost certainly an anti-tank shot, but it hasn't penetrated.

'A group of three Italian tanks crosses our front, presenting their flimsily armoured flanks to us. I halt and choose the first one and tell the layer. I know that his eyes are pressed up against the eyepiece of the sighting telescope. His left hand will be bringing the gun on to target and his right shoulder is elevating the gun. His was the task I enjoyed under training, and I can see it in my mind's eye as I wait for him to report that he is on target. He is moving the gun more slowly now searching through the telescope for the enemy vehicle and seeing it appear in the cross-wires of the sights. Through his mind will be running the details of how much to lay off because it is a moving target and then my "on", followed by my order to fire. Once again the crack of the 2pdr, a smell of cordite and then the clang as the barrel sharply recoils — to within about six inches of my stomach. There is a loud thump as the expended shell case falls into the deflector bag. I wait, but the Italian tank is still moving. I order him to fire again: another miss, and then a third time without success. I can't believe it, and then suddenly, urgently in my earphones, "Watch your left flank!" and then more urgently, "Your left flank!" As I turn, red tracer flashes slowly, almost lazily towards me and then flashes rapidly overhead. Everything now seems to run down to slow motion speed as I see the low, wide silhouette of a Panzer III and then the puff of smoke as its 50mm is fired.

'A second crash rocks us and a series of screams as the solid shot passes into our turret, killing the gunner and badly wounding the wireless operator. The driver and I bring him out but it is clear he has not long to live. The driver and I shelter in the lee of our tank and wait. Within a few seconds we are surrounded by German soldiers, grenadiers, who quickly remove what they can from the outside of the tank, unroll the bed rolls, open and eat our tinned fruit, smoke some of our cigarettes and hang about like people waiting for rain to stop before crossing a road. Then they are away, leaving us alone. We are not fussy about being prisoners; in an hour's time those panzergrenadiers might be our prisoners. The wireless operator dies, and then through the swirling dust and the crashing of shells there is a scout car — one of ours. The driver and I scramble aboard and the vehicle rushes us away, bouncing and bumping across the desert to where the colonel's tank is. There is a large group of our unit there, men from shot-up tanks. If it were not such a tragic scene it would be funny. Most of the men sitting in scrape holes or sheltering behind low sangar walls are like blacked up Christy's minstrels, faces blackened with cordite explosions. We are nearly all deafened by shell explosions and the engine noise. We dark-faced swaddies, shouting at each other, sitting in holes in the sand, must present a most unusual spectacle.

'I report to the colonel, and he gives me a tank from another troop whose commander has been killed. On the command set, the news comes in that a fresh regiment is coming forward to take over. Twenty minutes later by my wristwatch and a thousand years in terms of terror, the Grants roar past and we withdraw to the trigh crossroads where our 'A' Echelon has been set up. Quickly we throw out the empty rounds and load up with fresh ammunition. Then the machine is refuelled. (In those days fuel came in flimsy metal, four-gallon, square cans. Those containers were locally made and leaked through their poorly welded seams so much that nearly a third of the fuel was lost before it could be put into the petrol tank.) There is a reorganization of squadrons while we are in 'A' Echelon, and then we go forward again. This time it seems as if the enemy is weakening. Certainly we all think so, but really it is just another of his tactics. By avoiding battle he is drawing us farther and farther westwards. We pursue him into the setting sun, which shines in our eyes so that we do not see the line of anti-tank guns until they open fire.

'By the end of that day our regimental strength is down to seven fit machines. The crews of most of the others are safe and already in the laager when we reach the area after dark. The tank commanders are debriefed and then, totally exhausted, I creep under the tarpaulin bivvy that has been set up alongside the tank and fall instantly asleep. I am not on the morning patrol sent out just after reveille, but am sent to pick up new vehicles that the tank delivery squadron has brought forward. With those new machines, tanks repaired by the fitters and the seven from the previous evening we form two 'scratch' squadrons. Shortly after lunch we move forward again to relieve a regiment that has been in action since sun-up.

'The battlefield is a ghastly sight, with tanks on fire and the smoke clouds only torn apart momentarily as the ammunition inside them explodes. I can see in my mind's eye wounded men trapped inside their burning vehicles. . . . The tank stops and I am shaken out of my morbid reverie. We have developed a mechanical fault. There is no point in staying in the machine while enemy panzers are in the area. Having reported it as a non-runner, we walked away on a compass bearing, carrying a minimum of kit. (It was a standard operational procedure that certain pieces of equipment from the guns and from the wireless be removed before a tank was abandoned: the firing mechanism from the main armament and a valve from the wireless.) At TAC headquarters we hear that an enemy panzer column has overrun our 'B' Echelon and that there has been a flap among the ration column from division, whose trucks arrived at 'B' Echelon just before Jerry's tanks.

'Now there is the usual withdrawal to laager. Because of the likelihood of Stuka raids, we are in open laager, that is with 150 yards between each vehicle. The armoured fighting vehicles form a roughly circular-shaped perimeter with anti-tank guns positioned between the machines. Soft-skinned vehicles, dug-in to well above wheel axle level to protect them against aerial bomb splinters, occupy the centre of the perimeter together with TAC HQ. That night the news comes through that we are staying in position for a couple of days. We are like condemned men who have been given a reprieve, and that night we are in a very gay mood. We are still alive.

'What else is there to say? The difficulties of starting a cow of a machine in cold weather can be best imagined. We had to tow the damned thing and the metal towrope breaking under the strain sent a ship-like hawser crashing about with a force that could kill a man. There were fears, of course, that at some crucial stage of a battle there would be a breakdown. Fears of a hang-fire in the breech of the gun — oh, all sorts of things. Once in action though, the responsibility and the need to complete the job in hand submerged our fears. Quite irrational worries in action did obsess me, like choosing a new area when we had to change position. Quite often while we were waiting to go into action we would be spotted by a Jerry OP and shelled. If the shelling became too hot we would move position, and the fear of moving to a new spot was unnerving, just in case the next flight of shells did not land where you *had* been but on the place to which you had just driven.

'Being shelled by artillery was bad enough, but to be dive-bombed was terrifying. During the June '42 affair we were involved in fighting around one of the infantry boxes, and one morning bright and early we were attacked by Stukas. We had a very good air sentry system in the regiment, but he was confused by the Stukas coming in very high and from the east, what you might call our side of the battlefield. The aircraft were like little shining tadpoles. And then they started to come down. The feeling always was that they were aiming for one's own tank, and yet the aim was quite haphazard: artillery sighted and fired through rifled barrels, aiming direct; dive-bombers released their bombs on a general area. Yet of the two forms of bombardment the Stukas were the more frightening.

'It is strange when one considers the immense size of Libya and Egypt how the same places, a couple of miles square, were always selected as camping or staging grounds. Our regiment was particularly strong on the hygiene side of things. Our rubbish, food tins, old used equipment and the like, was always burnt and then buried. Areas in which our latrine pits had been dug were filled in and signposted before we left. Some other mobs left camping grounds covered with unburied food and swarming with flies. We used to burn out their latrines and desert roses with petrol; it was the quickest and least smelly way. When we left a site only the deep PAD pits into which the soft-skinned vehicles had been driven were left to show that we had been on the ground. We were also very hot on black-out, on wireless silences and on W/T procedures. There was one time when we had to tow a great number of our tanks in order to get their engines to start up. Jerry had broken up our 'A' Echelon, and the only fuel supplies from brigade were sufficient for half a tank full. A number of machines in the regiment were on listening watch, which of course drained the batteries. If we had had the petrol we would have run the tank engine all night to drive the dynamo so as not to drain the battery. As it was, the batteries on all the vehicles on listening watch were flat and had to be towed about until the engines caught on.

'In action we lived on tea and cigarettes, the tea sometimes laced with the tank commander's whisky from the NAAFI issue. The 50 free cigarettes that were issued to us every week would not have kept us going for a day in battle, and we used to buy British cigarettes made under licence in Egypt. We also got (but this was later on) Indian 'V' cigarettes and matches. An appalling combination.

'Conditions in the tank units changed dramatically when Montgomery came in. He stopped the charging about that tank units used to indulge in, and we used Rommel's tactics against him. No more cavalry charges; let the panzers hurl themselves on our guns and then finish them off. And, of course, by Monty's time we had the Sherman and the Priest SP gun. I had seen the Grant and thought it a poor thing, tactically; the sort of machine that is designed by a committee. Its main armament was set low down in a sponson in the hull so that its good gun had little lateral movement: thus, it had the disadvantage of an SP with none of that vehicle's advantages. In a Grant, owing to the gun's position, it was not possible to take a good hull-down position. The commander in his turret stood above the sky line like a fairy on a rock cake, visible for miles around.

'We eventually went into Shermans. They were roomier than the Crusader, even though there were five in the crew, and they felt safer. But somehow for me the abiding memory of armoured warfare in the desert will always be the Crusader with its large, Christie-type wheels, belting along some trigh with a cloud of dust rising high behind it. And the memory of life in an armoured regiment will always be one of men either black-faced with cordite or covered with a pancake layer of white limestone dust, eyes red-rimmed and bloodshot, lips unnaturally red against the white powdered cheeks.

'There was so much life, so much pleasure from simple things. A flower hiding in a crevice of a rock, the star-filled nights, the glorious companionship. We never had a special tank-crew song like the Germans had; I do wish we had had one.'

6.

THE GUNNERS AT WAR

In the desert battles, success or failure often depended upon the men of the Royal Artillery and the weapons they served. Chief among the pieces of ordnance on the British Army's establishment was the 25pdr gun/howitzer — a gun that was as feared by the Germans as their 88mm gun was feared by the British. Many German prisoners asked to see the 'artillery machine-gun' that could fire so fast and so accurately. They refused to believe that it was just an ordinary field gun and that it was the skill of the Gunners who served it that produced the accurate and high rate of fire they dreaded. The story of the barrage fired at El Alamein is well known, as is the fact that the greatest number of guns in the artillery regiments that fired that barrage were 25pdrs. This piece of ordnance fired a shell weighing 25 pounds for 13,400 yards on a low flight path or over a shorter distance with high angled fire. The weight of the gun ready for action was only 1.75 tons, making it a light, mobile weapon that could be brought into action in a minute and could be mounted to give a 360° arc of fire. In the hands of trained Gunners, the speed at which shells could be fired was so high that German prisoners-of-war asked to be shown the British guns that were belt-fed with ammunition. Capable of firing both high-explosive or solid shot, the 25pdr could be used in field or anti-tank roles and, if it lacked the fearsome killing power and range of the 88, the British piece had advantages that the most famous enemy piece lacked; chiefly, that a worn-out barrel could be replaced in situ and relatively quickly.

But there were other types of gun whose role may not have been so well recorded as that of the gun/howitzer. In particular, the men of the anti-aircraft artillery, who defended Eighth Army, have gone generally unrecognized. Their task of holding off the German bombers and of firing tracer ahead of ground attacks to point the direction to the attacking infantry are acknowledged here. So is the debt to the anti-tank batteries whose Gunners stood their ground under point-blank panzer gunfire, and whose devotion to duty broke up the attacks by the armoured fighting vehicles of the Panzerarmee.

Deep down in Egypt, meanwhile, there were other new weapons, among them self-propelled guns — not the mock-ups of earlier years, but turretless tanks fitted with the new and powerful 75mm gun. At last Eighth Army had an SP gun carriage as reliable as those on German chassis and mounting a gun far superior to any previous weapon fitted in a British armoured fighting vehicle.

Before mechanization came in, the traditional task of horse artillery in battle had been, through a combination of speed and skill, to bring its guns into the forward fighting zone, there to provide close support in defence or to form a mobile battering-ram during an attack. The speed of the horses, the daring and ability of the men — these were legendary. It was those attributes of fast movement, skill and bravery that were required when the time came for the horse artillery to be modernized as a result of the introduction of the internal combustion engine and of the rapid development of armoured warfare.

The armies of the world needed a weapon capable of being brought rapidly into action and one that bridged the gap between artillery and armour: in sum, a weapon with the advantages of both arms but without their defects. The self-propelled gun was the answer, and military thinkers of most major armies arrived at the same conclusion at about the same time. Their ideas on the design of the machines and the tactics that would have to be employed were very similar.

The SP gun was considered to be, quite simply, a gun that was carried rather than towed into action. In the inter-war years, the British Army in Egypt experimented with an 18pdr field-gun mounted on a lorry chassis, while on the German side the original idea of debussing a lorry-borne gun was found to be slow and dangerous. The lorry was a soft-skin vehicle and vulnerable to small-arms fire. The crew and the piece had to be protected and the cross-country capabilities of the vehicle improved. The next stage of development was to mount the gun on the turretless chassis of a tank. The artillery piece and its crew were protected from shell fragments and small-arms fire by a box made of tall steel plates. These enclosed the front and the sides, but as there was no roof air bursting shells could, and often did, kill or wound a whole gun crew. The early types of vehicle, primitive, cramped, unprotected open boxes, were eventually replaced by machines designed exclusively to be SP vehicles.

Self-propelled guns were less complicated in design than standard tanks and, being turretless, did not need the sensitive equipment that was essential in conventional armoured fighting vehicles. They were, therefore, cheaper and easier to produce, and found favour with those who demanded a simple but powerful weapon. The gun was, of course, fixed on the vehicle's chassis and had a very limited traverse, so in order to engage a target the whole vehicle had to be turned to point at the enemy. Priests, the SP guns with which the first regiments of Eighth Army were outfitted, were converted Grant and Sherman tanks and lacked the panzer ability to change direction quickly by spinning on a single track. It took longer for the US machines to engage a target, and although the delay was a matter of seconds only it was still a terrible handicap in a situation where the difference between life and death might hang upon fractions of a second. Indeed, only the 10.5cm gun that the Priests carried enabled them to fight and win, for that piece outranged the German 8.8cm, which had hitherto truly dominated the battlefield. Thereafter, British SP Gunners could meet their opponents on superior terms. They could stand off and bombard at ranges far above what the 88 could achieve, and under the covering barrage of 10.5cm shells British armour could advance to engage the panzers without fear of the deadly German piece.

Hundreds of field-guns had arrived from the United Kingdom by the time that Operation 'Lightfoot' began, but even more important than those were the supplies of the 6pdr anti-tank gun that were just coming into service in large numbers. To train the Gunners who would fire the new weapons in action, half a dozen ranges were set up where they could practise. Within a few weeks the guns and the men who served them were welded into a powerful partnership. Artillery regiments on the British establishment have no regimental colours, those mystic symbols of corporate identity carried by infantry regiments as a visible emblem of the soul of the regiment. To artillery-men, the guns replace the Standard, and to lose the guns to the enemy produces in a Gunner the same sense of blinding shame that an infantryman experiences with the loss of his regiment's colours. This mystic union between the men and the symbol is the reason why in so many accounts of battle the artillery pieces are recorded as having been served to the last man, and why Gunners will go to extreme limits of endurance and danger to save their guns from falling into the hands of the enemy.

Driver James Evans, once of the 50th Division Transport Column, relates an incident that occurred in one of the desert battles of the summer of 1942. One of the artillery regiments of the division was among a number of formations that had been trapped on the escarpment at Acroma. 'Jerry's armour was holding the low ground and had cut off the British units on the heights from the minefield gaps through which they might have escaped to reach the coast road and a quick run up to Tobruk. There was a choice. Either the guns, tanks and lorries could attempt to cross the minefields, knowing that a single explosion would alert the Afrika Korps, or else the units would have to give in and surrender. Some Gunners decided to try and escape down the escarpment. The rest of the trapped units decided to follow the Gunners' lead.

'A reconnaissance was carried out which revealed that it was an almost sheer descent down the escarpment. On the artillery quads (the vehicles that towed the 25pdrs) there were shovels and picks. By using every Gunner and enlisting men from other mobs, an attempt was made to create a narrow track from the top of the cliff. The men were at it all night. It wasn't that the rock was hard — if anything it was too soft, and the surface crumbled under every vehicle. It was a nightmare experience. Luckily there was moonlight by which to drive, but even so two men each armed with shaded torches walked along the track in front of each vehicle guiding the truck or tank or quad over the rocky surface and down to the valley. Everybody was shit scared. The noise of the shovelling, the engines roaring down in first gear and all the other noises must have been heard miles away, but Jerry made no effort to attack, and there were some companies of one of 50 Div battalions, keeping a look out.

'The whole of the group moved by fits and starts down the cliff face only to find that they were stuck in a wadi about 60 to 70 feet deep. Luckily, the far wall was not sheer, and the whole lot climbed up the far wall, which had a shockingly steep gradient − about 1 in 3. Some lorries boiled over during the climb or got their springs smashed as they drove over boulders. Once the column reached the top (this was about 6 in the morning) there was a bit of a wait until the infantry rearguard had climbed the steep wadi and had climbed onto the vehicles. There was a short drive, still downhill, onto the tarmac road. Every one of the guns was got out. Jerry took none of them.'

In that partnership of gun and men, the piece could be a hard taskmaster. Toughest of all, in terms of stamina, was intensive fire. 'That's a real madhouse. Open breech, slam one in, ram it, close breech, fire, open breech, catch the cartridge case as it comes out, chuck it away and while you are doing that another one is up and has been fired. That's how it goes on, minute after minute. You drip with sweat and all your limbs ache. The shells you fling into the breech begin to weigh a ton and that's why intensive fire lasts only minutes. Otherwise accidents begin to happen, and once you get out of the rhythm it's hard to get back into it again. When you are working at speed that's when fingers get caught and ripped open and fingernails are torn out. All the time you are working like stokers, shovelling in the shells. It seemed ages before cease-fire came, but when it did we were all shagged out. The trucks came round with tea, and while some of us cooled down the red-hot barrel with wet rags others cleared away the mass of shells that we had fired. We had also had a ten-minute rest every hour, and that pause helped to cool the gun.'

In addition to the sheer hard work, there was always the hair-raising possibility of a misfire: 'Our battery was lucky. Everything went like clockwork, but in one of the other batteries they had a misfire. This means that the cartridge hasn't fired. When the breech is opened it might be then that the cartridge chooses to explode. After a couple more unsuccessful attempts to fire it, the cartridge is withdrawn and taken to the rear. In one regiment they had a bore premature in the barrel. It killed or wounded a whole crew.'

The role that the army commander cast for the Royal Regiment of Artillery to play in Operation 'Lightfoot' reflected the memories he retained of the First World War and of the devastating effects of massed artillery fire. The morale-raising factors produced by huge, sustained and flexibly controlled barrages were incalculable. His own soldiers would have their hearts lifted; those of the enemy would be broken by the knowledge that their own artillery was impotent to reply to the challenge. There would be no fear that ground conditions would deteriorate under bombardment as they had at Passchendaele or on the Somme; nor would extensive urban demolitions or house-to-house fighting in built-up areas slow the army's advance towards the break-out point. It has been said that Rommel was a Second World War general who was forced to fight a First World War battle and that his opponent, Montgomery, was a commander who used the weapons of the Second World War in the fashion of 1914—1918. That may have an element of truth in it: but to say that the bombardment of El Alamein was only a miniature version of British bombardments of the First World War is only partly correct.

The disadvantage encountered in the Great War, that massed bombardment was inflexible and that the guns could not be switched swiftly from target to target, would be overcome at Alamein by the erection of a sophisticated wireless network running from the forward companies to the artillery and beyond. The Signals personnel were also intensively trained in the swift transmission of messages. With such equipment the danger that the barrage would outrun the infantry could be overcome; in any case, the infantry was being taught in training to advance so close behind the curtain of shells that they were 'leaning on the barrage'. The Forward Observation Officers, up with the infantry or riding in command tanks with the armoured regiments, could switch a concentration of guns from one target to another without the delays and accidents of former days: 'In position and with communications established, it needed only a single codeword from our FOO up forward with the Jocks and the whole battery would fire to order. There was a simple sequence of orders. The target would be described — say a gun position or a group of trucks. Then we would be told the type of shell we were to fire, HE or smoke. Then the charge was given. We were next given direction and distance and these were checked on our sights. Finally, we were told how many rounds to fire. During the time that these orders were being received, members of the gun crew would be setting the fuzes on the shells, the layer would be busy with the sights, and when all was ready No. 1 would raise his arm as a sign that we were ready. With the order "Fire", a troop, a battery or even the guns of a whole regiment could plaster a given spot in a matter of minutes.'

The aim of Eighth Army's artillery commander was not to pour out thousands of shells in huge 'sledgehammer' operations but to use the guns as delicately as rapiers, bringing down fire at a minute's notice upon targets of opportunity, such as sudden concentrations of enemy tanks, lorries or men. Such flexibility was the result of training as long and as thorough as that undergone by the infantry and tank men. The fruits of that training were to produce the barrages at El Alamein. This is not to suggest that every shoot would always be successful or that failures in communication leading to accidents would not happen. They did. But, by and large, the artillery support would be finer than anything that the army had had in the desert.

Indeed, for the Battle of El Alamein, the whole bombardment of that first night was perfectly synchronized and on successive days the set-piece attacks were each supported by concentrations of guns whose fire could be brought together, switched to a new target or halted with surprising speed. It was said, with absolute accuracy, that if communications were good, a planned set-piece bombardment could be changed as required within a time period of twelve to fifteen minutes. The last infantry battles of 'Supercharge' were evidence of this highly competent flexibility. The 5th Indian Brigade requested a postponement of the barrage which was to support its battalions only fifteen minutes before the programme was to be fired. The orders post-poning the opening sequences were passed to all units and sub-units with a minute to spare. It was a triumph of planning and training.

By the very nature of their role, FOOs were able to get a much wider view of the battle as it raged about them than the average Gunner sweating away in his gun pit. The FOO's perspective of the battle is provided by an article which describes the writer's time with an Australian artillery regiment.*

'Today we are to man a different OP. This one is well forward. . . . We have breakfast at the guns and set off across a marshy depression to the sea, then west along the coast for several miles. To our right, the Mediterranean washes gently against the sand dunes, only a stone's throw away; to the south the country is mainly low-lying and marshy. Soon a ridge appears to our left, that same ridge where fighting has been so bitter in the last few days. The western tip is Point 26 and then the long east-west rib depresses and rises to Point 33, the ridge finally petering out into enemy territory.

'We must occupy an OP forward of 26. We turn inland from the coast road towards 26, skirting wind-piled sand dunes and roaring across salty depressions. These Bren carriers become unbearably hot after a few miles. Occasionally, we see solitary crosses, sometimes in pairs. Maybe the graves are Australian, maybe Eyetie or German. All about this area there are infantry positions. One can only just detect the spoor of the army dug-outs and slit trenches. In the desert, armies disappear as if by magic. In the event of an attack, this whole area would leap to life, vibrant, expectant.

'We can detect the battery commander's armoured car with its fat wireless mast. Jim halts in a well concealed position behind the ridge. We collect our paraphernalia, climb the bare ridge that is Point 26 and settle down in a slit trench for the day's observation. We are on the forward slope. Back at the carrier, Jack gets his wireless operating and runs out a remote control to the OP. Aub., the OP sig., connects his 'phone to the gunline and another to the remote control. The other two

---

*'I saw a panzer attack', anonymous article in *Khaki and Green* (With the Australian Army at Home and Overseas), reproduced by permission of the publishers, The Australian War Memorial, Canberra, ACT.

batteries also have OPs on this forward slope. One is to the north and the other to the south of us, both within calling distance. Out in front, perhaps half a mile away, is . . . our artillery.

'Obviously, it will be a hot day. The sun is well up and blazing out. OPs should be relieved in darkness and our arrival after sunrise is unpopular with the major. The front is unusually quiet. Now and then mortar shells whistle over and burst south of us. We do little shooting. There is spasmodic shelling in the vicinity of our infantry positions. . . . We open up on an enemy mortar OP that has been directing fire onto our infantry. We range accurately and go to "fire for effect". For a time the mortars are silenced. Later they open up again and, as soon as they do, we give them a few more rounds. They are hard to hit, but we make them keep their heads down. After lunch it is very quiet. . . . I peer through glasses but can see no human being, only a faint shimmer shifting over the derelict tanks and vehicles scattered about the station. We just sit there quietly. The OPO passes a remark about the lull. . . . Seven Macchis roar overhead and swoop down. . . . to drop their bombs. . . . In the distance we can see enemy tanks. . . . Whole regiments of our guns open up on the tanks with terrific concentrations of gun fire. The sun is just setting and the attack has gathered full momentum. Behind us the guns belch flame, and everywhere over the coastal sector I can see the darts of burnt cordite from 25pdrs. In front the tanks are nosing closer to the station. Machine-guns are chattering all around us, anti-tank guns are barking sharply and shells from enemy tanks whizz overhead. Enemy field-guns are putting down a deafening barrage along the coast. This hellish noise is frightening. . . . Our infantry is taking a terrific pounding. The OPO orders ten rounds gunfire, then twenty, then thirty. Our infantry gives no ground. . . . I shall never forget the infantry about our OP. Their unconcern and nonchalance is unbelievable. Their officers stroll about from post to post; a couple of chaps are drinking beer while half a mile away a deadly battle is raging. Then comes the order for us to return to the gun positions. We do not want to go. Surely this looks like desertion to our infantry . . . It must look as if we're running away, the artillery leaving it to the infantry. We are still completely puzzled. . . . We flop into the vehicle pit. . . . pile in the last wireless battery and the last haversack and clamber aboard. Slowly we rev towards the coast road and Jim gives her the works. Those guns we can see belong to the 2/8th, they look brave and defiant spitting out shells, while other shells of a different calibre burst in among them. Just ahead of us more shells are bursting, right on the road too. Jim pauses until a group of shells bursts, then he puts his foot down on the boards. As he does so we squirm down into the carrier for cover. We get through all right. A little farther on we see the other carrier, which must have swung off the road and bogged down in the thick mud. We have a tow-rope and soon the carrier is out. We find a gap in the mine-field . . . having negotiated it we pause to light cigarettes. The barrage has not crept this far yet. . . . From every direction as we come out there are spurts of flame and our immediate aim is to find out which spurts belong to our guns.

'We find them and at the guns the noise is more violent than ever. The impression, despite the darkness, is one of untiring energy. The Gunners, stripped to the waist and covered in sweat, blackened with cordite and showered with dust all mixed with sweat which runs down their faces in dirty rivulets, are happy. They are happy because they have no time to think. We hear the orders coming through from the command post. Those tanks swinging to the east must be drawing closer. The object must be to wedge eastwards and then turn north to the coast, cutting off the long salient reaching out to 33. . . . I dash over to give a hand in carting ammo. As I stagger over with an armful of shells, the gun is fired. There is a roaring and a ringing in my ears. I have forgotten my earplugs. Others on the gun have the same trouble in spite of their plugs. I can see rather than hear their straining and shouting to get orders through. Although the gun is firing 'rapid', the only indication I have now is the vivid flash in the blackness, for my hearing is almost dead. One chap is carried away wounded. He fell cursing when a piece of shrapnel slapped through his foot.

'A big jagged piece of shrap has cut through the shield of the gun and other bits have damaged the sights, but the other Gunners are unhurt. Stan is laying and might be sitting in at a tea-party − bubble, line, bubble, line, steady as you like and with a cigarette we rolled for him drooping from his lips. I can feel the heat pulsing out from the gun, which is red hot. Around the pit there is a mass of piled cartridges and ammo boxes are scattered in wild disorder. Shells whine over and I duck involuntarily, but they are not close. The range lifts. That means the attack is turned. One can sense the elation, the air is almost warmer with victory. The range lifts again and still the guns pound away. Now I notice over the coastal sector fewer guns are firing. Gradually darkness settles and suddenly the guns in our area stop. It is like a jolt. Only five minutes ago the earth lived and now, amazingly, it is dead. The battle is over and once again the Hun has been repulsed. . . . I have seen a panzer attack, saw Australian infantry stand up to the tanks. . . . and I saw those Gunners sweating and confident when at any moment the tanks might loom up on the ridge a hundred yards in front of us. They were grand to watch. . . .'

*　　*　　*

With the men trained and proficient, detailed planning could begin, and did so during the first week of October. In order to reinforce XXX Corps sector, the one on which the maximum effort was to be made, three regiments of X Corps' field artillery was integrated by troops into the regiments of XXX Corps. The medium regiments were taken out of army reserve and put in to add power to the bombardment by the 25pdrs. In total there were 29 field regiments and seven of the

Royal Horse Artillery. To support the short-ranged 25pdrs, the army disposed three regiments of medium artillery. For immediate defence against armoured attack, there were ten regiments of anti-tank artillery and eleven light anti-aircraft regiments, together with two light anti-aircraft brigades to defend the divisions on the ground against assault from the air. Each infantry division had a minimum of three field artillery regiments on establishment, together with an anti-tank and anti-aircraft regiment. In armoured divisions the place of field regiments was taken by units of the Royal Horse Artillery, which had in bygone days accompanied cavalry divisions. Except for the title and a certain panache, there was little organizational difference between the two types of unit; both gave close support to the parent formation.

It was the medium regiments of artillery that would provide counter-battery fire during the battle. The precise and factual words of a report issued on counter-battery operations gives no hint of the tremendous task that was accomplished, although it does mention that to work out the programme took over 24 working days and that the master plan that was produced was so detailed that it had to be issued in five separate parts. Significantly, these individual sections refer to XXX Corps alone. The counter-battery work in XIII Corps sector was carried out by 25pdrs.

A total of 10,650 aerial photographs were taken showing the location of hostile batteries. From this mass of information, supplemented by traditional methods of sound ranging and visual spotting, a complete picture of the enemy's gun areas could be determined. On XXX Corps front, for example, all the Panzerarmee gun positions that were occupied were known on D minus 1. Only those few that might be moved to a new position during that final day could escape attack, and because of the known shortages of petrol very few batteries would change position. Such was the precision with which the air interpretation officers checked the photographs that the gun positions were located to within 50 yards or less. The types of guns in position and their arcs of fire could be determined and, consequently, the enemy batteries that could put down defensive fire in the sector of XXX Corps advance could be selected and bombarded. What this meant, in effect, was that fire could be poured upon the most obvious targets by a concentration of British guns to a ratio of up to 20:1 and that our shells would land within 50 yards. The enemy was unable to build up so accurate a picture of our gun defences and was absolutely unaware of the batteries that had been brought forward as part of the deception plan.

The chief difficulty mentioned in the report, and one that would be of the utmost importance in the battle, was that of locating anti-tank guns. The report admits that counter-battery operations could not expect to locate such weapons as they did not fire until actually attacked. The 88s could be detected without difficulty, but the lighter weapons in infantry strongpoints could not be seen except on blow-ups of aerial shots, although the probable area in which they were sited could often be deduced with reasonable accuracy.

The Royal Artillery played a very important part in fixing the time of the assault. Montgomery, appreciating how vital it was to destroy the enemy's artillery, most of which was beyond the range of the 25pdrs, was forced to rely upon the medium regiments. The CRA (Commander of the Royal Artillery) pointed out that the British observers could see the flashes of the enemy artillery only during darkness and in the early morning. As soon as the sun was well up, visibility decreased. 'The enemy artillery could open fire and shell our infantry off their newly-won objectives or cause them heavy casualties and CB could do little about it.' In order to give the infantry the longest time possible free from enemy shelling, and thereby provide the opportunity to effect the deepest possible penetration, the best time to start the attack would be as soon after dark as possible. The time selected for zero hour, ie, 22.00 hours was, therefore, ideal from the CB point of view.

Aware that the few medium artillery regiments on Eighth Army's establishment could not deal with all the enemy's guns, a total of 25 hostile batteries were selected as being the most likely to put down defensive fire on the sectors of the advance. These were given a very heavy concentration of fire in order to shatter enemy morale and cause so much damage that the hostile batteries would be out of the battle for at least the period of the main attack and probably for good. The success of this action can be gauged from the report, which mentions that during the main attack only two hostile batteries fired. Only about one half of the enemy's batteries concerned fired again during the remainder of the offensive, and the great majority of those did not fire more than once.

Almost every prisoner of war brought in during the first few days told of guns destroyed and heavy casualties among crews. The POW statements present an astonishing picture of CB successes. The 4th and 5th Troops of No. 2 Battery of 220th Artillery Regiment were reported as having been totally destroyed. The 53rd AA Regiment reported the loss of most of its personnel; killed, wounded or captured. No. 1 Battery of 46th Motorized Artillery Regiment suffered a 50 percent loss in its 100mm guns and a 25 percent loss in its 88s. The 354th Battery lost all its guns, as did 355th Battery, while 357th Battery reported the destruction of seven guns up to 28 October, and the total loss of all its pieces by the 30th. It is small wonder that most enemy gunners went to ground and stayed under cover until the hurricanes of British fire had passed. Some Italian gunners stayed in their concrete dug outs until they were taken prisoner.

A combination of careful planning and first class organization ensured that the Eighth Army went in under the best possible counter-battery fire programme. Flexibility provided the other ingredient for success. In one particular case, quoted in the report and testified to by prisoner-of-war statements, a bombardment was brought down upon a target within three and a half minutes of the receipt of information that an enemy battery had opened fire. It was this flexibility, careful attention to detail and sheer professionalism that enabled the Royal Artillery to be the umbrella of the other arms of service.

Artillery
at the Battle of El Alamein

XXX Corps

51st Highland Division: 126th, 127th and 128th Field Regiments; 61st Anti-Tank Regiment; 40th Light Anti-Aircraft Regiment.
2nd New Zealand Division: 4th, 5th and 6th New Zealand Field Regiments; 7th New Zealand Anti-Tank Regiment; 14th New Zealand Anti-Aircraft Regiment.
9th Australian Division: 2/7th, 2/8th and 2/12th Australian Field Regiments; 3rd Australian Anti-Tank Regiment; 4th Australian Light Anti-Aircraft Regiment.
4th Indian Division: 1st, 11th and 32nd Field Regiments; 149th Anti-Tank Regiment; 57th Light Anti-Aircraft Regiment.
1st South African Division: 1st, 4th and 7th South African Regiments; 1st South African Anti-Tank Regiment; 1st South African Light Anti-Aircraft Regiment.
Corps Troops: 7th, 64th and 69th Medium Regiments.

XIII Corps

7th Armoured Division: 3rd Royal Horse Artillery; 4th and 97th Field Regiments; 65th Anti-Tank Regiment; 15th Light Anti-Aircraft Regiment.
44th Division: 57th, 58th, 65th and 53rd Field Regiments; 57th Anti-Tank Regiment; 30th Light Anti-Aircraft Regiment.
50th Division: 74th, 111th, 124th and 154th Field Regiments; 102nd Anti-Tank Regiment; 34th Light Anti-Aircraft Regiment.

X Corps

1st Armoured Division: 2nd, 4th and 11th Royal Horse Artillery; 78th Field Regiment; 76th Anti-Tank Regiment; 42nd Light Anti-Aircraft Regiment.
10th Armoured Division: 1st, 5th and 104th Royal Horse Artillery; 98th Field Regiment; 84th Anti-Tank Regiment; 53rd Light Anti-Aircraft Regiment.

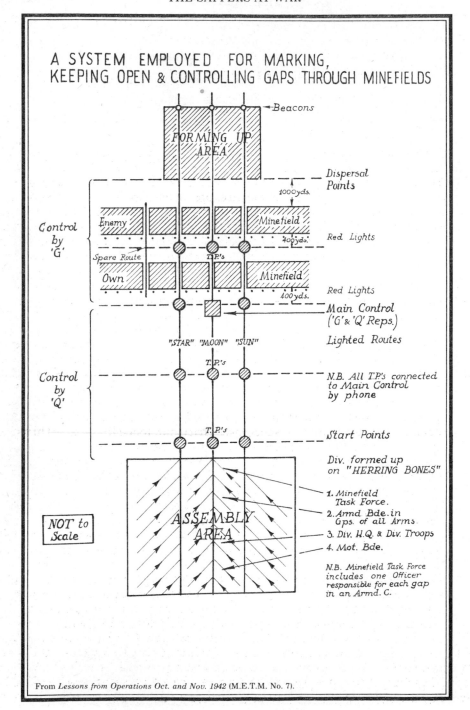

A SYSTEM EMPLOYED FOR MARKING,
KEEPING OPEN & CONTROLLING GAPS THROUGH MINEFIELDS

Beacons

FORMING UP
AREA

Dispersal
Points

1000 yds.

Control
by
'G'

Enemy

Minefield

Red Lights

400 yds.

Spare Route

T.P's

Own

Minefield

Red Lights

400 yds.

Main Control
('G' & 'Q' Reps.)

"STAR" "MOON" "SUN"

Lighted Routes

Control
by
'Q'

T.P's

N.B. All T.P's connected
to Main Control
by phone

T.P's

Start Points

Div. formed up
on "HERRING BONES"

NOT to
Scale

ASSEMBLY
AREA

1. Minefield
Task Force.
2. Armd. Bde. in
Gps. of all Arms.
3. Div. H.Q. & Div. Troops
4. Mot. Bde.

N.B. Minefield Task Force
includes one Officer
responsible for each gap
in an Armd. C.

From *Lessons from Operations Oct. and Nov. 1942* (M.E.T.M. No. 7).

The British armour prepares for battle. **Right:** Matilda cruiser tanks on patrol. **Below:** Men of the Royal Tank Regiment being instructed by American Army tank men on Grant tanks. The Grant was the first armoured fighting vehicle to engage the German panzer on equal terms, but it suffered from a major defect. The main armament was sponson mounted and had only a limited traverse, which meant that it could not take up a 'hull down' position without exposing much of the turret to enemy fire.

'The guns will open the way for the infantry. . . .' **Top:** A 25pdr gun opens fire upon enemy positions. Enemy shells are landing in the background. **Centre:** Field artillery in action, firing from well prepared positions. **Bottom:** Medium artillery being towed up an escarpment.

Mine and counter-mine, in theory and in practice. **Top:** Sappers of the South African Division combine the established method of prodding with a bayonet with the new technique of sweeping with a Polish detector. **Above:** An RE minefield gapping and marking detachment setting out just before dark to clear a lane through a minefield. **Below left:** An NCO of the Military Police filling hurricane lamps before issuing them to infantry and Engineer companies to light and put out along the desert tracks. Over 80,000 of these lamps were used by Eighth Army to light the gaps in the minefields. **Below right:** Two Sappers setting up a gap marker to indicate a cleared passage. The man on the left has the tape which will be run out to show that the area is safe.

'The enemy is to be totally deceived. . . .' In an attempt to deceive the commanders of the German/Italian Panzerarmee as to the strength of Eighth Army and the point at which its decisive thrust would be made in the British offensive, elaborate schemes were drawn up under the codename 'Bertram'. Dummy tanks were constructed of scrap materials or produced as inflatable rubber dummies. Across the length of the British battle line hundreds of tanks were disguised as lorries and squadrons of rubber tanks and guns were set out a long way from the front line. **Above:** A dummy tank being carried into position. **Left:** A light tank covered with a 'sun hood', a hessian frame to camouflage it as a lorry. It was this type of camouflage that deceived the Germans before the opening of Operation 'Lightfoot'. **Below left:** An officer in HQ 24th Armoured Brigade gives his men details of 'Lightfoot' and the part they will play in the battle. Note that the 'lorry' in whose shade he is standing is in reality a Sherman tank.

7.

THE SAPPERS AT WAR

The tasks facing the officers and men of the Royal Engineers in the desert fighting were varied and dangerous. Because there were no rivers in the North African battle area, the Sappers were spared the need to bridge waterways under fire, operations with which they were to become very familiar in Italy and North-West Europe. They were, however, faced with other nerve-racking duties, principally minelaying and minelifting. Both (and for the first time in the history of warfare) were not merely an important but a dominating influence on the course of military operations in the desert.

When the Front stabilized late in the summer of 1942, it was clear that both sides would set about re-equipping and rearming for new, possibly decisive battles. Mines were laid in thousands and then, as the situation developed, in hundreds of thousands. At first it was the British who laid out great barriers, and not in the forward areas alone. Lieutenant-Colonel Llewelyn Lloyd, at the time of El Alamein a major commanding a field company of engineers, recalled that defensive minefields were laid at Mena, near the Pyramids just outside Cairo. This was a measure of the way in which Eighth Army Command feared the next Axis thrust might end — with the Afrika Korps delayed but not halted by successive British defence lines, as it thrust for the Canal. Following the arrival in the desert of Alexander and Montgomery, it was clear that in the race to build up for a new offensive Eighth Army would not only be ready first but that its re-equipping would be on a lavish scale. Slowly the military initiative had swung in favour of the Allies. At Montgomery's order, a school was set up in which Sappers and then men from every arm of service were taught to identify and to lift mines. The methods used were not the same in each corps; what was common was the formation of a minefield task force.

In the history of warfare up to the Second World War, there had been little use of mines as a strategic weapon, to cover stretches along the front of an army, probably because of the unreliable nature of fuzes. Experiment and development in the 1930s had perfected not only the fuzes but newer and more powerful explosives, which could be packed into small containers. The principal enemy mine, and one with which the Allied armies were to become very familiar, was the German Teller or plate mine. This had a flat base and a slightly convex upper section, was about the size of a dinner plate and held several pounds of explosive. It could be fitted with any one of a small number of fuzes — for example, the tank fuze would not detonate the mine if a soldier walked over it. One variant of the standard fuze incorporated a ring fitted to a release switch. To that ring a wire could be fixed, and this would run to the casing of a second mine, some feet distant. The wire then served both as a trip wire to catch the unwary as well as an anti-lifting device. Wires could also be fitted to the underside of one mine and that mine would be laid on a second Teller. An attempt to lift the first would activate the release switch and detonate the lower mine.

While the Teller was essentially an anti-vehicle weapon, the S mine, which was not met in large numbers until El Alamein, was an anti-personnel device. It too could be fitted with a striker release fuze to serve as a booby-trap. And there were in the desert hundreds of thousands of such devilish things that had to be cleared from known fields, suspected fields and from unknown ones. It was not necessary to clear the whole area of a minefield during the course of an operation. Narrow gaps would permit assaulting troops to pass through and emerge to strike the enemy.

The Engineers could not be expected to carry out the tasks of clearing mines as well as of fighting off enemy interference, so it was essential that the Sapper groups gapping a field be protected by an infantry screen backed up by armour — a small bridgehead behind which the Sappers could carry out their 'de-lousing' tasks. This meant that the infantry had the frightening experience of being the first to cross an area they knew to be sown with mines. They crossed such fields with the full knowledge of the consequences of carelessness, and usually at night. Speaking from personal experience, it was a horrible feeling.

Dispersion was the way to minimize losses: dispersion and a controlled advance. In the early years when a party of Engineers cleared a field at night, they inched their way forward across the suspect area, each man lying prone on his stomach and feeling with extended arms, for wires. If the ground were free from trip wires, then a follow-up team of standing Sappers pushed their bayonets into the sand. Words cannot describe the awful feeling of sick hopelessness if resistance were met, for when the bayonet struck something solid this usually indicated the presence of a mine. The operator, sweating with the prospect of death or mutilation, would gently sift the sand with his fingers and . . . oh, the blessed relief of finding that it was only a piece of rock and not a Jerry mine! If no resistance were encountered to the bayonet thrust, then the operator would take another pace and dig the probe in again. If a mine were struck and then uncovered, and the absence of wires showed it to be 'clean', then it was gently lifted out of its bed and either stacked along the side of the swept track or else the fuze in the top of the casing was slowly unscrewed and removed. Fuzes could be booby-trapped, but that degree of sophistication was rarely encountered in the desert. Another night-time method was to crouch and to advance with the arms hanging loose and with the back of each hand brushing the surface of the desert, feeling for wires. This way was faster, but was less certain of completely clearing a suspect area.

The frightening situation of never knowing where a field began or ended, of not knowing whether the ground to be swept was sown with familiar devices or the uncertain products of some Middle Eastern light engineering shop, produced the demand for standard procedures in minelaying and lifting. Sapper training had to go back to fundamentals. There was no manual of instruction. Every idea, every tactic had to be tested under conditions in which the loser paid with his life. As the result of discussions between Engineer officers, a school was opened whose curriculum covered the plotting of fields, how to lay mines, how to lift them and how to deal with booby-traps. The short course taught Sappers and the Pioneer platoons of infantry battalions the drills that had been evolved to gap enemy fields. So effective were these courses that the lessons they imparted passed into British Army handbooks. The training of the Royal Engineers, like that of the infantry and the Gunners, was carried out by day and by night and, as for the battalions, on the same sort of ground that they would have to gap during Operation 'Lightfoot'.

When that time came it would not be too difficult for the Royal Engineer teams to widen gaps in the British fields to permit the passage of X Corps armour. It was the ground beyond that was the nightmare — across the wire lay an infested narrow strip of no man's land and then the deep 'marshes' of Panzerarmee's defences, old British or German minefields linking fresh belts of Teller mines, of S mines or of thermite and aerial bombs.

In the north of the German line, the most sensitive sector of the defences, a second belt of prepared positions had been constructed immediately behind the main minefields. The two separate belts were connected by transverse fields that had been designed with the object of channelling the British advance towards German guns. Behind those two extensive and sophisticated ribbons of death, running from the Mediterranean to the Deir el Meirar, a depression to the south-west of the German-held western end of Ruweisat Ridge, there was a third belt of defences. That extended from a point just east of Sidi Abd el Rahman and continued southwards for nearly eight miles. Around the freshly constructed defences of that third line were laid extensive belts of mines.

It was the task of the Royal Engineers to clear quickly all that vast area of sudden death. Behind the infantry shield and covered by the artillery barrage, the Sappers would be working at full pressure to open the way for the armour to pour through. Intensive training went on using established methods and newer ones. The conventional methods of detecting mines were not efficient, were slow and were not really applicable to the fields that had to be cleared. Speed was important, and improved mechanical methods had to be found. The solution was at hand in the shape of a detector invented by Polish officers. In this, the mine was detected by electrical impulses producing a high whine in the earpieces that the operator wore. But the introduction of the Polish detector produced a new problem: one of morale. The detector was shaped like a vacuum cleaner, and was swept across the ground in front of the operator, so the sweeper had to stand erect. It required more than the usual courage to be upright among the shot and shell that was flying across the battlefield, moving the detector arm backwards and forwards over the desert surface, listening for the whining noise that located the buried mine. Behind the sweeper came in number two, who had to mark the mine. Simple but effective markers, white painted cones made out of flimsy petrol tins, were designed, manufactured and produced in unit workshops. A whole team of sweepers was to go into action immediately behind and sometimes ahead of the infantry companies and would have to work there, defenceless in an area whose range the enemy artillery knew to a yard. It was an unenviable task, but one upon which the pace of the battle depended.

There were other methods employed in gapping the fields. The one described above was the method found most effective in the infantry units of XXX Corps, but even in that formation there were differences in approach by the two armoured divisions. The task force brought together by the 1st Armoured Division for the gapping of the fields on its sector was made up of infantry, Engineers and tank men. The force was under the command of an infantry officer with a Sapper advisor. The 10th Armoured Division favoured the employment of a senior Royal Engineer officer working with only his own men. In XIII Corps the 7th Armoured Division had received the flail tank, Scorpion, manned by the RTR, to clear the gaps in the southern minefields. The Scorpions were headed by a pilot vehicle, heavily sandbagged, which drove slowly over the desert. When the lorry blew up on a mine, this marked (possibly) the edge of another field. Then the Scorpion was put into action beating out a path. Behind the flail tanks came 'Snails', lorries laden with barrels of diesel oil, which was poured out over the rear tyres; this left an unmistakeable print in the desert and was visible even on moonless nights. There were, of course, variations of that tactic where Sappers on foot marched behind the Scorpions making sure that all the mines had been flailed and those men were followed by the Snails, marking a safe track.

Speedy and successful passage through minefields was vital to the deployment of the armour, and so a strict traffic control system was rehearsed. A major formation, for example a division, ordered forward would be formed tactically with a minelaying force at its head and with the other important units in order of priority in the forthcoming battle closely echeloned behind the leading groups. The formation would be deployed in three columns in an assembly area located at the approaches to marked, named tracks that led to gaps in the British fields; a fourth track would be cleared as a spare route in case of emergencies. The closest liaison was established at all important points by officers in armoured cars backed by men of the divisional provost companies. These policed not only the starting points of the tracks and a half way point along each track, but also a main control point some 400 yards short of the British minefield gaps. A set of red lamp signals indicated the forward edge of the British fields and another set of lights the forward edge of the enemy field. Each individual gap was marked by day with painted signposts and at night by the sort of illumination described by Corporal Harris whose narrative follows.

'By the middle of October it was obvious that we were about to undertake an offensive. Jerry had had two tries since Gazala (June 1942) and he had been held on both occasions. Now it was our turn, and we had time to gap our fields properly and to mark them. We were on the offensive and did not need defensive fields, but jump-off points for the new battles.

'I don't know how well the earlier battles had been organized, but the minefield gapping for Alamein was first class. Quite a lot of my unit had been on a Middle East mineclearing course, and so had all the unit officers. When we started, everything was done dead regimental. So far as I was told, earlier mineclearing had been a matter of prodding the ground with a bayonet, and when a mine was found then an NCO would lift it and take out the fuze. The empty mines were then laid in the open alongside the gapped area. But for Alamein we had detectors. We had seen some at the Eighth Army Mine Training School and we had a couple of the new Polish types issued to us. These looked like the old fashioned upright vacuum cleaners with a metal loop where the head is. That loop had an electric current and when the detectors passed over a mine a noise sounded in earphones which the operator wore so he knew where the mine was situated. The other types of detector that we saw in the Training School were really lash-up jobs and did not always clear a strip. There were also Scorpion tanks used although I never saw any that time, but I did hear that they made a lot of dust and did not always beat a clear path. The idea of the Scorpion was a revolving drum at the front of the tank which was fitted with chains that thrashed the ground ahead of the tank and, in theory, those flails would detonate the mines without damaging the machine. As I say, they were said to be unreliable.

'One of the most nerve-racking things in mineclearing was finding out where the front edge of the field was located. It was really a hit or miss affair, and to confuse us Jerry often mixed in the normal anti-tank minefields with anti-personnel mines. We were told about a new mine that they had just brought in. These were S mines, which were buried up to the depth of a three-pronged detonator. The whole thing looked like a tin of baked beans with a nozzle on top, but of course all that were visible were the three prongs of the detonator. When a foot trod on the detonator there were two distinct explosions. The first flung the mine up into the air and the second explosion was at waist height and it spewed out hundreds of ball bearings horizontally. You can guess the effect of those things and how we felt about them. There were other anti-personnel mines as well.

'For Alamein we were rehearsed in mineclearing with and without infantry co-operation. We had that training in addition to the course at the Eighth Army school and, as I said, the organization to gap a field during the battle was first class. The RE recce party went in with the infantry. I felt sorry for the infantry boys. They had to walk across the minefield and take up defensive positions to keep the Jerries off while our lads got to work. Then our recce party went in to find and to fix the forward edge of the field. Our officer then decided the area that was to be gapped. Behind the recce group were the tape men who ran out the tape for the first narrow gap. This was eight feet wide. The actual width of the gap when we were finished was 24 feet, and to make sure that the width was correct two men were roped at that distance and walked on compass bearings along the swept corridor.

'Then came the detector party: three sweepers who worked in staggered formation. Each operator had a mate, a marker who fixed a white painted metal cone over any mine that was detected in the gap. Behind the sweepers came the three-man lifting team, who knelt down on the desert and felt around the mine to make sure that it was a 'clean' one — that is, that it didn't have trip wires running from it or a booby-trap attached to it. That really was a dodgy operation because Jerry also had an explosive device that might be fitted under the fuze in the body of the mine. Anyway, once the mine had been defused, it was lifted out of the ground and placed outside the marking tape. The gap markers ran out their tapes to keep pace with the lifters, pegging down the tapes into position.

'Working at top speed, a team could work a two-hundred-yard strip in about an hour. The length of time taken was increased if we were under heavy shell fire; longer still if we were under Spandau fire; and even longer if we had casualties. Everybody moved dead slow then. Using the detectors we could stand up and operate them, but those of us who didn't have proper detectors relied upon the bayonet prodding method, although at Alamein my unit did no prodding. We had detectors and were standing all the time.

'There was always a little group of reserves, just in case we lost men on mines or to shell or machine-gun fire. This group, only a couple of men, stayed at the gap at the edge of the field and they used to brew up for us. It was really thirsty work in a gapping operation; it was fear I should think that made us so thirsty. The rottenest job, I think, was the actual lifting, because of the booby-traps that were fitted or the cunning anti-handling devices. In daylight one could often see the thin wires that led to another mine nearby, but at night one worked by feel, and a false move — one tug without being sure — and it was all over.

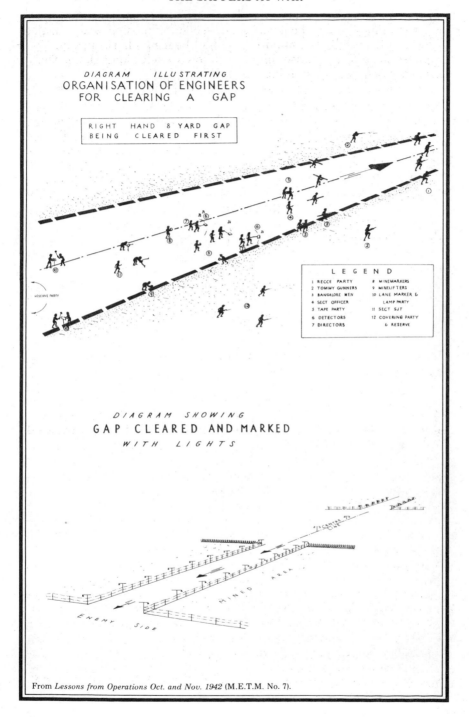

DIAGRAM ILLUSTRATING
ORGANISATION OF ENGINEERS
FOR CLEARING A GAP

RIGHT HAND 8 YARD GAP
BEING CLEARED FIRST

LEGEND

1 RECCE PARTY	8 MINEMARKERS
2 TOMMY GUNNERS	9 MINELIFTERS
3 BANGALORE MEN	10 LANE MARKER &
4 SECT OFFICER	LAMP PARTY
5 TAPE PARTY	11 SECT SJT
6 DETECTORS	12 COVERING PARTY
7 DIRECTORS	& RESERVE

RESERVE PARTY

DIAGRAM SHOWING
GAP CLEARED AND MARKED
WITH LIGHTS

From *Lessons from Operations Oct. and Nov. 1942* (M.E.T.M. No. 7).

'Because of the strain, we worked in half-hour shifts. Any longer than that and we lost our concentration and became careless. We did the Alamein gapping at night and put out lights to show the routes forward. Because of the sand, the smoke and the darkness, drivers would not have been able to see tapes marking the gaps, so a system of lights was set up. Our lighting party set up posts with a cross piece from which hung two empty petrol tins — the square flimsy type were ideal. A green light showed in one flimsy, and that marked the cleared side. An amber light in the other flimsy indicated the uncleared side. Of course, the lights — they were hurricane lamps with most of the glass blacked out and only a little disc of green or amber showing — only shone towards the British lines. There was no light to be seen on the side of the flimsy facing the enemy. There were supposed to be other lights set up, two blue lamps, one to mark the forward edge of the enemy minefield and the other to show where it ended, but we did not do that in my unit, or if we did I can't remember seeing them.

'The first gap we made was quite narrow, but then we extended this to 24 feet wide. We swept forward from our side to the enemy side, then came back in reverse, then swept forward again and came back again. The full width of the passage we made at Alamein was 48 feet, but we had an armoured mob coming through ours and they needed a wider gap than the infantry did.

'One of my mates drove a 15cwt truck that had its cab and floor covered with sandbags. He had sandbags under his feet, and because of the need for height the steering wheel was lengthened. To drive one of those trucks — really primitive mine-exploding devices — required strong nerves. The idea was that quite often the gapping team would not realize that it had crossed the enemy field and would continue to work forward blindly before being halted. To find out where the next field began it was not much use to go forward prodding or sweeping — that was much too slow. So the 15cwt was called up, and it was driven forward until it ran over a mine. That would indicate, or better said it might indicate, the forward edge of a new field. Then the sweeping, taping and gapping would start all over again.'

Mines were laid in places where they would be likely to cause the most damage and trouble to the enemy, such as airfields, verges or tracks around wells and camp sites. The few Arabs who moved through the area fell victim to the uncleared devices and it is likely that even today, forty years on, there are areas of the Western Desert under whose surface mines still lie ready to kill the unwary. Cynics say that the presence of mines altered certain social observances among the desert Arabs. Before the War, the husband rode or walked ahead of his wife, she following like a servant in his footsteps. The great expanses of mined areas and the possibility of being blown up altered the family formation: now the wife walks in front, a human mine detector.

8.

THE PLAN

During September 1942, Eighth Army had been training hard, preparing itself for the coming battle. In those weeks a confidence grew among the soldiers as they saw the mass of guns and tanks pouring into Egypt. Winston Churchill had promised ample reinforcements, and among them were the Shermans that had been promised to Auchinleck. Massive reinforcements had been promised and were being delivered, but the Prime Minister expected to see results flowing from his generosity to the desert army. His directive of 8 August to Alexander had been brief but clear, and the pith of it was contained in the words: 'Your prime duty will be to take or to destroy the German-Italian Army commanded by Field Marshal Rommel.' Following upon that order, the Prime Minister had made his usual impetuous, tele-grammed demands for prompt offensive action. But Alexander did not pass on these insistent demands, for he was as aware as Montgomery that Eighth Army needed time. It is a bitter paradox that former commanders of Eighth Army had been removed for their tardiness or lack of action, yet Montgomery who seemed just as dilatory was not sacked. Much of the querulous whining from London could be ignored once the Battle of Alam el Halfa had been successfully fought, but Churchill continued to ask the essential question — 'When will you attack the Germans?'

Churchill's concern was understandable. Operation 'Torch', the Anglo-American invasion of Algeria and Tunisia, was to be launched on 9 November, and it was imperative that the battle for Egypt should have been won by that date. A military success at El Alamein followed by the swift occupation of French North Africa would, the Prime Minister felt, bring to the British people the victory that was due to them. Even more important was the fact that Churchill realized how control of the War was passing out of British hands. The El Alamein offensive would be a British-run battle. Once the landings in French North Africa had taken place, future campaigns in the West would no longer be national affairs but Allied enterprises, and they would all be commanded by Americans. The Prime Minister needed a resounding victory to allow him to continue to influence the strategy of the War. To this end, although they did not know it, the regiments and divisions training in the desert were working. (Down in the Delta, American Army instructors had already been training British armoured and artillery units on the Sherman tanks and the SP guns that would be used in the battle. After El Alamein, stories would spread that some of the American instructors went beyond just training the British tank men and fought in the crews of the Shermans; some of them were said to have been killed in fighting.)

With the new month of October, it was time for Montgomery to assess the situation. He knew that the morale of his army was high and that his soldiers had completed the training of which they had stood in need. Supplies had arrived and were continuing to arrive in impressive amounts. The Royal Navy and the Royal Air Force had regained supremacy on the sea and in the air. He could now undertake the final planning of Operation 'Lightfoot'. He knew that the enemy troops were battle-tested warriors and that the best of them, the German contingents, were well forward, forming a shield. Montgomery's plan was to smash the troops forming that shield and to destroy them where they stood. Their destruction would lay open to him the almost undefended hinterland of Libya. Then only the difficulties of terrain and of distance would separate Eighth Army from its final objective, Tripoli.

The army commander had outlined his plan to the corps and division commanders shortly after the Battle of Alam el Halfa. In that and in subsequent briefings, Montgomery had explained that he would mount simultaneous thrusts in the north and in the south of the line with the point of maximum effort being in the north. The infantry of his northern corps (XXX) would carve passages through the enemy's minefields and defensive lines. Through those gaps the tanks of X Corps would pass, and on ground that it would select the British armoured force, fighting as a mass, would meet the panzers. A clash of armour would decide the outcome of the battle. Montgomery was confident that this would be in favour of Eighth Army. Then his tanks and infantry could turn against the Axis infantry divisions and destroy them at leisure.

During the first week of October — less than three weeks before the offensive was to begin — the army commander changed the concept of his battle. The planned breakthrough by XXX Corps in the north and the subsidiary attack by XIII Corps in the south remained: what did change was the priority that Montgomery gave to the destruction of the enemy infantry. In his words, they would be 'crumbled'. One after the other, the enemy infantry divisions would be attacked and destroyed until, as the Eighth Army commander confidently predicted, the panzer divisions would be forced to come to the rescue of their comrades in arms. En route they would encounter the British armour and would be destroyed in their turn.

That was the outline of Operation 'Lightfoot', and with certain amendments that was the plan that produced the victory. The plan would be in three distinct parts. The first would be the 'break-in'. During that period the infantry divisions supported by attached tank brigades would smash the Panzerarmee's defences and establish the conditions for the 'dog fight'. In that phase, the British armoured divisions would maul the panzers. Finally would come the 'break-out', the pursuit stage of the battle. The whole plan might take twelve days to complete.

OPERATION 'BERTRAM'

As he worked on the plan, there grew in Montgomery's mind the awareness of fresh and urgent problems. For example, to gap the enemy's minefields, did Eighth Army have sufficient trained men? If not, could these be produced quickly and in sufficient numbers to carry out the dangerous tasks of mine detection and lifting? In terrain so featureless as the desert, how could the infantry battalions know for certain whether they had attacked the correct objective and whether they had reached it. The artillery needed great amounts of ammunition: how could the huge dumps of shells be hidden? How could the new batteries that were coming forward to thicken the gun line be concealed? Considering these problems brought him round to the need to deceive the enemy as to the area in which Eighth Army's main attack would be made.

There was little natural cover in the desert and the problem of how to conceal the evidence of an impending offensive was a difficult one to resolve. The skilled interpreters of aerial photographs would soon note even from a single picture the signs of any build-up. A series of photographs taken over a period of time would indicate not only the possible direction of an attack and the strength of the forces to be used, but might even set a date upon which it would be launched.

It was vital for the success of Montgomery's offensive that the officers of Panzerarmee be deceived as to place, strength and time. To ensure that this happened, a simple but wide-ranging cover plan was undertaken. Since it was not possible to conceal the mass of guns, vehicles and stores, then what must be striven for was to hoodwink Panzerarmee leaders into believing that the build-up they could see on the photographs was evidence that the British main blow would be made in the south, when in truth it would come in the north. Deception on such a scale and playing such a vital role in the battle plan could not be left to ad hoc measures. The whole deception operation, codenamed 'Bertram' would have to be carefully planned, expertly orchestrated and faultlessly executed. Lieutenant-Colonel Charles Richardson of Montgomery's staff was given the task, and he drew upon the expert knowledge of camouflage units that had been in the desert since Wavell's day. The task he set them was to ensure that what the enemy saw was what they were supposed to see — shadow and not substance. Thousands of men were set to designing and constructing realistic-looking vehicles and guns out of hollow frames and netting. Such devices were neither new in warfare nor unfamiliar sights in the desert, for both sides had in the past used such disguises. It was the scale upon which Eighth Army operated its plan that was new.

While the dummy vehicles and weapons were being built, officers of Colonel Richardson's staff reconnoitred the sites on which the fakes were to be erected: the positioning and movement of each individual dummy was meticulously planned. Three weeks before the battle opened, hessian frames painted to look like lorries and tanks were erected in those areas where the deception would operate. Luftwaffe air-photographic interpreters poring over shots of the northern sector recorded the concentrations of trucks, and noted that over the course of weeks no significant changes in the composition of the mass had taken place. But the intelligence experts did not see the movements carried out at night: artillery units came forward to prepared sites, where each gun was hidden under a 'lorry'.

Major D. S. Elliott, M.C., then a lieutenant in a medium artillery regiment, recalls his unit's part in the deception plan. 'We spent several nights digging pits, which were then camouflaged. Before we left the pit area, we spent time smoothing out the desert surface so as to remove the tracks that our lorries had made. During the night before Alamein opened, our guns were taken forward to the pre-dug positions and sawn-off telegraph poles were left in the old positions we had left. This was to give the aerial photographers the idea that we were still in the old positions.' Gunner Vincent Knowles recalling those days wrote, 'We were told that we were going under camouflage, so we thought nets; but when we arrived in the area we saw what we thought were a lot of trucks. They turned out to be wooden frames covered with hessian. We lifted the back of the truck, pushed in the limber and then the gun. Then we were called together and told that there was to be absolutely no movement of personnel during daylight.'

Slit trench lines were dug in the British forward defence zones on XXX Corps sector, but these were not manned. The Axis intelligence officers became accustomed to see these empty infantry positions, unaware of their significance. The deserted trenches would be occupied on the day before Operation 'Lightfoot' opened and the infantry kept hidden inside them throughout the hours of daylight.

The great mass of stores that XXX Corps would require was moved by night to broken ground in the El Imayid area and stacked in pre-dug, carefully camouflaged pits. In a matter of weeks, 2,000 tons of petrol as well as food and water supplies had been brought forward and then buried. The huge mounds were covered with scrim netting and all traces of tyres or footprints carefully removed. The deception plan also worked in reverse: in XIII Corps area, the south, 7,000 tons of dummy supplies were piled up and badly camouflaged to deceive the enemy officers into seeing a build-up. Those Axis officers could see from the aerial pictures that a new British water pipeline running from El Alamein station was under construction. Progress on it was monitored over the course of weeks and showed that pumping stations had been set up and reservoir tanks dug. The officers also noticed that the direction in which the line was pointing was south, and they deduced from the pace of construction that the first week of November would be the earliest date upon which the pipeline could become operational and begin to supply the forward troops.

Gradually, the Germans were deceived into seeing an immobile mass of lorries and unmanned infantry positions in the northern sector of the line, while in the south there were what seemed to be quantities of guns, tanks and other vehicles. Photographs of the Munassib Depression showed there to be concentrations of artillery, but the eyes of the Luftwaffe experts were not sharp enough to notice that most of the real guns that had once been in position there had been removed and replaced by dummies made out of poles and sacking. No fewer than three and a half regiments of dummy artillery were fabricated and positioned, group by group and gun by gun. The great concentrations of artillery were not in the south, as the Germans believed, but in the north.

It was, however, in the efforts to hide from the enemy the existence and composition of the British mailed fist — X Corps — that Eighth Army's deception teams achieved their most astonishing success. Montgomery intended that the strength of X Corps should be an unpleasant shock when its full force was unleashed against Panzerarmee. The mass of X Corps vehicles could not be hidden, nor could they be dispersed. At some stage before Operation 'Lightfoot' began they would have to be assembled. Then their presence would betray the direction of the coming British thrust. By early October, more than 2,000 vehicles had been assembled in the corps training area. Hoods painted to resemble heavy trucks were made and placed over a great number of the tanks. The remainder of the armoured force was left in the open for the Axis to photograph and to record.

Then, during 19 October, part of the two divisions of X Corps undertook a daylight move from the training area, and entered the staging areas behind XIII Corps front. They were located so far back as not to be seen as an immediate threat, but yet not so far back as to be supernumaries in the forthcoming battle. From the position of the regiments sitting astride the complex of tracks in the south, the Luftwaffe experts concluded that it would take the British armour two days to reach the front-line in XIII Corps area. The Panzerarmee would thus have two days clear notice of any British intention — sufficient time to prepare a strong defence. But at night tanks were moved out of the staging area and replaced by dummy vehicles. The real ones then went north to be concealed in some of the dummy lorry frames still standing immobile on the northern flank. On 21 and 22 October, according to Major Elliott, his unit transport and everybody else's on the northern sector was sent south to create a dust cloud and give the impression that Eighth Army was preparing to undertake a 'left hook'. 'In the meantime we had seen the incredible sight of more and larger tanks moving up to the FDLs in a skin of plywood making them look like 3-ton lorries.'

In addition to these physical indications, wireless messages were used in the deception plan. The Axis intelligence officers monitored the traffic passing between units. They did not know that these were cadres of the non-operational 8th Armoured Division busily engaged in sending out fake signals. Listening to the weight of traffic, the German officers concluded that there was a large concentration of armour in the southern part of the British line.

There was painstaking attention to detail. All signs of movement by armour were swept away. There were no tyre marks where none should be. Special vehicles were sent out to make false tyre marks and tank tracks in the desert. There was no excessive movement by the infantry. All these precautions went to produce the desired result. The enemy observers saw what it was intended they should see — preparations for a thrust in the south. It cannot, of course, be determined with complete accuracy to what degree the deception plan was successful, but it is clear that two Axis armoured divisions were held in the south as a result of the faked intelligence. It is also clear that General Stumme, temporarily commanding Panzerarmee in Rommel's absence, predicted that the British offensive would come in somewhere around the Deir Munassib sector. The fact that not until 26 October did the Axis commanders determine the direction of the main British thrust points to the conclusion that Operation 'Bertram' was a brilliant success.

BEYOND THE MINEFIELDS

What of the enemy? Facing Eighth Army was a mass of battle-hardened men, most still confident of victory. The German and Italian soldiers assumed that the fighting had been halted until the rumoured new equipment, the expected reinforcements and the fuel that had been promised all arrived. Once those things had come in, they confidently believed, the offensive would roll again. This time they would only halt on the Nile. The new assault would take them out of the arid deserts of Egypt and into its fleshpot cities.

Until those stores and reinforcements had arrived, the Axis units were forced to lie behind extensive, well laid out minefields. They were short of material things; they lacked entertainment and were even short of necessities. The water ration was low and very poor in quality. Every drop had to be brought by road from Mersah Matruh. Rommel considered water less important than fuel, and it is a strange but significant fact that the Germans had neither brought boring equipment to drill for water nor had they laid a pipeline from Matruh to bring it into the forward areas. Lack of water meant less chance of personal hygiene, and dirt equalled lice. There was jaundice, too, and dysentery, the result of the poor food and low standards of hygiene in the Italian army. But, those things apart, the Germans felt confident, fit and ready: the new Panzer IV Special with the long 75mm gun had been received, plus a brigade of paratroops and a new infantry division, the 164th. All in all, they could consider themselves well pleased with life. Nor were the Italians out of spirit: to their establishment there was added not only the Folgore Parachute Division but also a number of line infantry formations to replace the units lost during the fighting of the summer and the early autumn. The Axis was at the peak of its power. In Russia the German Army Group South was heading towards Stalingrad and into the Caucasus. In the Far East their Allies, the Japanese, were going from victory to victory against the Anglo-Saxons. At sea and in the air, Axis forces seemed to be victorious. In the Mediterranean Malta was under pressure, and in Africa the Tommies had their backs to the Nile. As soon as the petrol arrived it would once again be the claim that the song made for them, *Panzer rollen in Afrika vor* ('Tanks are rolling forward in Africa').

The German contingent of the Panzerarmee consisted of two panzer divisions, two light divisions, a parachute brigade, an anti-aircraft division and several miscellaneous independent groups of armour and reconnaissance units. Two armoured divisions, one motorized, five infantry divisions and one of paratroops made up the Italian element.

According to a report issued shortly after the Battle of El Alamein by the 15th Panzer Division, the situation of the Italian XXI Corps, with which it was at that time serving, was as follows: 'The 164th Light Division and the Italian Trento Division were in the front-line with the Italian Littorio Armoured Division and the 15th Panzer Division in the second line.' The strip of coast through which passed the road and railway track was held by elements of a Bersaglieri regiment. South of them ran the front of the German 164th Division and then Trento Division holding Miteiriya Ridge. West of the Rahman track the 15th Panzer was positioned behind the 164th Division and the Littorio was in the rear of the Trento Division. The battle report continues: 'The four divisions covered the whole of the width of the sector. There were no divisional boundaries. . . . German and Italian troops were to be intermingled . . . down to battalion level. The individual formations were split up and then reformed into three individual battle groups. . . . The 164th Division was responsible for the defence of the whole northern sector of the Alamein line. . . . There was no definite task for the 15th Panzer Division. That formation was to be used as the situation developed, either as a fixed defensive force in the rear of the main line or as a mobile reserve for either corps or army. At the beginning of the battle, tank strengths of the two armoured divisions of XXI Corps were 120 German and 90 Italian machines. In addition there were sixteen self-propelled guns of 7.62cm calibre and eight of 15cm. There were also 78 anti-tank guns, 70 of them of 5cm calibre and eight of 8.8cm calibre.

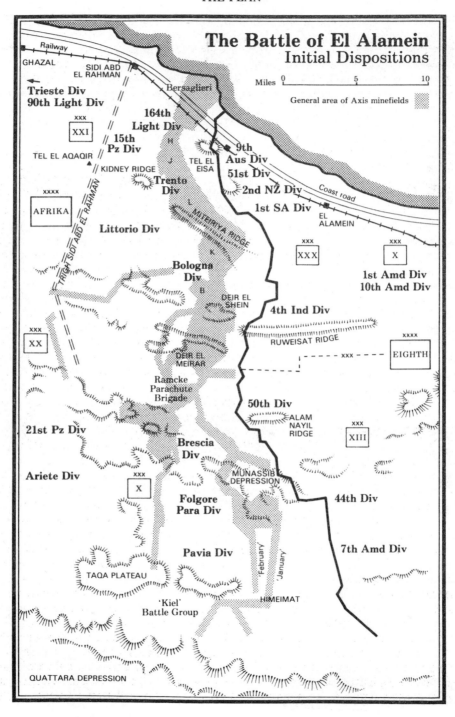

The Battle of El Alamein
Initial Dispositions

GHAZAL

Railway

SIDI ABD
EL RAHMAN

Trieste Div
90th Light Div

Bersaglieri

Miles 0   5   10

General area of Axis minefields

164th
Light Div

xxx
XXI

15th
Pz Div

TEL EL AQAQIR

KIDNEY RIDGE

H

J

TEL EL
EISA

9th
Aus Div

51st Div

Trento
Div

2nd NZ Div

Coast road

1st SA Div

EL
ALAMEIN

xxxx
AFRIKA

Littorio Div

L

MUIERIYA RIDGE

xxx
XXX

xxx
X

1st Amd Div
10th Amd Div

Bologna
Div

K

B

DEIR EL
SHEIN

4th Ind Div

RUWEISAT RIDGE

xxxx
EIGHTH

xxx

xxx
XX

DEIR EL
MEIRAR

Ramcke
Parachute
Brigade

50th Div

ALAM
NAYIL
RIDGE

xxx
XIII

21st Pz Div

Brescia
Div

MUNASSIB
DEPRESSION

Ariete Div

xxx
X

Folgore
Para Div

44th Div

Pavia Div

February

January

7th Amd Div

TAQA PLATEAU

HIMEIMAT

'Kiel'
Battle Group

QUATTARA DEPRESSION

The map opposite shows clearly the length of front held by the infantry divisions of XXI Corps. Located much farther to the west behind the first and second lines of corps were two other divisions: the German 90th Light, which straddled the road and railway lines west of the Rahman track, and to the south of the 90th Light was the Italian Trieste Division. On the right of the Italian XXI Corps was another Italian unit, X Corps. This formation also held a vast length of front. The Ramcke Parachute Brigade on its left wing was intermixed with the regiments of the Bologna and Brescia Divisions. South of that grouping was the Italian Folgore Parachute Division with Pavia Division and, finally, in the deep south of the Axis line, the German Kiel Group of armoured and reconnaissance vehicles. Behind the Axis infantry divisions in the southern half of the front was the Italian XX Corps, whose establishment was the 21st Panzer Division and the Italian Ariete Armoured Division. These were positioned behind the centre of the Panzerarmee front: the 21st Panzer behind the Brescia, and the Ariete behind the Folgore.

The men, tanks and guns that made up Panzerarmee stood deployed to meet an assault that the German and Italian commanders knew must come; from intelligence sources they knew that supplies and reinforcements had been delivered to Eighth Army, and even if they were unaware of the exact details of the new equipment (particularly of the Sherman tanks) they could have been in no doubt that vis à vis the British they were already in an inferior position, and that their position could only deteriorate. Since Alam el Halfa they had been on the defensive, waiting for the fuel, which alone could release them to fight a mobile battle against the British. Without it they were condemned to wait until they were destroyed. This is not to say that Panzerarmee was totally committed to the defensive, however. There were flurries and attacks, local in character; but bitter enough for those who fought them. The supply famine restricted such aggressive operations to minor offensives.

*   *   *

Meanwhile, a few miles to the east, Montgomery was putting the final touches to his plan. His front-line was held by two infantry corps with the armoured corps behind them. The northern corps, XXX Corps, would have as its principal task the creation of gaps in the enemy minefields through which would pass the X Corps armour, while in the south XIII Corps would mount a series of diversionary attacks. These were aimed principally at holding two Axis armoured divisions in the south so as to prevent them moving northwards against XXX Corps. The secondary task of XIII Corps would be to drive its own passages through the minefields so that when Panzerarmee began to retreat the 7th Armoured Division could strike northwards to cut off Rommel's shattered forces. While the Sappers of XXX Corps were making the minefield gaps, the infantry battalions would have gone on to secure a bridgehead beyond the Axis forward defence zone on the western side of Miteiriya Ridge. That perimeter would be consolidated along a map line that was given the name 'Oxalic'. The armour would pass through the infantry and reach its first-bound objective, a line called 'Pierson'. The attaining of that line would mark the end of the 'break-in' stage of Operation 'Lightfoot'.

XXX CORPS

On the right wing of XXX Corps, in the coastal sector, was the veteran 9th Australian Division. Its task was to strike forward from the positions its battalions held at Tel el Eisa, to advance westwards across the 1,000-yard strip of no man's land and to continue that movement across some 6,000 yards of enemy-held territory, to reach 'Oxalic'.

Each of the brigades in the Australian Division had its role to play; all three were committed to action, but only two, the 20th and the 26th, were to advance against the enemy. The task of the 24th Brigade holding the narrow strip of marshy land between the coast and the railway, was to mount 'Chinese' attacks, supported by bombardments from heavy mortars, and through those noisy demonstrations to hold the attention of the Axis troops on that sector. While that diversion was proceeding, other brigades, the 26th on the right and the 20th on the left, would strike westward until the 'Oxalic' line had been reached. Thereupon, the 26th Brigade would turn to face northwards and thus act as a guard to Eighth Army's right. This operation, the covering of the army's open flank, was vital; but the numbers of infantry in the 26th Brigade would be too few to cover the whole length of line when it wheeled to face north. Inevitably, there would be a gap, and this open space would, in the words of Lieutenant-Colonel Weir, commanding 2/24th Battalion, be covered by 'our good friend Lieutenant-Colonel MacArthur-Onslow of Australian 9th Division Cavalry, who will have a composite force under his command and will occupy a series of posts on our flank as we advance, to discourage any untoward adventures of the enemy in this direction'. The posts that the men of the composite force would occupy were to be well constructed and set up for all-round defence with wire and mines. Each of them would be garrisoned by infantry anti-tank gunners and by machine-gunners. On the division's left wing, the task of the 20th Brigade would be to open a gap for the armour to pass through and the brigade would then exploit westwards to Point 33, a slight hill to the north east of Kidney Ridge. This operation would be achieved in two phases. In the first, the 2/15th Battalion on the left and 2/17th on the right would open the assault and carry it forward. At a certain point, 2/13th Battalion would take up the running, pass through the halted battalions with tanks and then go on to attain the final objective.

To the south of the 9th Australian Division lay 51st Highland Division which was, in conjunction with its Australian neighbour, to drive across the desert and to form the northern corridor through the enemy's minefields. To accomplish this, the divisional commander proposed to attack with 153rd Brigade on the right and with 154th on the left. The 152nd Brigade was to be in reserve. That formation's role before the offensive would be limited to the unexciting but vital tasks of clearing minefields and, in the last few hours before the barrage opened, to laying tapes to mark the mine gaps and the unit starting lines. Some of its battalions also had a third task, that of manning the front-line trenches until the men of the spearhead formations took them over just before Operation 'Lightfoot' began. The division's final objective was, like that of the Australians, a line on a marked map, but this was not known by the name 'Oxalic', but was called 'Blue' line. It ran north-eastwards from the northern end of Miteiriya Ridge to the edge of Kidney Ridge, and to reach that line the assaulting brigades would have to advance about 7,000 yards. The capture of the objective could only be accomplished if certain small but very heavily fortified pieces of ground were overrun and held during the attack. There were a great number of those tactically important German defensive positions located between the starting line and the 'Blue' line. They can be seen on the map on page 159 showing the task of the 51st. For many of the Highland Division, this was to be the first experience of war. Most companies in the infantry battalions had been introduced to the rigours of active service life when serving with the Australians and New Zealanders in the weeks of training during August and September. Operation 'Lightfoot' was, however, to be the division's first chance of action since the campaign in France and Flanders, and the Highlanders were determined to avenge the surrender of the original division to Rommel at St. Valery in June 1940.

The New Zealand Division holding the ground on the left of the Highlanders was so seriously short of infantry that its establishment was only two infantry brigades. To increase its firepower and to help it achieve the task which it had been set, the New Zealanders were given the British 9th Armoured Brigade. The armoured fighting vehicles of two regiments, the Royal Warwickshire Yeomanry and the Royal Wiltshire Yeomanry, were each to support a New Zealand brigade, while the 3rd Hussars were held in reserve. The Yeomanry was allotted by troop, each of which was to move behind the spearhead infantry along a cleared track while the remaining squadrons took out any pockets of enemy resistance or dealt with any interference by Axis armoured units.

The advance of the New Zealand Division was to be on a south-westerly line with the intention of gaining the north-western section of Miteiriya Ridge. To accomplish that task, 5th Brigade was on the right and 6th Brigade on the left. A single battalion from each brigade would lead the assault. The 5th Brigade would have 23rd Battalion in

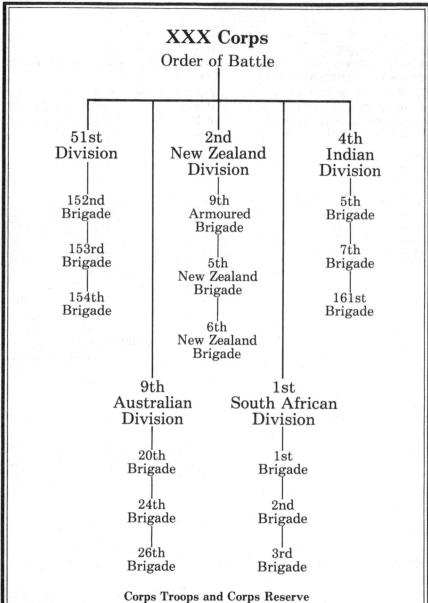

XXX Corps
Order of Battle

51st Division	2nd New Zealand Division	4th Indian Division
152nd Brigade	9th Armoured Brigade	5th Brigade
153rd Brigade	5th New Zealand Brigade	7th Brigade
154th Brigade	6th New Zealand Brigade	161st Brigade

9th Australian Division	1st South African Division
20th Brigade	1st Brigade
24th Brigade	2nd Brigade
26th Brigade	3rd Brigade

Corps Troops and Corps Reserve
23rd Armoured Brigade Group; 4/6th South African Armoured Car
Regiment; 7th, 64th and 69th Field Regiments; 8th, 40th, 46th and
50th Royal Tank Regiment; 121st Field Regiment, Royal Artillery;
168th Light Anti-Aircraft Battery; 295th Army Field Company, Royal
Engineers.

front, with the 21st and 22nd Battalions as a second line. The 24th Battalion would spearhead the advance by the 6th Brigade, and behind it would be the 25th and 26th Battalions. As with the attacks by the other divisions, there would be a halt made during the advance as each of the leading battalions tired. Then the second-line formations would pass through them and take the attack to the line of the final objective. To ensure that no enemy pockets infested the rear of the advance, men of the 28th Maori Battalion were to sweep the ground behind the assault wave. It was the Maoris who, before the barrage opened, danced the 'Haka', that ceremonial 'toning up' dance with its stylized movements and frenzied eye-rolling. The other New Zealand battalions, too, felt the drama of the occasion and rose to its challenge. We shall see from the casualty figures the price that the 2nd New Zealand Division paid for that warrior spirit.

The 1st South African Division, on the New Zealand left flank, was fortunate in that the distance its battalions would have to cover during the advance to the final objective of Miteiriya Ridge was only 5,000 yards. In the South African plan of battle the final objective was codenamed 'Mango', and the intermediate line was known by the name 'Part'. For the assault, the 2nd and 3rd Brigades were 'up' with the remaining brigade carrying out the same type of operation as the 24th Australian Battalion. The battalions of 1st South African Brigade were to make demonstrations and to mount 'Chinese' attacks on the division's left flank. Such activities, it was hoped, would divert the attention of the enemy and draw some of his strength away from the sector on which the assault by the 2nd and 3rd Brigades was being made.

The last division of XXX Corps, the 4th Indian, was positioned around Ruweisat Ridge. The 4th was one of the most experienced formations in Eighth Army, but for Operation 'Lightfoot' its task was to be a purely diversionary one. With the exception of vigorously fighting patrols and demonstrations, its battalions were to take no major part in the opening phases of the offensive.

XIII CORPS

The second major formation of Eighth Army was XIII Corps. This held the ground running south from the far side of Ruweisat Ridge to the Quaret el Humur. Its order of battle was the 50th Tyne Tees Division, 44th Home Counties and 7th Armoured. Two foreign detachments held its outer wings: the Greek Brigade under the 50th Division on the right wing, and the Free French under the command of the 7th Armoured Division on the extreme left wing.

Because XIII Corps was weaker in numbers and its potency was, therefore, less than that of XXX Corps, it had been given a less vital part to play in the battle. Its principal task was to hold the Axis armoured divisions — the 21st Panzer and the Ariete Division — and to prevent their movement northwards to where the main brunt of the British blow was to fall. In order to accomplish this, XIII Corps, but especially the 7th Armoured Division, would act aggressively and try to secure a passage through the minefield, to capture Himeimat and the high ground to the west and to carry out reconnaissance as far west as possible. On the right of the 7th Armoured Division the 44th Home Counties Division was to protect its northern flank, using only one of its infantry brigades, while the 50th Division cleared enemy resistance around Munassib.

There was an important proviso to this battle plan. In 'Memorandum No. 2 by the Army Commander' issued on 6 October, it was stressed that the 7th Armoured Division was to assist in the task of destroying all the enemy in the area between Deir el Anqar, Himeimat and Taqa, but that it had to be 'kept in being on the southern flank so as to ensure balanced dispositions throughout the army area; it must not be destroyed. . . .' This meant that in the event of meeting really determined enemy resistance the armour was not to be too heavily committed, but was to be held back for any task of exploitation that the army commander might decide.

The most northerly of the infantry divisions of XIII Corps was the 50th Tyne Tees, and the role it was to play in Operation 'Lightfoot' was a minor one. It will be recalled that in the Gazala battles of May and June this division's 150th Brigade had been destroyed. This left only the 69th and 151st Brigades on establishment, and to bring the division up to strength for the October offensive the 1st Greek Brigade had been taken under command. That unit held the right of the divisional line. Next to the Greeks and holding the centre position were three battalions of the Durham Light Infantry, constituting the 151st Brigade. On their left was the 69th Brigade, made up of the 5th Battalion of the East Yorkshire Regiment and the 6th and 7th Battalions of The Green Howards. The unusually wide area of front that the 50th Division had to cover extended from just south of Ruweisat Ridge to the area of the Munassib Depression. Between the 151st and 69th Brigades there was a great gap, and that unmanned area was covered by mines and by patrols.

One of the sensitive sectors of the divisional front was the Munassib Depression, which had been strongly fortified by Eighth Army so as to form one of the chief defensive 'boxes' in the southern part of its pre-battle line. It was lost during the Axis summer offensive of 1942, and was converted by the Germans to form an important forward defence position on the right flank of the Panzerarmee. The area was garrisoned by part of the Ramcke Parachute Brigade and elements of the Folgore Parachute Division, and it was against those determined formations in well prepared positions that the battalions of the 50th Division operated during Operation 'Lightfoot'. In view of the well known strength of the Munassib defences and the aggressive nature of its garrison, the role of the 50th Division on the first night of the El Alamein battle was restricted to offensive patrols carried out by the Durham Light Infantry and to threatening demonstrations by the Greeks. The future employment of the Tyne Tees Division was conditional upon the success of an attack that the 44th Home Counties Division was to undertake.

The 44th Home Counties Division, on the left flank of the 50th Division, was the unluckiest formation in the El Alamein line. Its run of misfortune had begun with the Battle of Alam el Halfa, when, fresh out from the United Kingdom, it had been flung into action against the battle-hardened units of Afrika Korps, and had been severely mauled. The official history of the Queen's Own Royal West Kent Regiment, two of whose battalions were on the divisional establishment, states that it had seemed to many who took part in the fighting at Alam el Halfa that 132nd Brigade 'had been thrown away in a suicidal attempt to cut off the retreat of the enemy'. Shortly after the division's bloody initiation the 133rd Infantry Brigade was taken off the division's strength and posted to the 10th Armoured Division, leaving the 44th reduced to only two brigades. Then, before Operation 'Lightfoot' opened, the 2nd Buffs were detached from the 132nd Brigade, bringing down that formation's strength to just two battalions.

In the weeks preceding the Battle of El Alamein, the units of the 44th Division played an important part in Operation 'Bertram', the

XIII Corps
Order of Battle

44th Division	7th Armoured Division	50th Division
131st Brigade	4th Light Armoured Brigade	69th Brigade
132nd Brigade	22nd Armoured Brigade	151st Brigade
133rd Brigade		1st Greek Infantry Brigade

The 131st (Queen's) Brigade and the 133rd (Royal Sussex) Brigade were posted away from 44th Division: 131st went to the 7th Armoured Division and 133rd to the 10th Armoured Division.

deception plan. Day after day battalions that had been carried into the division's rear areas by truck at night, were brought back again in broad daylight, those movements affording proof to German observers that an infantry build-up was taking place in the southern half of the El Alamein line. The task of the 44th Division in Operation 'Lightfoot', as outlined in 'Divisional Operations Order No. 6', dated 21 October 1942, was: 'To support with divisional artillery the passage of 7th Armoured Division through the minefields; to take over with 131st Brigade and attached troops the minefields and the bridgehead running to the west from 7th Armoured Division and to hold this area at all costs.' The distances that the infantry would have to cover to accomplish those orders were vast. From the British forward lines to the final objective was 16,000 yards (nearly nine miles), and the greatest part of that march would be across the minefields, codenamed 'January' and 'February'. These had been laid by the British, but had been captured by the Germans at the same time as the Munassib Depression positions and converted by them to be a barrier against a British advance.

X CORPS

The third great formation of Eighth Army was X Corps, the armoured fist made up of the 1st and 10th Armoured Divisions. The 8th Armoured Division, which should have formed part of the corps, never became fully operational, but its Signals units played a part in the weeks before the offensive opened. These were in the deception plan to fill the air with wireless traffic and thereby to give the sound and impression of an armoured division 'in being'. To aid in this hoodwinking of the enemy, certain officers with distinctive voices were brought back at intervals to the division's supposed concentration area to give orders to non-existent units over the command network.

The task of both armoured divisions of X Corps was to pass through the gaps in the Axis minefields that XXX Corps troops would have made. The 1st Armoured Division was to use the northern corridor and the 10th Armoured Division the southern one. Once through those gaps, the armour was to pass through the infantry, who would be on their objective line, and continue to advance to their own objective line, codenamed 'Pierson'. This would be located about a mile ahead of the XXX Corps infantry.

The mass of tanks, covered by their own anti-tank gun units and defended on either flank by the battalions of their lorried infantry, would then move forward about 7,000 yards to a second line, codenamed 'Skinflint', along which it was intended they should bring the enemy armoured divisions to battle. In this connection it is interesting to note that in the post-battle report produced by the 15th Panzer Division, the significance of 'Skinflint' escaped the Germans:

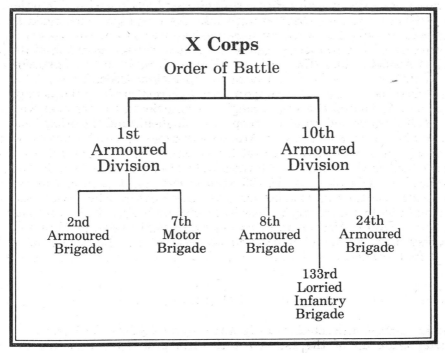

'. . . it is too large to be an assembly area for XXX Corps. It is too far forward to be X Corps assembly area. *Before* the battle and *after* the battle it is unnecessary. . . .'

The 1st Armoured Division had an armoured brigade, the 2nd, the tank units of which were all line cavalry regiments — The Bays, 10th Hussars and 9th Lancers. By a strange paradox, even the motor infantry battalions of the brigade was a former cavalry unit, the Yorkshire Dragoons. The great strength of the 2nd Armoured Brigade lay in its 92 Sherman tanks, but the remaining 69 vehicles on establishment were Crusaders, some of which were still armed with the puny 2pdr gun. The 7th Motor Brigade was made up of London Rifle regiments, the 2nd and 7th Rifle Brigades and the 2nd Battalion of the King's Royal Rifle Corps. This brigade had only recently been transferred from the 7th Armoured Division.

The 10th Armoured Division had two armoured brigades, the 8th and 24th, plus a lorried infantry brigade, the 133rd. This consisted of three battalions of the Royal Sussex Regiment, which had been formerly part of 44th Infantry Division but which had been transferred to the 10th Armoured to form its infantry component. The 8th Armoured Brigade's establishment was a regular battalion of the Royal Tank Regiment, the 3rd, and two yeomanry regiments, the Nottinghamshire and the Staffordshire. The 1st Battalion the East Kent Regiment formed the brigade's motor battalion. The 24th

Armoured Brigade had under command three battalions of The Royal Tank Regiment, the 41st, 45th and 47th, and the 11th Battalion The King's Royal Rifle Corps as motor battalion.

X Corps was thus a balance between the regiments of line cavalry, territorials of the yeomanry and the Royal Tank Regiment. It was an interesting combination of a professional elite and dedicated civilian soldiers.

* * *

By the end of the second week of October, Eighth Army was ready — although for what enterprise it had been prepared was known only to its senior officers. It was clear to all ranks, however, that a new and great offensive was in preparation. The army stood like a huge battering-ram, a mass of men, tanks, guns and trucks extending from east to west across 40 miles of desert between Burg el Arab and the British forward defence line, and from north to south from Tel el Eisa to the Quattara Depression.

One can see on the map on p.128 the power of just one element, XXX Corps. That formation's area extended from the British minefields to its rear headquarters at El Hamman and within it the units were concentrated, tensed like a spring ready to thrust forward. Dotted along the depth of XXX Corps, on an east-west line, were the so-called 'boxes', constructed as defences against the advance by the Axis forces and, in the event of a breakthrough by Panzerarmee after the Gazala battles, would have been the only obstructions to the enemy advance upon Alexandria. Now, in October, the 'boxes' were obsolescent. No longer would they be needed for any sort of defensive role. The initiative now lay with the British, and the 'boxes' had become bases which would nourish the attack. Each of them held concentrations of tanks, vehicles, stores, masses of shells and men — all waiting for Operation 'Lightfoot' to begin.

Most of the rear troops were encamped along the coast. Immediately to the west of Burg el Arab lay the concentration of medical stores. Near Dawar Abdullah were the sectors for the New Zealand divisional transport; then farther westwards were areas set aside for the 9th Australian, 51st Highland and 1st South African divisional transport. Armoured brigades were echeloned behind 4th Indian Division which was holding Ruweisat Ridge. The whole of XXX Corps waited merely upon the order to advance. When it came, each of the transport groups would move out and take its place in the long columns heading westward behind the advancing spearhead units. And, as early as 20 October, the armoured mass of X Corps had begun to 'thicken' its forward areas with real tanks, replacing the dummy machines strewn across the desert, maintaining always the same vehicle density so that the enemy would see neither a reduction in numbers nor a build-up.

Such a mass of transport as would use the trigh required that the track surfaces be strengthened and improved. Between the 19th and

22nd, teams of road building engineers went out and, literally in the last days and nights before the offensive began, built 120 miles of fresh road. From El Imayid railway station, an undistinguished wayside halt, there began the battle tracks, arteries that would exit in the mine-cleared passages of the German forward defence zones. Through Shamman Halt, another railway station, the tracks passed close together, and then on the 890 grid line, each of them became a single, named lane — 'Sun', 'Moon', 'Star', 'Bottle', 'Hat' — along which the advance would flow.

XXX Corps was Eighth Army's strong right arm; the left arm was XIII Corps, and the powerful muscles that would smash the Panzerarmee was the armour of X Corps. Now, as the hour approached, the divisions of Eighth Army stood ready for the orders that would take them from the form-up areas behind the front-line. In XXX Corps alone fifteen battalions of infantry would form the assault wave and marching behind them would be more than twice that number, ready to take up the battle as the elan of the leading formations was lost as a result of heavy losses or simple exhaustion. An infantry battle, even a set-piece one like Operation 'Lightfoot', would not be a coherent affair but rather a complex mass of small clashes conducted by isolated groups of soldiers. The reason for this incoherence is obvious. As we have seen from earlier pages, an infantry division generally would not have put all its brigades into the front-line at the one time, but would hold at least one in reserve. In like fashion, a spearhead brigade would commit only part of its strength to the assault, and a battalion would put in only a number of its companies. The nine battalions of infantry on the standard divisional establishment were thus reduced considerably — with only two brigades 'up' and with only two battalions from each brigade forming the assault group, the number of battalions making the attack on a divisional front would have shrunk to four. In numbers, too, the same reduction in strength would have occurred. Before a battle the cadre of LOBs, the left-out-of-battle group, would have been withdrawn and this removal would have brought the fighting strength of a rifle battalion down to about 300 men.

The serious shortage of infantrymen and the great width of the enemy front that had to be attacked meant that each unit had to fan out in its advance from the starting-line. By the time that a battalion reached the final objective, it was holding a much greater length of front than it covered at the opening of the attack. And it held that extended front with fewer men, for there were inevitably casualties.

An infantry battalion fighting its way forward across enemy territory would have insufficient numbers to take out all the enemy posts scattered across the ground over which it would pass. Those by-passed positions would contain soldiers who, once recovered from the effects of the barrage, would rise up to man their guns and oppose the follow-up companies. The undefeated opponents who would have appeared between the spearhead and the supporting groups would have to be fought down, leading to bitter little actions all over the battlefields: encounters between the men of a single platoon and the crews of a couple of Spandau machine-guns; a grenade battle for a sandbagged position; a short charge with rifle and bayonet to subdue a still defiant enemy. All those fire-fights would be part of the confusing pattern that constituted a modern battle. Most of those struggles would be carried out during thundering bombardments laid down as the attackers struggled to pass through cunningly laid minefields or through a web of defensive positions. And most would be fought out in the dark — in a fog of sand and dust.

9.

THE BARRAGE

It was now 21 October. The battalion commanders had had their briefing from Montgomery and from their own divisional commanders. They had liaised with the units on either flank. The 7th Black Watch, the formation on the left flank of the Highland Division, had arranged with the right-hand battalion of the New Zealand Division that in the event of doubtful encounters in the dark of the desert night battle, the challenge 'Kiwi' would be answered by the identifying response 'Jock'.

The day of the 21st was devoted in most units to a formal parade, in the course of which each commanding officer outlined the battle, quoted from the statistics that Montgomery had produced and then went on to the specific part that would be played by the battalion. Usually a sand model was displayed, showing the ground over which the unit would advance during Operation 'Lightfoot'. Most men recognized the model as being that of the terrain over which they had made mock assaults in September, and the realization came to them of how thorough and detailed had been the preparation for this offensive. Some models were incredibly detailed and showed every known enemy position, the dug-in guns and the minefield defences. There were, inevitably, some enemy positions that were not known or that had been incorrectly identified, and these were to cause severe and unexpected losses in the early hours of the assault.

In the battalions of the Australian and the New Zealand Division there was an exceptionally high feeling of resolve and most commanding officers, responding to the exultant mood, expressed themselves consciously or unconsciously in a pattern of words that are part of the British heritage. Did Lieutenant-Colonel Weir, commanding 2/24th Battalion of the 9th Australian Division, recollect Henry V's speech before Agincourt, fought on 25 October 1415? Certainly the concluding words of his address were very similar to those that Shakespeare put into Henry's mouth. The Australian colonel said, 'If there is a man among you who hasn't the guts to fight shoulder to shoulder with us, and who hopes in some way to dodge his share of the job, let him go and let no one stop him. We will take no one into this fight who is not dedicated to the task.' Shakespeare has Henry say, 'Rather proclaim it . . . through my host that he which hath no stomach to this fight let him depart; his passport shall be made and crowns for convoy put into his purse. We would not die in that man's company that fears his fellowship to die with us.'

Filled with this resolve, and aware of the trials that lay ahead, some mens' thoughts turned for comfort to religion. In many units there were church services for those who wished to attend and, where the unit was too small to hold one, men were encouraged to attend the services in other units. This arrangement was not carried out without some difficulty. R. P. Hill, formerly of the RASC, found that his intention to attend Holy Communion did not meet with complete approval. 'On Part I orders it appeared that any man wishing to take Holy Communion was to report to company office and ask the sergeant for transport at 7.30. Reporting at the office . . . I received a mouthful of abuse and words to the effect that if I thought they were going to put on a truck for one man I had had it. I stood my ground, and in the morning a 15cwt Dodge turned up and took me across the desert to where I saw one person standing. It was the padre. The altar was a blanket over two corned beef cases, with a portable cross. The pair of us waited until 07.55 when another Dodge drove up and a second lieutenant joined us. We took Communion together, just the three of us. As far as I knew that was all who took Communion from the whole of XIII Corps before the battle.' Mr. Hill's feelings were to be further outraged. 'I remember the padres blessing the 25pdrs before the attack started. This sickened me.' Such a benediction must have been rare, probably unique, for no other unit history or personal correspondent mentions it.

For obvious reasons of security, the men holding the front-line positions were not privy to the information about the imminent battle, to intelligence that had become common knowledge to the rest of the army. Security was absolutely tight. Military police patrols kept away the natives from the battle area. The troops were isolated. In accordance with the army commander's instructions, 'on 21 October, a definite stop will be put to all journeys by officers or other ranks to Cairo, Alexandria, or the other Delta towns, for the purpose of shopping or any other reason', no unit trucks drove eastwards. No word of the impending operation must be betrayed to Axis agents. Eighth Army was encapsulated, shut off from the world.

Within this little world there was urgency. Now, made confident and buoyed up by the knowledge of the battle plan the troops prepared. Colonel Weir had told his men of Montgomery's words: 'Battles are won before they are fought, and this battle is already won.' He and his battalion, with memories of so many former promises and forecasts, nevertheless had faith in this new prediction. They anticipated the end of Panzerarmee Afrika.

After dark the moves began, westward to the lines of slit trenches, pre-dug, camouflaged and waiting to be filled with troops of the battalions that were to lead the assault. From Colonel Weir's speech to his men, 'We move from here to occupy a laying-up area in camouflaged diggings. . . . This area is sited sufficiently far forward so that we will be involved in the least possible movement to our start lines for the attack. I warn you all that after occupation of those diggings tomorrow night there will be no movement whatsoever during the following day. The last thing we want to do at this stage is attract the curiosity of the enemy.' Starting on the 21st and continuing through the days and nights after that date, the controlled and continual movement took place, reaching its climax during the night of 22nd/23rd.

During the hours of darkness that night, the spearhead units made ready. Infantry battalions moved forward, some riding in darkness, the trucks so shrouded in the dust and darkness that a watcher at the side of the trigh, although knowing that troops were passing, would have seen nothing through the swirling clouds, and would have had only his ears to help him identify that regiments were going up to the Line. He would have heard first, that watcher at the trigh, the noises of lorry engines; and then, perhaps, singing, which would vanish into the night to be swallowed up by the roar of the trucks and muffled by the dust. Some distance from the front-lines, the troops were debussed and began a foot march to the slit trenches. There were other battalions that marched the whole distance, moving by stages from concentration and assembly areas far back in the rear areas, trudging steadfastly in single file across the cold night desert, until the first companies reached and occupied the pre-dug slits. In those narrow graves the men then crouched, hidden throughout the whole of 23 October, sleeping fitfully, unable to stretch or to move about even for the calls of nature. All activities during that long, long day had to take place within the confines of the sandy walls of a slit trench.

In that final day, the Gunners, concealed under hessian frames that disguised their guns as light lorries, made their last minute preparations. Behind the gun lines, some of which were only 1,500 yards from the front-line zone, there were Sappers with masses of tape (130 miles of it would be unrolled in the battle), posts and lamps (more than 80,000 were used to illuminate the minefieid gaps) and with detectors (there were 500 brought together for the operation). Some of them remember the last minute training and instructions they had been given. Sapper A. Rowlands of 21st Field Squadron recalled how 'three nights before the actual onslaught, some of our Sappers were sent out to lay bully tins as mines. The rest of us were then to go out with Polish mine detectors to find them. I enjoyed it really, although I know it was just practice for the real thing. On the morning of 23 October, a senior officer came to see us. There were about 184 of us — and he asked what we thought about the laying of bully tins a few nights before. We all laughed. Then he dropped a bombshell in our laps. He said, "Well, lads, tonight at 9.45pm you Sappers are going to open the minefields that Jerry has laid, and you won't find any bully tins there. In fact, I know I'm speaking to young men only about 20 or 21 years old, but I have to give it to you straight: right behind you is a whole division relying on you Sappers to open the lanes for the tanks and infantry to pass through. Also behind you are a thousand guns. They will put up a terrific barrage as you Sappers go in. Some of you will be killed, or lose an arm or leg, because Jerry will be trying to stop you. There will be mortaring, Stuka dive bombing and the rest.'' I must have smoked twenty cigarettes in about ten minutes. I was shaking, saying my prayers and wishing it was only a dream.' That night Sapper Rowlands, as part of the task force in 44th Division area, was to find that there were, in truth, no bully tins hidden in the 'January' and 'February' minefields, but deadly devices laid out in patterns across miles of desert.

Dotted about the Forward Defence Zones were more than 2,000 military policemen preparing themselves to direct traffic through the minefield gaps. In that duty they were to win unstinting praise from men who had formerly seen the provost corps as officious killjoys. The sight of the Redcaps calmly directing traffic through the gaps, immaculately dressed and scorning to wear steel helmets, convinced many who fought that day that a policeman's life was not a happy one. Corporal E. Goulden of the provost was to spend 36 hours on 'Hat' track, helping to get the units to their start lines. Farther back still, east of the 'Springbok' track, the mass of armoured fighting vehicles, X Corps, had also begun to move forward. The whole Eighth Army was in motion.

Dawn on Friday 23 October broke cold but bright, forecasting a sunny day. Slowly the sun moved out of the east, passed overhead at midday, and then late in the afternoon began to go down behind the German lines. It sank slowly, and most remember that vivid red ball that seemed somehow reluctant to leave the sky. At twilight a Khamseen blew, not a very strong one, but enough to be annoying . . . and then the wind went, leaving a bright starlit night.

At last it was fully dark. Out of their narrow slit trenches, rapidly cooling in the night air, the infantrymen rose, stretched and grouped round their platoon leaders. As the darkness became full night, ration parties arrived, the sound of their coming as well as that of the approaching armour obscured by the noise of aircraft flying low overhead. 'On the night of the assault, a Wellington squadron equipped with radio jamming equipment was using our airfield,' recalled W. Marsh, formerly of 223 Squadron, RAF. 'The task of that squadron was to fly above the German tanks and to prevent radio communications between them. They were also to fly so low so as to drown out the noise of the tanks moving forward. The squadron air crews got a bit browned off seeing so many targets and spending ops only jamming radios. They asked for volunteers to test the bomb gear and to put bombs on the machines that were still working. This we did, although none of us had ever worked on Wimpeys. We managed to get half to three-quarter capacity loads on them. Tragically, probably due to inexperience of flying with a bomb load, one aircraft crashed on take-off and the bomb load went off.'

144

In most units, the final meal before battle was eaten — nothing more elaborate than Machonachies stew and hot sweet tea. The soldiers then rested on the ground, waiting with the patience of the ordinary swaddy who knows his fate is in the hands of his superior officers. The minutes ticked by. 'Get dressed!' Small packs swung into place between broad infantry shoulders. Long files of men began to approach the start lines, where teams from the battalion Pioneers had located pegs that had been driven, nights earlier, into the hard ground. Between those pegs the Pioneers unrolled wide white tape, which marked the point from which the battalion's attack would begin.

Already, in the broad belts of the British minefields, squads of Sappers were continuing the work of widening the gaps sufficiently to allow the armoured columns of X Corps to pass through at least two vehicles abreast. In the artillery lines, the hoodwinking canvas had been flung down and towed away, exposing the lines of guns ready and facing towards the west. Around the gun pits, small parties of men were searching for the marker poles that indicated the position of stocks of shells hidden in past weeks. These would be dug up, dusted off and set in piles upon laid-out sheets. Other Gunners were hard at work setting fuzes, fitting the aiming lamps, testing communications and, in a dozen or more ways, preparing for the barrage that they would soon fire. The detailed plotting had already been carried out. Sheets of paper filled with calculations had been passed to the gun commanders, giving such arcane information as barometric pressures and wind forces. It was with certain pleasurable expectancy that the officers and men of the Royal Artillery looked forward to the thunder of gunfire that would broadcast the largest barrage fired by the British Army since 1918. In the armoured regiments, released now from the need to be hidden under concealing hoods, the fighting vehicles had begun the slow movement towards the front. In the vehicle parks of the RASC, lorries with fresh supplies of shells and other ammunition were preparing to drive forward into the battle zone. In the darkness of the desert night, from the sea to Quattara and across the whole width of Eighth Army's fighting area, men were at work, committed to one single enterprise: Operation 'Lightfoot'. The Sappers and Gunners, intent upon the successful execution of their tasks, had no time to speculate upon future issues. There was too much to do at the moment to consider long-range prospects. Their concentration was total.

Quietly, and with the dignity of men who know that they are committed to an undertaking in which their very lives are at stake, the infantry battalions began their short moves nearer to the front-line. The rifle companies of 2/24th Australian Battalion moved off at 20.30 hours, and more than an hour later the Highlanders marched silently through the night to take up their positions. The battalions that were to lead each brigade were well forward of the 25pdr gun lines, but the follow-up units for the most part would be held in the artillery belt until the attack was under way. This was not to the liking of the waiting infantrymen. They knew that once the British barrage opened the guns of Panzerarmee would respond with counter-battery fire, and that the fury of this bombardment might well fall in their ranks. They could accept shellfire while making an attack or defending a position, but to suffer a barrage impotently disquieted them. (It is a paradox that, although the soldiers of each branch of service felt that the men of the other arms had an easy life, none would willingly have changed places. No infantryman would have wanted to serve in a tank crew; nor would any Gunner have wished to fight as a rifleman; and the prospect of fighting on foot and unprotected by armour plate was something that tank crews preferred others to do.) The battalions that lay on the dusty trigh waiting to move forward felt insecure in the gun lines, and waited impatiently for the assault to begin so that they would be clear of this dangerous area before the 'incoming shit' started to fall.

In the artillery positions the calculations had been completed, the shells primed and ready, and the Gunners, many of them still in greatcoats against the cold night air, stood or sat in the gun pits by the side of their silent, gleaming masters. Soon the exertion of heaving the shining shells into the hot, dark breech would cause the Gunners to sweat profusely despite the October chill: off would come the overcoats, then the battledress blouses and finally the shirts. It was no easy duty that lay ahead of them. Theirs was the physical task of loading and firing at least 600 rounds for each gun in that single night, together with the mental strain of working out range increases at precise intervals; for the fire plan was elaborate and complicated. An intensive barrage would be fired. Such intense heat would be produced during the five and a half hours of firing that for ten minutes in each hour the guns would have to be rested to cool them. Buckets of water also stood to hand to sponge the breeches, for if these became too hot there was the danger of premature explosion. The task would be a hard one. And this night's barrage would be only the first of a series if Operation 'Lightfoot' really were to last twelve days.

By 21.30 hours the batteries were ready. The desert lay quiet except where in the west there was the far-off drone of aircraft engines and the dull rumble of aerial bombing and anti-aircraft gunfire. The order came for gun detachments to take post. In some regiments, this command was acted upon with the snap and precision of a parade ground in 'Blighty'. In other detachments there was less drill book exactness, but instead the ease of familiarity and an exactness born of years of experience, the smoothness of which was concealed by casual movements. The acolytes knelt round the weapon they would serve during the coming fight. Already the fuzes had been set for detonation on impact. In each pit the same scene was enacted. The breech swung open; the shell was swung in and rammed home; the charge followed; the breech was closed. The layer worked out his calculations, aiming throught the sights at the shrouded lamp hanging on the aiming mark and setting the first range on the plate. The sights came on; the gun was loaded and aimed. Now the crews waited until the tardy second hand on the watches of the battery officers moved towards 21.40 hours. Up and down the length of the battle-line men were peering at their watches. It was so close. Now all the planning, the training, the exercises, and the preparations were over. Nothing could now halt the onset of the operation, for only seconds separated the events that would transmute the ordinary day of 23 October 1942 into a date famous in military history. The waiting Gunners strained to hear the voice that would unleash them into a fury of activity.

Then it came — 'Fire!' And in response to that order issuing from hundreds of throats, hundreds of hands responded and struck the firing handles. The barrage had opened. Some who were there retain the memory of a single gun being fired, and then this premature shot being followed almost immediately by the general bombardment. Whether this is true or not is unimportant, but at the exact time there was a thunder of gunfire as the British Front erupted in a single flame, which then became a flickering fire as the crews loaded, aimed, fired, adjusted, loaded, aimed and fired again, and again . . . . The guns had begun to speak, and the sight and sound of that great barrage has become a memory deeply enshrined in the minds of those who experienced it.

Determined to give the attacking infantry of XXX Corps the maximum artillery support, Montgomery had massed 834 25pdr guns and all of the 48 medium pieces at that time on the establishment of Eighth Army. To achieve the fullest concentration, he had taken from X Corps its artillery regiments and added these to the strength of XXX Corps. The greatest concentration of batteries was behind the 9th Australian Division, which was facing the strongest German defences. Much of the barrage techniques were new to the younger Gunners, but the older men had memories and experiences of barrages fired during the Battles of the Somme and of Passchendaele. They were able to compare those with the bombardments fired during Operation 'Lightfoot', and they were to witness at El Alamein a flexibility in 'orchestrating the symphony' that had been impossible during the First World War. For the course of this new battle, control of the artillery was centralized so that the fire of the greatest number of pieces could be directed swiftly and precisely to defend a threatened sector, to bombard a decisive point, or else to lift the infantry onto their objectives. A whole fire plan could be laid down, altered or cancelled within twelve minutes.

On the 12,000 yards of front held by XXX Corps, the guns fired for twenty minutes at intense rates upon enemy positions that had been located and fixed in the weeks preceding 'Lightfoot'. These were saturated with a hail of shells, and each enemy gun was attacked by concentrations of British pieces on a ratio of at least 10:1 and more usually 20:1. The whole of the counter-battery programme had been organized and planned to a depth formerly unobtained in the Second

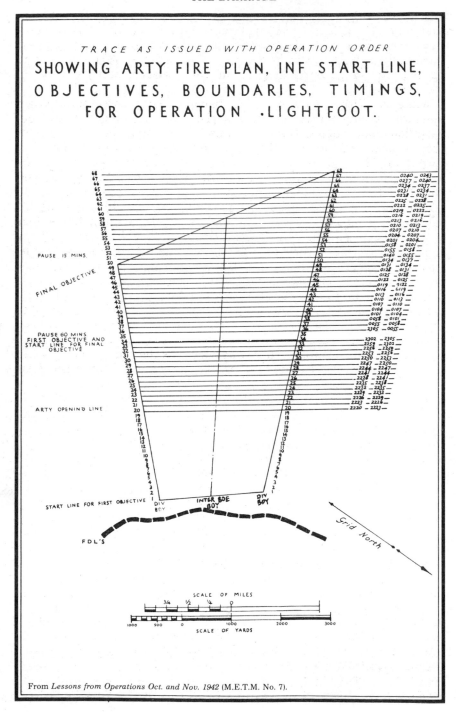

TRACE AS ISSUED WITH OPERATION ORDER

SHOWING ARTY FIRE PLAN, INF START LINE, OBJECTIVES, BOUNDARIES, TIMINGS, FOR OPERATION .LIGHTFOOT.

From *Lessons from Operations Oct. and Nov. 1942* (M.E.T.M. No. 7).

148

World War. In the event, most of the enemy batteries were silenced well before the fifteen minutes of intense fire had ended. There was a five minute pause to bring down the ranges and to rest the guns. Then, punctually at 22.00 hours, the guns of Eighth Army spoke again, and opened up on selected targets in the forward defence zone of Panzerarmee.

While the fifteen minute counter-barrage had been crashing down upon the enemy's artillery, the British infantry of the assaulting battalions had reached the white tape that marked the start lines of their attacks. At the tape, they shook out into attack formation with correct distance between each man, and then the soldiers stood waiting, silently, for the order to advance. Theirs was a daunting task. Ahead of them stretched menacingly the enemy's positions, within which there lay, some nine or ten miles distant, the objective line. To reach that point they would have to cross uncleared minefields, face the bullets of enemy machine-guns and the bombs of his mortars. They would have to pass through curtains of fiery steel erected by the enemy's artillery. Mile after mile they would march in a dust fog, seeking to maintain direction and pace, striving always to keep up with the barrage — for to lose it would be to lose security. They would do this nightmare march burdened down with equipment and ammunition, grenades and weapons. If wounded, they would have to lie alone in the crashing bombardments untended until a stretcher bearer came along.

Suddenly, unexpectedly, there was silence as the counter-battery fire ended. In that relative quiet before the guns opened upon the Axis forward lines, many Australians and New Zealanders record that they heard, shrill upon the night air, the sound of bagpipes: the battalions of the Highland Division were approaching their start lines. And then the sound was lost, submerged in the roar of explosions as flights of shells smothered the enemy's outpost line. For the next three and a half hours the guns would fire at varying rates. To begin with, there would be the firing of a timed programme, and when that plan had been completed the artillery regiments would engage targets selected for them by the Forward Observation Officers who would be marching with each infantry battalion headquarters. There would be no rest for the Gunners — even if their own infantry had no tasks for them to undertake, they would certainly be called upon by division or by corps to participate in concentrated defensive fire tasks.

*　　*　　*

Now, as the salvoes go crashing down upon the hapless enemy infantry, the desert that had seemed to be empty is a mass of movement. The men, guns and vehicles concealed within wadis and broken ground have emerged and have filled the battle area with life. Back, a long way back from the flickering line of gunfire, the tank crews of X Corps and of the other armoured formations are checking their guns and warming up the engines to test their reliability. Ahead of them are the trigh, each lit by lamps suspended from poles and covered with an empty flimsy petrol tin upon whose face has been punched the design that identifies each track. Across the dark desert, the armour, following the scout cars and preceding the soft-skin vehicles, creaks and rattles its way forward. By dawn, the tanks must be in position.

Nearer to the gunfire there are the reserve battalions of infantry, moving forward now in open formation. Each battalion is disposed tactically in a box pattern. The two assault companies advance side by side, and immediately behind them comes the small box of battalion headquarters. Close behind that command group follow the other two rifle companies of the battalion, like the assault companies, marching side by side.

Imagine then, these small boxes of men (a whole battalion with two companies 'up' covers a front of only about 600 yards) marching through the night towards the sound of the guns hidden almost completely in the dust clouds that the explosions have raised. Dimly, through the night and the murk, red patches glow. These are the flaring muzzle flames, dulled almost into invisibility by the dust. We are now in the artillery belt of the 25pdrs. Silhouetted against those glowing patches of gunfire are the slow columns of the second-line infantry battalions at last moving forward. Ahead of them there is the activity of Pioneers or of the minefield task force setting up lamps to illuminate the tracks forward, or laying tapes that will mark a centre-line for those who will soon follow the trails into enemy territory. Farther ahead still, the skilful Sappers concentrating, listening for the betraying hum of a detected mine in the earphones of their detectors, are already at work gapping the enemy's minefields. Sapper Rowlands, formerly of 21st Field Squadron, was one of them. 'At 20.45pm we went towards the barbed wire. I turned round (to see the barrage) and could see the flashes from our guns spewing out death. I wanted to lie down or run off, but before I knew it I was just inside the minefield, knocking the iron stakes into the sand with a heavy hammer, the lamps on the posts showing two greens to denote ground clear for our tanks to pass through. Screams, shouting, blood, being strafed and mortared by Jerry. It was a terrifying experience. Some of us came back to our lines at 4.30 in the morning. It had been a nightmare. My hands didn't stop shaking for nearly eight weeks.'

Hidden by the darkness are the extended lines of infantry from the leading battalions, tramping stolidly and fatalistically across the broken, mine-strewn ground. The pace in the Highland Division has been fixed as 100 yards in two minutes on the approach march to the edge of the first Axis minefield, and 100 yards in three minutes across the gardens of death.

Briefly outlined against the flashes of enemy explosions are the short, squat figures of the infantry; as the lines vanish into the dust of the explosions along the length of the Scottish line, the sound of the pipes can be heard. Of all the battle-line, this is the only part that has gone in with music. On the fronts of the other divisions there is only the sound of battle: the explosion of shells, the rapid bursts of Spandau fire from some sandbagged post and the detonation of exploding mines. Operation 'Lightfoot' has entered the infantry phase.

* * *

Meanwhile, on the other side of no man's land, all unconscious of the plan that had been hammered out to destroy them, of the preparations that had been made in pursuit of that plan and the deceptive ruses that had been played upon them, the Germans and their Italian allies had seen 23 October as just another day in the desert war. The chronicler of Panzerarmee War Diary wrote of the continuing bomber raids against troops in the forward areas and against Luftwaffe aerodromes. The 21st Panzer Division reported less air activity than usual and only light artillery fire. The 164th Afrika Division merely mentioned that there was bombing. The Afrika Korps War Diary, seemingly seeking to record something noteworthy on that day, included the visit to Quattara by the corps commander and a Colonel Liss of the Army High Command's department of Intelligence that dealt with Western foreign armies. The Diary probably stressed the visit of Colonel Liss to show how out of touch with reality was the Army High Command, for the OKH appreciation of the situation, as expressed by the Colonel, was that no major British offensive operations could be expected in the immediate future. This astounding forecast was at variance with Panzerarmee's own assessment. But even its leaders were surprised at how quickly their fears were to be realized.

At regular intervals of time throughout the day, flights of Bostons and Mitchells, of Wellingtons and Beauforts had taken off from airfields west of Cairo and Alexandria and had droned over Egypt to bomb almost at will. An army that forfeited air superiority paid a terrible price in human and material losses. Now it was again the turn of Axis troops to lie impotent while aircraft 'shining white like moths against the deep blue sky', as one German wrote, dropped bomb load after bomb load upon camouflaged artillery concentrations, upon the Luftwaffe's forward airfields and upon the deep defences in the limestone, dug out with drills or blown out by explosive, within whose claustrophobic confines the immobile army lay and suffered the fury of the British bombardment.

The hot day had passed. Slowly the sun had set and there was a period of cool blackness. The moon had risen, and in its bright cold light the whole desert had lain wrapped in an intense and uneasy stillness. The desert at night was always a deeply quiet place, but on that particular night the stillness had seemed to many to be a fearful one. Then along the whole British line the guns opened a furious cannonade. German war diary entries give conflicting times. That recorded by Panzerarmee was 20.40 hours; Afrika Korps gave 21.12

hours as the time of the first report; the 90th Light recorded the time as 20.50 hours; and 21st Panzer as 20.30 hours. The times may vary, but on one point all reports were agreed — that a sudden and furious drum fire of artillery had saturated the Panzerarmee front. Within an hour, a reduction in the intensity of the bombardment was noted in the southern part of the line, but an increase in the scale of the gunfire in the northern sector was reported.

With a better choice of words than his colleagues, but still in the restrained prose of a historian witnessing contemporary events, the chronicler of the 90th Light Division Diary wrote, 'The muzzle flashes from our batteries and from those of the enemy guns, together with the flares that were being dropped by enemy aircraft, illuminated the whole area of the El Alamein position.' The 90th Light was in reserve near El Daba, west of the Rahman track and astride the railway line, but Erich Stock, a grenadier of that formation recalled, 'The noise and the spectacle of the "drum fire" woke us. It was not so much the sound of the explosions, but rather a strange throbbing and trembling in the earth. The sky was alight along the whole length of the Front.' (Leonard Bratten, at that time a Lance Bombardier in a light anti-aircraft artillery regiment, recalled that from his battery's position near Alexandria the barrage could be heard as a continuous rumble of thunder.)

Telephone links from the forward battalions of Panzerarmee to division as well as those between division and corps were torn up. The Panzerarmee War Diary stresses how little information was received, but sufficient had come through for the general staff to make a preliminary assessment of the situation. From the 15th Panzer Division there was news that British infantry and armoured thrusts were being made on a ten-kilometre front, along the railway line and between mine 'boxes' B and K, K and L, and L and J. The 21st Panzer and the Ramcke Parachute Brigade unit in the south of the line reported no major movement except for a British attack in the central sector between mine box S and the Deir el Shein defensive positions. Another appreciation was made at 22.00 hours, and in a discussion with commanders at corps HQ the conclusion was reached that a major two-pronged assault was in progress on the northern sector of the line. The British attacks between the railway and the coast road had been halted, but the German outpost line had been overrun at certain other points. Local penetrations had also been made in two of the mine boxes, J and L, as well as in the area of the front-line positions held by the Italian Folgore and Trento Divisions. The 90th Light War Diary also recorded that aerial reconnaissance had disclosed the presence of British warships some 12 miles north of El Daba: two ships were heading eastwards, and five were sailing in a westerly direction. Italian aircraft were ordered to attack the targets. The 90th Light Division commander put his formation on full alert in anticipation of an assault from the sea.

In the north of the Axis line, Italian infantry, overwhelmed by the violence and the duration of Eighth Army's artillery fire, began to abandon their trenches and to flee into the rear areas. On the 164th Division front, British advances had overrun the panzergrenadier outpost line. There were fires blazing where the bombers of the Royal Air Force had hit a target, and strewn across the desert were those who had been caught out of their prepared positions when the barrage first struck and who now lay dead or wounded from shell or bomb blast.

With the situation so unclear it was still too early to commit the panzer force, but the whole Afrika Korps was put on full alert, and the men of the formation not yet engaged in battle stood facing eastwards, watching the lightning flashes of gunfire wax and wane. Dimly seen against the muzzle flashes, red signal flares rose above the German front-line, passing the message, 'We are under attack', as British infantry and tanks, covered by a barrage of high-explosive shells and aircraft bombs, moved towards their first objectives. Soon it would be 24 October, the feast of St. Raphael, patron saint of pilgrims and of crusaders.

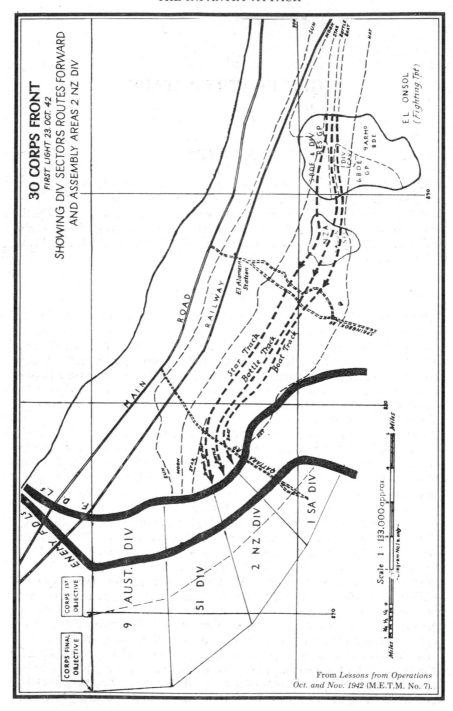

30 CORPS FRONT

FIRST LIGHT 23. OCT. 42

SHOWING DIV SECTORS ROUTES FORWARD
AND ASSEMBLY AREAS 2 NZ DIV

Scale 1 : 133,000 approx

Miles

From *Lessons from Operations
Oct. and Nov. 1942* (M.E.T.M. No. 7).

154

10.

THE INFANTRY ATTACK

XXX CORPS

A Panzerarmee intelligence summary dated 10 October 1942, assessing the fighting capabilites of the British units in the line, concluded that the Australian troops were the finest troops in Eighth Army. It is not surprising, then, that the northern wing of the Axis position facing the 9th Australian Division, which held the right flank of the British line, was strengthened.

THE AUSTRALIANS

The Australian Division would field two of its three brigades; while its third brigade, the 24th, held the coastal strip, the assault would be made with the 26th Brigade on the right and the 20th Brigade on the left. It is the 2/24th whose actions have been spotlighted in the following pages as representative of the 26th Brigade. Its story is one of almost unbelievable bravery: of companies reduced in number to a remnant, still going forward taking out enemy posts and battling on to achieve their given objectives.

During the night of 22 October, the assaulting troops of the 9th Division had marched into a laying-up area south of Tel el Eisa station and occupied the pre-dug slit trenches. Dummy lorries had been removed and real ones brought up. Before first light the area had been clear, and there had been no sign that the ground was in fact occupied by masses of troops. Nightfall on the 23rd brought the battalion to life, with the riflemen and the men of HQ company platoons preparing themselves for the advance to the forming-up line. At 20.30 hours the four rifle companies marched on compass bearings along a track of tape and lights laid out and lit by the regimental Pioneers.

The battle plan was simple: 'B' and 'D' Companies would march behind the barrage and reach the first objective; the remaining two companies, 'A' and 'C', would leapfrog them and advance upon the battalion's final objective. The battalion would then consolidate and begin to prepare for a further attack on the following night.

The barrage opened and most of the men stood silent watching the pinpoint lights of exploding shells fade and vanish completely in the dust and sand that the barrage had raised. Even the bright waves of light from the gun muzzles behind them were soon obscured, and the

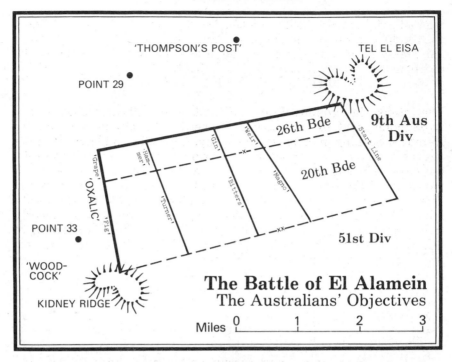

'THOMPSON'S POST'

TEL EL EISA

POINT 29

9th Aus Div

26th Bde

20th Bde

'OXALIC'

POINT 33

51st Div

'WOOD-COCK'

KIDNEY RIDGE

The Battle of El Alamein
The Australians' Objectives

Miles 0 1 2 3

waiting troops were wrapped in their own thoughts. Then, shortly before 22.00 hours, the battalion began to move forward, 'B' Company on the right and 'D' on the left. With correct distances between each man, the two companies extended for only 800 yards across the desert. Punctually, the leading troops crossed the tape and the battalion's attack swung forward across no man's land. It was to be no uncontested advance. The Panzerarmee High Command had strengthened the coastal sector and reinforced the German troops in the front lines. These called down a defensive fire from their field artillery.

The leading Australian Companies marched quickly across the uncharted, unflagged and unswept minefields of no man's land, moving at such speed that at the German wire a halt had to be made — the Eighth Army artillery barrage was still pounding the enemy front-line positions. The 2/24th stood waiting. There was a sudden silence where seconds before there had been all noise. The barrage was lifting. Back in the gun lines, sweating artillerymen were spinning the elevating wheels to lengthen the range. 'On', 'on', 'on', came the reports. 'Fire!' And then flying low above the infantry came that sibilant whispering of shells heading into enemy territory — 'outgoing shit'. The Australian line resumed its advance.

Once across the wire and the battalion was in enemy territory proper. There had been little direct opposition in the crossing of no

156

man's land, but once inside the German wire and the night was alive
with sudden, crashing mortar bomb explosions; lines of tracer coloured
like pretty beads flew out of the fog of the enemy's outpost positions
as Spandaus traversed the battalion's front.

*   *   *

The intense fire coming from the right front indicates that it is a
strongpoint held by a determined enemy. A platoon goes in, its
members working in unspoken harmony. Grenades and bayonets take
out the post, but not without loss. The wounded are made comfortable,
but have to be left — a rifle stuck muzzle down deep into the sand will
indicate to follow-up stretcher bearers where their comrades are lying.
There is no time for delay. The 2/24th Line is advancing through a
second minefield, and above the shell explosions can be heard clearly
the angry buzzing of bullets. Only yards ahead there is a group of
Spandau machine-guns swinging back and forth across the narrow
front of the two Australian companies. There is the flat crack of
grenades as the platoons move in. More fire from the Spandaus;
mortar fire and thunderous detonations as mines explode, set off by
shell fire or by the bodies of men flinging themselves down to lie
beneath the traversing machine-guns.

There's a bastard of an obstruction ahead, a real pig of a post. It's
surrounded by mines and wire. The call goes back for Sappers. Men of
2/7th Field Company come up carrying a bangalore torpedo. Snaking
low, the Sappers push the thin tube through the wire and slide
backwards into cover. A crashing detonation, a bright flame, figures
silhouetted against a glare in the sky, and then prisoners begin to
come out. These are not the first: several have been encountered
already during the advance by the companies across no man's land,
and others have been taken from posts knocked out in the advance.
Walking wounded 'Diggers' escort the dishevelled Italians and
disconsolate Germans. Here is evidence of how closely the enemy's
troop units are intermingled. 'B' and 'D' Companies have nearly
reached the points at which the reserve units will leapfrog them and
take the attack, over the final 1,800 yards of ground. 'A' and 'C' had
crossed the start line only 23 minutes after the leading companies, and
in their follow up had taken prisoners of their own and carried out
section or platoon attacks on positions overlooked in the advance by
the forward troops. 'A' and 'C' pass through, take over the lead and
fight their way forward across a mile of defensive complexes and
mines. The line halts. There is nothing to mark it, but the battalion's
objective has been reached. 'A' Company wheels through a 90° arc to
face north. To close the gap between the left wing of 'A' and the right
wing of 'C', the depleted ranks of 'B' Company move forward, but even
with the gap in the battalion line now closed the position cannot yet be
considered secure. Another gap yawns between 2/24th and its
neighbour 2/48th Battalion. The gap must be closed, and the tired men

of 'C' Company, who have already dug their positions once, have to rise out of their slits, to move a few hundred yards. Then the whole battalion, now facing north, digs in, prepared to defend the open flank of XXX Corps.

'THE JOCKS'

On the left wing of the Australian Division, the battalions of the 51st Highland Division were drawn up waiting for the time at which they would move forward to their start lines. Pipers stood on the flanks of each leading company, while others were with battalion headquarters. The whole Highland Division, the scrim-netting Cross of St. Andrew across each man's pack clearly visible in the strong moonlight, waited in silence for the guns to open the battle.

The order of the attack was the 5th Black Watch on the right flank and then, from right to left, the 5/7th Gordons, 1st Black Watch, 7th Argyll and Sutherland Highlanders, a reconnaissance regiment, and the 50th Royal Tank Regiment, with the 7th Black Watch and two companies of the 5th Camerons on the left divisional flank. Once the opening attack had crossed the enemy front-line zone, there were three further bounds to reach before the final objective of 'Blue' line was cracked. In view of the distances to be covered, the losses that had to be anticipated and the need to keep the impetus of the attack rolling, the lead battalions were to halt on given lines so that the reserve battalions could pass through them. Thus 5th Black Watch, on the right flank, was to halt on 'Red' line to allow 1st Gordons to leapfrog them. On the division's left wing, the two companies of 5th Camerons were also to halt on 'Red' line so that the 7th Black Watch could pass through and carry the attack to the final objective. The 1st Black Watch and 5/7th Gordons, in the centre, would halt on 'Black' line to allow the other battalions to press on and advance to 'Blue' line.

Scattered across the enemy's area from start line to final objective were strongpoints, each given the name of a town in the recruiting area of the battalion that was to capture it. The diagram opposite shows the number, name and location of the enemy positions that lay across the division's front and would have to be taken before the Highland battalions could consolidate on the western side of Miteiriya Ridge. When 'Blue' line had been attained and while the battalions on the objective were consolidating or regrouping, and while behind the divisional front-line undefeated parties of the enemy were being mopped-up, fighting patrols would go out in front of the divisional line to beat down the Axis troops and, by dominating them, to assist the passage of the 1st Armoured Division past the Highlanders.

The pace of the advance was set at 200 yards in two minutes for the march to Panzerarmee's forward belt of mines, but this rate would have to be slowed down to 100 yards in three minutes for the movement across the enemy's mine 'marshes'. (That information is

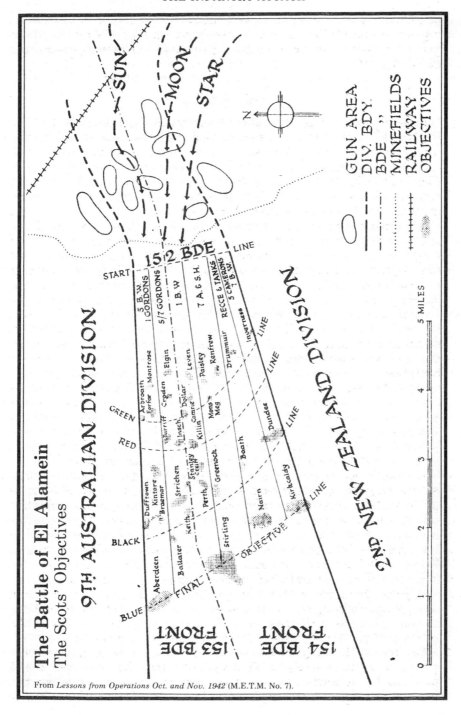

The Battle of El Alamein
The Scots' Objectives

From *Lessons from Operations Oct. and Nov. 1942* (M.E.T.M. No. 7).

159

stressed, for in the accounts that follow we shall see how the buoyant Scottish advance was so rapid that at times the rifle companies arrived at a given line while the barrage was still pounding it, and the infantry had to wait for the guns to lift to the next line.)

At this point it should also be stressed that the divisional commander believed in the positive effect of morale and in the techniques of advertising. He obtained authority from Montgomery for the men of the 51st to put up the divisional sign and to paint that boldly on any available surface. The Highland Division may have been known scurrilously as the 'Highway Decorators', but no one was unaware of its presence in the desert, and nor were its units hard to find. To raise further the already high morale of his men, the commander brought up the regimental pipers so that during Operation 'Lightfoot', but particularly on that historic first night, units on the Highland Division's flanks heard the stirring music, as the pipers, marching in front of the advancing battalion lines, played their comrades into battle. Bob Scott, formerly an anti-tank gunner in the 51st described how the pipes were 'made for the desert. During the lulls in the barrage you could hear them all along the Front. As one stopped another would start up. I remember hearing someone playing *The Road to the Isles*, and thought to myself, this is a far cry from Loch Tummel and Loch Rannoch.' But not everyone who heard them was pleased with the sound of the pipes. Scott talked to one New Zealander, a Private Etetau of the 28th Maori Battalion, who said that the sound of the pipes playing *Hielan' Laddie* produced a barrage of shell fire from German gunners. It was not always battle music that was played, however, and D. F. W. Smith, formerly a sergeant with the 69th Medium Regiment, RA, recalled the emotion of hearing a pipe major of the Highland Division playing a lament for the fallen on the El Alamein battlefield.

Let us then accompany two of the Highland battalions as they step out aross the tapes that mark the start line. We shall be following, particularly, the fortunes of the 5/7th Battalion of the Gordon Highlanders, one of the units on the division's right wing, and of 7th Black Watch, the formation on the extreme left. Across the whole area of the division's advance, similar battles to those which will be detailed were being fought out on that first night — including the inevitable mistakes. At one point the British barrage fell short, and the 1st Gordons marched on through its intense and shattering fire, accepting casualties in order to close with the enemy. The pace of the Scottish advance was too fast for the mineclearing Sappers to keep up, and as the Engineers fell behind the storming infantry so did the Valentine tanks of the 50th RTR, which should have accompanied the Highland battalions. The armour could not keep up; the infantry went on alone.

The battalions in the centre and south of the division's line had more cunningly laid minefields to cross than the units on the right flank. To augment the minefields, the Axis engineers made great use of aerial bombs — the sort dropped by aircraft. By October, there were vast numbers in store, which could not be dropped owing to the shortage of aircraft. So these large pieces of expensive material were fitted with the usual anti-handling devices and left to be activated by a trip-wire. They were a frightening element, for their detonations killed and wounded men over a wide area. Whole sections of infantry were killed when a single aerial bomb exploded, and groups of men fell stricken by flying balls of steel when the invisible S mines flew out of the ground and exploded at waist height. But mines, mortars, machine-guns or artillery fire — nothing could hold back the 51st. As with the Australians on their right and the New Zealanders on their left, there were instances of sections and platoons going in with the bayonet.

The 5/7th Battalion of the Gordon Highlanders together with 1st Battalion of that regiment and the 5th Battalion of the Black Watch formed the 153rd Brigade of the Highland Division, the brigade that would attack on the Division's right wing. Of the three battalions in the brigade, the 5/7th would carry the attack from the start to the 'Black' line. After the usual approach to the forward defence zones, companies occupied front-line slit trenches, each of which held food and water. This was not a bonus supply but the ration intended to be consumed during 23 October, the day on which no movement was allowed in the front-line. Each man's water bottle would have to be full when the time came for the infantry to advance and for the first crucial 24 hours of Operation 'Lightfoot'. It was not expected that the water trucks would be able to reach the battalion during the first day of battle.

Within an hour of sunset, the companies of the 5/7th had been formed up, and at 19.15 hours the leading sections began the short march along 'Sun' track, cleared and taped by units of the reserve brigade. By 20.25 hours, in the light of the moon, the battalion was in attack formation with 'A' Company on the right, 'B' Company on the left, battalion headquarters behind them and the other two rifle companies side by side and immediately behind the headquarters group. Behind the opening barrage the Gordons moved forward to the attack, and of all the unit records only the 5/7th mentions that a section carried night marching lamps to guide the companies. The impetuous pace of the advance soon brought the battalion to the first objective, but they were ahead of schedule, for artillery shells were still falling in the enemy's front-line. The leading Gordon companies lay down in the desert waiting the long minutes before the barrage lifted onto the next step. Then up again the Gordons rose and moved across the second enemy minefield to rush and capture two enemy strong-points, codenamed 'Elgin' and 'Croden'.

The pace of the advance was still fast, and so close were the leading companies 'leaning on the barrage' that the dazed enemy had no time to man their guns before the Highlanders were among them. 'A' Company was particularly successful in taking out a number of

Spandau posts. Within 90 minutes of crossing the start line the leading companies were on the 'Green' line and again they had to wait until the barrage lifted. But by this time the enemy artillery had steadied, and his guns began to pour down a hail of fire along the battalion front. Casualties, until now relatively light, began to mount, and not only among the Gordons but also among the Sappers wire-cutting and wire-laying in this, the main section of the German defence complexes. There was now a planned halt to the forward movement.

At midnight the advance was once again resumed, and now the battalion came up against strongly-held positions, surrounded by wire and mines and each post forming part of an interlocking defence system. It was in this web that the Germans expected to hold the British attack. Fire was coming at the battalion from all sides — direct fire from the front, enfilade fire from the flanks and even from the rear where German posts, still holding out, were firing into the High-landers' backs. Shadowy forms were seen on 'A' Company's flank and, by one of those tragic accidents which inevitably arise in the dark and confusion of a night attack, parties of men from the 5th Black Watch were thought to be the enemy and were fired on. The incident was soon over, and in the final storming advance by 'A' and 'B' Companies two enemy strongpoints, 'Insch' and 'Turriff', were rushed and captured. The two companies had reached 'Red' line, and their storming advance had smashed through nearly three miles of German defences.

It had been planned that 'C' and 'D' Companies would take over the lead once the 'Red' line had been reached. The forward units waited for the follow-up units to leapfrog them, and meanwhile were subjected to a heavy and accurate mortar fire. By 01.00 hours on the 24th, 'C' and 'D' had passed through their depleted sister companies and had advanced through crashing barrages of enemy defensive fire for nearly a thousand yards. Then the attack faltered in the concentrated fire of German machine-guns and mortar fire on the forward edge of strongpoint 'Strichen', which lay completely across the battalion's front, obstructing the forward movement. 'C' Company was ordered to carry out a frontal attack, covered by the fire and movement of 'D' Company on the left flank. The men of the two companies rose, regrouped and moved off. The thin line of 'D' Company passed into the thundering detonations of the German barrage, into the smoke, the sound and the dust. They were never seen alive again. Caught in a minefield, brought under fire by heavy machine-guns firing on fixed lines and bombarded by mortar bombs, they fell. 'C' Company could make no further advance without close support weapons, and these were back in the rear. Mortars and machine-guns were ordered forward. Until they appeared in the front lines, the survivors of 'C' Company held on in hastily-dug positions behind a screen of anti-tank mines.

* * *

The 7th Battalion of the Black Watch was one of the units that did not open the infantry attack of 51st Highland, but took over at the 'Red' line. Together with the 1st Black Watch and 7th Argyll and Sutherland Highlanders, it formed the 154th Brigade which was placed on the left of the Highland Division's line. The 7th moved from its concentration area at 21.30 hours and towards the start line through the 25pdr positions. In the artillery belt the battalion halted, and experienced the usual infantryman's dislike of being in the gun lines. That naked feeling was felt more strongly when the barrage opened all round them. 'The noise was deafening and the flashes in that black night were blinding. We were all pleased when we had gone through, but then we felt the blast as our section passed near the gun muzzles.' At 23.10 hours, 70 minutes after the spearhead battalions had crossed the start line, 7th Battalion's 'C' Company on the right and 'B' Company on the left stepped over the pegged-down tape and committed themselves to battle.

Somewhere ahead lay the first battalions of the division, whose leading companies were now on 'Red' line. It was clear that the first phase of the attack was going well, for in their advance the leading companies of the 7th met little opposition. But if there was little opposition on the ground, the German artillery fire was unusually heavy and seemed to be directed upon the sectors through which the 7th was advancing. Particularly severe were the losses among the pacers, those men up with the leading sections having no fighting role in the battle but playing an important part in maintaining direction and keeping tally of the distances marched. Six pacers were killed or wounded in the first few hours.

The companies of the 7th walked forward through a curtain of enemy fire across a second and uncharted minefield. Now there were casualties, caused not only by shell fire, but also by the carpets of S mines that had been laid and by the aerial bombs — huge monsters filled with 200 pounds of explosive. The staggering casualties caused a change to be made in the battalion's attack plan. It had been the intention that 'C' and 'B' Companies should lead the battalion's advance up to the 'Black' line and that 'A' and 'D' would then lead the assault up Miteiriya Ridge, over its crest and on to 'Blue' line, which lay on its far side.

Even before 'Black' line had been attained, the scale of losses had required that the battalion regroup its depleted forces. The remnants of the three companies 'A', 'B' and 'C' were amalgamated into a single detachment, and these together with 'D' Company marched on to the objective, 'Blue' line, a strongpoint codenamed 'Kirkcaldy'. It was a battalion shockingly depleted in number that at last reached the 'Black' line. As the sections and platoons moved up the arid slopes of the ridge, preparing to drive on to the last position, the final objective, Point 33, they were met with concentrated fire from the German defenders holding carefully sited and excellently built positions.

There was no pattern in the bitter struggles that raged that night on Miteiriya Ridge. Out of the darkness, brilliant flashes of tracer would suddenly appear. They were coloured red or green and seemed to approach slowly, almost languidly. Then they increased speed, appeared to accelerate, and the shining sparks whistled and cracked above the Highlanders pressed to the ground. As the men of the 7th Battalion lay pinned beneath the scything sweeps of one pair of Spandaus, there were crashing detonations as the German grenadiers sought with stick grenades and light mortars to drive the Scotsmen back. Men desperate to reach the battalion's objective slithered forward to the barbed wire that surrounded the enemy's positions, cut the strands and pulled them aside. A flurry of bombs burst among the defenders, amidst the screams of men mortally wounded and dying in agony. Behind the thunder of Mills bomb explosions, the leaping and vengeful figures of the Black Watch came out of the dark, determined to avenge St. Valery in 1940 and their more recently fallen comrades.

Who were the heroes of that night? Who knows. . . . The actions of the men of this battalion were no different to the deeds that were being enacted along the whole British front, in every battalion in both XXX and XIII Corps. The sudden swing of an arm and a well aimed grenade silences a machine-gun that has held up a company's advance. A burst of Bren gun fire cuts down a group of the enemy gathering for a bitter little counterattack. Who threw the grenade? Who fired the burst? Who knows. . . . It is all part of the soldiers' trade to battle in darkness and not to know that any action may have saved a battalion or speeded the advance of a brigade.

Foot by foot, the men of the 7th fought their way up the crumbling sandy slopes of Miteiriya Ridge and passed over the crest, battling against defenders on the reverse slope who had been relatively unaffected by the British barrage. On that western side of the ridge, fighting reached new heights of fury. The German positions had inter-locking fire zones. Each post defended the other and was sited to give maximum protection. But, slowly and skilfully the Highland companies — reduced by losses now to less than platoon strength — took the German positions. On the left of the battalion line, one of 'D' Company's sections saw shadows and movement. 'Kiwi' they called at the dark shapes. 'Jock!' came back the reassuring response. The left flank of the 51st Highland Division and the right wing of the 2nd New Zealand had made contact. The line was firm on that sector.

It was time for the depleted battalion to regroup and to gain its second wind, preparing to consolidate the gains it had made and to defend these against Axis counterattacks. But the situation was serious: 'D' Company had lost more than 50 percent of its strength; all its officers were casualties, although the four wounded subalterns rejected the idea of evacuation and stayed with their men. Behind the battalion's front, the stretcher bearers were busy collecting the wounded or marking the places where the Highlanders had fallen in action. The words of a 51st Divisional song come to mind: 'They buried him out in the desert, and his body lay deep in the sand. On his head was that famous balmoral, with the red hackle clutched in his hand.' There were lots of red hackles lying on the 7th Battalion's front.

Behind the line, the adjutant and the regimental sergeant major had been busy. Across two uncharted minefields came Bren gun carriers with food and ammunition. The journey forward to the groups of men holding the line (for they could no longer be called companies) had been arduous. Shell fire had destroyed much of the system of track marking that had been erected so painfully, and the drivers of the battalion transport had had to be led on foot for much of the trip. The men of the Pioneer platoon who had come up with the carriers moved out beyond the battalion's forward line and began to lay chains of mines. The 7th was consolidating and had to be protected against probable enemy counterattack. Fighting patrols went out to sweep the captured area and to destroy the last remnants of opposition. Dawn was not far away, and in the dark of the October night the men of the 7th Battalion, The Black Watch, stood to and awaited the almost inevitable enemy counter-blows.

THE NEW ZEALANDERS

The war establishment of the 5th New Zealand Brigade (whose attack we are now to follow) consisted of the 21st, 22nd and 23rd Battalions, with tanks of the Royal Wiltshire Yeomanry in support. Troops from 'B' Squadron of that regiment were to move behind the leading companies along tracks cleared for them by Scorpions, while the other squadrons of the Wiltshires were held ready to take out enemy strongpoints.

In common with the attacks being made by other divisions, the New Zealand battalions that started the assault would halt at a given time and place in the advance to let the second wave battalions pass through. In the 5th Brigade it was 23rd Battalion that was to open the attack, and it was the task of that unit to seize the first objective, strongpoints laid out more than a mile behind the Axis easternmost minefield. With the attaining of the intermediate line, the first objective of the attack would have been completed and the barrage would continue to fall while the assault companies reorganized and awaited the arrival of the other two battalions, which would take the assault forward. Between the ending of phase one — the capture of those defences — and the opening of the second phase, there was to be a pause, at the end of which the 21st and 22nd Battalions would move forward on to Miteiriya Ridge, the final objective.

The opening assault by the 23rd Battalion made progress despite fierce fighting, and was completed on schedule. The one slight impediment to the perfect unfolding of the battle plan was that, because visibility had been reduced to 30 yards maximum, the success

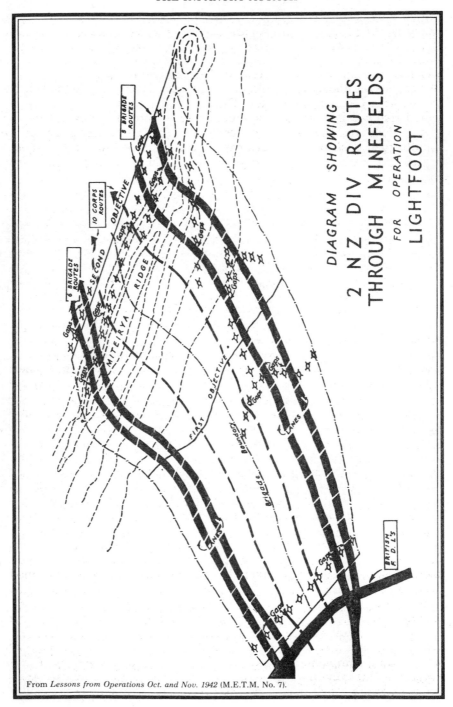

From *Lessons from Operations Oct. and Nov. 1942* (M.E.T.M. No. 7).

signal announcing 23rd Battalion's arrival on the intermediate line could not be seen, and the divisional commander was unaware of the progress of his troops. Nevertheless, the support battalions had begun their advance from the British artillery belt and, moving some distance behind the 23rd Battalion, had crossed the gap between the Allied and the enemy minefields and had passed through the 'marshes' of the first German minefields. During their advance they had seen how fierce had been the battle fought by the 23rd. The angular dead, lying alone on the desert or crumpled around a Spandau in a sandbagged position. The patterns of rifles muzzle-down in the sand, which had marked the position of wounded comrades, now mercifully removed by stretcher bearers to regimental aid posts.

At times, the controlled pace of the advance had been slow enough for the men to see, shining clearly in the bright moonlight, the sinister round shapes of Teller mines, and even the trip wires leading to booby-traps were visible. Then a bank of smoke, dust and sand would blow across the advancing line, concealing so much that each man felt that he alone was carrying out the advance. In that darkness and deadly murk there could be no sight of mines, and the riflemen plodded on in their foot-tingling forty minute advance towards the take-over line. Dimly seen ahead, glowing weirdly through the darkness, the follow-up battalions could see a line of blue lights, hurricane lamps suspended from picket posts. The Pioneer platoon of the 23rd Battalion had done its job well. The lamps marked the forming-up area for both battalions, the point from which they would make ready to continue their advance. Ahead of the line of blue lamps, the depleted companies of the 23rd Battalion lay in the sand, as just ahead of them the barrage continued to pound the Axis positions. Smoke from the explosions and the desert's abrasive dust choked them as they lay waiting upon the arrival of the two sister battalions. The concussion of the explosions drove the very air from their lungs, and the New Zealanders were wheezing and spluttering in the foul murk. To add to the horror of that night, it was realized that some of the 104 guns that were firing in support of the 5th Brigade's attack were firing short and inflicting casualties on the waiting companies. Messages passed and then the whole barrage lifted. The second stage of the division's attack opened.

Precisely at 00.55 hours, the extended lines of the 21st Battalion on the right and 22nd on the left crossed their start line and, marching along compass bearings taken by their 'pacer' officers, marched towards the objective nearly 3,000 yards away, an objective that was protected by a complicated web of defences. Emphasis had been laid during training on keeping close behind the creeping barrage, and the 5th Brigade began to 'lean on the barrage' so closely that the forward companies were soon advancing through Eighth Army bombardment. The leading companies moved swiftly up the crumbly slopes of the ridge, but this impetuous pace needed to be braked, for casualties were being caused by their own shells. The troops were moving too quickly, but this had an advantage remembered by one veteran: it was not possible to distinguish whether the shell bursts were 'ours' or 'theirs'. The speed of the assault was slowed down and the extended lines, moving at 100 steps in three minutes, met and overran in smoothly executed attacks the defended positions of the enemy. It will be recalled that the attacking front of each formation would widen during the advance, and in some cases the length of each unit's line would double. The gun density was not sufficient to take out by bombardment all the enemy positions, and it was realized that some Axis defences would inevitably remain untouched and therefore manned by unshaken and resolute panzergrenadiers.

Thus it turned out, and the two-battalion advance was struck by machine-gun fire from front, flank and rear. Streams of tracer cut through the dark dust clouds, approaching slowly but then whistling overhead to disappear at the same languid pace as they had approached. The attacks from front and flank were dealt with by the battle drills that had been taught, and from out of the stormed defences dishevelled and wounded prisoners began to emerge. The posts still holding out behind the advancing companies did not hold out for long. The silent Maori warriors of the 28th Battalion were quickly in among the desperate enemy, and much of the killing was with the bayonet.

At 01.40 hours on the morning of 24 October, the creeping barrage halted again while the battalions reorganized and took stock of the situation. Artillery fire continued to fall on the enemy positions meanwhile, and thus laid a curtain of fire between the tired New Zealand infantry and the possibility of an enemy counterattack to drive them from the ground that they had so hardly won. The centre of the 22nd Battalion had suffered severely: 'C' Company, which held the centre position between 'B' Company on the right and 'D' Company on the left, had met such opposition that its strength was only 30 men, so 'A' Company was brought forward from reserve to take over. At five minutes before 02.00 hours, the creeping barrage moved forward again, and as it did so the infantry instinctively took great gulps of air into their lungs. Just ahead was the crest of Miteiriya Ridge and behind it lay the battle-hardened German infantry, untouched by the barrage and ready to sweep the comb of the ridge with machine-gun and mortar fire. As the men crossed the high ground they were struck by a hail of fire, a bombardment from the enemy artillery of an intensity that would have deterred most other soldiers. But it had the opposite effect on the New Zealanders. They began to move downhill at a faster pace so as to close with the defenders. In their speed, the men of the 5th Brigade again entered into their own barrage, but they did not halt — they were prepared to accept casualties from their own guns in their determination to overrun the enemy.

Not everywhere were they successful. Once again scattered across the ridge were enemy posts untouched by the barrage and posts out of which strong-nerved defenders, with the bombardment still crashing about them, fired their Spandaus. Working their way on their stomachs under the sweeping layers of machine-gun bullets, the leading files came to within grenade range, and then as the bombs exploded the New Zealand infantry went in with bayonet and Tommy gun to face the grenades and machine-pistols of the German soldiers, fighting now not merely to hold the position but for their very lives.

'It was some scrap this time, believe me', wrote E. M. Scott in a letter home. 'So far as I can see, the Masterton boys [the men of 22nd Battalion, who were recruited from that part of New Zealand] came through fairly well. . . . The first few days were the worst; the night attack was really grim. Went in that night with 25 in that platoon and reached the objective with twelve. It is remarkable the stuff we went through that night without sustaining a great number of major casualties. Some, of course, were unlucky and some grand soldiers and great mates are no more. . . . The rotten part about an attack is that it must go on, and if your best mate goes down beside you you can't stop. It seems hard and callous, but it's unavoidable. The stretcher bearers and the lightly wounded following up attend to them. The infantry certainly carried the fight to Jerry in the initial stages, and it was a stiff tussle for a while. Without the support of the artillery it would have been a much harder job to get him moving. . . . The barrage that they put over on the night of the attack (23 October) was terrific; it is impossible to describe what it was like. No one who was within miles of the front will ever forget those guns. We were lying at the start line awaiting zero hour when, with one mighty roar, hundreds of guns . . . went into action almost as one. The whole half-circle of horizon behind us was lit up by the flashes, the ground shook, and to make a man hear you it was necessary to shout into his ear. This went on without a break for four hours.

'In the first fifteen minutes they plastered Jerry's gun positions behind his front-line and they dropped on to his trenches starting at his FDLs and working back. At zero hour we began our advance, keeping 200 yards behind the barrage, and as we moved forward we saw the effect of concentrated artillery fire. The desert was pockmarked every few feet with shell holes; his wire was blown to bits. He must have found it fairly unhealthy in those trenches. That the Hun was taken completely by surprise was obvious from the fact that his front-line defences were clear of the enemy when we reached them − that is, live ones. . . . Also some of the prisoners were in stockinged feet. There weren't many prisoners taken that night. I often try to imagine their feeling and thoughts that night when they were so rudely awakened. Picture to yourself a dirty big Hun peacefully snoozing . . . then all at once he is awake and the very desert is trembling from the thunder of guns and the air is filled with screaming messengers of death. . . . What must have been their thoughts when the front sprang to life in a half-circle of blazing, roaring destruction?

In the middle of the bombardment and counter-bombardment, in dust storms thrown up by shell and mortar-bomb explosions, the Dominion soldiers and their enemies were locked in battle. In the fog and confusion, touch was lost between companies, so that each fought its way forward in isolation, smashing down the enemy wire, taking the sandbagged posts or stone sangers one after the other. In the 21st Battalion, 'A' Company on the right met fierce opposition and its advance encountered not only the strong machine-gun fire of the defenders but deep belts of anti-personnel mines and concentrations of mortar bombs brought down upon pre-determined areas. Then, with relief, the platoons, seriously reduced now in strength, felt level ground under their feet. Ahead, the terrain was flat. Only 600 yards separated them from the line of the final objective.

By 02.35 hours, the companies of 22nd Battalion were on the objective; in the 21st Battalion, 'C' Company on the left of the battalion line was first to report itself in position. The success signal was fired at 03.00 hours and company runners were sent back in case the Verey lights had not been seen at brigade headquarters. The information that the 22nd Battalion had reached its objective could not be signalled until 03.15 — the Verey lights had been destroyed in the hard-fought advance — but at last the golden light soared into the dark, and beneath its glare the men of the 5th Brigade began to dig in. There was an urgency in their work. The brigade had taken the ridge and had advanced to level ground about 1,000 yards west of the ridge, but the whole area was swept by the most savage bombardment, so fierce in fact that the 22nd Battalion headquarters had to retire behind the crest to positions which the heavy weapons units had also taken up. 'D' Company of the 21st had no chance to consolidate, for its task, once the battalion had reached its objective, was to sweep the front of the area with fighting patrols. Each of these was equipped with detonating charges to destroy those enemy weapons that might be captured during the patrols but could not be brought back into British lines. The patrols were outstandingly successful, and in addition to four heavy guns that were rushed, seized and destroyed, the fighting men of 'D' Company also blew up anti-tank guns, machine-gun posts and took 90 prisoners.

Shortly before the flares announced that the 5th Brigade was on its objective, armoured fighting vehicles of the Royal Wiltshire Yeomanry had begun to pass through the gaps in the first enemy minefield. Now the regiment was waiting with anticipation, resignation or impatience for the second belt to be gapped so that the tanks could get forward to link up with the infantry with whom they had practised just such a liaising manoeuvre in the months of training. By this time too, some support weapons had got through, chiefly 2pdr anti-tank guns. These had been man-towed across the 7,000 yards of battle area, through soft sand into which the pieces sank up to their axles, or else across stony desert littered with large and unyielding rocks. The guns were brought into position behind Miteiriya Ridge to form the firm backbone of the British defence. The night was well advanced. When day dawned, the hurricane of fire would not be indiscriminate: it would be directed by observation officers and aimed and fired with precision by veteran Gunners to whom every shot was important. And with daylight would come the inevitable counter-attack. In the broken ground before the New Zealanders, the enemy's panzer force would assemble and attack to drive back the defenceless infantry across the ridge they had so recently captured. With daylight would come danger, and the New Zealand infantry dug with a will, hoping that before first light they would have their slits dug to a safe depth. The 21st and 22nd Battalions were strung out along a plateau in front of Miteiriya Ridge, both units on the objective. The north-western section of the ridge was firmly held, but the 6th Brigade on the left was still some hundreds of yards short of its final line. The failure of the 6th Brigade, of the South African Division and of 51st Highland Division to gain the final line meant that the 5th Brigade was holding a salient − and one that could be expected to find itself under the most severe pressure as soon as the enemy commanders realized it.

It was now the darkest part of the night, two hours to dawn. On the plain the battalions of the 5th Brigade were completing their trenches. A short way behind the ridge, where the battalion headquarters and heavy weapons were positioned, the New Zealand divisional commander, desperate for news and anxious about his men, had come forward. Back over the ground across which the brigade had advanced, there were all the signs of a hold-up in the advance. Scorpions were flailing in the dark, the dust from the beaten ground rising in suffocating clouds around them. At the edge of one gap in the minefield a small group of disabled tanks, victims of an attempt to bypass a stranded vehicle, stood shattered by Teller mines. Some of them were burning. Bren gun carriers trying to tow 6pdr anti-tank guns through the murk ground slowly through the night, often knocking down the picket posts and lamps that lit the safe route forward. Groups of infantry machine-gunners plodded along carrying the heavy barrels, tripods and ammunition for the Vickers with which they would support the front-line companies. Shell bursts, fires from stricken vehicles and dumps behind the advance . . . and the ever-present unspoken fear of walking or driving across a mine.

Meanwhile, the medics had their hands full. A stretcher bearer in the 22nd Battalion recalls the horror of what he saw: 'It is after midnight before we get our first casualties, the walking wounded who are sent on their way back. We feel sick. The remnants of two platoons lie dead or wounded. In the distance one can see a machine-gun post. It's bloody murder. I start sorting the wounded from the dead. After we stop the bleeding, we move the wounded in close to the sandbags that made up the machine-gun post. I make sure the wounded have a water bottle. I suggest to the other two stretcher bearers that we climb into the machine-gun pit and have a smoke. The only place to sit with one's head below the level of the parapet is a dead German lying on his back. I sit on his chest and light a cigarette. We all get a hell of a fright. The dead body speaks! We jump to our feet and the German slowly gets up. Apparently the force of the shells hitting him had thrown him against the side of the dug out making him temporarily unconscious. The German starts to protest. . . . We all say together, "You bastard!" and point out to where our dead are lying. Then, suddenly, we realize how ridiculous it is having an argument with an enemy soldier in the middle of Alamein.

'We climb out of the machine-gun pit and set off for the front-line. By the dead and wounded lying on the sand we knew we were going the right way. . . . It is eighteen hours before we get back to that machine-gun post. The wounded are still there. . . . I can still see the look in their eyes. They thought we had deserted them. . . . impossible to carry so many wounded so far (to the RAP). Minefields everywhere. One of our tanks drives onto a mine. A body appears in the flames . . . I can still hear the scream as he falls back into the tank.

'The Germans start to shell our forward positions. Four lads from 'D' Company bring in a wounded mate. A shell bursts among them. We go across to give first aid. One of the casualties has both legs and an arm blown off. The right arm is thrown out at an angle and is held onto the body by a piece of skin. While I stand there he regains consciousness and starts pleading, "Kill me, God, please kill me." I find I am incapable, and with tears in my eyes cover the body with a greatcoat, thinking how small he looks. Move on to the next casualty. His right arm is blown off at the shoulder. I cover the wound, put a cigarette in his mouth. The wounded soldier apologises for trying to remove the cigarette with his missing arm. Complains of a sore backside. I turn him over. . . . one cheek of his ass has disappeared.

'We heard later that they all died . . . only 27 of the original battalion left.'

*　　*　　*

We cannot leave the area of the New Zealand Division without some mention of the 6th Brigade and the part its battalions played in the fighting on that first terrifying but exhilarating night. P. W. Briant, formerly of the 25th Battalion, served in a Bren gun carrier and had as part of his battle task the duty of leading the brigade support group forward and onto the final objective. The support group was made up of two carriers, a Scorpion, a troop of tanks from the yeomanry and a second group of carriers bringing up the rear. Recalling the sights, sounds and experiences of that night of battle in which he was wounded, Mr. Briant describes how the lines of Bofors tracer that marked the divisional boundaries between the New Zealanders and the South Africans on the one flank and the Highlanders on the other, were clearly visible. The sound of the pipes could be heard in the intervals when the barrage stopped for a short time. Of the barrage he wrote, 'I held my arm above my head and found that I was unable to hold the hand still, because of the vibration caused by the guns.'

The support group was waiting to move up, but congestion in the minefield gaps held the little unit back at the entrance to the field. 'It must have been getting on to midnight when we were given the OK to lead off. About a mile after the start line we came across a minefield, so the Scorpion was sent on ahead.' The flails went into action whirling round and round and thrashing the ground raising great clouds of choking dust. 'After the dust had settled we followed through the gap, and found that the Scorpion's flail was badly tangled with barbed wire. The crew said that they would have to clear it, so we went on without them.' Fire was coming from enemy strongpoints that were still holding out. 'The infantry kept calling for tanks, and so we moved on for about another mile, and then I reported that I couldn't see the second Bren carrier that was behind us.' By this time visibility had dropped to only a few feet, as explosions and vehicles created the conditions of a London pea-souper. 'We turned back and found that the second carrier had run over a mine. The driver was fairly badly wounded and I gave him a morphia injection from the first aid kit. The other two men were OK. We were obviously in a minefield, and the tank crews refused to go on until a gap had been cleared.' The nightmare journey forward had taken hours as the vehicles snaked their way through the British minefields, across no man's land and then through successive German mine 'marshes'. Now, approaching the objective, the tanks would not accompany the support group because of the danger of unswept mines. 'Miteiriya Ridge (the division's objective) was about a mile ahead, and dawn was just starting to break. It was not long before we could see the Engineers clearing a gap for us, and soon we were on the ridge having some breakfast. A mortar bomb burst close by, and our driver had a fairly bad leg wound. I also had a wound in the leg as well as small pieces of shrapnel in my hand and chest − a pay book and notebook in the breast pocket of my shirt stopped the pieces of shrapnel from wounding me there. I was taken back to the RAP and spent about three weeks in hospital.'

THE SOUTH AFRICANS

The task of the two spearhead brigades of the 1st South African Division was to capture part of Miteiriya Ridge before first light on 24 October, and with that objective firmly in its hands its brigades were to drive southwards. It is with the 3rd Brigade that we move forward in this narrative and specifically with the 1st Battalion of the Royal Durban Light Infantry which was, in conjunction with the Imperial Light Horse, to take up the advance from the Rand Light Infantry and to carry it to the final objective.

It is surprising how often the unit war diaries or individual accounts of the days in the desert mention music. Just as the Highland battalions each had their pipers and the 28th Maori Battalion performed the 'Haka', in the South African Division it was the Durbans who produced a musical memory. It was a tradition in that regiment that at sunset the regimental bugler played the famous hymn *Abide with me*. It was a particularly poignant reminder on the night of the opening of the El Alamein offensive, and those who heard it and have described it write of its effect with deep emotion.

The companies of the Durbans were on the start line to the rear of the Rand Battalion, and the soldiers lay down and waited until the roar of the barrage told them that the battle had opened. The Rand Light Infantry moved expertly into the attack, and the results of the opening phases augered well for a successful outcome. Their swift-paced advance brought them forward more than 700 yards in seven minutes. Soon the infantry had swept up to the wire fences that enclosed the first German defence complexes and, by bayonet and bomb, had burst their way into the northern side of those positions within half an hour of crossing the start line.

The programme of the attack was that the two reserve battalions would pass through the Rand lines when it halted at 22.45 hours and then with the Durbans on the right and the Imperial Light Horse on the left the assault would continue until barrage line 'B' had been reached at 23.00. There would be a pause in the advance of a quarter of an hour and then the attack would roll on to reach barrage line 'C' at 23.35 hours; to 'D' line at 00.25 on 24 October; to 'E' line by 01.45; and then to 'Mango', the final objective, at 23.50. Only fifteen minutes past their expected time, the success signal was fired to indicate that the battalions were on the 'C' line; from then on there were difficulties that could not be completely overcome, as the determination of the enemy infantry and the fury of his bombardments slowed down the advance.

On the 3rd Brigade's sector, the Axis artillery had opened fire on the area behind the spearhead infantry, causing a number of casualties to the Durbans before they had crossed the start line. Staggered by the concentration of shells that fell upon them, the Durbans then encountered the first of a series of uncharted minefields and enemy strongpoints defended by tenacious grenadiers. The two battalions, the Durbans and the Light Horse, battled their way forward, bombing the enemy posts and going in with the bayonet to clear out the last of the German defenders. But, forty minutes after midnight, the advance of the inner flank of the 3rd Brigade was halted. The battalions of the 2nd Brigade on the right had crashed into a large enemy strongpoint, which had been incorrectly identified before the offensive as a series of dumps. As a consequence of that faulty intelligence, the area had not been subjected to any of the selected bombardments. The grenadiers in those positions directly in the path of the 2nd South African Brigade proved their determination by flinging back all attacks. The firm German defence threatened to create a salient on the inner flanks of the assaulting brigades — a salient, moreover, that would be enfiladed by a mass of fire poured out by the determined Germans armed with heavy machine-guns and mortars into the advance of the South African battalions.

Not until 02.50 hours could the 3rd Brigade move forward again. The South African advance was now more than an hour behind schedule, and as the Durbans struggled on they were fired at from front and flank. The impetus of the attack had been lost in the enfilade fire and in the terrible bombardments that were still pounding the divisional rear area and had stopped the forward flow of the heavy weapons detachments. Behind the start line there was serious congestion. Uncleared minefields and narrow gaps restricted the flow of the division's vehicles.

The 'E' line was reached at 03.05 hours and the intelligence was passed back to brigade HQ by Aldis lamp. Just after 03.40 there was a sudden and inexplicable reduction in the volume of the enemy's fire, and in this welcome interlude the Durban's spearhead companies made a faster pace. Then, as the first files approached the 'F' line they were met by a withering storm of fire. Summoning up their last reserves of energy, the Durbans went in chanting a Zulu war song: they rushed across the barbed wire surrounding the position and went in among the enemy machine-gunners with the bayonet. Now there remained only 500 yards to the objective on the ridge, but it was ground swept by a hurricane of shells and mortar fire, spread with a blanket of bullets, covered by mines and surrounded by barbed wire. There could be no smooth-paced advance up that deadly glacis, but instead the application of battle drills. In short, sharp rushes the survivors of the Royal Durban Light Infantry (for now all that was left of the battalion were remnants) fought their way forward up the ridge, each section's rush covered by the fire of other groups until, at 04.00 hours, the first men of 'C' Company reached the 'Mango' line and fired the success signal. 'A' Company, still under enfilade fire from the right flank, did not form on the objective until 06.00 hours and in broad daylight. The 3rd Brigade was on its objectives, but the 2nd Brigade's battalions had still not managed to gain theirs.

Bouncing their way along the narrow track swept through the enemy minefields came part of the Durban transport platoon, bringing a welcome breakfast of coffee, porridge and bacon. There was more than enough. The cooks at 'B' Echelon had prepared food for all the men who had crossed the start line only hours before: seven of the Durbans would never eat again, and 44 others were wounded and had had to be evacuated. When it is remembered that the strength of the battalion at the start line — its strength in 'bayonets' — had been just over 300, then it can be seen that the Durbans had lost one man in six of those who had gone in on the first night of Alamein.

XIII CORPS

The role of XIII Corps was, as we have seen, less dramatic than that of its more powerful partner XXX Corps, and the accounts of the actions fought in the south of the line are, therefore, less spectacular. But an incident representative of the actions of the 50th Division is recalled by an NCO in the Royal Sussex Regiment, W. J. Giddings. As part of a pre-battle decoy group out in no man's land, he saw the barrage very much as the Germans and Italians would have seen it, and was impressed by its fury. 'My platoon was made up with men from the Ox and Bucks, and although they appeared decent soldiers I wondered how they would react under fire. So when I heard a buzz that a volunteer platoon was needed for a job I volunteered. I reported to battalion headquarters and there I was introduced to an officer whom I had not met before. He told me that the Free French were going to attack the 'Sugar Loaf', one of the high peaks on the Quaret el Himeimat, and that we were to be a decoy. There would be five Bren gun carriers: two of those would be taking 3-inch mortars and bombs, two with Vickers machine-guns manned by the Cheshire Regiment and one to take any casualties. My platoon had to take their groundsheets. Why was at that time a mystery to me.

'We went through the wire about 20.00 hours — after stand down — and, after travelling about a mile into no man's land, the officer said, "This place will do." The groundsheets that we had brought were laid out covering the sand and the mortar bombs were then laid on top of the groundsheets. This enabled the bombs to be picked up cleanly and quickly. My platoon was sent approximately 100 yards ahead and spread out in a semi-circle so as to protect the carriers and crews from enemy patrols. At 21.00 hours the officer gave the order to fire, and the mortars and the Vickers did so. The officer said to me, "Come on Sergeant, we will try and see what damage we are doing." But then the enemy started to send up Verey lights and to return our fire. The two of us settled on a small ridge and watched our mortar bombs exploding. After a while the officer said to me, "Keep looking behind you, Sergeant. You will see a sight you will never experience again." I kept looking, and could see nothing but darkness, so I wondered what the hell he was on about. But at 21.40 hours I looked behind me again, and it looked as if the whole horizon was on fire. Then there was a few seconds silence and then a sound of whistling in the air, followed by the "crump" of shells exploding in the German lines. The Battle of El Alamein had started. When the last bomb and the last round in the Vickers had been fired the officer said to me, "Bring your men in, Sergeant, and let's go home." '

Down on the left flank of the Tyne Tees Division, the 44th Division was preparing for its part in the battle. The advance by the Queen's brigade began badly. 'Even before we crossed the start line we were under fire from Jerry artillery. The battalion had moved in single file

'The monstrous thunder of the guns. . . .' **Top:** The guns of Eighth Army blanketed Axis artillery positions with shells before moving on to bombard the enemy's forward defence zones. The barrage at its height, towards midnight on 23 October. **Above:** A view looking back at the barrage from no man's land. **Right:** The guns have softened up the enemy and the infantry wait for the order that will take them into the attack.

Infantry — queen of the battle-field. **Above:** Infantry consolidating on the objective. The first task is to dig in. **Right:** A British infantryman in a well dug and fortified German position. The MG 34 is projecting only inches above the surface of the ground.

Vignettes from the days of battle. **Top:** Gunners of an anti-tank detachment firing their 6pdr at German armour. **Centre:** Crusader tanks, armed with the 2pdr gun, move up a trigh towards the battle area on 2 November 1942. **Left:** A 15cwt lorry comes under fire as it negotiates a gap in the enemy's minefield.

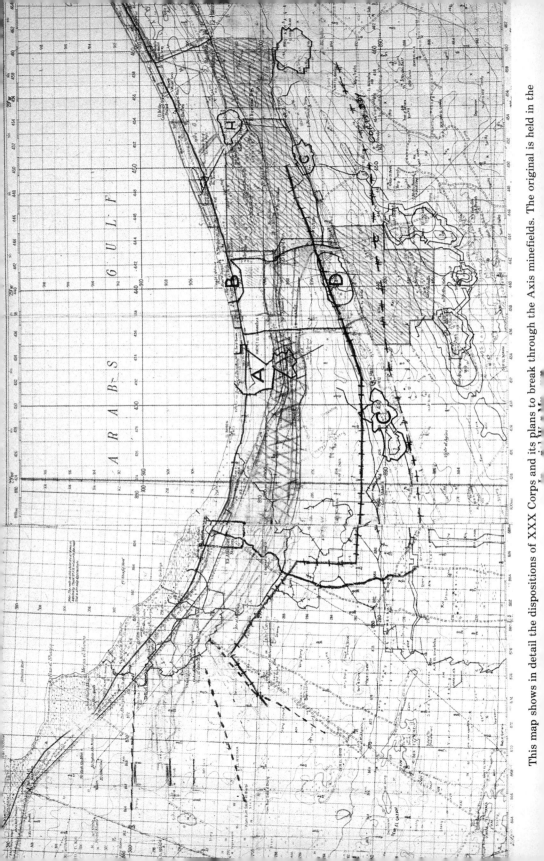

This map shows in detail the dispositions of XXX Corps and its plans to break through the Axis minefields. The original is held in the

down through the Twyford Gap in our 'Nuts' minefield, that is the field nearest to the enemy. (The most easterly of our fields was called 'May'.) The track was lit with little amber lights on poles, and at the far side of the minefield we halted and formed up. Our barrage had been firing for a long time, but we were soon aware that the enemy was firing back. It was not possible to see the shell bursts except when you were very near them. The dust that they flung up hid the flashes of the explosions, but men were falling all over the place, hit by shrapnel. Then the farther we got into the minefield the more fierce was the fire. And it wasn't only shells, but mortars and machine-guns firing tracer. We had two companies up and one in reserve. Behind us was the gapping detachment. By the time we had slogged across no man's land we were very tired. The going was terrible. It was mostly very soft and hard to walk through. You know how tiring it is to cross a sandy beach at the seaside. Well, this beach was just as tiring, and it was miles wide.

'Then we were in the "January" minefield. At least, we were told that we had entered it. There was no difference as far as I could see between no man's land and the Jerry minefield, but once we knew for sure that we were in unswept areas we all had a horrible feeling. I can't describe it, but you have the fear that the next step you take is going to be your last. Of course, most of the mines were anti-tank, but we all knew that among them Jerry would sow some anti-personnel ones as well, and there were lots of Red Devils about — you know, the Italian hand grenades. There were lots of empty slit trenches about, which must have been enemy infantry forward positions. We had been told at O Group that the Italian troops were brought up by night to those slits in front of, and in, the minefield, and just dumped there with orders to hold the gaps to the last man.

'The battlefield was completely empty of the enemy, so far as I can remember. I can't remember seeing any enemy — dead or alive. There were so many explosions and, of course, I was concentrating so hard upon looking out for S mines that nothing else seemed to matter. I remember the enemy bombarding us. He seemed to be trying to cut our companies off from each other and, that way, to isolate them. The Jerries and Eyeties were firing tracer from their machine-guns. A lot of it was fixed-line fire so that it was quite possible to walk alongside the tracer line — not too close, of course — knowing that we were in safe ground. It was clear to us, later on, that by avoiding the tracer bullets we were being forced into ground that Jerry was saturating with mortar fire. We were being controlled and herded to where he would be able to kill us.

'We seemed to have been marching for hours, and then there was a certain amount of confusion and we began to dig in. It seemed that we had passed through the "January" minefield and that we had reached the objective. The regimental history says that some of the battalions headquarters and part of the forward troops were counterattacked by the Folgore Division and taken prisoner. Whatever it was, the rest of us were pulled back to guard the gap that had just been pushed through the minefield, and after a couple of hours we were ordered forward again. It was all very confusing.'

There was confusion, piled upon confusion, as the paratroops of the Folgore Division, backed by German heavy artillery, smashed the first British assaults. The individual explosions could no longer be distinguished and combined to form a single, continuing and deafening roar. Visibility was down to a matter of feet and yards. Visibility even in the British lines was so bad that nothing could be distinguished. 'We were towing a 2pdr anti-tank gun,' wrote T. V. Pulland, 'and by accident moved across the front of a battery of 25pdrs which, because of the smoke, the dust and the noise, we never saw until they opened up over our heads. I thought to myself, this is a ruddy good start. . . .'

'What do I remember distinctly?' In his reply, H. L. Matthews, formerly of 1/7th Battalion, The Queen's Regiment, painted a vivid and dramatic word picture that enlarged upon the event described in the regimental history as: 'Battalion headquarters was counterattacked and its men killed or taken prisoner.'

'I remember shells and mortars coming from the other way. Advancing through the bursts and through the smoke and dust at a rate of 100 yards in three minutes. We were approximately five yards apart. A runner coming up to me and shouting in my ear, "Mr. Davies is wounded. Take over." Mr. Davies was my platoon commander. Suddenly realizing that our numbers were getting fewer. Then it was the Colonel and Major Colbrook, my company commander. The Colonel called us to him shouting, "We are in our own barrage. Back 100 paces." We regrouped, but there were only about twelve of us. The Colonel said that we had reached our final objective, but we would not be able to hold the position. Everyone else had been held up.

'We decided to turn south and try to link up with the Free French, who were to advance on the left of us. They had not got to their objective. We stumbled into the rear of an Italian strongpoint that turned out to be manned by part of a battalion of the Folgore Parachute Division. We were captured. We spent the night lying under guard, but in comparative quietness. In the morning they tried to march us away, but we decided to try for a break. We were suddenly fired on by our own tanks, which appeared like little lumps on the skyline about a mile away. In the confusion we made a break, running a few yards and then down flat. Then we ran on again and again fell flat. We were nearly half way when it got lighter and our tanks started firing at us again. We just had to lay there not daring to move, holding up a couple of steel helmets towards our tanks hoping that they would see that we were British. I think it was an hour or so before they stopped, and then a carrier and a Honey tank started to move out towards us. By now the Colonel, who was next to me, had been killed. Major Colbrook was fatally wounded and had been left with the

Italians, who had a doctor. Major Mills, near me, shouted, "When I say go . . . go." Again we did a mad dash, a few yards at a time. I made for the carrier, reached it, and leapt inside. It was commanded by a corporal of the rifle brigade. I remember him standing in the carrier while we were cowering at the bottom of it. He stood there as we turned towards our own lines and, with tracer whizzing past, even anti-tank tracer, gave the Eyeties a rude sign with his two fingers. I heard him shout, "They couldn't hit **** all." He took us back through the tanks and infantry to peace and quiet behind the ridge.'

The 1/7th Battalion advanced at 05.30 hours and took up position facing north to protect the gaps in the 'January' minefield. There they lay all day under continual fire, preparing to move forward again and to undertake a second attempt at gapping the 'February' field.

The 1/7th Battalion of the Queen's advanced again at 05.30 hours and took up positions facing north, so as to protect the gaps the minefield task force had made. With the onset of daylight there was little chance that the other two battalions of the Queen's would be able to force the 'February' field, and the second stage of the brigade attack was called off. The armour that had come forward through the gaps could not move out of the confined passages and was grouped, congested, in the 'January' field. The tanks and the supporting infantry battalions echeloned behind the spearhead battalion were under accurate fire, directed by enemy observers on Himeimat.

There were other memories, which may have been of less dangerous happenings but which nevertheless have remained firmly imprinted. T. V. Pulland recalls the attack carried out by the Queen's on the 24th: 'The Queen's attacked the "February" minefield and reached a point about 800 yards on the far side. Here they were pinned down. . . . It was very uncomfortable for everyone concerned. I myself was lying face down in an Eyetie slit trench that had been used as a latrine. My mates never came near me for days afterwards. One of our casualties was a man who took cover under a 2pdr anti-tank gun. A Jerry shell went through both tyres and the gun went down on his back.'

Little happened in XIII Corps area throughout the long and bitter 24 October, but the corps had fulfilled its role: the Axis armoured divisions were still held in the south and had made no move to aid the northern group of 15th Panzer and Littorio.

11.

THE ARMOUR ATTACK

1st ARMOURED DIVISION

It was the task of the 1st Armoured Division to advance through the swept passage at the junction of the Australian and the 51st Highland Division. The objective for the Armoured Division was the 'Pierson' line, on the far side of Kidney Ridge, and that had to be gained before dawn on 24 October. To describe the first night of Operation 'Lightfoot' from the armoured perspective it is the 2nd Brigade whose actions we shall follow. In the days before the offensive opened, the armoured regiments moved to their assembly areas near El Imayid station and Hamman, where they crept under the canvas covers that disguised them as lorries. Thus hidden, the squadrons prepared for battle. The crews tuned the tank engines and checked the tracks.

On 23 October the final details of the battle plan were announced at formal parades, and in the Queen's Bays a church service was held at which Holy Communion was taken. 'It was in a mood of sombre anticipation that we prepared to drive out that night,' was the comment of one man who served in the regiment, and his description fitted the feelings of most of the men who fought in the armour. After last light on the 23rd, the regimental areas became scenes of last-minute preparations. The 'sun shades' (the hessian covers under which the fighting vehicles had been concealed) were cast off. Engines were started, and in single file the machines moved out from their positions behind the British front and into the marked and lighted tracks. Three of those had been set aside for the 2nd Brigade's advance. On the right, 'Sun' was to carry the machines of the Bays; along 'Moon', the centre track, would pass brigade headquarters and the 9th Lancers; while 'Star', the left track, would bear the 10th Hussars.

Far ahead of the Bays, on 'Sun' track, the left-hand battalion of the 20th Australian Brigade would be fighting its way forward, while behind the 5th Black Watch, the right-hand battalion of the Highland Division, would be the 10th Hussars. Behind the spearhead infantry formations and in front of the armoured squadrons, the all-arms minefield task force would be at work. (The duties of the force have been explained in an earlier chapter, but to recapitulate briefly, the infantry component was to protect the minelifting Sappers. The task of the military police was to control the flow of traffic through the gapped areas, and the allotted tank troops from armoured units were present to protect the others from immediate threat by enemy armour. In the 1st Armoured Division, the infantry of the minefield task force was made up of men taken from the 2nd Rifle Brigade.) The squadrons of the 10th Hussars were the first of the two leading regiments to move off from the brigade concentration area. At 21.00 hours they marched. Half an hour later, the Bays moved out. Brigade head-quarters followed, trailed by the 9th Lancers.

The columns were still on their approach march to the gaps in the British minefields when the barrage opened, but most crew members were unaware that the guns were firing. The noise of the tank engines drowned out all other sound, and only the commander, standing upright in the turret, could see that the skyline ahead of him was lit across a 40-mile arc with flashes of gunfire. At 22.00 hours, in single file, the leading armoured cars of the Bays crossed the start point, closely followed by the regiment's tank squadrons. For two hours the slow-paced advance continued. Attempts to lay the dust by using water carts had not been successful, and visibility was down to a matter of feet. In the darkness and the murk, there were frequent but minor collisions between vehicles as drivers moved along a track whose lights could hardly be seen through the clouds of dust.

Some time after midnight the regulating area on the 'Springbok' track was reached and a halt was made. The tired drivers gave themselves over to resting after the ordeal they had undergone. At the regulating point, the crews carried out the last-minute preparations before they were committed to battle. The fuel tanks were topped up and muzzle covers were taken off the guns. There was still some time to wait. The night was a bitterly cold one, and the crews sat around smoking, waiting and watching the barrage. That spectacle soon palled, and most settled down to sleep. Some slept outside their tanks; others preferred the warmth of the tank compartments, resting their tired heads against the steel framework. The only light visible was the strange diffused glow from the wireless sets illuminating the faces of the operators, who sat with headphones on, waiting for orders. In the rear of some tanks, billycans were boiling over small Benghazi fires. God alone knew when the next brew would be.

Shortly before 02.00 hours on the 24th, the regulating area was filled with noise as the powerful engines were re-started, and then in obedience to simple commands the columns headed out, each unit driving down between the little sparks of light that indicated the gapped area of the minefields. The British fields were negotiated; then no man's land was traversed; and finally the leading elements entered into the corridors that the task force was making in the German fields. The noise inside the tanks and the sounds of the British barrage kept most of the tank crews in ignorance of the fact that the enemy artillery had begun a furious counter-bombardment, and that much of it was being directed at the armoured columns as they made their slow way forward into battle. Only the glowing red 'cricket balls' slapping against the armour plates of the leading Shermans or the whistling, white-lightning streaks that were the path of 88mm solid shot showed the tank commanders that the regiments were under fire. The infantry and the task force, outside the security of inches of armour plate protection, had been aware of the enemy's retaliation for some time.

One of the team of lamp lighters, helping to set up the lights along 'Moon' track, the path along which the headquarters of the 2nd Armoured Brigade and 9th Lancers would pass, was keenly anxious to complete the dangerous task of setting out the lamps. Former Rifleman Suckling, of the 2nd Rifle Brigade, with his mate Bill Milligan, was seated in a 3-ton truck lighting the hurricane lamps and handing them to other riflemen, who then placed them inside the petrol tins and hung them on pickets. When the tanks arrived, the enemy's response was immediate and heavy. There was a severe 'stonk', and the area was swept with shell fire and machine-gun bursts. It was no safe job sitting in a soft-skin vehicle under shell fire with a 40-gallon container of paraffin. The two men in the truck became, understandably, keen on completing the task in the shortest possible time. Inside the truck's canopy the noise of battle seemed magnified, and the vehicle shook as shells crashed down in the desert. 'I'm saying to my chum, this I don't like. At least let's keep our tin hats on. We decided that instead of lighting one lamp at a time we would light two or three so as to get the task over quickly. It was hell outside. Next thing that happened was one of the lamps turned over. Whoosh! The kerosene was blazing and the track of the flames was making for the 40-gallon drum. There was plenty of smoke and confusion. We did our best to extinguish the flames, but to no avail. The truck would go up any minute. We baled out, hit the sand and crawled away before it went up. There was plenty of small-arms fire coming at us from the enemy. We managed to crawl to a slit trench, and there we were pinned down until dawn. Then we withdrew to positions behind the minefield to cover gaps for our armour to go through at some time.'

The slow-paced advance — 3mph was the regulation speed — brought the leading squadrons through the first Axis minefields, but then came a stop. Ahead of the second minefield there was a third which had not yet been gapped. There were also enemy strongpoints that had not been captured. Resistance from these was halting the move forward. The situation was confused. No clear picture could be gained at first, but slowly the details were sorted out. The 1st Battalion of the Gordon Highlanders had suffered such appalling casualties that the advance had been brought to a complete halt. The battalion was about 3,000 yards short of its final objective, a defended area named 'Aberdeen', located on the south-eastern corner of Kidney Ridge. The survivors of the shattered companies were digging in, determined to hold the ground that they had won.

The whole forward movement stopped. If the assaulting infantry could not advance, then neither could the task force complete the gapping. Until it did so, the vehicles, both wheeled and tracked, had to wait. It was a frightening situation. The cleared track was only eight yards wide, and vehicles could not pass each other. Nor could tanks turn round and drive back to areas in which they might be hidden from the observant officers of the enemy artillery. In daylight those observers would be able to direct accurately the fire of their batteries upon the three long columns of vehicles. There were three choices of action. They could advance into the unknown blackness ahead, with the probability of being blown up on unswept mines and the certainty of being destroyed by the anti-tank guns of the enemy. Alternatively, the columns could stay where they were and present the Axis batteries with an unmoving 'dream' target. The third choice was to risk being blown up on mines by deploying into the ground on either side of the gapped area. To stay and be a target was unthinkable. To push on would be to invite disaster and to waste the armoured potential. The orders came to deploy, and the great armoured machines lumbered into unswept desert on either side of the white tapes. The Hussars carried out their deployment without loss; so did the 9th Lancers, but the Bays came under fire from a 5cm anti-tank gun, and the leading group was hit. Leaving 'B' Squadron to advance as a screen, the other squadrons spread out into the broken ground across which the bleak light of day was breaking.

All too soon it was daylight, and as visibility improved there was an immediate increase in the shelling. The 1st Armoured Division was stuck in its corridor, and was not on its objective.

10th ARMOURED DIVISION

The 10th Armoured Division's great mass of AFVs and soft-skin vehicles was in position to the east of the 'Springbok' track. For the drive through the minefields and the advance to battle, the divisional commander placed the 24th Brigade on the right and the 8th Brigade on the left. Echeloned behind the 8th Brigade came the division's lorried infantry component. The task of the 10th Armoured Division was to pour through the southern gap in the minefields, to cross Miteiriya Ridge and reach the 'Pierson' bound. That line lay, so far as 10th Armoured Division was concerned, on open ground some two miles ahead of the New Zealand infantry objective.

The story of 10th Armoured Division differs only in slight detail from that of 1st Armoured: for both divisions the first night was one of waiting. In the concentration area east of the 'Springbok' track just before 02.00 hours on 24 October, the engines of the huge mass of vehicles were started and the regiments began to move along the marked tracks. The 8th Armoured Brigade led the divisional group, followed several hours later by the 24th Armoured Brigade. Towards dawn, the lorried infantry of the 133rd Brigade crossed the 'Springbok' track, heading west and entering into the maelstrom of noise and danger that was now the El Alamein battlefield. Across no man's land and then into Panzerarmee's minefields, the squadrons made their slow way. There was a halt in the first enemy minefield, and the squadrons waited nose to tail in the narrow swept lane, as the Engineers of the minefield task force worked desperately to open the road forward. The Sappers made good progress, and shortly before first light they had cleared gaps through the fields in which the vehicles of the Sherwood Rangers were lined up. Now the Rangers could move out of the last enemy minefield and across Miteiriya Ridge.

The army commander's plan proposed that through the swept corridors the armour would advance, hidden in the darkness of the October night, to debouch behind the enemy's rear. Montgomery's plan proved in the event to be an unrealistic one, for it was predicted upon the ability of the Sappers to clear minefields at a rate of 100 yards in three minutes. This was a difficult pace to maintain at any time, even under optimum conditions. It was totally impossible under the conditions that obtained on the El Alamein battlefield. The enemy's principal minefields were known. What was unknown was that, for weeks before Operation 'Lightfoot' opened, Axis engineers had laid out new fields, and had not only fitted existing ones with sophisticated booby-traps but had thickened and deepened the original mine 'marshes'. The widening belts and those other fields of more recent growth were unknown to British intelligence, as were the great number of gun emplacements in the solid rock that Italian engineers had dug and were continuing to dig. Into those positions, Axis artillery and anti-tank guns could be relocated once the direction of the main British thrust had been established. The German plan was to delay the British advance by new minefields; once these had been cleared and the armoured regiments resumed the advance, they would meet freshly-dug gun lines. Eighth Army's advance would be dearly bought. The artillery positions had been dug so deep that the guns within fired at just above ground level. The pits were almost undetectable from ground level, and were safe against anything but a direct hit. They were laid out so as to dominate the areas through which the British tanks would have to come, and they were supplemented by infantry strongpoints of solid construction and well sited.

So ahead of X Corps armour there were the known German minefields, plus other fields of which Eighth Army knew nothing, plus new and unsuspected gun lines. Those obstacles the regiments would have to overcome. If they could break out from the gaps during the dark of the October night, then smoke shells, dust clouds and the darkness might give some protection, might reduce the risk of being hit, and might allow some tanks to form a bridgehead that could be built up. There was, however, a limit to the number of passages the Sappers could make on the first night. The passages would be few and they would be narrow. Even assuming that twelve tracks could be cleared, that these were divided equally between the northern and southern corridors; and that each could accommodate two armoured fighting vehicles; even then, as a maximum, no more than 24 tanks at any one time could exit from the cleared passages and fan out for the advance to 'Pierson' bound. The squadrons would have to be clear of the minefield lanes before first light. Any attempt made in daylight to cross Miteiriya Ridge or to reach the line at Kidney Ridge would be nothing but a senseless and tragic waste of armour, for the tanks would be under the direct and accurate fire of the Axis anti-tank guns.

It was exactly this situation that faced the squadrons at first light on 24 October. Take the Sherwood Rangers as an example. The regiment had advanced through the New Zealand Division, suffering the sudden and frequent halts with patience, moving slowly forward, enveloped in dust clouds and smoke. Then the Sappers reported that the track through the last minefield had been cleared. The final gap markers were hammered in and the Sapper officer gave the 'all clear' for the Sherwood Rangers to move forward. The night was so far advanced that the first vehicles had cleared the gap exits and had passed into open country the sky was already lightening.

Urged on by the minefield task force officers, the column passed over the crest of the ridge and moved down the slight slope towards the 'Oxalic' line. Through the cleared exit gap, the Crusader tanks of 'A' Squadron poured, halted, reformed and revved up ready to swing southwards and advance upon the 'Pierson' bound. A sudden storm of fire struck them. The squadron was surrounded by well concealed anti-tank guns. Some of these then opened fire from only 50 yards away. Their gunners had practised excellent fire control. Five of the nine Crusaders were hit almost immediately and then 'B' Squadron, which had come up to support the stricken 'A' Squadron, lost five of its Grants in a matter of minutes. The situation was untenable. There must be an immediate withdrawal. Infantry would be needed to fight down the Bersaglieri anti-tank gunners, but the division's lorried infantry was a long way back. Unsupported armour could not hold the ground. It had to be withdrawn or else it would be annihilated. Under the hurricane of fire, the other troops of the Rangers tried to turn their vehicles in the narrow channel of the minefield gap and then withdraw to a safe position on the reverse slope of the ridge. Sixteen tanks had now been destroyed — more than a third of the regiment lost in a matter of minutes. The survivors of 'A' and 'B' Squadrons came back behind the crest, and in its shelter the Sherwood Rangers regrouped. Then the depleted squadrons took up the battle again.

Military Medal winner B. Dudley, who served with the 3rd RTR, had the unenviable task of driving the CO's jeep, which meant that he had to be immediately behind his officer's tank at all times and to be 'The only person in an unarmoured vehicle in the whole area. On the first night of Alamein we drove along "Bottle" track, which marked the gap in our minefield. The RSM was travelling with me, and I took up my position behind the CO's Grant tank, moving along the track in fits and starts, blinded by the dust kicked up by the tracks of the regiment of tanks of which we were a part. Soon we came to a halt, and I drove up close behind the Grant in front of me for protection. I looked at the RSM beside me, wondering if he was as afraid as I was. We were in a bad position and could go neither forward nor back and were jammed in by tanks and other vehicles. Nor could we escape to the side because of the mines on either side of us. He seemed quite unperturbed, so I felt better. "Must be nearly time for the balloon to go up", I said. He looked at his watch. "Ten minutes or so yet," he said. We knew that in a few minutes thousands of shells would be fired at the enemy. That would start the ball rolling with a vengeance, as the Axis was bound to reply with all they had got. Just then, a string of flares appeared in the sky over "Star" track on our right, and we could see the bombs exploding among the packed transport. "Looks as if the Staffs Yeomanry are catching a packet", I said. "Hope it isn't our turn next." A moment later our guns opened fire with a deafening roar, and the horizon in front became a sea of flame as far as the eye could see.

'As though linked to the guns, two powerful searchlights were switched on behind us, pointing up into the sky in the form of a great V. "What are they for?" I asked the RSM. "So we know which way we're going if we get lost", he replied. Not much danger of that, I thought, as I watched the shells exploding in front of me. The tank ahead of me moved forward, and I drove up close behind if for cover until the blue flames from the exhaust were almost setting fire to the jeep. I looked across at the RSM. He was huddled down in his seat, his jaw set. "Don't get too close, Dudley", he said. "If he hits a mine we've all had it." I dropped back a few yards, but the dust was so thick that I couldn't see the white tape that was all that was between us and the mines. "Can't see where I'm going, Sir", I told the RSM. "I'll have to go in close again." He agreed and we drove on, easing our way past burning vehicles, all kinds of vehicles, which were partially blocking the track. A nightmare journey that seemed never ending and was further enlivened by the enemy shells, which were by now bursting among the mines on either side of us and setting them off with further explosions. The sky began to lighten. "Soon be dawn", the RSM shouted above the clamour. "It'll get really warm then."

'We emerged through the last of the marked minefields in daylight, and the tanks fanned out into open formation. Something went wrong and they were soon halted by a rain of shells that fell among us. The RSM leapt onto the Colonel's tank to confer with him and told me to leave the area until things had become quieter. I pulled away and lay in a trench of sorts until things were under control. We moved forward again, the tanks took up their battle positions, and for three days and two more nights we were in constant engagement with the enemy. Then we were pulled back for 24 hours' compulsory rest, and I spent that time directing unit fitters to broken-down tanks and leading replenishment lorries with petrol and ammunition.'

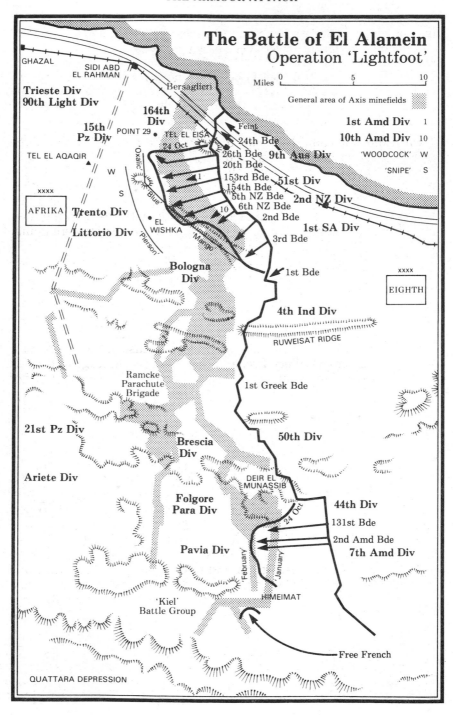

The Battle of El Alamein
Operation 'Lightfoot'

GHAZAL

SIDI ABD
EL RAHMAN

Bersaglieri

Miles 0   5   10

Trieste Div
90th Light Div

General area of Axis minefields

**164th
Div**

**15th
Pz Div**

POINT 29

Feint

1st Amd Div   1

TEL EL EISA

24th Bde

10th Amd Div   10

24 Oct

26th Bde   **9th Aus Div**

'WOODCOCK'   W

TEL EL AQAQIR

20th Bde

'SNIPE'   S

W

153rd Bde   **51st Div**

154th Bde

xxxx

S

5th NZ Bde   **2nd NZ Div**

AFRIKA   **Trento Div**

6th NZ Bde

2nd Bde

Littorio Div

EL
WISHKA

3rd Bde

1st SA Div

**Bologna
Div**

1st Bde

xxxx

EIGHTH

4th Ind Div

RUWEISAT RIDGE

Ramcke
Parachute
Brigade

1st Greek Bde

21st Pz Div

**Brescia
Div**

50th Div

Ariete Div

DEIR EL
MUNASSIB

**Folgore
Para Div**

24 Oct

44th Div

131st Bde

2nd Amd Bde

Pavia Div

'February'

'January'

7th Amd Div

HIMEIMAT

'Kiel'
Battle Group

Free French

QUATTARA DEPRESSION

'Oxalic'

Blue

'Pierson'

Mango

188

12.

CONSOLIDATING

24 AND 25 OCTOBER

Dawn could not come too soon for some. The horrors of the night might not be so hard to bear in daylight. Private Crane remembers with relief the dawn of the 24th. He had not feared to go into battle for the first time. Every fighting soldier he knew had to undergo his baptism of fire, and the advance on the first night of El Alamein had been noisy and eventful. 'By dawn on the 24th, with the morning mist and the smoke from gunfire, it was a job to see where you were going. Before breakfast we had to dig-in, in case there was a counterattack. Daylight came, and no sign of any Germans or Italians. Only the dead. My impression at that moment was to look out at the open spaces of desert sand and be thankful to be alive. We stayed all that day in a dug-out, resting. During the day, column after column of German and Italian troops passed us on their way to the prison camps. I felt we had won the war.'

But dawn on the 24th brought with it an increase in the weight and accuracy of enemy artillery fire, and there was no shortage of targets at which to aim. Almost any shot would be certain to score a hit either directly or else by showering with splinters the great masses of men, vehicles and tanks that covered the surface of the desert to the west of El Alamein.

What was bewildering to most men who saw that first dawn was the great numbers that thronged the area. 'I had thought myself to be alone in the desert, or at least with just the blokes from my own unit. But when the light grew stronger during 'stand to' I had a look around, and the whole desert was covered with stuff.' It was a feeling that R. Scott, formerly an anti-tank Gunner in the 51st Highland Division remembered well. 'A squadron of Bostons flew over in perfect formation. Then about an hour later a dozen Baltimores arrived just as Jerry reorganized . . . and that went on all day. On one sortie a Boston or Baltimore began to lose height and smoke poured from its tail. One crew member jumped, then another, and as the last man got out a mighty roar went up. Up till then I thought we were the only ones around.' The feeling of being alone facing Panzerarmee is a recurring theme. 'What struck me as odd was that we had been told about the dangerous minefields, and yet all over the place there were tanks roaring about, 25pdrs coming into action, trucks coming up with food and ammo. I had never seen so many people and stuff in one place before. There seemed to be miles and miles of nothing but our army.'

'Stand down' came, and those battalions that had good quartermasters and lucky 'B' Echelon drivers enjoyed breakfast which, even if it was predictable, tasted that much sweeter for the simple fact of just being alive to eat it after the experiences through which they had passed. And not only through which they had passed, but which they were still enduring. Shells came over, sometimes in a hurricane of explosions, often singly, and the enemy never seemed to be short of mortar bombs or machine-gun bullets. What surprised most Gunners was the speed of German reaction. To D. F. W. Smith, formerly a sergeant of the 69th Medium Regiment, 'It was a shaker when he hit back first thing in the morning.' In addition to the high-explosive shells there were fiery balls, all of them armour-piercing and deadly, whizzing about and flinging up showers of sparks when at last, their mad momentum spent, they struck the rocky surface. Then the Stukas came. The Afrika Korps War Diary may have reported that the Luftwaffe had so few fighters that only a handful of Stuka raids could be launched, but this is not the way that the troops on the ground saw it. Raids were frequent, heavy and destructive, and each dive-bomber seemed to aim directly at *you*. 'The barrage continued until first light and then the Stuka raids started and low-level bombing, which gave me a chance to have a go at them with a Browning machine-gun taken off a tank', was the memory of L. Wink, Gunner in the 144th Field Regiment. James McNally of the 68th Medium Regiment recalled that 'there were as many as thirty Stuka raids each day'. With Stukas, low-level bombers and fighters, artillery and mortars, life was hectic in the forward positions that morning.

The word went round that the generals had come forward to see for themselves how the battle was progressing. And, while those in authority made their plans, those who had no say in this talk of life and death relaxed, so far as they could with the knowledge that death might be only inches or seconds away. They relaxed and talked, reliving the frightful things of the previous night, trying to talk them out of their minds . . . but yet, even now, forty years later, to listen to them in pubs or in home surroundings is to be taken back to that dusty, dirty desert filled with noise and danger.

It would not be a day for moving about in the open unless movement was absolutely necessary. Axis artillery units had been ordered to conserve ammunition by not bombarding British concentration areas before the battle opened. With Eighth Army now poised on Miteiriya Ridge and threatening to drive westwards, this restraint upon the Axis artillery regiments was lifted and the morning was filled with storms of fire from guns, directed by OPs holding high ground positions. One phenomenon observed in the Trento Division's area was an Italian artillery observer sitting on a chair at the top of a very long pole — a quick battery 'shoot' brought him down from his perch. Those who were required to move about on foot across the desert and through the enemy's artillery fire included Sappers widening the minefield corridors and fighting patrols and battalions of infantry, chiefly of the Highland Division, undertaking attacks to gain the uncaptured objectives.

'We were on Miteiriya Ridge by dawn on the 24th', recalls Frank Compton, who served with 'A' Squadron of the 47th RTR, part of 24th Armoured Brigade in the 10th Armoured Division. 'The scene as the light became good amazed our crew. There were tanks as far as you could see, all jockeying for position so that they could 'hull down' on the ridge, which was by now under very heavy shell fire. The battalion sat on the ridge all day under heavy shell fire, for Jerry had got over the shock of our barrage. On the 25th we went over the ridge onto 'Pierson' bound to engage the enemy Mark IIIs and IVs of the 15th Panzer Division. We were straddled between the 51st Division and the New Zealanders.

'I shall never forget as we drove over the ridge, about 20 or 25 feet high and onto the level ground, how our infantry looked with horror at us as we ran over the slit trenches they had dug in the soft sand. We fanned out under fire from very well concealed 88s and dug-in tanks. Tank after tank of ours was knocked out, and the desert was filled with men trying to get clear of the burning vehicles. I had a go at everything my tank commander put me on. I saw two 88s off in three minutes. It was clear that we were breaking through their screen. My tank commander was hit by an air burst that exploded just above our turret. He had been badly hit in the chest and fell on top of me as I served the 75mm gun, stripped to the waist. I was covered with his blood. I called over the intercom to the driver to back up the ridge. We backed up the slope and stopped among a group of Sappers. We couldn't manhandle our commander out of the turret, so I asked some of the Sappers if they would give us a hand. Then their major came up and told us to get the tank out of it, as we were drawing enemy fire. But the men helped me and put our commander in a trench with them, and I took over command, put the co-driver in the turret and went back in among what was now left of the squadron. What a sight it was. Tanks knocked out all around me, everywhere. What could tanks do against well concealed 88s? I just could not believe the great Shermans could just get it like this. But there it was. I rallied with some of "B" Squadron. We moved towards enemy tanks we saw in the distance, but again those unseen 88s started taking toll. As the day drew on, I realized that I was in a broad but shallow depression and was brought to a halt. We got back to the ridge and sought cover. The RSM, Mr. Lindley, spoke to us and gave us a large slab of chocolate. "Compton," he said, "we have suffered heavy casualties." The Queen's Bays took our Sherman and complained about the blood on the turret floor. The battalion was then broken up, and I was posted to the 8th RTR in time for Operation "Supercharge". The most miserable moment of my life was that day seeing the tanks of my squadron being decimated by 88s.'

As the day drew on, the units began to consolidate under the intense shell fire. Former Trooper Johnson of the 41st RTR, was one of those who had a lucky escape. 'First light on the 24th, everyone began sorting themselves out. During the night I had thought I was lost, so when first light came two infantrymen asked me what I was doing there. They were front-line infantry. I noticed then some of our mob waving to me about 30 yards away and I drove over to them. I heard the whistle of a shell and heard it explode. My pals said, "Just look where that bloody thing landed!" It was right where I had stopped my truck, where the two infantrymen were. Now both were lying dead.'

S. J. Ayckbourne of the 2nd Rifle Brigade had a more frightening escape. 'There were three of us in a Bren gun carrier, and we were in the middle of no man's land. Suddenly, a Jerry SP (self-propelled gun) came up over the hill. He had a very large 75mm gun, and he pointed it at us for well over twenty minutes. Then suddenly he backed away, and once he was down the slope we raced away.'

The artillerymen were exhausted from the effects of the barrage. From 22.00 hours they had been firing almost without pause. For many regiments, once the night's bombardment had finished and the huge piles of empty shell cases had ben cleared away, the orders came that brought them forward into the great moving mass of Eighth Army. Many units, wise in the ways of desert life, had sent off a couple of experienced old sweats who searched around until they had found a clean piece of desert in the area to which their batteries had been allotted, and had had it swept for mines and marked out for their own unit. 'A clean piece of desert' seems an odd phrase, but there were quite large strips of ground that were foul. Those that had been staging points or even semi-permanent sites might very well contain filled-in latrines or rubbish pits with the refuse of one or the other armies that had passed that way. Then there were the dead. Gunner Leveridge of the 7th Medium Regiment recalled the well-manicured hand of an Italian officer projecting through the sand and another dead Italian officer, immaculately dressed and lying face down in a waterhole.

If one looked, the dead could be seen everywhere. D. F. W. Smith of the 69th Medium Regiment looked into one Italian tank and saw the skeletons of two Italians. In other tanks there were the bodies of men who had been caught before they could escape from the vehicle, burned black and shrunken. To many, this was a ghastly way to go. 'If I had to get killed, I prayed it would be quick. Nothing lingering or frightening. Just a bang and that's that.' Gunner Wink recalled, 'Near to where we were firing at El Alamein there was a burnt-out tank still smouldering. One of ours. There were four bodies that had been thrown out. Two with no legs and arms. The tank had had a direct hit on the petrol tank. Our troop commander asked me to bury them, as there were millions of flies on them.' It was not surprising that so many of the British armoured fighting vehicles blazed like torches. The American machines were fitted with engines that ran on aeroplane fuel, and a white-hot armour-piercing shell striking the petrol supply would send them up in seconds. 'As I watched from my slit trench, the tank was hit in the wheels and slewed round. Its turret began to swing round and then it suddenly shook and vibrated. Then there was a loud explosion and flames burst through the hatch like a blow-torch. All I could think of was "Christ help those poor sods inside it." I tell you, I was very glad I was below ground. Those things were absolute death traps.'

James Smith, Gunner in a light anti-aircraft unit, saw just such an incident. 'I was in a battery attached to the KRRC. The fighting was terrifying. There were rifle shots to the left and right of you and men being bayoneted at the side of you. A German hand grenade exploded in an ammo truck belonging to the KRRC. In the cab there were two young soldiers who couldn't get out. We could not get close enough to get them out. All we could hear above the noise were the cries of those two soldiers, and they were screaming, "Mother, Mother, help me! They've got me! Mother!"'

There were others who could not bear the strain of the shocking sights that they had to see and the fear of sudden and horrible death. In Rifleman Suckling's unit there was 'one chap, bomb happy, who every time he saw anything flying would run across the area shouting, "Collapse your bivvy's, they're on you!" We lost many a brew over him. To him, anything that flew was an enemy plane.'

Battle exhaustion was not an exceptional phenomenon. Its causes were strain, fear and tiredness. There were men who fought day after day on tea and cigarettes and laagered at night sleeping immediately and soundly as soon as they lay down. With a primitive sense, they would waken at the first sound of the wireless chattering. Infantrymen, exhausted and on only an hour's sleep, would wake, instantly alert, at the whispered order, 'Stand to', and the muscle-weary Gunners could sleep through thundering barrages. According to the former lieutenant of the South Notts Hussars, RHA, D. Elliott, M.C., 'After two days I could sleep through any noise except the executive command "Take Post!".' In Vincent Knowles's battery of the RHA there was a system. 'One man on stag per gun with a round in the piece. If the Verey lights were fired in a specific sequence, the gun had to be fired. The peculiar thing was that, although the guns were firing all the time, we were able to sleep until our own gun was fired. Then it was "Take to your post!".' The battery of Sergeant Wilson, formerly of the 58th Sussex Field Regiment in the 44th Division, was kept awake by a Gunner who went round each gun pit 'so that we would be ready to fire. When the order came, every gun fired as one. The barrage that followed left us choking with cordite fumes. We had no water to drink and began coughing and spitting, as round after round was fired. Suddenly, above the smell and noise, the troop cook appeared with a bucket of tea. Never has tea tasted so good.

He asked if he could fire a shell, and when I gave the order he pulled the lever. He had played his part in firing the barrage.'

This, then, was 24 October, the second day of the El Alamein offensive. The ordinary soldier did not know whether he was on his objective or not. All he knew was that he had walked a long way westwards during the night and that wherever he was it was dangerous and noisy. The whole army had in fact taken a huge pace westwards, but it had not been a big enough step, and for the generals the first night of Operation 'Lightfoot' had not been the complete success for which they had planned. Down in XIII Corps area the attacks to seize Himeimat and to pass the armour through the deep minefields of 'January' and 'February' had failed, but the principal objective, to hold the 21st Panzer and the Ariete Divisions in the south, had been successful. Both enemy armoured divisions were still in place and had not been moved northwards. In XXX Corps sector about 80 percent of the ground it had been planned to capture had been taken, but the armour had not gained the 'Pierson' bound and was held immobile. At several places the infantry had not succeeded in reaching the 'Oxalic' line, and where they had failed the Sappers had been unable to sweep a passage through the enemy minefields.

There had been too many mines and too little time to clear them. The opposition had been too strong. The men of Panzerarmee had not been crushed even by the biggest British barrage since 1918, but resiliently had sprung back to man the guns and to defend their positions. Then, as always, the speed of German reaction had been swift. Even with Rommel absent and its temporary commander, Georg Stumme, missing, the German staff officers had pulled the front together and were sealing off the British penetrations with infantry and artillery fire. Already, in front of that area in which it was clear that Eighth Army intended to make its break-out, German anti-tank guns were being brought into positions drilled out of the solid rock weeks before, and the infantry had begun to occupy concreted strongpoints that Rommel had helped to design. Engineer troops were laying mines in pre-dug holes — an operation not without danger, as witness an accident in which a great number of the 33rd Engineer Regiment were killed and wounded, which was recorded in the Afrika Korps War Diary.

Reviewing the fortunes of the divisions from north to south, it can be seen that the 'Chinese' attacks by the 24th Australian Brigade had successfully diverted the enemy's attention and had allowed the 26th Brigade to advance and gain its objectives, thus holding firm the open flank. From the 26th Brigade front-line, which was on the 'Oxalic' position — XXX Corps objective — the line swung sharply south-east where the 20th Brigade had failed to reach the objective. The right flank of the 51st Highland Division conformed to the sweep back of the Australian line, but then its left wing swept forward again and touched the objective line. This was in the south of the Highland

Division's sector where the 7th Black Watch had taken the strong-point named 'Kirkcaldy' and had gone on to pass beyond the 'Blue' line. The New Zealand Brigades were in front of Miteiriya Ridge with the 21st Battalion of the right flank brigade and the 26th Battalion on the left firmly in position. Only on the division's deep left flank did the line swing back to conform with the line of the South African Division. (It will be recalled that the right brigade of the Union Division had struck a massive German defensive complex, and that uncaptured position was still holding up the South African advance.)

Since the objective line had not been gained at the junction of 9th Australian and 51st Highland Division, there was no exit to the corridor along which the 1st Armoured was now strung out and enduring the bombardment of artillery and aircraft. The 10th Armoured Division had indeed cleared its corridor, but it had been halted by the onset of daylight before its regiments could reach the 'Pierson' bound. It was a bitter disappointment. With all the great superiority in weapons, with assured supplies and armed with accurate knowledge of the intentions of Panzerarmee, the British blow had still been insufficient to smash through and rout the enemy. A second attempt would have to be made. But for the 24th it would be a matter of reorganization, of gathering together scattered units and expanding corridors in the minefields.

On the Axis side, the dawn of the 24th found Panzerarmee without its leader. The Panzerarmee War Diary in its final paragraphs recorded, 'The Deputy Supreme Commander and the Panzerarmee Signals Officer set out at 08.30 hours to check the enemy penetrations near mine box L. The Deputy Supreme Commander has been missing since 09.30 hours. The General Officer Commanding Afrika Korps has taken over command. The Supreme Command of the Armed Forces (OKW) demands information and advice as to whether Rommel should return to Africa.' For, on 23 September, Rommel had flown home to Germany in poor health. When Operation 'Lightfoot' opened, he was on the Semmering in Austria, convalescing. His position as Supreme Commander of the Panzerarmee had been taken by General Georg Stumme, a specialist in armoured warfare who had been brought from Russia. The destruction of the German communications network as a result of the British barrage had forced commanders to go forward so as to gain a clear picture by personal reconnaissance in the front-line. What had happened to Stumme is uncertain, but the vehicle in which he was travelling was fired upon and in the fire-fight Stumme suffered a fatal heart attack. The Axis forces were bereft of their commander early on in the battle, but smoothly the next senior officer took over — another panzer general, von Thoma — and carried out the standard German Army riposte to an enemy thrust. The 15th Panzer Division was ordered to counterattack.

So the British, when faced with a setback, reorganized and planned for a continuation of the failed attack along exactly the same lines. The

Axis, faced with the loss of their FDL, decided on counterattacks to win back the old front-line. Plus ça change. . . .

*   *   *

The volume of the Official History of the Second World War that deals with the Battle of El Alamein says that very little happened on the ground during 24 October and that the principal activity was in the air. Such an assessment will not have been shared by those on the ground who were still lifting mines under fire; by those who were exchanging shots in tank-versus-tank duels; who had to carry out infantry attacks against well sited and courageously defended strong-points; nor by those others who, in a multitude of ways, were engaged in fighting, which grew in intensity with every hour.

The highest level of command was determined that the initiative that Eighth Army held must not be lost. Where a given objective had not been gained, attacks would be renewed to achieve it. During 24 October and the days succeeding it, operations by XXX Corps were to be a matter of aligning units in order to accomplish the supreme commander's plan. This meant that the northerly corridor through the enemy's minefields had to be cleared so as to allow the 1st Armoured Division to pass through and to occupy the 'Pierson' line. As we have seen, the southerly corridor had in fact been opened, but the tanks of the 10th Armoured Division had not crossed Miteiriya Ridge and thus had not advanced to 'Pierson'.

The 'crumbling' stage of Montgomery's plan was now to be under-taken, and in order for it to begin in XXX Corps sector it was vital that the armour was well forward. In that way the tank regiments could protect the New Zealand units that had been ordered to drive south-westward from Miteiriya Ridge. It was up to the armour to advance and to gain its targets quickly. In discussions with his senior commanders, Montgomery left the commander of X Corps in no doubt that the armour must get forward and that losses would have to be accepted.

XIII CORPS

The operations of XIII Corps, in the south, were destined to be drastic-ally reduced. It will be remembered that its operations were subordinate to those of XXX Corps and that the main task of XIII Corps was to hold two Axis armoured divisions in the south. Its commander had also to ensure that its own tank formation, the 7th Armoured Division, did not become involved in heavy fighting, but was retained 'an armoured division in being', to undertake whatever employment the army commander found it. However, the fighting that took place in the southern half of Eighth Army's battle-line during 23 and 24 October led to the fear that the 7th Armoured Division might suffer heavy losses. The corps commander reduced the scale of its operations. But without armoured back-up the infantry could not fight a modern battle, and slowly XIII Corps activities were run down and units withdrawn to reinforce XXX Corps. But that is to anticipate events. . . .

The task was to clear the ground so that the 'February' minefield could be gapped, and activity in the south was devoted to that end. Shortly after breakfast — a sketchy affair eaten in the lee of vehicles by the more adventurous and in the tank itself by those who were not — the British artillery opened up on the Italian FDLs and, under cover of the bombardment, Sappers of the mineclearing detachments went forward to continue clearing 'February'. For hour after hour the work went on. The teams were relieved at half-hourly intervals and many of the mentally exhausted Engineers lay where they were and fell instantly asleep, oblivious to the gunfire, the bombs and the bullets. 'It was a difficult day to describe. There was so much noise and dust and confusion. As a runner I was sent back to brigade HQ and stopped while the shelling was going on. Jerry was flinging over some really heavy stuff. There were some Sappers near me and I asked them why they were prodding with bayonets. We had been told of the new equipment that had been sent out to the desert to detect mines. They told me that none of the mechanized gadgets worked well. They had had tanks that smashed chains onto the desert to explode the mines. All that happened was that the chains flung the mines onto the tanks and that Jerry barbed wire got caught up in the drums. Even the detectors were not much cop. So it was back to bayonets.'

For one trooper in 44th Recce, the day ended, as it had for so many others, in pain. 'I rode up to the start line on the top of a tank,' recalled former Trooper Jakes, 'along a desert track that had a double bend in it where it passed through two low hills. There were the splattered remains of men, blown at the rock face, where some poor devils had been too near a shell burst. In the open there was a truck 'brewing up' and it was in our path, highlighting each movement of ours to the enemy. As we approached a minefield the great barrage opened, and it was as though the greatest firework display of all time was flashing all along the line as far as the eye could see. Whoever laid out that minefield knew what he was doing. He had straddled a ridge with it so that to cross it you became a sitting duck on the skyline. A mortar bomb fell on our Bren gun and one of my friends, a corporal, lost part of the top of his skull. I put on a shell dressing and tied it under his chin like a bonnet. It must have been about that time that a metal fragment went through my hip, escaping through the left buttock, but I felt nothing at the time. I half rose, ready to dash forward, when I felt a frightful searing pain in my leg, or rather two pains, one when the bullet went in at the front and one when it emerged at the back. This bullet fell out of my hose top when I was being cleaned up at the dressing station.

197

'In no time I felt a big bang on my right thigh as a red-hot piece of shrapnel hit a glancing blow. After those experiences I decided to lay low awhile, and then made my way back. Hours later, after our morphia 'shot', a great many of us wounded were lying out on the sand and the firing had almost fizzled out. We had great difficulty in getting the American volunteer ambulance drivers to get us away. Every time a shell passed overhead, which was not all that often, they took flight. In all fairness, I must say that they had probably never heard a shot fired in anger. A sniper was installed in a foxhole somewhere nearby and more than one poor lad met his death. From now on, for me, the battle was over, and after a very rough ride we arrived at the main dressing station.'

With daylight the enemy's fire increased both in tempo and in accuracy, and the vehicles of the armoured brigade had to be moved from point to point to avoid anti-tank guns whose solid shot struck repeatedly against the armoured plates, practically concussing the crews at every impact. The gunners of the Folgore Division may not have been numerous, but they made up in aggression for the deficiencies they suffered in manpower and equipment. Other Italian units may have lacked the sticking power of the paratroops but the men of Folgore were good and they knew it. Keen, determined and skilful, they were the best Italian formation on the strength of Panzerarmee, and their attitude stiffened the resolve of the units around them. Resistance to the advance of the British armour was firm and unshaken wherever they were.

Throughout the long day the armoured fighting vehicles of the 7th Armoured Division and their infantry support, together with the infantry battalions of the 44th Division, lay out in the open under the observation of enemy posts on the high ground. The attempt by French infantry to seize Himeimat had met and had been repulsed by the crack German armoured battle group 'Kiel'. The French did not gain their objectives. There was little that the soldiers of XIII Corps could do but wait for darkness to fall so that they could attempt once again to force the armour into the open.

With the night, the front of XIII Corps awoke and two battalions of the Queen's went in under a barrage to carry the attack through the 'February' field. The depth of their thrust was just over 1½ miles, and as they consolidated on the objective — a map reference beyond the western edge of 'February' — it was clear that they were in a salient and under fire from three sides. The battalions suffered heavily, and one vicious burst of shelling caused heavy casualties to one battalion's headquarters company. The Sappers accompanying the Queen's were equal to the occasion. 'It was my first real battle', J. W. Harris, formerly of the 21st Field Squadron, RE, in the 7th Armoured Division, recalled. 'Our unit's task was to open gaps in the minefield. On the second night of battle I was ordered to take over a Bren gun carrier belonging to the Queen's Regiment. I followed a flail tank with a team of Sappers on board. Soon they were at work lifting mines and marking out clear lanes with wide, white tape. The Germans and Italians let fly at the flail tank with everything they had. I was then told to take a crowd of Queen's infantry walking wounded to a forward aid post, and drove back with them all hanging over the carrier. I had to find my way back through the dark and the thick choking smoke. To do this I had to pass through our own advancing tanks. It was a nightmare drive, and I was almost run down by our own tanks a few times. After finding the aid post and handing them over to the medical orderlies, I stopped for a minute or two for a cigarette and to relax a bit: it was then I discovered how scared and tired I was. Still soaked in sweat, I started back to find my Sappers, and found them just as it was getting light, crouched near the top of a low rise. Being inexperienced at that time, I drove too high up the rise and drew heavy machine-gun fire, which nearly blew off my head. Stuck on the dashboard of the carrier was a photo of a nice young woman, presumably the original driver's wife or sweetheart. I glanced at this from time to time throughout the ordeal. It seemed to be the only real thing in a bad dream, and I drew comfort from it.'

In the dark and dust of the night of 24/25 October, there was a great deal of confusion, and an error occurred of the sort that was to be repeated during future operations by XXX Corps: this was due to the inability of the men on the ground to locate their positions with total accuracy. In XIII Corps during that night, a difference of opinion on map-reading led to the assault lanes of the Queen's and of the Sappers to follow different directions. This meant that between the two tracks there lay pockets of determined enemy, who brought the leading troops under severe fire. The British paid heavily for their error. The Panzerarmee also brought forward fresh batteries of field and anti-tank guns to support the men in the strongpoints, and the hail of fire that these newly arrived weapons brought down smashed the armoured regiments as they strove to break out of the corridors. One German tactic was to fire smoke at a minefield exit so that the vehicles of the armoured brigade were silhouetted and formed perfect targets as they emerged from the gap. Lashed by the furious gunfire, the brigade advance halted to seek their tormentors, but as the tanks stood on the open desert they were shot to pieces. In the County of London Yeomanry, 'C' Squadron was destroyed in minutes, while most of 'B' Squadron and regimental headquarters were badly hit. In desperate attempts to deploy and to escape the punishing fire of the anti-tank guns, some vehicles ran onto scattered Teller mines and were disabled. Within minutes the strength of the CLY squadrons had been reduced to those of troops, as tracer shells and armour-piercing shot screeched across the battlefield. The area to the west of the 'February' minefield was dotted with vehicles gushing dull red flames, and columns of smoke marked the location of the burning tanks of the 22nd Armoured Brigade.

A. J. Medlar, then a tank crewman in the 5th Royal Tank Regiment, a unit with a high proportion of regular soldiers, recalled earlier battles where British 2pdr shot had bounced off the German armour, and contrasted those actions with the terrible power of the German anti-tank guns. How frightening it was to be under fire from German guns is remembered all too clearly by many of those who were in Eighth Army's fighting vehicles. 'The solid-shot shells of the 88s coming at you were a white streak. So was that of the Russian 7.62, but the 5cm PAK shell glowed red like tracer. Not that you really registered it consciously. By the time you had seen it, the shell had flashed past. The 88 travelled at thousands of feet per second — it was just a flash and a bang if it hit. The intelligence bulletins put out by Eighth Army said that tank crews tended to claim falsely that they had been fired on by 88s. None of us was in any doubt when we were under fire that it was 88s we were up against. Being hit was a nightmare experience. The Grants and the early Shermans ran on high-powered aircraft fuel. It was dangerous stuff — highly inflammable. A white-hot shell entering into the vehicle turned it into a sort of fire-bomb. You see, all our vehicles carried extra tanks on the outside of the turret. It would almost be true to say that when they were hit the American tanks blew up. They were horrifying sights, and I hated the booming sound as they went up. Luckily, both types of US machine were well armoured. I never saw it myself, but I was told that when an 88 struck the energy that was propelling the shot would be converted into heat, so that the shell literally burnt its way through the armour. Apparently, at the point of impact the plate would quickly turn bright cherry red and then turn white hot. Then the shell would come through into the fighting compartment. When you were hit then it was PDQ to get out. Hitting a Teller mine was less dangerous but the dust that then flew about was choking, and every protruding part of the vehicle seemed to have the edge of a cut-throat razor.'

Shattered by the appalling losses, the CLY was pulled back to the eastern side of 'February' and into the open ground between the mine-fields. There the remnants of the squadrons were reorganized. The Yeomanry now had only 26 'runners' left, and of that small number nineteen had only the 2pdr as main armament. From these vehicles a single squadron and a headquarters detachment were formed.

The confined space between the two minefields was now seriously congested with the vehicles of the armoured brigade as well as the other trucks and lorries that were trying to make their way forward with supplies and reinforcements. Inevitably, such concentrations of vehicles attracted the attention of the German and Italian artillery. Lorries blazed in the minefields and in the ground between them. 'In a semi-circle of vision, the eye could see little but those terrible black candles of smoke that marked another burning tank.'

Being out of the firing line did not mean to be inactive, and late in the afternoon the remaining tanks of the CLY were brought forward and swung in an arc southwards to face Himeimat, to give support to yet another attempt by the French to seize that eminence. Then there was a further change of direction to face westwards to guard the minefield gaps.

The casualties that had been suffered by the armour of the 7th Division had reduced its strength considerably, and the corps commander, mindful of Montgomery's orders to keep the 7th Armoured as a division in being, gave instructions for the regiments to be withdrawn east of the minefields, leaving the infantry in position. After dark the Queen's battalions, reduced by the terrible casualties they had suffered, were relieved by the units of the Kent brigade. The Queen's were then reorganized and reinforced. They were, on 1 November, to be taken onto the strength of the 7th Armoured Division as that formation's infantry component, beginning a partnership that was to continue until the division entered Berlin in 1945.

Operations in the southern part of the line were run down, the only exception being an attack in the night of the 25th/26th by the 50th Tyne Tees Division on the Munassib Depression. The XIII Corps had thus far succeeded in its principal task, and the 21st Panzer and Ariete Divisions were still held on its front; but German intelligence officers were quick to sense the slackening in XIII Corps effort. Both Folgore and Ramcke signalled their confidence that they could hold, unaided, the British attacks on their sectors: indeed, the tenor of Panzerarmee's sitrep at midday on the 24th was a confident one. For the future, XIII Corps was to be the source of manpower from which XXX Corps would draw the units it needed to carry out its own operations. And there was ample need for such a milch cow. Losses to the British infantry had been high, and there were already signs that the troops were becoming tired. Montgomery decided to create a reserve that would produce fresh units, and he began to withdraw certain formations from the line; when the time came for a new hard-hitting blow, then his refreshed reserve would supply it.

XXX CORPS

All along the front, the enemy had not remained inactive. The Panzerarmee's assessment of the situation was that the British thrusts had been generally held all along the line, although there had been penetrations at some places. Local attacks would clear these. At 06.15 hours, the Afrika Korps was ordered to mount a series of assaults against the penetrations by XXX Corps, using elements from the 15th Panzer and Littorio Divisions, both of which had moved nearer to the front during the night. According to Panzerarmee War Diary, the counterattack by its sub-units recaptured many areas of the original front-line that had been lost, but on other sectors British tank and anti-tank gunfire stopped the Axis assaults. The diary also reported that some Italian troops had abandoned their positions and that panzergrenadier detachments had needed to be put in to close the gaps. The diary then records the very high losses in material that had been suffered. From the tenor of the sentences, it is clear that the Germans realized very clearly that this was to be a battle of attrition.

The Panzerarmee's counterattacks came in against the 40th RTR, supporting the Australian Division, and post-battle reports state that the panzers had carried out a fire and movement advance with the armour working forward slowly, covered by a bombardment laid down by 88s. The Australian reports speak of the Bostons, which had been called up to bomb the German armour and artillery, but which dropped their loads on their own troops. To the physical losses suffered in the Axis counteroffensive and the morale blows caused by the Bostons' error, there was the additional misery of the Khamseen, which blew all morning. 'By and large, the 24th was a miserable day, and when the dust storm had blown itself out we could see on our side of the line our burning tanks.' One of the few inspiring sights for the Australian troops was the passage of the regiments of the 10th Armoured Division on their way to carry out the next stage of Montgomery's plan.

The sector of front held by the 51st Division needed a certain amount of tidying up, but the Highlanders were frustrated in carrying out the attacks were intended to bring them onto the 'Oxalic' objective by the counter-offensive of the 15th Panzer Division. This brought unpleasant surprises for both sides — for the British, to be attacked by an enemy they thought to be smashed; for the panzer men, to encounter the Shermans and the Priest self-propelled machines. The panzer attacks on the 51st Highland sector were intercepted by the 2nd Armoured Brigade, one of whose regiments, the 10th Hussars, reported that among the vehicles engaged were Panzer IV Specials, and that these had been fired upon with effect at distances up to 3,000 yards. On other sectors of the front, and to the end that objectives uncaptured on the first night of Operation 'Lightfoot' were to be taken, the minefield task force of the 1st Armoured Division was put in during daylight. The Sappers pushed forward to such effect that by evening most of the 'Oxalic' line between the 51st and the Australian Divisions had been reached. There were, however, still obstinate pockets of resistance in the Highlanders' area, which were to hold out for several days.

Behind the task force, the 2nd Armoured Brigade advanced to the crest of Miteiriya Ridge, not without casualties from undetected mines or from the armour-piercing shells that whizzed across the crest. By late in the afternoon the tank regiments had cleared the minefield gaps and were spread out some way in front of Kidney Ridge. There they were attacked, shortly before sundown, by the 15th Panzer Division, whose battalions came in with the sun behind them. The battle was fought out over ground already occupied by the units of the Highland

Division. The Scottish infantry, unable to intervene in this clash of armour, could only lie in their slit trenches enduring the storm of shells and bullets that criss-crossed the battlefield. At last light the panzers pulled back. The day had gone to the British, whose demolition teams then went out to destroy the German vehicles lying on the brigade front. The 15th Panzer Division had lost 26 machines in this particular attack — vehicles it could not afford to lose.

The 10th Armoured Division, the 24th Armoured Brigade on its right, the 8th Brigade on its left (and with the added support of the 9th Armoured Brigade to the far left), was ordered to advance, descend the slight decline of Miteiriya Ridge, cross the valley and ascend the low Wishka Ridge. The attack would go in after dark and under a heavy barrage, accompanied by a night bombing programme of the RAF upon ground targets.

Right from the start, at 22.00 hours, the 10th Division's advance went wrong. The enemy was no more the surprised and overwhelmed foe of 23 October, but a vigorously reacting opponent who knew that the British advance had to be made across Miteiriya Ridge and had deployed his anti-tank guns to counter it. The number and depth of the minefields on Miteiriya Ridge were greater than had been believed, and the lifting teams were under heavy and concentrated fire from the start of the attack. Enemy opposition was not confined to artillery fire, but included direct attacks upon the Sappers by enemy infantry. The standard defensive weapons of Panzerarmee had become the anti-tank gun and the mine. Mines — 'silent soldiers', as they were known in the German Army — required little effort to put down and could be laid to produce strategic results. A handful of determined and skilful Engineers with a lorryload of 'silent soldiers' could halt a complete armoured division or force its vehicles into channels where anti-tank guns could kill them.

It was the slowness with which the minefields were being gapped that constrained the British armour within the confines of the narrow channels. It was while units were thus waiting in a narrow corridor that a string of bombs, dropped by a Luftwaffe night bomber, hit and set fire to the supply lorries of the Sherwood Rangers. The vehicles, loaded with petrol and shells, burnt fiercely, attracting the attention of the German gunners and other aircraft whose crews could see as clearly and as if it were day the long columns of guns, lorries and tanks that were held fast in the corridors. The road forward was blocked. The chaos caused by the bombing not only prevented the 8th Armoured Brigade from following the barrage and thus taking advantage of its cover, but provoked a crisis that seemed to Montgomery to indicate a lack of moral fibre in the senior commanders of the armoured force. Reduced to simple terms, the role that Montgomery had given to the tanks for Operation 'Lightfoot', was for them to advance, if necessary in broad daylight, against successive lines of guns. Such an action was, to the corps commander and his immediate subordinates, the generals

203

commanding 1st and 10th Armoured Divisions, a total misuse of armour. It can, therefore, be no wonder that they lacked confidence in the army commander's plan. Their known scepticism was one reason why Montgomery had spoken earlier to X Corps commander stressing that the armour must get forward even if it suffered casualties.

In the early hours of the morning of the 25th, it seemed to the brigadier commanding the 8th Armoured Brigade that his regiments would be caught by daylight, undeployed and prime targets for the Panzerarmee's guns. He expressed his fear to General Gatehouse, commander of the 10th Armoured Division, who at first rejected the request that the attack be cancelled. But then Gatehouse began to have doubts about the feasibility of Montgomery's plan. His proposal to pull the armour back behind Miteiriya Ridge was passed back to Eighth Army headquarters, where the Chief of Staff woke Montgomery and asked for a decision. At a conference called for 03.30 hours, General Lumsden, commanding X Corps, was told that the armour would either get forward or new commanders would be found to ensure that it did. There was to be no change in the plan and the armour *would* succeed.

Some tank regiments had in fact got forward and had linked, so that elements of both armoured divisions were deployed in front of the minefield gaps inciting the Axis armour to attack them. But along other parts of the ridge the story was a different one. The night that had begun badly for the 8th Armoured Division, with the loss of so many soft-skin vehicles of the Sherwood Rangers, worsened. Initially, of its three armoured regiments, only the Staffordshire Yeomanry had crossed Miteiriya Ridge and the desert floor. There the squadrons halted and deployed at the foot of Wishka Ridge, enduring a hurricane of fire. The Staffordshire squadrons were joined by detachments of the 3rd RTR, and together they advanced up the slight incline of Wishka. The opening stages of the advance were uneventful, but then fire was opened upon the tanks by 88s positioned on both flanks and at close range. Shermans and Grants began to burn, and regimental headquarters of the Yeomanry ordered its squadrons to pull back. That movement took back with it other parts of the brigade.

The shattered regiments rallied on the reverse slope of Miteiriya Ridge, and there they held the line against the forceful attacks of the panzer divisions, which came in on that day and on succeeding ones. The 9th Brigade sat out all day forward of Miteiriya Ridge and was then pulled back. The British armour on the left of the line was back on the positions from which it had advanced. Just as in the XIII Corps area, the sector of XXX Corps lining Miteiriya Ridge now went over to the defensive. Operation 'Lightfoot' was at an end. It was time for a fresh move. First there would have to be a period of reorganization. The 10th Armoured Division was taken out of the line and the 24th Armoured Brigade passed under the command of the 1st Armoured Division.

With the scale of operations along Miteiriya Ridge now slackening, the Eighth Army commander swung the main effort from the 'crumbling' operations by the New Zealanders to the northern sector, where the Australians held post. He ordered them to undertake a series of attacks against the enemy formation that was defending the coastal sector of the Axis front. There were to be three separate assaults, and their principal intent was to hold the attention of Panzerarmee's commander by pretending that Eighth Army's principal effort was to be made along the coast road. The immediate objective of the first attack was to seize Point 29, a dominant hill on the Australian's northern front. A second target was the heavily fortified defensive complex known as 'Thompson's Post', slightly to the east of Point 29. Both places were bastions of the northern salient, which was held by grenadiers of the 164th Division.

Rommel returned to Africa during the 25th, and according to the war diary took up post again at 20.30 hours. A series of briefings from his senior lieutenants illuminated Panzerarmee's situation. There was the usual fuel shortage, which would be temporarily alleviated by the arrival of tankers the next day. The immediate supplies of fuel were three issues (one issue being the equivalent of about 60 miles of driving). One of the issues was held at Benghazi. Experts at OKW had considered that for a formation of the size that Rommel commanded, and undertaking the type of operation in which he was engaged, the minimum requirement of fuel would be 30 issues. So far as the new British offensive was concerned, its ground attacks had lost impetus, although activity by the RAF persisted unabated. The British ground forces had lost heavily, but it was certain that they would continue the assault and that the most likely area in which this would be made was to the north of Ruweisat Ridge. The leaders of Panzerarmee were confident they could hold, but Rommel's private feelings were less optimistic. In a letter he was to write to his wife, he described the fight as uneven. 'We are being suffocated by the enemy's superiority', he wrote. 'I am struggling to retain at least part of my army. I am racking my brains to find a solution, to find some way that the soldiers can escape from the terrible situation. . . .'

The Panzerarmee's sitrep on the 25th reported only 81 German 'runners', although the Italians had 197 tanks fit for action. Rommel knew that he was bound to lose any battle of attrition, and he was to write that, 'those two days, the 25th and 26th, decided the outcome of the battle. In that short space of time we lost nearly 200 armoured fighting vehicles. The army had been so battered that there remained nothing it could do but to evade the enemy by moving westwards. . . .' Already in Rommel's mind there was the realization that his hold on the El Alamein position was a tenuous one, and the question was no longer *if* he could be forced to withdraw from it, but *when*.

The situation as he saw it required that he reduce as far as possible all unnecessary movements by his armoured forces. The German defence would be based on anti-tank guns and mines, and the former would be deployed along the most obvious lines of advance. These were the approaches to Wishka Ridge, in front of Kidney Ridge and along the Sidi Abd el Rahman track. Surveying the whole front, he knew — as a result of the reported British reduction of effort in the south — that he had no need to consider any threat from that sector. It was clear that the main British effort would be made in the north, and he considered whether to bring north his two armoured divisions currently facing XIII Corps. The central sector of his line was covered by batteries of guns that could be moved from sector to sector via the Rahman track. He issued his orders. The armour, which had been put into weak and local counterattacks, was to be held back. British armoured attacks were to be halted by artillery fire, chiefly that of anti-tank guns. Only in the area of Point 29, which overlooked the coast road and the railway, was any ground lost to be regained. A heavy panzer counterattack was to be launched to drive back the British bulge, particularly in the northern sector of the line, for that was the sector, so the German leader forecast, where the decisive actions would be fought. Rommel was back and had taken a firm grasp on the battle.

13.

ROMMEL'S LAST TANKER

While on the ground the scale of the fighting had been reduced, air operations continued. On the 27th, one mission was to destroy the chance of the Axis army to fight a mobile battle: the Royal Air Force sank at sea the last remaining tankers bringing fuel for Rommel's panzer force. Petrol was crucial to the Panzerarmee, and the sinking of the tankers was a major factor in forcing Rommel to withdraw from the El Alamein positions. The fuel situation for the Axis troops was so critical that the fate of the Panzerarmee literally hung upon just one ship reaching Tobruk and discharging its cargo. The Panzerarmee War Diary entry for 25 October, includes the sentence, 'if the tanker that is due on the 26th does not arrive, a crisis will develop. The Italian fuel position is already critical. . . .'

The vessel whose arrival was so keenly anticipated was destroyed before it could reach harbour by Ralph Manning, now a retired historian and former Assistant Curator at the Canadian War Museum, but in those days a pilot in No. 42 Torpedo Bomber Squadron. His unit was en route to the Far East, but while in transit through Egypt had been held back to support the RAF effort in Operation 'Lightfoot'. The crews of 42 Squadron that had already arrived in Egypt were then amalgamated with those of 47 Squadron, another unit that flew the torpedo-carrying Beaufort.

Flying such machines in torpedo attacks was a highly skilled business. When the aeroplane was running in to attack, the pilot had to keep it straight and level at a height of 70 feet. The speed had to be exactly 140 knots, and the torpedo had to be released not farther from the target than 2,000 yards and not nearer than 500 yards. Failure to co-ordinate any of these requirements might result in the expensive device plunging to the bottom of the sea, or bouncing in the water and failing to run true, or even of not arming itself in its passage so that it would fail to explode on impact. The task of bringing together all the pre-requisites of height, speed and stability required concentration and bravery of a very high order. It was also such an extremely dangerous job that RAF authorities anticipated a 95 percent replacement of aircrew every three months.

It was, of course, to be expected that the Germans and the Italians would take every possible precaution to ensure that the tanker reached Tobruk safely, by escorting it with ships and aircraft. Through 'Ultra' sources the British authorities knew not only the composition of the convoy but also its route and what its ships were carrying. It was vital that they be sunk. In order to avoid the possibility that 'Ultra' would be compromised, and the flow of highly secret information that had fed the British government since the outbreak of war be lost to them, a cover plan was devised and put into operation. British reconnaissance aircraft would 'discover' the convoy, and the usual naval and air operations would ensure that it was attacked. In this particular instance, 47 Squadron, operating out of its base near Alexandria, would under take the strike.

Manning was the pilot of aircraft Y for Yorker, and his crew was Norman Spark (navigator), Charles Bladen (wireless operator) and Cecil 'Nimmy' Nimerovsky. Command of the amalgamated 42/47 Squadron was invested in Wing Commander Sprague, an officer new to torpedo bombing who relied for advice upon Flight Lieutenant 'Auntie' Gee, a veteran pilot. The crews of 47 Squadron were at Gianaclis, an advanced Coastal Command strike force field, made up according to Manning of 'lots of sand and a few tents'. It was to that dusty aerodrome that four of 42 Squadron's Beauforts were ordered on 24th October, and it was from that place that the torpedo-strike aircraft took off.

Although Operation 'Lightfoot' was in its third day, and even though it was clear that a major offensive was in progress, Manning states that 'no-one had any details [of the Eighth Army's big push] or knew what success the soldiers were having. . . .' Security about the battle was still very tight. But the crews did know of the German intention to run a tanker into Tobruk. The information was 'pukka gen' — it must be, for Air Marshal Tedder, Chief of Mediterranean Air Command, had ordered that the tankers be sunk at all costs. It was to carry out Tedder's orders that the missions were flown. From notes that Ralph Manning made at the time, and which he has since expanded, comes the following account of the raids.

'October 26. Breakfast is just over when Duff comes running down to the Mess to say that 47 Squadron's four crews are wanted in Ops room immediately. Oh, Oh. Looks like a daylight strike. The thought of that makes my stomach contract somewhat!

'Briefing is being done leisurely. Seems as if we have all morning. We are to have a Beaufighter escort, which won't arrive until noon. Seems as if the target is a small MV (motor vessel) of 800 tons which is carrying tins of aviation petrol for Rommel. It is sneaking eastward along the coast for Tobruk. It's going to be very hard to hit that with a torpedo. Why don't they use a low-level bombing attack? Seems as if four Blenheims are to come along with bombs. They certainly want that little ship — apparently it's being escorted by a destroyer. It has been shot up once this morning by Beaufighters. Torpedoes are to be set at six feet.

'Beaufighter pilots are here at last. They are to fly with us at sea level until the target is sighted, then to climb to 1,000 feet to give fighter cover. One is to shoot up the destroyer. That's not right. If just one goes in it's a suicide job. That's what the Beaufighter boys say, but they are told to do as they are ordered. Everything is ready at last. The striking force consists of four torpedo-laden Beauforts, four Blenheims with four 250-pound bombs and six Beaufighters. Take-off time is 13.15 hours.

'We are the last Beaufort off and it is a blind take off. The airdrome is covered with clouds of dust. We are all in the air now and in loose formation. We cross the coast at 100 feet and will do the trip at 50 feet. The sun is bright and the sea is very blue. It's so holiday-like that you are apt to forget you are on a mission of death and destruction. Two hours have gone by, and expectation increases. In a few minutes we will make a landfall near Tobruk and the fun will be on.

'There's a low red coast ahead. We are going in close to the shore. The Beaufighters have climbed up. Black puffs appear in the sky as the Tobruk ack-ack goes into action. Can't see Tobruk — the harbour is around that neck of land. There is a launch or something ahead. Men are standing up waving to us. We are circling it. A Blenheim cuts me off and I have to turn away. Why waste time looking at it on this dangerous coast? Why not go and find our target? Well, we'll circle it too. Norm is taking pictures. A Blenheim goes in to bomb it. We are too close to the shore. I can see machine-gun bullets hitting the water under us.

'Out to sea after the other aircraft. I suppose they will reform and go on. No. They seem to be going back towards Egypt. Not for me to wonder why; we're with them. Company is good when you are in enemy territory. Home at last, and on the good old ground. Somebody comes over and says we still have our torpedo. Of course we have our torpedo. Then he yells that the others have dropped theirs. My God, don't tell me they wasted £2,000 torpedoes on that rowing boat!!!

'I go over to see McKern. He tells me the Wingco dropped so he dropped. I'm irritated, and tell him the Wingco is new to the game and that he (Mac) should have more sense. The torpedo would go under that boat; it wouldn't draw six feet. Mac isn't so sure it is as small as I think. 'Auntie' Gee, when questioned, is evasive about the size of the ship. Damn these people. If they all say it was the ship in their reports, it is going to be embarrassing for me. Thank goodness, Norm took photographs. We will take them over to the photographic section.

Debriefing is over. The old Group Captain seems to think we got the ship, although our crews didn't say so in so many words. Three of the Blenheims didn't bomb because they thought the boat was too small, even for bombing. Still I'm worried. Eight o'clock and the photographs are ready. What a relief. The boat is still as small as I thought it was. Too bad for the Wingco that he 'boobed' on his first trip. No. 39 Squadron will be inclined to sneer, but they can't say much. They have been up here a week, yet when they want any 'ops' done they get the despised 47 Squadron.

'Well, enough excitement for one day. Guess I'll go to bed. Five more of our crews arrived this afternoon.

'October 27. Another bright morning. Something seems to be up, but the Wing Commander says we won't be on it. Our aircraft, Y for Yorker, is due for an inspection and we must take it back to Shandur. Don't know whether to be pleased or not. Figure 'ops' are too dangerous to be fun, but again, if the boys are going out you like to be with them. Will hang around to see them off. Preliminary briefing is over. Now for the 'gen'. The Wing Commander has just leaned over and told me to get ready. The Group Captain has authorized an extension of time on our aircraft. Well here we go!!!

It is another daylight strike off Tobruk. This is getting to be a habit. There is a convoy of two merchant ships; one large, 10,000 tons, and the other small, 900 tons, and a tanker of 4,000 tons with an escort of four destroyers. All available aircraft are to go. That will mean eight of our Beauforts, six Blenheims from the South African squadron and six or seven Beaufighters. Briefing is very much as yesterday. There are at least two Ju 88s guarding the convoy, and it will have protection from shore-based flak as well as being able to call on shore-based fighters. The Group Captain has made a speech in which he says we can definitely play a part in the great battle now waging in the Western Desert. That tanker is carrying fuel for Rommel's tanks and transports, and he is desperately short of oil. We must get it at all costs. The Blenheims can do a diversion by attacking the small merchant vessel with bombs. Plan of attack is to go for the tanker and nothing else. He wishes us good luck.

'The Wing Commander has made a nice little gesture in telling F/Lt ("Auntie") Gee that he can lead the formation. I will be on "Auntie" Gee's immediate left. Out to the aircraft and a quick take-off. Hal Davidson yells "good luck" just before I get into the aircraft. Arnold Feast was over to say goodbye. The squadron is to go out in two hours time to make sure the job is done.

'We are all airborne in a short time and on our way. I try not to think of what it is going to be like at the other end. I have a feeling it is going to be a shaky "do". Two hours later and we make a landfall. The navigation was a little out and we are slightly east of Tobruk. A pity. Jerry will know we are here and it will give him more time to get fighters in the air. We follow the coast to the west. Just past Tobruk we see boats ahead. Is it the convoy? We cut in towards it. There are about twelve boats. They look like power-driven barges — and are they sending out some flak! Up and down and sideways we go. We're not going to be a sitting target. The shore defences have opened up, too, but it is "heavy" flak and not so dangerous. Charlie is firing at the barges with a side gun. Nimmy with a bored voice tells him to save his ammunition as they are too far away. Passed them at last. There was no need to go so close to them, we could tell they were not the target from at least three miles away. On up the coast we go. What is that ahead? Two aircraft circling and it looks like ships below. Oh, oh, we're for it. It must be the convoy. They are hugging the coast. We are about three miles from the shore; they are about a mile offshore. It looks like a small MV and a destroyer, then a large MV and a couple of destroyers. I think I see something further along. At this moment "Auntie" Gee does a steep turn towards the shore and the ships followed by the other aircraft. I pull up sharply and go on. I'm irritated; there is no tanker and since we haven't passed it it must be farther along. I'm also a little scared; fighters are overhead now and we will have to go on alone. Also, if what is ahead isn't the tanker we will have to go back and attack the convoy single-handed.

'Thank God, two of the Blenheims have caught up with us. It is comforting to have some support. Norm has picked up the camera. We are almost abreast of the third ship, and sure enough it is the tanker with one destroyer on its port beam. We turn into it to make our torpedo run. I don't know where the Blenheims are. There is quite a bit of flak from the destroyer. I'm almost in position but the ship realises its danger and is turning towards us spoiling our shot. There is a strong temptation to drop, but it's important to get the tanker. We must be sure, so we will carry on into the land and attack from the other side. The destroyer is turning inside of me, firing all the time. Into land, and now we are coming on the ship from the landward side, as close as we can before dropping. Just enough distance for the torpedo to arm. Seven hundred yards and I push the button. Almost at the same time a Blenheim streaks for the ship; pulls up sharply. The foremast goes. He has cut off his wing. A second Blenheim is across. The first stick of bombs explodes. Out of the corner of my eye I see puffs of white on the destroyer. A Beaufighter had dived on it and given it a burst. So much happens that I'm forgetful of the danger of exploding bombs on the ship. At the last second I pull as hard as I can on the stick and we gain height. A helluv' an explosion and a jar. Then that awful moment when you wonder whether you have motors or not. We are still flying. Half a minute later a shout from Nimmy: "A hit", he yells. A great explosion. I don't hear any more. The intercom is bad. I'm thinking that we have got away with it. Nimmy yells to take more evasive action, there is still flak coming our way. There are aircraft to our port side. We make for them and formate. Soon there is a good party of us and I feel better as we speed out to sea.

'The boys are all talking about the affair. I hear for the first time that a Macchi at a thousand feet was going to attack us at one time and then attacked someone else. Later we are to figure he gave us a brush, because we find one petrol tank is holed and the main spar damaged by a couple of armour-piercing shells. While this talk is going on, a bright flash from the sea catches my eye. I yell to Nimmy, asking what it was. In a shocked voice he tells me that a Blenheim and a Beaufighter have collided, exploded and fallen into the sea. The Wing Commander is now flying on my left and "Auntie" Gee on my right.

There is a great gaping hole in the Wingco's rudder. I wonder what our casualties are. All our aircraft aren't in this formation, but maybe they were separated and are going home on their own.

'Two hours go by and the pink skyline of Alexandria is in sight. We can feel safe at last. As soon as we have landed, we go over to 'ops' room and the story of the attack is sorted out. Hal Davidson and crew were shot up, and crashed immediately after dropping their torpedoes at the small MV. All the other aircraft with the exception of F/O Meechem, F/O Hearne-Phillips and ourselves, dropped at this ship. F/O Meecham dropped at the larger ship. Hearne-Phillips followed the attack on the small MV, but realised it wasn't the tanker and didn't drop, but carried on around to find the tanker. A cannon shell came through the fuselage and pierced the fuse box, shorting the whole electrical system, and the torpedo fell off. Damned bad luck.

'Results weren't observed from that attack, but both McKern and "Auntie" Gee saw our torpedo run and hit. Our losses were five aircraft among the Blenheims and Beauforts. One Blenheim lost when attacking the small MV, another on the tanker and another in the crash with the Beaufort. We lost Hal Davidson and it was Garrioch who was in the collision. Very sad indeed; it was the first "ops" trip for both of them. The surviving Blenheim of the two that came with us was piloted by Major Pidsley. They came along with us to draw the flak from the destroyer. It take guts, say I. In a few days time he is to be awarded the D.S.O. for this "do".

'In the evening, 39 Squadron come back. They only went out as far as the barges. Three of them dropped torpedoes on them — which would be futile. The Wellington squadron is sending out a torpedo striking force. They will be doing the trip there in daylight, which they don't like. Good luck to them.

'October 28th. Big topic of conversation is still yesterday's strike. The Wellington boys last night found the convoy. The small MV was missing; the big MV was stationary, and farther east was the red glow which was all that was left of the tanker. They hit the big MV with two torpedoes and it went sky high. They only lost one aircraft.'

14.

THE 'SNIPE' ACTION

27 OCTOBER

26 and 27 October were days of confusion and sudden alarms. For the Germans, the 27th was to see the halting of their counterattack aimed at driving the British back. For the British, the 27th was the day during which an infantry battalion of a motorized brigade demonstrated how, with firm control and armed with effective anti-tank guns, it could defeat German armour. This unit was the 2nd Battalion, The Rifle Brigade, one of the three battalions of the 7th Motor Brigade in the 1st Armoured Division. One role of such units in armoured divisions was to form a screen to protect the tanks, and for that task each battalion had its own 6pdr anti-tank gun detachment. In addition to that group on the 2nd Battalion's establishment during the battle there were Gunners of the 239th Battery of the 76th Anti-Tank Regiment together with Sappers of the 7th Field Squadron, Royal Engineers. A second duty of motorized battalions was to be light and mobile, carrying out reconnaissance duties ahead of the armour, so the infantry were carried in Bren gun carriers or light lorries. These infantry, organized into three motor companies, were backed by a platoon of Vickers machine-gunners and a 3-inch mortar platoon. There was a higher than usual establishment of wireless sets distributed throughout the battalion. Although low in numerical strength, a motorized battalion was a unit of highly-trained specialists controlling a tremendous firepower.

For the opening nights of Operation 'Lightfoot', the 2nd Battalion had formed part of the minefield task force of the 1st Armoured Division (and we have seen Rifleman Suckling in his role as lamp-lighter during that stage of the battle). The three motor companies of the battalion had each been allotted to defend the gapping Sappers — 'A' Company had been put in on the Australian sector, 'B' and 'C' were on that of the Highland Division. From last light on the 23rd to last light on the 24th, the riflemen had been on minefield duties, and then they had been taken away and put onto traffic control to direct the passage of the 2nd Armoured Brigade. It was these men and the other battalions of the 7th Motor Brigade, exhausted from days and nights on duty, to whom was given the job of capturing two important features that lay in front of the 1st Armoured Division.

Montgomery's orders for the 26th had directed that divisions were to work towards their 'Oxalic' line objectives, and had included instructions for X Corps to gain ground to the west and to the north-west. It was in pursuit of those orders that the units of the 7th Motor Brigade went in to capture the positions codenamed 'Snipe' and 'Woodcock', both of which formed part of a larger feature, Kidney Ridge. Since these were all still in enemy hands, the execution of Montgomery's orders would involve the battalions in a fast advance through enemy-held territory, the seizure of the two strong-points and the determination to hold them until relieved. That relief would come when the armoured brigades of the 1st Armoured Division moved forward.

Not for the first time in Operation 'Lightfoot', nor indeed for the last time, was the problem of pinpointing one's exact location to bedevil attack plans, although it is a consolation to know that this was a problem that also affected the Axis troops. This problem of imprecise location was to cause the most acute problems during the 2nd Battalion's attack. The feature known to the British as Kidney Ridge had gained its name from the shape of its contour line on War Office maps. But the ridge itself was so undistinguished a feature that the British official history states that opinions differed widely over where the ridge was actually located — and even whether it was a ridge or not. Thus, units had been, and were in future to be, sent in against some low and unremarkable elevation whose precise location was a matter of conjecture and dispute.

Of the two objectives of the 7th Brigade assault, 'Woodcock' (target for the 2nd Battalion, The King's Royal Rifle Corps) lay about a mile to the north-west of Kidney Ridge and 'Snipe' (the objective of the 2nd Battalion, The Rifle Brigade) was about a mile to the south-west. The 7th Battalion of the Rifle Brigade was held in reserve. The attack was timed to begin at 23.00 hours on the 26th, and the battalions would go in under a bombardment fired by the artillery of X and XXX Corps. Once the infantry had consolidated on the objectives, the 2nd Armoured Brigade would move onto 'Woodcock' and the 24th Armoured Brigade of the 10th Armoured Division would drive onto 'Snipe'.

In the few hours that remained before zero hour, the scattered companies of the 2nd Rifle Brigade had to be reformed and a reconnaissance made of the ground over which the advance was to made. During the O Group discussions, Colonel Turner, commanding the 2nd Battalion, discovered that there was a difference between his battalion's reckoning of its position and that of the Highland officers from whose sector the riflemen would be attacking. If the riflemen were right, the barrage that was to accompany the battalion's assault would fall ahead of them and take out the enemy positions. If, however, the calculations of the Highlanders were correct, then the barrage would fall not in front of the rifle companies but more than half a mile away to the right. In that case, the enemy ahead of the battalion, waiting in the darkness, would be unaffected by the bombardment. A fudged-up compromise was reached. If the barrage fell dead ahead — that is in accordance to the Rifle Brigade's judgement of where they were — then the battalion would carry on. If, however, the shells fell to the flank — the Highlanders assessment of the position — then the 2nd Battalion would change direction and follow the curtain of shells. It was in such a cloud of uncertainty that the riflemen prepared for action.

While on the British side preparations were being made to seize the high ground across which the armoured brigades would drive, on the enemy side Rommel had begun to concentrate his forces for a counter-attack intended to push back the bulge that XXX Corps had created. For this counterattack the Panzerarmee commander brought forward formations that had thus far remained generally uncommitted to the battle. Rommel had tried, at last, to concentrate his armoured forces, particularly now that there was no threat in the south. The 90th Light Division was ordered to attack in the northern sector of the front against the Australian penetrations, and the 21st Panzer Division was to thrust across the 'Snipe' position to drive in the Highland Division's salient. The Ariete Armoured Division was to co-operate with 21st Panzer Division and both the 15th Panzer and 164th Divisions were to participate in the offensive. The counterattack was timed to begin in the afternoon of the 27th, and the advance would be preceded by dive-bombing attacks and a short but heavy artillery bombardment.

As the 2nd Rifle Brigade prepared for its task, the commanding officer found that only 'C' Company had arrived at the start line in good time, for the other sub-units had had little chance to organize themselves before the barrage opened. As the companies formed up under enemy fire, it was observed that the barrage was falling to the right, as the Highland Division had predicted it would. The companies changed direction. But this manoeuvre so delayed the start of the attack that the barrage was already a long way in advance of the battalion before it crossed its new start line.

The spearhead of the advance was made up of two carrier platoons leading in the rifle companies, a tactic that flung up dust and not only obscured visibility but choked the riflemen who were following on foot. For more than half a mile of the advance by 'A' and 'C' Companies, only shell fire and dummy minefields obstructed progress. At one barbed-wire fence that marked a minefield (a dummy one as it turned out) the carriers halted, and the attack was continued by the rifle companies moving forward on foot at a very brisk pace. By 00.15 hours, Colonel Turner judged himself to be on 'Snipe'. The success rockets were fired and the anti-tank guns, together with the supply trucks that had been held back on the start line, moved forward. The wait by the support echelons had not been without incident, and a bombing raid had brought casualties: while the battalion's medical officer was attending to the victims of the bombs, the anti-tank guns moved off to 'Snipe' and the doctor was left behind — a loss that was to be keenly felt in the battle to come. The passage of the anti-tank guns from the start line to the battalion positions was more than usually difficult. In addition to the darkness of the night and the dust fog, there were slit trenches into which some trucks fell; there was soft going and shell fire, all of which taken together combined to slow the forward movement so much that it was not until 03.45 hours that the guns were in position, the stores had been unloaded and the lorries sent back.

Taking stock of the situation, Colonel Turner established that thirteen guns from his own 'S' Company and six of the 239th Battery had managed to reach the positions in which his companies were deployed. Each company had been allotted an arc to defend of about 140 degrees. 'A' covered an area from north-west to north-east. 'B' from south-west to south-east and 'C' Company held the western side of the battalion 'box'. The guns were deployed around the perimeter, with a small reserve held at battalion TAC headquarters. A reconnaissance by the carrier platoons, made after the rifle companies had dug their positions, established that the 2nd Rifles were between two laagers of enemy armoured fighting vehicles: one was situated about 1,000 yards to the north, and there was a second laager to the south, made up of vehicles from the Italian Littorio Division. Seemingly aroused by the British offensive spirit, the Italian formation, the 12th Battalion of the 133rd Tank Regiment of Littorio, moved north-eastwards to join the remainder of the German battle group 'Stiffelmaier', which was under orders to attack 'Snipe'. According to the Rifle Brigade diary (but not confirmed by that of the Italian unit), the north-easterly advance of the Italian battalion was bombarded by the 2nd Rifle's anti-tank guns and a tank and an SP were knocked out.

At first light, the combined German/Italian Stiffelmaier group moved westwards away from 'Snipe' and was fired at by the British battalion's guns, which claimed a number of vehicles destroyed. The battalion area was then swept by German gunfire from light and medium-range artillery, and to add to the confusion Sherman tanks of the 24th Armoured Brigade opened fire upon the riflemen. Not for an hour were the riflemen able to halt the tank fire, and there seemed to be a general misunderstanding among units that morning. To be fair, the whole British front was now under heavy shell fire as the Panzerarmee artillery opened the barrage behind which its divisions would counter-attack XXX Corps. Meanwhile, the Royal Artillery's forward observation officer with the 2nd Battalion suddenly disappeared and turned up later back in the main army area. His absence from the 'Snipe' perimeter meant that it was not possible to bring down fire on the German artillery, nor to attack the panzers that could now be seen preparing to move against the battalion.

Before the panzer assault came in, certain guns that lacked a good field of fire and others that had been sited on very soft sand were resited — a difficult and dangerous task in the circumstances, but one that was efficiently carried out. What was more important was that Colonel Turner realized that not only was the battalion not on the objective, but that a hill to the south-west, Point 37, dominated the area. Behind Point 37, a strong force of panzers was drawn up, ready to bombard the Shermans of the 24th Armoured Brigade, which had ceased bombarding friendly troops and had come forward to support the rifles. The tanks were not to stay long in the British perimeter. Their presence brought down upon 'Snipe' a hurricane of fire. Rommel's counterattack could not be jeopardized by these British intruders, and every type of artillery piece was brought to bear against the tank squadrons. The German guns then fired smoke to blind the Shermans and to hide from the British the movements of their own tanks. (Another tactic used to great effect by the Germans was to fire a single smoke shell to select a particular British machine upon which a concentrated fire was then brought.) Seven Shermans were lost during the German bombardment; the remainder withdrew.

The Italian battalion's war diary quotes that at 06.30 hours (their time) it made ready to attack, and that its strength was nineteen tanks and seven self-propelled guns. 'In front of us are at least ten anti-tank guns dug-in flush with the ground. Distance of the guns from our start line, 2,000 metres.'

There was, once again, a confusion of identity that brought danger to the Rifles garrison when British artillery, deceived by the large number of vehicles that could be seen in the area occupied by the battalion, assumed these to be a concentration of Axis vehicles and bombarded them. A number of thrusts that the Stiffelmaier group had undertaken against 'Snipe' had been only a prelude, and later in the morning a strong force of 24 vehicles struck at the 24th Armoured Brigade and thereby cut off the battalion. Now, with the garrison isolated, strong assaults went in against them from the south and south-west. Under the fierce and unremitting shell fire that was being poured onto the battalion, its losses in men and guns multiplied.

This was part of a double thrust launched by the 8th Panzer Regiment and the Littorio. Colonel Teege, commanding the Stiffelmaier group, appreciated that any advance by his panzers against the 24th Brigade would be taken in flank by the defenders on 'Snipe', and to neutralize these the Italian tank battalion was ordered in. The war diary records, 'The 12th Battalion attacks. In spite of the violent enemy fire and the resultant initial losses of tanks and men, the battalion advances firmly, keeping a certain distance from the anti-tank guns, which are extremely well dug-in and camouflaged. Suddenly there is violent fire from a further eight or ten anti-tank guns hidden on our left and located in depth. Their fire claims a number of victims and the battalion advance comes to a halt. Enemy fire becomes more and more violent. The survivors then give incredible proof of valour. Second Lieutenant Camplani from the outside of his vehicle urges his tanks on to the attack, and at their head drives his own machine at full speed at the most advanced anti-tank gun. A belt of mines halts him and then a shell strikes his tank and breaks its tracks. The vehicle commanded by Second Lieutenant Stefanelli is hit and explodes; that of Lieutenant Pomoni is struck as he advances at the head of his company; Lieutenant Bucalossi's tank is hit and set on fire. At 11.30 hours Colonel Teege orders a withdrawal back to the start line. The vehicles that have been brought back are dispersed in a wadi and the damaged ones, except the burnt-out ones, recovered. Colonel Teege's adjutant and his interpreter follow the action from their own tank and report the battalion's actions to their commander. Colonel Teege expressed his admiration for the magnificent courage shown by the battalion and for the way in which Captain Preve commanded the movement of his own tanks and the SP artillery.'

To counter the Italian attack, two 6pdrs were brought forward, and in the concentrated fire that this movement attracted a number of riflemen were killed or wounded. As the Italian attack recoiled, the Rifles anti-tank guns opened fire upon Teege's tanks, taking them in flank. When the tanks turned to engage the 'Snipe' garrison, they then presented their flanks to the Shermans of the 24th Brigade.

Throughout the day the fury of the fighting rose and fell. The battalion's perimeter, no more than 400 yards at its widest and just over 800 yards in length, was littered with knocked-out guns, burning carriers, tanks and dead — the German ones of the previous evening and the more recently fallen of the 2nd Rifle Brigade. The area was covered with smoke from the knocked-out carriers and with dust flung up by the shell bursts. It was a long and wearisome morning. Inevitably, the casualties had reduced the gun teams, and many pieces were being served by scratch crews. Shortly after noon the Italians came in again, and this time against part of the perimeter that was covered by only one gun — and the crew of that gun was reduced to its NCO commander. Two men ran across to crew the 6pdr; one of them was Colonel Turner, the commanding officer of 2nd Battalion. At 600 yards the gun opened fire and hit and stopped in succession five of the oncoming Italian vehicles. The remaining three enemy tanks were now frighteningly close, and there were only two rounds left in the locker. Realizing the critical situation, one of the battalion officers ran through the shell fire to bring up the jeep that was loaded with shells. A deluge of fire fell on the moving vehicle and soon it began to burn. Colonel Turner and his two man crew left the gun and salvaged some of the ammunition, and while the trio was carrying out this dangerous duty a shell burst close by and wounded the commander in the head. His place at the gun was taken by a corporal. By now the Italian machines were only 200 yards away and closing fast. The sergeant commanding the gun laid on, and with three shots destroyed them.

The Germans and the Italians, desperate now to destroy this centre of resistance, smothered it with shell fire throughout the whole long,

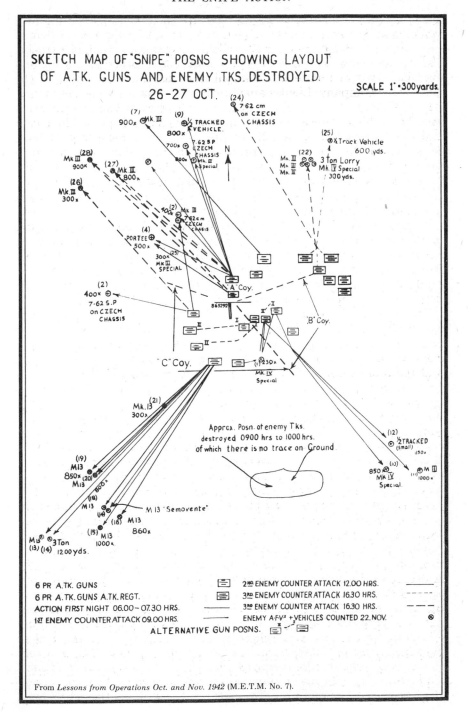

SKETCH MAP OF "SNIPE" POSNS SHOWING LAYOUT
OF A.TK. GUNS AND ENEMY TKS. DESTROYED.
26-27 OCT.

SCALE 1"·300yards.

From *Lessons from Operations Oct. and Nov. 1942* (M.E.T.M. No. 7).

hot afternoon. It was not long before all the officers on the western side of the battalion perimeter were dead or wounded, and the colonel, who had insisted on visiting his men's positions to encourage them, had eventually to be physically restrained for his own safety. Late in the afternoon the 2nd Armoured Brigade appeared out of the east and made the same error in identification as had the 24th Brigade and the Royal Artillery. The tanks and SP guns of the 2nd Armoured began to bombard the 'Snipe' garrison. As if this were not enough, movement to the west showed that Rommel's armour was forming up for the general counterattack that he had ordered. All that had occurred during the day had been only skirmishing — this was to be the real blow.

A force of more than twenty tanks and SPs was drawn up into two groups, and at 17.00 hours the northern group of panzers, drawn from the 21st Panzer Division, struck south-eastwards to engage the 2nd Armoured Brigade. In making this move the German tanks passed broadside on past the guns of the 239th Battery. It was clear that the Germans were unaware of the British battery's location, and when the four 6pdr guns opened up at 200 yards a dozen tanks were soon hit and destroyed. The Panzer IVs turned head on to meet the challenge from 'Snipe', but at so close a range that the British guns could penetrate the front armour. Under the furious and accurate cannonade, the panzers halted. Then, aware of the threat posed by the tanks of the 2nd Armoured Brigade that were now moving forward, they pulled back. The German second wave then made its effort, approaching in a more cautious fashion, using dips in the ground to full advantage. At first only two of the anti-tank guns could bear upon this new threat, but then a third gun was swung round to face the slowly approaching enemy. At point-blank range the guns opened up, and the four leading panzers were knocked out. Then three more were hit and began to burn. The remainder turned away to take up hull-down positions from which they raked with machine-gun and shell fire the now almost undefended perimeter.

But, with the repulse of the second attack, the panzers had had enough. More than sixty armoured fighting vehicles, German and Italian, were littered around the perimeter, and dotted about on the desert were the dead bodies of tank crews and infantry. Within the garrison area there were seven Shermans and a single German tank hulk (from an earlier encounter), together with the shattered chassis of sixteen Bren gun carriers and ten anti-tank guns. Still determined to resist the enemy thrusts, the riflemen waited . . . and waited. . . . But the panzers were next seen heading for night laager, and the defiant garrison engaged them at 1,200 yards, scoring a hit on one of the vehicles. With the onset of darkness the perimeter was pulled in to hold it against an infantry attack. But none came. At 23.15 hours, having waited in vain for the promised relief by the 133rd Brigade, the Rifle battalion was eventually pulled back. The 'Snipe' action was over, and it had demonstrated that the panzers could be held off and defeated. The action had also crucially reduced the number of Rommel's armoured vehicles, and the number of 'runners' in the Afrika Korps had dropped to 77. The 'Snipe' battle had been important, and the award of the V.C. to Colonel Turner acknowledged that fact.

The following account by Rifleman Suckling recalls his part in the operation. 'I went in as a Bren gunner with a foot platoon, loaded with spare mags and hand grenades. There was no number two on the Bren. The other lads were carrying spare mags. Our objective was about 2,000 to 3,000 yards ahead. The Bren carriers were forward of us. We were on our start line at about 23.00 hours; there wasn't much moon, and we stood waiting. As we waited for the word to advance, the thoughts of how and what's going to happen went through my mind: we were all the same, nerves taut, parched lips and throat. Then suddenly we were off, with the artillery giving covering fire and all hell was let loose. Our carriers were advancing, firing their light machine-guns at targets or at least at anything on our front. You didn't realize what was coming at you for the noise; you could only think of what is hitting the enemy. Our advance was cautious, and every so often we hit the deck. We'd have a quick look for targets and then we'd give a quick burst, just to reassure ourselves. When we passed slit trenches it was a quick pull of the hand grenade pin and in with it. It wasn't just to get rid of the weight, but in the hope that you'd knocked some of them out. We didn't bother to wait to find out if there was anybody in the slit, as the line was moving on in the advance. It was a rather flat area, and there was as good as no cover: camel shrub was about all there was, but once behind a bit of that and it seemed like an oak tree. Any small mound seemed as big as a hill.

'There were casualties, but we couldn't stop — the stretcher bearers were following us in and would tend to them. Eventually we reached the objective, or so they said, and we were ordered to dig in. The sand was quite soft, so we soon had a section slit trench dug. It wasn't easy to do this, as we had to lay on our stomachs to dig. To stand up or to kneel was to make yourself a bigger target. There was LMG and rifle fire and heavy stuff flying everywhere, balls of smoke from knocked-out vehicles and tanks. Our anti-tank guns were doing their stuff. Without them we would have been useless. We could never have done it fighting with just small-arms alone. In the hours of darkness the firing was quite nerve racking. Of course, you couldn't see targets, so you watched for tracer coming from the enemy LMGs and fired at the end of the tracer line, or else you aimed at the gun flashes. We got no rest at all during the night, and lay there hoping that dawn would give us some light on our front and, perhaps, relief. Dawn came, and some of us began to doze off. We hadn't had much rest in the past few days, what with two nights of grafting in the mine task force.

'Our section was facing a north-westerly arc of fire. Dawn came and with it the thought that there might be a counterattack. Jerry didn't come in for a couple of hours and when he did it was mostly tanks and mobile guns. Our anti-tank guns did their good work with these. The 6pdrs stopped them cold. Then the crews began to bale out and we opened up at them. We only fired at targets that we could see on our immediate front, for we had used a lot of ammunition and had to conserve what was left. All this time no-one actually knew how the whole battalion was faring. There was not much communication between platoons. It was a day of alertness, with plenty of action. Our bombing shuttle service was a picture to behold, blasting any heavy formation of vehicles or tanks. We could see the bombs dispersing them.

'About five in the evening another counterattack came in. By the sound, there wasn't so much fire coming from our anti-tank guns. Whether they had been knocked out or were just short of ammunition, we didn't know. We found out later it was a combination of both. Again, the remaining anti-tank guns did a wonderful job. Round about this time I glanced back behind me, and to the right rear was a Panzer III. I told the lads to keep their heads down. This was our lot. Out front there was quite a lot of movement of vehicles, but our thoughts were on the enemy tank at our rear. We knew that there was a 6pdr anti-tank gun to our right and facing the front, but there was no firing from it. Presuming the crew were knocked out or were out of ammo, if one of us were to crawl to it, perhaps we could have a go at the panzer. We did a John Wayne, raising a tin hat above our slit trench. We did this and the tank gave it a burst from his MG. It would have been suicide for any of us to get out and have a go. All of a sudden there was an explosion over our position. We all thought this was the tank firing at us with his 75. Deeper we crouched in our position. Then there was a pall of smoke and the smell of burning rubber. We looked over the edge of our trench. . . . The panzer was burning. This was the tank that Sergeant Swann knocked out. We didn't know this at the time, but what a relief it was!

'About this time, we heard that we would be getting out as soon as conditions improved and a relief to take over could be got up. We got out about 11pm, moved back to a safe area and got a meal and some rest.

'Next day we moved to a rear area, had a pep talk regarding the action at "Snipe" given by General Lumsden. There were many awards and our colonel, Vic Turner, got a V.C. He was a great commander and a compassionate one. It was a whole battalion effort, especially the anti-tank gunners. To think it could have been a disaster . . . because we heard afterwards that we had gone off our bearings to the objective. Battalion HQ said that we had to fight it out at all costs. Luckily, it turned in our favour. There is no doubt the infantryman has one of the worst jobs, but with good leadership and especially the comradeship one builds up, a lot can be overcome. This was shown at "Snipe".'

During that night of 27/28 October, there was another disaster in the area of 'Woodcock'. Units of the 10th Armoured Division had begun to relieve those of the 1st Armoured Division, and one of the Sussex battalions of the 133rd Brigade had gone forward to take over the 'Snipe' position from the Rifle Brigade battalion. The relief was bedevilled with the usual problem of being unable to locate a position and, as we have seen, the Sussex unit did not take over the 'Snipe' position. To be fair, the location of the 7th Motor Brigade was not precisely known, and no reconnaissance of the ground over which the Sussex Brigade was to advance had been made because of enemy fire. It was only later on the 27th that the brigadier commanding the 133rd Brigade was told that neither 'Snipe' nor 'Woodcock' had been captured and that it would be up to his brigade to gain these. The brigade assault, again no fault of those who undertook it, went hopelessly awry. The barrage had to be postponed until 22.30 hours in order to give the Sussex battalions sufficient time to form themselves for the assault. The infantry went in under the barrage, but within a short time tragic accidents had begun to happen. Companies of the 4th Sussex mistook parties of the 1st Gordon Highlanders (through whose battalion area they were advancing to the attack) for the enemy. The Sussex men opened fire upon the Gordons and casualties occurred. On the battalion's left flank, another company of the Sussex was lost in battle with German grenadiers and was destroyed in the fire-fight that followed. At first light, a counterattack came in, spearheaded by panzers and supported by panzergrenadiers. The combined assault force overran the 4th Sussex and destroyed it.

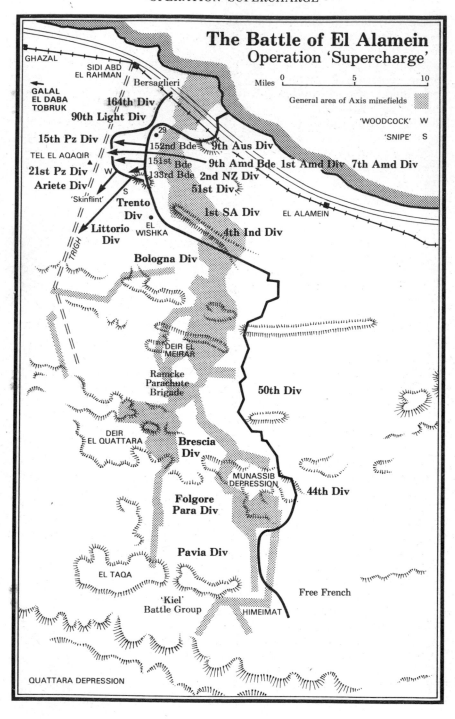

The Battle of El Alamein
Operation 'Supercharge'

Miles 0   5   10

General area of Axis minefields

'WOODCOCK' W

'SNIPE' S

GHAZAL

SIDI ABD
EL RAHMAN

Bersaglieri

GALAL
EL DABA
TOBRUK

164th Div

90th Light Div

29

15th Pz Div

152nd Bde   9th Aus Div

TEL EL AQAQIR

151st Bde   9th Amd Bde   1st Amd Div   7th Amd Div

21st Pz Div   W

133rd Bde   2nd NZ Div

Ariete Div

51st Div

'Skinflint'   S

Trento
Div

1st SA Div

EL ALAMEIN

EL
WISHKA

Littorio
Div

4th Ind Div

TRIGH

Bologna Div

DEIR EL
MEIRAB

Rameke
Parachute
Brigade

50th Div

DEIR
EL QUATTARA

Brescia
Div

MUNASSIB
DEPRESSION

Folgore
Para Div

44th Div

Pavia Div

EL TAQA

Free French

'Kiel'
Battle Group

HIMEIMAT

QUATTARA DEPRESSION

15.

OPERATION 'SUPERCHARGE'

Montgomery was now looking for ways in which the flagging Eighth Army assault could be revitalized. The 'crumbling' stage of the operation was in train, and those units not engaged in it could slacken their efforts. The scale of operations along parts of XXX Corps front could be reduced while the main emphasis of the attack was switched northwards to the area of the Australian Division. The enemy forces in that sector who were to be 'crumbled' were the 164th Division and several Italian formations, chiefly Bersaglieri, all of whom were deployed in strength along the salient that projected towards the British lines to the west of Tel el Eisa. There would still be intense patrolling along XXX Corps front and concentrated artillery fire, to form a screen behind which the army commander could withdraw certain formations and regroup them for a new, hard blow at the enemy.

The most important of this regrouping of forces was to take from the battle line the 1st Armoured Division, the 9th Armoured Brigade and the 2nd New Zealand Division. The gap caused by the movement of the New Zealanders was covered by the 4th Indian Division and the South African Division, each of which took over a wider sector of front. A second series of withdrawals and reorganizations was undertaken later on the 27th, and when that was concluded the 7th Armoured Division and certain infantry brigades of the 44th and 50th Divisions had moved out of the south and into the northern sector.

Montgomery's attention was now concentrated upon the next stage of the battle plan. It was important that the Australian Division's 'crumbling' attacks should continue in order to draw Rommel's attention towards the north, and there was evidence that this part of the plan was working well, for intelligence sources reported orders to the 21st Panzer Division to move even farther north. While the German commander was moving forces to block a thrust on the left of his line, the British forces were being regrouped to re-open the attack. Montgomery retained until quite late in October the intention to use the Australian sector as the base-line from which to launch his new attack. Once again XXX Corps would carry the burden, with the armour of X Corps protecting the desert flank from the panzers.

The native track known as the Trigh Sidi Abd el Rahman, or more simply the Rahman track, now began to dominate the story of the Battle of El Alamein, for its significance was considerable. The trigh ran from the white-walled mosque of Sidi Abd el Rahman on the coast down deep into the desert: it was thus a lateral highway running along the back of Panzerarmee, so that along its dusty length the Axis commanders could quickly deploy their units, men and guns. The Rahman track was vital to the Germans, and it was only to be expected that the enemy would base his strongest opposition to a British advance in front of this very sensitive area. Rommel had lined the most obvious lines of approach to the track with a series of gun positions, and it was the speed with which anti-tank guns could be brought from one threatened point to another, to counter British tank thrusts, that now overshadows this narrative.

While in the north the Australian attacks 'crumbled' the enemy, the question was raised at the highest level as to whether or not it was better to shift the main point of Eighth Army's new thrust some way south of the coastal sector through which Montgomery had proposed that it should go in. From his intelligence officers, Montgomery learned that Rommel expected it to be the area of the British attack and had gathered his forces to defend it. Eighth Army's intelligence summary for the night of 29 October reported the movement of the 90th Light Division to the Sidi Abd el Rahman sector. German strength in the north was now overwhelming, and the policy of 'stiffening' the Italian formations with German detachments seemed to have been generally discontinued. There were now two different types of Axis troops facing Eighth Army: in the north, the under-strength but able German and Italian panzer and motorized divisions; farther inland, the almost immobile Italian infantry mass of low morale and obsolete weapons. It was pointed out to Montgomery that a quick thrust through the Italian formations would allow Eighth army to pass its armour into the Axis rear areas, to cut the Rahman track and Aqaqir Ridge, which ran behind it. Once across the track and over the ridge and X Corps armour would be in open country. Once through, the tank divisions could move quickly, trap the Germans and pin them with their backs to the sea. Montgomery appreciated immediately the power of the proposals put to him, and changed the point at which the main effort would be made. But, to ensure that Rommel did not become aware of this change of emphasis, he ordered the Australian attacks against the 164th Division to be intensified.

THE AUSTRALIANS' 'CRUMBLING' ATTACK

It will be recalled that the plan of Operation 'Lightfoot' foresaw that the 26th and 20th Brigades of the 9th Australian Division were to advance in the general assault, leaving the 24th Brigade to divert the attention of the watchful enemy. The 26th Brigade would march westwards into the desert, presenting its right flank to the Panzer-armee and forming in the north the strong 'shoulder' of Eighth Army's attack. We have seen how successful was the Brigade's advance. As a consequence of the attacks of the first night, a German-held salient projected into the British line, from a point just westwards of Tel el Eisa and reaching back to the 'Oxalic' line. Within that salient lay both the railway and the coast road. It was against this salient on the northern flank of XXX Corps that the 'crumbling' operations were to be undertaken. The impetus to Montgomery's decision to switch the 'crumbling' from the western front of his army to its northern flank can, perhaps, be found in the sensitivity which Rommel showed to British moves in the coastal sector.

On 25 October, a short, sharp tidying-up operation carried out by 2/48th Battalion of the 26th Brigade had captured Point 29, a low hill to the west of Tel el Eisa. The loss of this eminence produced a strong reaction from the Germans, who launched a series of strong attacks to recapture that lost hill during 26 and 27 October. The realization that Rommel considered the coastal sector to be vital to the Axis defence plans tied in perfectly with Montgomery's own intention to 'crumble' the enemy's forces. Rommel could be hoodwinked into spending his energies defending the worthless northern salient while Eighth Army regrouped and prepared to fling its divisions across the Sidi Abd el Rahman track, the last line of German resistance on the Alamein front. To hold Rommel's attention to the coastal sector it would be necessary for the 9th Australian Division to mount attacks designed, ostensibly, to pinch out the Tel el Eisa salient and to capture or to destroy its aggressive garrison. Thus, the 9th Australian Division was now to advance northwards to the sea, on a line 90 degrees to its original axis of advance.

Once again, we must compress the records of valour and the details of days and nights of bitter fighting into a single brief narrative. In this short account, one name will occur again and again: 'Thompson's Post', a name that in Australia is synonymous with unexampled bravery and devotion to duty. 'Thompson's Post' was a German defensive complex covering half a mile in extent, and skilfully laid out. Its positions were mutually supporting, and the whole network of trenches, dug-outs and machine-gun posts dominated the area around it. When the panzergrenadiers finally abandoned 'Thompson's Post', the whole area was carpeted with Australian dead. The fighting ability of the 9th Division and the price that the Eighth Army seemed prepared to pay to take the 'Post', reinforced Rommel's conviction that, for both strategic and tactical reasons, the northern salient was the area of decision. Whether it was for either reason is immaterial. The Australians attacked and continued to attack for days on end, and were met by equally determined German resistance. Men did not fall in ones and twos but in tens and twenties in the most bitter fighting of the whole offensive. Rommel wrote of blood being poured out for a piece of miserable desert marsh so lacking in importance that not even the poorest Arab would have wanted it.

The task facing the 9th Australian Division was to achieve the coast road. The attacks that would accomplish this were to be launched from the area around the recently captured Point 29; that is to say, from ground to the west of 'Thompson's Post'. The Australian attack would first come in behind the Axis defenders, and while one prong of the assault continued a second prong would turn eastwards to bottle up the panzergrenadiers and the Bersaglieri. The assault would be a two-brigade operation. The 20th would first attack and seize two low hills in the area of Point 29, and their capture would form a base area through which 26th Brigade would pass. Once on the main road, its battalions — tank support was promised — would turn eastwards to destroy the Axis garrison.

It should be understood that the battalions allotted to carry out this intricate series of operations were not fresh units at full strength, but the survivors of five days and nights of battle and bombardment. Many of the sub-units were at only one third of their strength. Indeed, it was only the determination of the lightly wounded not to leave the line but to stay with their comrades in the fight that helped to maintain the belief at HQ that these small groups of exhausted men were rifle companies.

The first of the attacks went in at 22.00 hours on 28 October. In bitter fighting, the 2/13th and 2/15th each reached and consolidated on their objectives, the high ground near Point 29. The 2/23rd Battalion was not so fortunate and lost men to a field of S mines. Against strong resistance that was met soon after the battalion had crossed the start line, the companies of the 2/23rd pushed forward, but the delay made it impossible for the attacks to be completed that night. It was hoped that the operation might be resumed on the night of 29/30, but difficulties of supply forbad that. It was, therefore, not until the night of 30/31 October that the operation was resumed. The 2/32nd Battalion of 24th Brigade was attached to 26th Brigade for the resumption of the operation and was given the task of opening the first stage of the attack; that of cutting the railway line and driving the enemy from the area so that the 2/24th and 2/48th Battalions could concentrate there. Later in the night they would swing eastwards towards 'Thompson's Post', and as they moved eastwards the 2/3rd Pioneer Battalion would resume the drive northwards to the sea.

The artillery tasks connected with the three-stage operation were varied and complicated, and the guns were to be the infantry's only support. The armour could not be deployed for this operation. The battalions would have to advance over mine-strewn ground in the dark, for the attack would go in before moonrise, against an alerted, strong and determined enemy holding well prepared positions from which he would pour fire into the front and flanks of the advance. Shortly before 22.00 hours, the guns opened up on the grenadiers of 125th Regiment and the leading companies of 2/32nd Battalion stepped out across the start line. Swiftly, the Australian infantry moved forward and had soon begun to penetrate the enemy line. The opposition of the grenadiers was fierce but the élan of the men of 2/32nd was fiercer still, and soon they had crossed the road, gaining their objective and establishing themselves in the area from which the other battalions would take up the assault. Through the consolidated area to the north of the railway line, 2/24th, 2/48th and 2/3rd Pioneer Battalions passed. The first two sorted themselves out into attack formation and halted on the form-up line, ready to begin their advance towards 'Thompson's Post'. The Pioneers stood waiting on their line, ready to trudge forward to the sea. The strong German opposition to the Australians increased in power and, as the companies of 2/24th and 2/48th stood waiting at the start line, they endured a concentrated bombardment, which has been described by one survivor as 'a positive volcano of fire'. At this point it must be pointed out how close was the liaison between the grenadiers and their artillery. From OPs located on small areas of high ground just behind 'Thompson's Post', the German gunner officers responded immediately and with vigour to the flares that rose up into the dark night sky — the calls of the hard-pressed German infantry for artillery support. From batteries established along the whole length of the Tel el Eisa salient the fire rained down on the small Australian groups, who stood waiting to go in under their own artillery's barrage. Shortly before 01.00 hours on 31 October, the twinkling lights on an arc running to the south and west of the Australian positions heralded the opening of the artillery phase of the second stage of the battle. Soon the crash of detonations and the choking clouds of dust showed that the British barrage was on time and on line.

A hand waved and the attack was on. The German bombardment that the battalions had endured at the form-up line was nothing compared to the hurricane of fire that poured over the thin lines of infantry as they walked through curtains of shrapnel towards their objectives. From 'Thompson's Post', fire from machine-guns, mortars and artillery swept the ground over which the Australians were advancing. Bombarded with artillery fire, swept by small arms fire and reduced in numbers by losses to S mines that infested the area, blinded by dust and disorientated by the dark, the battalions of the brigade soon lost contact with each other. Then cohesion between companies within battalions was lost. Slowly the attack began to peter out, and the commanding officers of the battalions decided that their units were too weak in number to hold the ground that they had gained at such cost. The battalions withdrew.

The Pioneers luck had been equally as bad. At 04.35 hours, in the dark of the night, the men, for whom this was to be the first experience of infantry warfare, moved out and were faced with concentrated machine-gun and rifle fire. Against this single battalion was now turned the full force of the German defensive fire, and it soon became clear that the Pioneers' attempt to drive to the sea could not be concluded. With too few men under command to force the attack to a successful conclusion, the advance was stopped. The Pioneers were pulled out of the dangerous salient, and joined the other units of the brigade to endure with them the bombing and shelling.

The battalions were by this time exhausted by days and nights of unceasing combat, but although they were reduced in strength to cadres and were suffering casualties with every German barrage, patrolling went on. At first light, a fighting patrol drawn from two of 2/32nd's companies went out to mop up enemy posts that were still holding out in the battalion area. In this sweep they rounded up more than a hundred prisoners from the German garrison. By the morning of 31 October, the situation was that a narrow and tapering Australian salient, running generally north to south, had been driven into the German east/west salient. The Australian salient did not, as was believed at divisional headquarters, extend to the sea. A narrow corridor remained in German hands and along that corridor passed reinforcement and supply to the grenadiers and Bersaglieri in 'Thompson's Post'. To maintain their salient, the Australian commanders packed the north/south salient with anti-tank guns and field artillery and brought forward tank battalions to meet the counterattacks that would soon come in if Rommel reacted as Montgomery had predicted. He did, and 31 October is recalled as a day of high danger by those who survived it.

A probing attack came in against the fragile western wall of the Australian salient shortly after first light. This was little more than a strong reconnaissance and was broken up by artillery fire. At 12.30 hours a strong German armoured attack was launched. This was a typical German ad hoc grouping of SPs and panzers with some artillery and grenadiers all drawn from 21st Panzer Division. The first group of panzers in this midday attack drove over 'B' Company of 2/32nd Battalion, destroying it as a fighting force. Valentine tanks of 40th RTR, which had been engaged to the east of 'Thompson's Post', were alerted and came forward. In the face of this opposition, the German armour pulled back. How easy the words make the scene. In reality, it was a hell on earth. The Australian infantry, reduced in number, exhausted by the lack of sleep and almost continuous battle, stood to arms, ready to repel the German armoured attack. Looking across the rim of their slit trenches, dug with the last reserves of energy only hours before, they could see a bleak and desolate waste land on which the bodies of the fallen lay like so may bundles of rags. Some of the dead were rotting and stinking from days of exposure. The more recent ones were beginning to swell as the gases in the bodies expanded in the midday heat. The thought, 'What support do we have?', must have been present in all the living, for there seemed to be only a handful of men left to oppose the oncoming panzers.

The whole arena of battle was a mass of destruction, some of it from the immediate past. The battalion transport, smashed by shell fire during the previous night, were examples of that. There was detritus from other battles, from air attacks or from bombardments of earlier days, weeks or even months, for the Tel el Eisa salient was one of the most hotly contested sectors of the whole battle line.

Shapes appear from out of the distant heat haze to the west. In the distortion of the shimmering waves, they take on enormous height and look like black tower blocks. With a sickening feeling at the pit of the stomach comes the realization that the point at which they are coming in is your own company front. Already the German artillery is firing and, under the shelter of exploding shells, the tanks and SPs crawl slowly forward. To add to the confusion, smoke shells begin to fall, hiding the battle so that the desperate infantry soldiers, fighting with rifle and bayonet against the grenadiers, do not see the wounded lying in their shallow slit trenches watching in horror as the great steel belly of a Panzer IV crashes down upon them. ' "B" company was overrun.' What pictures that simple phrase evokes. Of men wounded, perhaps; or trotting across the grey sandy grit of the Tel el Eisa salient, flopping down to open fire on a Spandau, throwing grenades with sick despair as the grey shapes of the German armoured fighting vehicles close in. ' "B" Company was overrun. . . .' What unknown deeds of heroism and devotion to duty are enshrined in those four short words.

Against the lightly armed Valentines, the heavier German machines, crewed by veterans of years of desert fighting, pulled back. Competent and devoted crews do not pull back from battle with weaker foes, except when the lightly armed enemy has achieved a moral superiority. And this the tank men of 40th RTR had gained. Through their determination and their willingness to accept losses, they had shown themselves to be unconquerable. At the end of that dreadful day, the 40th had lost 25 tanks, but they had driven the veterans of 21st Panzer Division from the field, not in the midday attack alone but in the other assaults that came in before sunset halted the fighting for that day.

The 31 October can be seen, in retrospect, to have been the day of crisis for the success of Operation 'Lightfoot'. Although the main German minefields had been breached, the British armour of X Corps was not yet able to exploit the gaps and begin destroying the mass of German troops who were now crammed into the northern sector of the Panzerarmee battle line. The operation that would accomplish that destruction was imminent. The success that was, eventually, achieved can be attributed in great measure to the tired, exhausted troops of the 26th Australian Brigade who had fought on and on. During the night of 31 October/1 November, those survivors were to be relieved by battalions of 24th Brigade. The difficulties of a night-time take over from a unit holding front-line positions can well be imagined. The difficulties are, naturally, increased when those who are to be relieved are scattered about in a loose and unclear pattern and in an area over-looked by an enemy who is within hailing distance. These were the problems facing the commanders of the battalions of 24th Brigade. The 2/28th, for example, had no guides from the 2/24th, the unit it would relieve, and the incoming men set out 'with no sense of adventure but the uncomfortable feeling of unpreparedness for the dangers which lay ahead'.

The situation on the ground was different from what the incoming battalions had been led to expect. Units that should have been positioned to support the 24th Brigade were not in their allotted areas, and it was soon established that there were, in fact, no Australian troops holding the area between the road and the sea. All the battalions holding the salient were scattered in a confusing jumble. Some sort of order was established between 04.00 hours, when the relief operation was completed, and first light, but the situation still left much to be desired. There was no line communication between units, and the temperamental wireless sets communicated, when they did, only fitfully and quixotically. Units miles away could be picked up on the air — companies half a mile away might just as well been on the moon.

The positions of 24th Brigade were set in a shallow depression overlooked by the watchful, aggressive and competent enemy, who was within grenade-throwing range — a fact that he soon demonstrated. That the enemy was aggressive was soon evident for, exhorted by Rommel, the panzers and their grenadiers came in before lunch under a short but intense bombardment. The first blows struck at the junction of 2/28th and 2/43rd Battalions, but the grenadiers were soon driven to ground and began immediately to dig in. Meanwhile, a new thrust was coming in against 2/43rd's company, which was holding positions near the coast road, and then the panzers with grenadiers riding on the outside of the steel colossi came driving in from the east. Rhodesian anti-tank gunners fought down the determined armoured thrusts and, in the absence of artillery observation officers up with the infantry, helped the inexperienced officers of the battalions to bring down the fire of British guns upon the dream targets that constantly presented themselves. There were groups of German infantry trudging forward into the attack, field guns coming up to engage the Australian defenders at close range, sp guns and tanks that rolled slowly across the gritty salt marsh. As one attack was repulsed at one place, it was succeeded by another on a new sector. The errors arose that inevitably accompany such close fought actions. One of 24th Brigade's units reported that it had been dive-bombed by RAF aircraft, and another battalion was bombarded by shells from British batteries. All day the noise and fury of battle rolled and thundered across the waste land upon which Rommel had set his gaze and to hold which he was committing piecemeal the élite troops of the 90th Light Division.

But Montgomery had by this time decided to make his break-out drive not along the coastal sector but deeper inland, and was concentrating his armour for the thrust towards the Sidi Abd el

Rahman track and Aqaqir Ridge, the last natural barrier that the Panzerarmee could hold. With Aqaqir in British hands, the enemy would be forced to withdraw or to suffer destruction. Thus, while troops in the coastal plain, concentrated within the confines of the two salients, battled for supremacy on a sector that had neither tactical nor strategic advantages, the remainder of Eighth Army, coiled and ready, was preparing to open Operation 'Supercharge'. It is, therefore, to other sectors of the battle front that we must now turn our attention, but it would not be in order to leave this account of the fighting in the coastal sector without a final reference to 'Thompson's Post'.

Throughout 1 and 2 November, the Australians and Germans met and clashed in savage patrol battles. There was now no longer the driving urgency to capture the 'Post' — the point of maximum effort was being made elsewhere — and patrols on 3 November reported a weakening of German resistance. The enemy was thinning out his troops, and later that day patrols brought back news that the Axis troops were moving westwards out of the salient. It was nearly over. Later in the night, 'Thompson's Post' was found to be empty. The grenadiers had vacated it. The area was desolate. Dead bodies, fragments of men, torn clothing, wrecked vehicles and the débris of war littered the ground. The most abiding memory is of the dead. From cemeteries in the area the survivors of those terrible ten days of battle can look across the desolate sands and see the slopes on which they endured and upon which their comrades fell.

The army commander's plan for Operation 'Supercharge' was to be a re-run of the operation of the first night of El Alamein, but fought on a narrower frontage. He would, once again, employ a combined force of infantry and Sappers to breach the Axis front and thereby to create a salient. Driving out of this would be an armoured brigade that would destroy the enemy gun lines and hold open the door of the salient through which 1st Armoured Division would pass. Then, in a great wheeling movement, the tank regiments would take up position on 'Skinflint', there to meet the challenge of Rommel's panzer force. It had been the intention of the army commander to open Operation 'Supercharge' on 31 October, immediately following the last Australian 'crumbling' attack, but time was too short to organize so complex a battle. Zero hour for the new offensive was fixed for 01.00 hours on 2 November 1942.

INFANTRY 'SUPERCHARGE'

From among the formations that he had placed in reserve, Montgomery found infantry brigades that had thus far played little direct part in the fighting. The first of these was the 152nd Brigade of the 51st Highland Division. It will be recalled that its battalions, the 2nd and 5th Seaforth Highlanders and the 5th Cameron Highlanders, had not been put in on the opening night of Operation 'Lightfoot', but had been employed in other vital but less spectacular duties. The second of the two fresh formations was the 151st Brigade of the 50th Tyne Tees Division: its constituent units, the 6th, 8th and 9th Battalions of the Durham Light Infantry, had earlier been detailed for a XIII Corps attack, but this had been aborted. It was chiefly upon the fighting ability of those six battalions that success would lie in the opening stages of Operation 'Supercharge'. Montgomery had intended that the New Zealand Division should provide the infantry for his new offensive, but the battalions were both overtired and understrength through the heavy losses they had suffered. However, it was still considered a New Zealand operation, for it was led by General Freyberg, the Dominion division's driving force, and used that division's organization and fighting services.

It would be the task of the two British brigades to push a 4,000-yard-wide salient into the enemy line, and to take this forward to a depth of 4,000 yards. The infantry objective line was a mark on a map that would, on the ground, be a point some 800 yards east of the Rahman track and a little to the north of Tel el Aqaqir, the highest point on the low ridge of Aqaqir. The walls of a salient are its weakest parts, and it was to be expected that the enemy would strike vigorously against these by pouring enfilade fire into the flanks of the advancing brigades. To beat down such opposition, other infantry units would be employed. On the left, or southern wall of the salient, the 133rd Brigade's three Sussex battalions would storm 'Woodcock'; on the right, or northern wall, the 28th (Maori) Battalion of the New Zealand Division would attack and seize a German defended area on and around the dominating height of Point 29. Armour would give close support to the infantry and Sappers who would carry out the assault, and the 8th and 50th Royal Tank Regiment, each with 38 Valentines, were deployed. Both these battalions had formed part of XXX Corps reserve, and both had accompanied infantry divisions in the opening night attacks: the 8th had been with the South Africans, the 50th with the 51st Highlanders.

The whole operation would be covered with a massive blanket of artillery fire. Montgomery assembled the guns of two armoured divisions, of the 51st Highland Division, those of the New Zealand Division, and added to the whole a regiment taken from the Australians. So that the shells would carpet all the ground from the British front lines to the objective, the infantry battalions were withdrawn from the front-line trenches. The first flights of shells would be fired at 01.05 hours, ten minutes after the two brigades had crossed their start lines, and would fall upon the evacuated British forward zones until the infantry battalions had closed up to them. Once the attack was under way, a proportion of the artillery would fire upon known enemy gun positions, while the remainder laid a steady barrage across the ground over which the battalions were advancing. Even before the guns began their bombardment, a 'softening-up' process would begin. A seven-hour long series of air raids would be carried out upon the Rahman track and Aqaqir Ridge. With such a weight of shells and bombs ahead of them, it was anticipated that the infantry would meet little opposition as the companies tramped across the desert to reach the objectives. As on the opening night of Operation 'Lightfoot', the battalions would march at a speed controlled by 'pacers', and direction would be maintained by the passage of tracer shells above the heads of the advancing infantrymen. If the attack went as planned, the battalions would be on their objectives by 04.00 hours. The 9th Armoured Brigade would then pass through the salient to charge Panzerarmee's gun lines. At 05.45 hours, covered by a creeping barrage and hidden by the darkness of the night, the tank regiments would climb Aqaqir Ridge, the objective of 9th Armoured Brigade. Then, to conclude that part of Operation 'Supercharge', through the corridor the infantry and the 9th Armoured had opened the regiments of the 1st Armoured Division, reinforced by those of the 8th Armoured Brigade, would sweep into the open country, behind an advanced guard of armoured cars whose task it would be to harry the enemy and allow him no time to form a rearguard line.

The desert over which the two British infantry brigades would be attacking was not thought to be so heavily and so cleverly mined as had been the ground on the opening night of Operation 'Lightfoot', but it was certain to be littered with small fields of devices, indiscriminately sown. Set among those scattered fields there would be well-sited infantry positions equipped with machine-guns, mortars and probably with tank turrets dug into the hard rock surface, there to give immediate and local support. Behind those positions it was known that Axis engineers had constructed successive lines of gun pits, sited so as to give supporting crossfire and directed by command posts dug deep underground. It was known that the lines of anti-tank guns extended to a great depth both in front of and beyond the Rahman track, but most of the positions were of such recent construction that details of their location had not been precisely determined by intelligence. Also, they were so well dug-in and concealed that from ground level they were almost undetectable except at close range.

It was axiomatic that infantry had to be employed to attack and take out enemy artillery positions. Only as a last resort, or in the fluid movement of armoured warfare, was it in order for tanks to confront directly an enemy gun line. In such desperate circumstances, the 'attacking front' of the tanks had to exceed by a very large margin the 'gun density' — in other words, there had to be a lot more tanks than enemy guns. Montgomery, lacking sufficient infantry to attack the gun lines in front of the Rahman track had decided, reluctantly, that he would have to employ armour in precisely the way that it should *not* be used. The armoured unit that would have to carry out the task of charging the guns would be certain to sustain the most severe losses.

The most saddening concomitant of battlefield command is for an officer to know that he is sending in men to almost certain death. But there comes a time in the life of every leader when he is aware that only flesh and blood can prevail, and that young mens' bodies must achieve what aerial bombardment, artillery barrages, tactics, fire and movement and sophisticated weaponry cannot. And then, with heavy heart, he must send for the best he has and lay upon them the responsibility for victory. For those so selected, it is just as bitter to receive such an order. Keen and ambitious officers may convince themselves that the glory to be gained from such an enterprise is worth the sacrifices. The general feeling among most units, however, must have been not so much 'we have the honourable task', but rather more 'sod our horrible luck!'

Those in senior echelons of command may point out to the commander that the execution of his orders will result in severe casualties. The rank and file do not enjoy the privilege of dissent; but, to be honest, neither do their regimental officers. At a battlefield conference in which details of 'Supercharge' were being given, the question was raised as to the wisdom of tanks attacking an unbroken gun line. The commander of one armoured regiment pointed out that his unit might well sustain 50 percent losses, only to be told by Freyberg that the army commander was prepared to accept 100 percent, but that the objectives must be gained. This ruthless decision was repeated in orders that, even if the infantry failed to gain its objectives, the armour would and must achieve theirs. The knowledge that Montgomery was prepared to accept such high losses was given only to officers; the realization that they were entering into some new 'Charge of the Light Brigade' was thought to be too much for the men to bear. Montgomery had selected the 9th Armoured Brigade, and had given to its regiments the unenviable task.

This then was to be Operation 'Supercharge': a break-in by the infantry, followed by a self-sacrificing charge of an armoured brigade carrying out an infantry task, and succeeded by the drive of an armoured mass, which would break out into the open desert to gain 'Skinflint' — the ground on which the massed British armour would meet the panzers and destroy them.

For the 5th Seaforth Highlanders, the infantry phase of the fighting that opened the new offensive was the first chance that they had had to strike a blow. It was their first action. Roy Cooke was one of their number: 'We were relieved by the 2nd New Zealand Division during the night of 30/31 October, in preparation for the operation that was to take place during the night of 1/2 November. As we made our way back past our battalion commander he was heard to say, "Cheer up lads, you'll get a smack at them tomorrow night." 1 November was spent getting ready. . . . We all wrote our farewell letters home, as in those days none of us really expected to see 'Blighty' again. . . . There was a general air of expectancy. . . . After a last hot meal, we made our way towards the start line. Before we set off, we all received a rum ration for the first time.'

The assault by the Highland Brigade went quickly and, certainly in the initial stages, without the heavy casualties that had been feared. The battalions were to cross a start line consisting of a line of cairns surveyed and erected with special care so that the confusion that had marred other attacks should not be repeated. Roy Cooke makes no mention of the thunderous explosion when the 360 guns opened fire, producing so concentrated a bombardment on that 4,000-yard wide front that a shell fell every twelve yards. Then, when the first, mad five minutes gunfire had been exhausted, a creeping barrage was laid by 200 guns, and this led the infantry in. Perhaps, like most infantrymen, Cooke's concentration was so firmly fixed on reaching the objective that he saw and heard nothing of the guns that were lifting his battalion onto its objective.

'Whilst awaiting the order to move forward, we all lay down on the desert with safety catches on and bayonets fixed. Suddenly, we were all on our feet and moving forward. As far as could be seen, to both left and right of us, men were advancing with their rifles in the port position, their bayonets glinting in the pale moonlight. Full moon had been days ago so the night was quite dark. . . . As we advanced, the feeling of pride and exhilaration was unmistakeable. We didn't realize or think of the danger we were in; we were doing a job, and the thought of being killed or wounded was far from our minds. We just felt happy to be doing *something* to help win the War. There were reddish coloured explosions ahead of us and bullets, both tracer and otherwise, coming our way. I remember seeing forms sink to the ground, but our orders were to keep going and not to stop for wounded or dying. Later we passed slit trenches with forms slouched over them facing in our direction. Inevitably, we came up too close to our moving barrage and had to wait for it to move forward. Above all the din, the sound of the pipes could clearly be heard, and even an Englishman can feel proud to belong to a Scottish regiment when he hears the shrill warlike sound of a pipe tune above the racket all round him. It sounded so incongruous, yet it was just what was needed to keep up one's spirits for what lay ahead.

'Our objective was about two miles ahead of us, and all too soon we were upon it. Before we reached it we met both Germans and Italians coming towards us with their hands in the air, and I aired my schoolboy German telling them which way to go. The Italians were terrified and kept calling out, "Madre!" It was a very cold night and we were only wearing our KD shirts and shorts, yet we were all in a sweat. We reached our objective, and before we were ordered to dig-in some of us were standing around, not sure of what to do next. It sounds crazy now, but a young German came up and started to chat to us in English. He told us how glad he was to be out of the war and wanted to compare notes between wartime Germany and England. He was well educated and had been to university. At the time, nothing seemed more natural than to chat with this young German . . . then a Kübelwagen, the military version of the Volkswagen, raced round us blazing at us with a submachine-gun, interrupting our discussion.

'It wasn't easy to dig-in, as the ground was almost rock-hard and there was too much stuff flying about to allow us to dig deeply, certainly not as deep as we should have been. It wasn't long before the sun shot up and we could hear our first tanks approaching. This was the 1st Armoured Division, who were soon among us, over us and then in front of us. I had never seen quite so many tanks at one time before. They were Shermans and they pushed on full of confidence, so it seemed to me. Once they had passed through us there was no peace for anyone. We were constantly trying to dig deeper, but it was no use . . . two feet down one would hit solid rock.

'I shall never as long as I live forget 2 November, 1942. It was the longest day of my life. Never was I more pleased to see the sun go down that day and to be thankful to be still alive. We in no way changed the course of the battle once we were on our objective, as we were just pinned down in the open, very close, indeed, right in the middle of a hard-fought battle between the 1st Armoured Division and Rommel's dug-in panzers and anti-tank guns. We had to stay put from the moment the tanks went through us until the sun set. The shelling and mortaring were unceasing, heavy and accurate. All day long we expected every minute to be our last. I had left my haversack and mess tins above the ground. When the firing eventually did die down, I found they were both riddled with shrapnel. I was hit once in the leg, but managed to bandage myself with a field dressing. Others were less fortunate. Apart from many wounded, some of whom died later from wounds received, we had 48 officers and men killed outright. By the time the sun did eventually set, the horizon was filled with 'brewed-up' tanks, mostly Shermans. . . . Eventually, the remaining tanks withdrew for the night and we were left alone, constantly expecting a Jerry counterattack. . . . We didn't think at the time that Jerry was beaten. . . . After sundown I ate as much as I could, as no one had felt like eating since the previous evening. At dawn on 3 November the Shermans came up again, but this time the battle had passed farther away to the west and the worst was over. We began collecting prisoners, both Italian and German, and could not help marvelling at the splendid dug-in positions for panzers and 88s that the Germans had left behind them. Our total casualties on 2 November were 12 officers and 165 other ranks killed and wounded. After a day or two to get reorganized, we followed the rest of Eighth Army in troop carriers, firstly up the Rahman track, then along the coast road towards Mersah Matruh. We met long lines of POWs coming from the opposite direction, and on the coast road there were many trucks coming eastwards, crammed full of Afrika Korps men in the back with their light desert uniforms and long peaked caps. . . .'

The Highland Brigade's attack had gone well, even though the 5th Seaforth's leading companies had been fired on by dug-in tanks, which they had then stormed and captured. On the right flank of the advance, by contrast, the Durham Brigade's assault had struck bitter opposition. The area through which the 151st Brigade had to advance was one on which the skilful German engineers had expended much time and expertise. It was the most important defence line in the northern sector of the front, and the well-designed positions were garrisoned by veteran panzergrenadiers who met the determined thrusts of the north countrymen with equal determination. Each position had to be fought for in close-combat assault. 'A lot of the Jerries fought to the end, and there were bodies flung about all over the place. From what I saw when daylight came, the dead outside the positions were mostly Italian. They had been caught by our barrage as they tried to run away from their trenches. Around one position in particular there were so many dead that it had obviously been a platoon position. Our intelligence officer had told us about some Eyetie defensive system called a "fire centre", a sort of all-round defence, and this must have been one. There must have been a score of dead, and what was sickening to me was that even when they were dead shells still fell on the bodies and mashed them up.' In this bitterly-contested battle, the Durham losses were staggering: one platoon of the 8th Battalion had only five survivors. Even so, the Durham Brigade was only minutes late arriving on its objectives.

The infantry units on both flanks had also fought a hard battle, but the Sussex on the left and the Maoris on the right had both gained their objectives. Now it was the speed of the Sappers that would determine the time at which the 9th Armoured Brigade would move into its charge. Enduring bombardment, machine-gun fire and frequent close-range fire-fights against the unshaken and aggressive Germans, the Sappers followed the infantry and worked methodically, detecting, gapping and lifting devices from the scattered fields. Behind the Sappers the tanks of the 9th Armoured Brigade inched their way in slow progress along the swept tracks, while farther eastwards the regiments of the 1st Armoured Division were approaching the entrances to the corridors.

ARMOUR 'SUPERCHARGE'

The difficulties that the armour encountered in that night drive cannot be fully explained or totally comprehended. The nearest description was that of a former RTR man, John Nickalls. 'It was like driving blindfolded through the rush hour. Through the intercom our officer would shout directions, but half the time he couldn't see anything himself. Remember, it was pitch dark and we were in a very thick cloud of dust. It was a real pea souper.' There were frequent and annoying halts. The lane was blocked by burning vehicles, victims of the enemy's bombardment, for not all the Axis artillery had been knocked out by the barrage. During the advance to contact by the 9th Brigade, some of the soft-skin vehicles and carriers belonging to the infantry component had been hit. There were heavy casualties, but more serious still to the overall scheme of things was the delay that such obstructions caused. Attempts by tank drivers to swing round the blockage often resulted in the vehicle moving into unswept ground: machines ran onto mines and had their tracks blown off. As an illustration of the difficulties that attended that drive, from the 79 Shermans or Grants and the 53 Crusader tanks that moved off that night from the concentration area near El Alamein station, only 94 took part in the attack. Confusions and delays retarded the forward movement, and the Warwickshire Yeomanry failed to reach the start line on time. Because of their absence, the advance of the 9th Armoured Brigade to the Rahman track was delayed. Thanks to the sophisticated Eighth Army signals techniques and to the flexibility of its operation, the artillery barrage under which the armour should have charged did not fire on schedule, but was held back until the regiments of the brigade had concentrated at the minefield exits. There was, however, one thing that waited upon no-one and which science could not control. This was the onset of daylight. The half-hour's delay imposed upon the brigade meant that the tank advance would not take place cloaked in the dark of night, but in the growing light of a new day.

The reverberating noise of nearly 100 tank engines could not be muffled even by the fury of the barrage still firing to cover the infantry, and neither the tank crews nor their opponents could have been in doubt that the attack would be made and that preparations had been made to meet it. It is not hard to imagine the feelings of the men of the British tank regiments. They may not have known, those of the rank and file who were not privy to the truth about the death ride they were about to undertake, but they would certainly have suspected that there would be guns to the left of them, guns to the right of them and ahead of them. And they also knew that they had to smash through the lines of those guns to reach the objective. Darkness should have been their main concealment, and the night was now far gone.

For the enemy gunners, the prospect must have been equally daunting. They were about to be attacked after enduring days and nights of bombardment and barrage, assaulted from the air and on the ground, by an armada of tanks. They could doubtless have confidence in their guns and in the splendid defences within which the weapons were sited. Many of the positions were dug-in on reverse slopes of the slight rises that undulate across the desert. There the gun teams lay hidden, listening to the clattering roar of the approaching British armour, waiting and holding their fire until the tank reared up to breast the rise. Then, seeing it as a dark shape against the sky, the

The new 6pdr weapon gave British anti-tank gunners a fighting chance against the panzers. **Above:** Knocked out German armour in the 'Snipe' area. **Right:** After the 'Snipe' action only one 6pdr anti-tank gun survived and it was withdrawn only after the last round had been fired. **Below right:** The men of 2nd Rifle Brigade fought an anti-tank action on 'Snipe' during 27/28 October, during which they destroyed more than fifty enemy machines. Here some of the survivors are telling the editor of *Crusader* about the action.

The price of war is death. **Above**: Temporary graves of two of the fallen of 51st Highland Division are marked by rifles buried muzzle first in the sand and the Balmoral or steel helmet set on the butt. **Below left**: The dead crew of a knocked out Sherman are buried temporarily alongside their tank. **Below right**: German dead in a communication trench.

'Lightfoot' and 'Supercharge' are over. **Right:** Prisoners of the Black Watch being taken to a POW cage. On the left of the photograph is a cairn of stones which served as one of the map reference points in the desert. **Below:** Wrecked British and Italian tanks in the area of Tel el Aqaqir after the Afrika Korps armour had been smashed during Operation 'Supercharge'. **Bottom:** In one of the well constructed Axis positions an Italian 47mm anti-tank gun projects so little above the surface of the desert that it was almost undetectable by tank crews.

The aftermath of battle. **Above left:** Lieutenant-General Ritter von Thoma, commander of Afrika Korps, was taken prisoner on 4 November. Here, he is seen leaving Eighth Army TAC HQ on the following day. **Above right:** A British soldier is puzzled at an enemy unit sign. **Below:** On the El Alamein battlefield men of a native African unit and of the Highland Division bury the fallen.

gunners would fire a shot into the thin metal belly, and a sudden gusting and a ball of fire would show where another British machine had begun to 'brew-up'. If, in the excitement, the panic, the fear of the moment, the gunners fumbled the shot, then the machine's huge bulk would smash down upon them with a shattering thump, squashing both gun and crew. The thoughts of both sides at time of crisis can only have been anxious ones as each waited in the darkness of the November night.

There was only a minimum of time for the commander of the 9th Armoured Brigade to dispose his regiments for the charge. On the right wing he placed the 3rd Hussars; the Wiltshire Yeomanry held the centre, and the Warwickshire Yeomanry were on the left flank. The brigadier himself took post in the first line of tanks. In the regiments there was a last minute shuffling, as squadrons that had suffered losses in the night drive were replaced in the battle-line by those at full strength. The vehicles' wheeling and revving-up flung clouds of dust into the air, which shrouded the whole brigade. Then the movement ceased.

The dust settled, and in the dying minutes of a fine, starry night the black shapes of other tanks in the line became visible. Ahead of the regiments, on the far side of the Rahman track, there were fires to be seen in the German area, the product of hours of bombing by the Royal Air Force. Behind the regiments there were also fires on the British side of the battlefield, where in the minefield gaps soft-skin vehicles, carriers and some tanks hit by the German counter-bombardment were still burning. Across the dark night, anti-tank shells suspired, then shells flashing like shooting stars, and the air was filled with the rumble of tank engines and the smell of exhaust fumes and explosions.

Punctually, at 06.15 hours, the guns opened up the bombardment under which the 9th would go in. 'Driver — advance!' And with pennants flying the lines moved forward at controlled speed, keeping close to the curtain of shells, 'leaning on the barrage', each tank commander standing upright in his turret, his eyes searching intently the dark desert surface for enemy mines and guns. The charge was on, and yet the greatest number of those who crewed the Shermans, the Grants and the Crusader tanks that rumbled across the desert towards the Rahman track saw nothing of the battle that followed. At best, they followed the progress of their own tank's battle through the intercom and the wireless, absorbing the instructions, orders and commands that crackled through the earphones. Drivers, half blinded by the dark and the dust, were only dimly aware of the clustered hand-fuls of the bewildered enemy who stood at the side of the tracks, dazed by the fury of the barrage. How many of those submissive groups were machine-gunned in error or run down by accident? Then again, how many of those who had seemed to be surrendering had rushed back to man their guns once the first wave of tanks had passed them to take under fire the next squadrons that roared towards them?

The night was now nearly gone, and silhouetted against the paling eastern sky the British regiments thundered towards the Rahman track. Enemy gunners whose pits had not yet been affected by the British barrage manned their pieces, and then, in concert with other artillerymen who had survived the bombardment, they began to fire upon the squadrons as they made their deliberate way westwards.

There then ensued a Calvary for the 9th Armoured Brigade, of whose agony it is not possible to give a detailed or precise account. 'There could be no concerted nor planned action. Each tank fought for itself, and every duel that was fought out between the German gunners and our armour could only end with the death of one of the duellists. Then the victor had to go on and fight a fresh duel with a new opponent.

'As you know, we should have attacked in the darkness; instead we went in at dawn. That half-hour's delay cost us dear. We were like so many targets in a shooting gallery. At one time during the attack, the dawn wind came up and blew the sand away. It seemed to me that there was a half-circle of guns firing at us, and not just a single line of guns, but row after row of them. And they all seemed to be firing at once. There were white streaks, red flashes, green lights and all the time violet coloured flares, their Verey lights, exploding in the sky.

'I do not consciously remember seeing the desert covered with shell holes, although when I was knocked out and waited to get away across the desert I could see that the whole surface looked like a rather dirty bank holiday beach. There were craters everywhere.

'There was for me no excitement in the charge. I'd seen it all before, and after a certain time you look round the faces of your mates and you realize with a shock how few of the original mob are left. Then you know its only a matter of time before you get yours. All I wanted to do was to get across that bloody ground and through the guns. As I passed one position — the gunners were prostrate, I think with fear — I saw that the gun couldn't be swung around very easily. They were only good for "action front" — well they had a little bit of a traverse, about 15 degrees either side of a zero line, I should think. So once we were past them they couldn't really shoot us up the arse. They were banking on their forward firing to get us all.

'We bucketed up and down. It was a really rough ride, and once we nearly "bellied" in a position. That was really frightening. We just lay there at an angle and we were all shouting at the driver as if he'd done it on purpose. We were hit about four times, but nothing penetrated and we finally got under way again. I really felt sorry for the ammo truck drivers and those driving the petrol lorries. They had to come through the same shit as we did, but they did it in unarmoured vehicles and their cargo was dead lethal. One hit and it was curtains.

'Just to the right of my machine, diagonally that is, there must have been an 88 or something very heavy. Bang, bang, bang, just like that — and a whole troop went up in flames. In fact, the whole ground ahead of us was full of burning tanks and we knew that we were next.

'I could see one cruiser tank fire at a Jerry gun without effect, and I could well imagine the commander's fury, having such a stupid weapon — for he just swung the tank around and ran over the pit. The gun stuck almost straight up into the air. The tank was out, and so too must have been both crews. I didn't see anybody get out. Even in daylight you couldn't see the guns until they fired, and then if they missed you had to get them with your first shot or you were dead. There was no mercy shown to crews — tank crews or gun crews. We shot them up as they ran — they did the same to us when we baled out. It wasn't such a gentleman's war as a lot of people like to make out it was.

'Oddly enough, there were patches of calm in all that frightening fury, and there were jeeps racing about, organizing something or the other, I suppose. The infantry didn't like us. First of all we attracted shell fire, and any "overs" usually pitched onto them. I felt sorry for them just sitting there in all that shelling without being able to hit back — it couldn't have been nice.

'There was a line of telegraph poles, which I took to be the Rahman track, but this was some sort of branch line, and the remnants of our squadrons reformed along them, and then we rushed up towards Aqaqir Ridge and straight into one of the panzer divisions that Rommel had put in to drive us back. There was a big bang and then I was outside the tank, dazed but not hurt, smoking a cigarette and watching our tanks going up like torches. I seemed detached from it all — it was probably a slight concussion.'

Fighting its way forward, the brigade overran some enemy positions, firing at point-blank range at others. Tanks were hit and their crews were shot at by desperate defenders as they scrambled out of the blazing tanks. There could be in that bewildering confusion little quarter given. The intention of the battle was simple: the British had to reach Aqaqir Ridge, and the gunners of the Panzerarmee had to stop them. In pursuit of those orders both sides fought and died.

For the 9th Armoured Brigade, now diminished in number, there then entered a new factor into the battle. Advised by its forward units of the British assault, the Panzerarmee commander ordered forward and into the attack the 15th and 21st Panzer Divisions. The counterattack was led by General von Vaerst, and the intention was to sweep back the British tank thrusts. Soon the panzers had come in, firing from both flanks and threatening to pinch out the salient that the 9th Armoured Brigade had created. The regiments were still holding the door open for the 1st Armoured Division, but in the early morning light no columns of British armour could be seen coming from the east.

Looking eastwards from the back of his shattered tank, an NCO of the 3rd Hussars recalled that so far as he could see the ground from the brigade start line to the Rahman track was a total graveyard of tanks and guns. Gun barrels were stuck in the air from positions across which Shermans and Grants had rolled. Tanks were dipped by the bows into some gun positions and were burning where they had been hit as sitting ducks by other anti-tank guns. At some places, two or three tanks together were on fire, evidence of a well-defended series of gun positions, and everywhere there were the dead. Straggling across the desert were short lines of prisoners or tank crews, walking wounded and infantry runners. Across the surface of the desert, tracer flickered, seemingly only a foot or two above ground level, and already in the air the flights of Bostons flew majestically westwards, en route to some new bombing raid. 'Looking at the faces of the men around me I wondered if we would ever be clean again. Each of them had a grey face from the sand and dust being flung up, and the gunner's face was blackened with cordite. Our hands were filthy with oil, grease and the dirt that somehow seems to be associated in my mind with fighting. Christ, it was a miserable sight. Wherever I looked all I could see were those tall black clouds of smoke from our tanks.'

And to add to the anti-tank guns that continued to fire with effect upon the small number of British tanks that had survived from the charge, there were the German panzer battalions moving forward at their usual slow pace under shelter of a barrage of 88 shells. Against the heavily-armed Panzer IIIs and IVs some of the British tanks could pitch only the useless 2pdr. Undaunted by the experience they had gone through and that which they still had to suffer, the survivors of the British armoured regiments turned to face the oncoming panzers. How long would they still have to hold open the door? That there were still some tanks of the brigade in action shows that the army commander's sombre evaluation of a 100 percent casualty rate had not been realized. But he was not far wrong. Of the 94 tanks that went into the battle, 75 had been knocked out. Casualties among the crews were more than 50 percent, with 203 being killed, wounded or missing out of the 400 men who had gone into action that morning. The handful of tanks still remaining waited anxiously for the 1st Armoured Division to arrive.

16.

THE BATTLE OF AQAQIR RIDGE

The 1st Armoured Division had come late to battle. The reasons were many, but the chief one was, perhaps, that at senior level it had not been appreciated how slow was the passage of a single vehicle through the narrow minefield lanes when the drivers were as good as blinded by dust that was now inches deep on the surface of the tracks. Multiply that delay by a thousand. . . .

The diaries and accounts by the tank regiments that made up the 1st Armoured Division all deal with the difficulties of that approach march. It was unusual, and it was therefore worthy of very special mention. The battle that followed was the usual routine of a tank man's life, and the events that occurred during it are less lengthily dealt with. Several accounts detail the difficulty of driving out of a minefield gap that the enemy had blanketed with smoke and into which he was pouring shells from 88mm guns firing on fixed lines. For the rest, however, the diary entries are a sober story of losses and successes, reported without drama.

The battles that ensued on 2 November and were carried on during the 3rd have passed into British military history as the Battle of Tel el Aqaqir. The two brigades at that time under the command of the 1st Armoured Division were sent out: the 2nd Armoured Brigade to hold an area two miles north-west of Tel el Aqaqir, and the 8th Armoured Brigade (transferred from the 10th Armoured Division) to occupy the Tel itself, which rises as a small peak a little above the level of the ridge. The surviving tanks of the 9th Armoured Brigade were posted to the northern flank. The walls of the salient that Eighth Army had forced were lined on its northern side by the battalions of the Durham Brigade and in the south by the Highland Brigade. The western wall was made up of the armour. It was against that salient that Rommel ordered his panzer forces to attack. That phase of the battle had come for which Montgomery had planned: the British tank force would meet that of the enemy and would destroy it. Of course, the British should have been in possession of Aqaqir Ridge and X Corps should have been on the 'Skinflint' bound . . . but the most important factor was that the Axis forces were concentrated and were coming to battle.

It was important now that the British armour should not be let loose to engage in any type of unchecked 'cavalry' charge. The panzers must be allowed to waste themselves in attacks. This they did, and soon. The whole of the British salient was then swept by a hurricane of fire under whose fury the British infantry crouched in their shallow slit trenches and cursed the tank squadrons for bringing down a 'stonk' on them. 'We were up the sharp end with a vengeance. I'd never seen any shelling like that before. We had hardly got into position when tanks began passing through us. The shell fire was the worst I'd seen, and every time it died down the tanks would roll forward again to our slit trench line and fire their guns. Then they would pull back and Jerry would send some stuff back, all of which fell in our area. The battalion's anti-tank guns had it very bad. For a very long time they were out in the open and unprotected. Then we were told off to capture the ridge. After laying out in that shell fire all day long, now we had to throw Jerry off the ridge.'

Montgomery had appreciated that the crisis of the battle had come. In preparing for the stage that would follow upon the destruction of the Axis armour, he had no doubt as to the outcome of the battle. 'Ultra' decrypts told him that, if nothing else. To Eighth Army's superiority in armour and guns he could add command of the air over the battlefield, which allowed his bomber squadrons to smash enemy concentrations, his torpedo-carrying planes to attack the ships that tried to run the blockade, and his fighter aircraft to drive from the skies the attempts by Stuka bombers to support the counterattacks by the panzer divisions. Montgomery carried out a reorganization of the attacking forces. He ordered the formation of an infantry 'fist' by assembling the Durham Brigade, a brigade of Highland battalions and the 5th Indian Infantry Brigade. The attacks those units were to undertake would be launched south-westwards from the salient, to bypass the gun lines in front of Aqaqir Ridge and to pass the armour through the funnel and round the Axis flank. For the pursuit stage, he brought the 7th Armoured Division forward and placed it under the command of X Corps and strengthened the 7th Armoured with the Queen's Brigade from the 44th Division; a brigade of New Zealand infantry was made ready and converted into a lorried unit ready to exploit the breach; and finally a force of armoured cars was ordered to infiltrate the enemy line and to create confusion in his rear areas. But certain prerequisites to the next stage of operations needed first to be obtained. To strengthen the southern sector near the south-western break-out point, the Eighth Army commander moved the 8th Armoured Brigade from its position on the north of the salient and ordered it to face west and south. The walls of the salient would have to hold so that he could bring the killing force forward to launch it in the break-through attacks. To initiate these required that two tactical features be seized. These were the 'Snipe' position and a ring contour, 'Skinflint'.

The infantry operations were launched, and they succeeded. The 2nd Battalion of the Seaforth Highlanders advanced under a barrage fired by eight regiments of artillery and captured 'Skinflint', while to the east of that feature the Sussex Brigade took 'Snipe'.

The War Diary of the 15th Panzer Division recorded that all the German attacks during 2 November had broken against the solid wall of British tanks, and it went on to forecast that there was no way in which the British could be prevented from breaking through. At a higher level, the Afrika Korps Diary reported that only 35 tanks were still operational, that British armoured cars had broken through in the area to the south of Tel el Aqaqir and that the main battle-line had been gapped at several places. The Panzerarmee ordered the Ariete Armoured Division to take up position at Aqaqir Ridge behind the thinnest part of the Axis line. Rommel, surveying the situation, realized that the battle was lost, and gave orders for a slow withdrawal, by bounds, to a new line farther to the west. The disengagement from Eighth Army would begin on 3 November, and he advised OKW and his other superiors of his intentions. Two small pieces of intelligence lightened the picture for his opponent, Montgomery. Reports from XIII Corps in the south and from the Australians in the north of XXX Corps line reported that the enemy was thinning out his front — such moves were the prelude to withdrawal. The Eighth Army commander issued orders that units from his infantry reserve were to strike southwestwards to outflank the German line. Through the gap that those assaults would make, the British armour would pour; a gap that already existed in part and through which armoured car patrols of Eighth Army were already filtering to create confusion in the rear of Panzerarmee.

The three-stage operation ordered by Montgomery was placed under the control of 51st Highland Division, and it was stressed that speed of execution was all important. The armour must be in the open before the enemy, now committed to the north, could be switched southwards again. For the attacks, the equivalent of two infantry brigades were to be employed; three battalions from the Highland Division, who would form the right of the attack, and 5th Brigade of 4th Indian Division whose units would constitute the left flank.

Looking at the short battle line from right to left, the assaulting units would be 7th Argyll and Sutherland Highlanders: the task of that battalion was to attack and seize Point 44, the Tel el Aqaqir, the highest point of the ridge. The Argyll assault would go in at 05.15 hours on the 4 November. On the left of the Argylls, the 5/7th Battalion, Gordon Highlanders were to advance and, together with the 8th RTR, cut and hold an area of the Sidi Abd el Rahman track, approximately two miles to the south of the Argylls. The 2nd Seaforth Highlanders would be in reserve to the other two battalions. The 5/7th Gordon attack would be the first of the three 'unlocking' assaults and would go in during the late afternoon of 3 November. Battalions of 5th Indian Brigade, 1/4th Essex, 4/6th Rajputana Rifles and 1/10th Baluch, together with 50th RTR, were to make the second of the three assaults and would attack at 01.30 hours on 4 November. Their objective was a stretch of the Rahman track two miles to the south of the sector that the 5/7th Gordons would have captured. The attack by the 7th Argyll and Sutherland Highlanders, to which mention has already been made, would set the seal on the whole operation. The battalions would be moving on a general west-southwest/southwest line from positions that had been reached during Operation 'Supercharge'. The narrow area of front that marked the assault area was bounded in the north by the Tel el Aqaqir and in the south by Kidney Ridge. The battalions would, therefore, be moving into and across 'Skinflint', the original final objective.

At the western end of the salient, the moves were being undertaken that would launch Eighth Army westwards, but at the eastern end of the bulge there was, at last light on 2 November, confusion and chaos. The salient was crammed with vehicles. The area of ground between the minefield exits and the British front-line was filled to capacity with all sorts of units. In the confines of the minefields, whole formations were forced to wait, unable to move either forward or back; nor were they able to deploy into the unswept areas. There they were forced to wait, subjected to shelling and occasional air raids that somehow seemed, under such circumstances, to be more than usually frightening. The length and width of the salient was littered with the debris of battle, with the vehicles of the fighting echelons and with the infantry battalions. There was no room for anyone else. The only way in which the army could gain such room was by ensuring that during 3 November it had crossed the Rahman track and had taken Aqaqir Ridge. The plan produced by X Corps commander was for his infantry to capture the ridge so that through the gap that had thus been created he could pass the tanks of the 1st Armoured Division westwards. They would halt at a point about four miles east of Aqaqir. Then, through the funnel that they had created, he would pass the 7th Armoured Division, whose units would wheel north-westwards towards the coast. The whole outcome of the operation depended upon the 1st Division's motorized brigade, who must hold the ridge while the panzers were destroyed by the Eighth Army armour.

The rifle battalions of that brigade went into an attack over unreconnoitred ground and literally at a few hours notice. They had lain under bombardment all day, and were beginning to feel the strain of the eleven-day long battle. The attack, launched at 01.15 hours on 3 November was a failure: the advance by two battalions on the right was broken by German artillery fire and by infantry resistance. The shattered battalions were pulled back. On the left, however, the 60th Rifles had gained what it believed to be its objective, had dug-in and was quickly supported by tanks of the 10th Hussars. It was a start.

3 November was a day of complete frustration for Eighth Army. Despite fresh efforts, the 1st Armoured Division could not break across the low ridge. In the south, two German anti-tank battalions, ordered forward to close a gap and to intercept the infiltrating British armoured cars, were suddenly presented with the 8th Armoured

Brigade advancing and unaware of the presence of the German gun line. Meanwhile, behind the ridge, the Ariete Division had come forward and was playing its part in stiffening the Axis line. Behind that screen, however, the first evacuations were taking place, as Italian and German rear echelon personnel were taken back. The combat troops would hood to the last, although German war diaries echo Rommel's orders that no German fighting soldier would be left behind. The first stop in the westward movement would be Fuka, where the narrow pass dominated the coastal road. It was a good defensive position.

Then, at 15.30 hours in the afternoon of 3 November, the worried commander of Panzerarmee was thrown into complete despair. He received telegrams from his superiors at OKW and in Rome. In reply to his report that he intended withdrawing to new positions, there came peremptory orders from both Hitler and Mussolini to hold his ground. Rommel was in a quandary. To obey such senseless orders would result, as surely as night follows day, in the total destruction of his army. But to disobey was unthinkable. Following discussions with von Thoma, the commander of the Afrika Korps, Rommel compromised and ordered a reorganization of his forces, withdrawing some of them slightly westwards. Once that rearward movement had been completed, then the Ariete was to take post on the right flank of the 15th Panzer Division, and the mass of the Italian XX Corps was to conform to that movement.

While on the German side political bullying was placing in jeopardy the lives of German and Italian soldiers, a tragedy marred the afternoon for the British. The attack by the 5/7th Gordon Highlanders failed — not through any fault of the infantry or the armour that supported it, but because of faulty intelligence. The day had not begun well for the Gordons. It had been attacked by dive-bombers and by fighter aircraft during the morning. At 15.00 hours the companies began a three-mile approach march across unswept minefields, and arrived at the forming-up point to find that the tanks with which they should have been co-operating had not yet arrived. Then came information from brigade headquarters. According to reports from the 1st Armoured Division, the enemy was withdrawing. An artillery barrage or air support would, therefore, not be required by the Gordons. Smoke would be laid to identify the target. To the brigade HQ suggestion that some infantry should ride on the outside of the tanks, the commanding officer of the 8th RTR made the strongest objections, but he was over-ruled and three platoons of Seaforths were carried on the armoured fighting vehicles. In fact, the enemy was not withdrawing in that particular sector, but had in position a gun line of 88s attached to 15th Panzer Division. The tanks of the 8th RTR ran into a well-laid trap. Six vehicles were destroyed within minutes and eleven were badly damaged. The Highlanders on the outside of the tanks, exposed to the shellfire, suffered heavily. In one company, all the officers were killed or wounded. The attack was halted and the Gordon survivors dug-in along the Rahman track. It was a bitter afternoon.

The second of the two attacks was that of 5th Indian Brigade and this too opened in confusion, but unlike that of the Gordons, the Indian assault ended in success. The battalions were in position on the Miteiriya Ridge and for them to reach the new attack area they would have to cross the width of the battlefield forcing their way across the east-west flow of the army. It was at 10.30 hours in the morning of 3 November that orders were received that 5th Brigade was to move down into the area of the Highland Division. Two hours later the officers of brigade HQ together with the colonels of the battalions had arrived at TAC HQ of 51st Division and less than ninety minutes later they had been put in the picture and were out on a reconnaissance of the ground over which they would have to advance. The attack would be made on a very narrow front, but, before the battalions could under-take the advance, fresh gaps would need to be made in the minefields to the southwest of the Tel el Aqaqir.

To bring the units forward would require the most rapid organiza-tion, for the attack was to go in at 01.30 hours on 4 November. At 14.30 hours the officers of 5th Brigade were still out on recce inspecting the ground of the advance. Within ten minutes of their return, the two Indian battalions were ready to undertake the 12-mile approach march over unreconnoitred routes to a debussing area. From that point they would have a 5-mile foot march to the form-up line. The brigade officers and the colonels were making their final plans in the sector held by 2nd Seaforth Highlanders before 16.00 hours, and had soon coordinated plans concerning minefields; liaison had been carried out with neighbouring and supporting formations, the form-up line was being taped and all made ready to receive the battalions that began to move at the time. These moves began in an atmosphere of foreboding, for the leading companies were attacked by Stukas as they set out on their south-westerly drive from Miteiriya Ridge.

Two and a half hours later, the teams went out that were to light the road forward. A simple V was chosen as the symbol that would glow gently through the darkness and light the way forward for the vehicle drivers. By nightfall the columns were moving along the 'Sun', 'Moon', and 'Star' tracks, each now a foot or more deep in gritty dust. The thickness of the dust and the dense curtain that it flung up had the same effect upon the Indian battalions as it had had on the remainder of the army and, soon after the start of the drive, the transport of the Baluch battalion became bogged down. Stuck fast in the narrow mine-field lanes, the vehicles became targets for German artillery and for the Luftwaffe's Stukas. The Rajputana Rifles then took over as lead battalion, but such were the difficulties connected with the advance that it became apparent that the 5th Brigade would not be able to begin its attack as planned, at 01.30 hours. At 00.55 hours, with only half an hour to spare, urgent orders went out to the artillery to hold the barrage for an hour. The Rajputs joined the Essex battalion, which had arrived at the form-up line at midnight. Both units were quickly briefed and moved forward to their start lines.

Their task was to advance to a depth of over four miles. The barrage that led them in was a finely tuned instrument, the result of long days and nights of Gunner endeavour. There was no hesitation nor confusion. The infantry went in from the form-up line at 02.30 hours. Despite the poor visibility, which reduced to 10 yards in places, and the difficulties of the foot march, the attacking battalions gave an exemplary demonstration of an infantry night attack, as they moved up to, into and across the enemy's territory taking out anti-tank guns, mortar pits and strong points in their opposed but unstoppable advance. They consolidated on the objective and, still protected by the artillery's concentration of fire, waited until they could hear coming out of the east and clearly audible above the sound of the barrage, the noise of tank tracks. In broad daylight, across the thin lines of infantry slit trenches, the armour of 22nd Armoured Brigade swung into the gap that the infantry had created, accompanied by a South African armoured car battalion.

Robert Kelly of the Essex saw part of the armoured force go through. It was then about 09.00 hours and a bright sunny day. 'They flew pennants. I did not know that these little flags had any meaning. I thought they were typical of the bullshit bravado of tank mobs.' These pennants and guidons did have a significance, for they served to distinguish friend from foe, indicated the seniority of the officer in the vehicle and, of course, could be used to pass visual orders or information. The position, colour and meaning of the pennants was detailed, usually on a daily basis, by a senior formation. Identity or seniority was established chiefly from the way in which the pennants were flown. In the unusual visual conditions of the desert colour, identification was not easy. Nevertheless, colour coding was widely used within armoured formations. Red was normally the colour of the commander, with yellow, blue, green and white being the colours of the successive stages down to the junior unit. This hierarchical system applied between division and brigade, brigade and regiment and regiment and squadron. Flags could be shaped as pennants, could be swallow-tailed or square. On the field of the latter, a number might be found: that of the unit or even its tactical sign. These formation flags, flown with such signal flags as 'Rally', 'Disperse' or 'I am out of action', clearly informed nearby troops of the state of play or who was in the area. Montgomery's own armoured fighting vehicle, a Grant, flew the standard red pennants for commander and, on a smaller staff at the rear of the turret, the square flag striped, horizontally, red, black and red, which indicated the GOC.

While Kelly was watching the 7th Armoured Division pour into open desert, the last of the three infantry attacks, that of 7th Argyll and Sutherland Highlanders had gone in. The battalion assault was covered by the fire of seven artillery regiments whose guns were concentrated so that the barrage fell on the 600yd-wide area which was the battalion's frontage. A line of telegraph poles could be seen from the slit trenches that marked the battalion's forward positions. These were an illusion. Not an optical one, for they were certainly tangible, but several units, on seeing them had thought, in error, that they followed the Trigh Sidi Abd el Rahman. The Argylls would advance across the desert and pass through the column of poles, behind which lay the Rahman track. On its western side the ground rose slightly to form the Aqaqir Ridge, at whose southern end lay the Tel, the objective of 7th Argylls. The barrage would open at 05.15 hours on 4 November and would fall for an hour on the line of telegraph poles. Precisely at 06.15 hours the bombardment would lift to form a zone around, upon and beyond the final objective. There would be no tank support.

Reveille was early on 4 November, and in the pitch darkness the companies moved forward to the form-up line. Dawn was breaking as they reached the area, only to find that they were wrongly positioned. They were also late, for the barrage was already firing. Without delay the companies led off, changing the direction of their advance from northwest to west-northwest to compensate for the errors at the start line. The advance went well. Under cover of smoke the telegraph pole line was crossed on schedule, but then it was feared that cohesion would be lost as platoons and companies vanished into the thickening white clouds. Fortunately, the danger did not develop and, when the leading company reached the objective, they found that the German grenadiers had pulled back. Sniper fire and sporadic shelling had been the only opposition, but even this barely contested attack had cost the battalion 8 dead and 23 wounded — victims of their side's shell fire.

The area of the objective had been a German headquarters that in its haste to depart had not had time to evacuate stores of drink, which the Highlanders immediately began to consume. There had been time — so it was believed — for the thorough German pioneers to rig up the usual booby traps. Urgent signals from Royal Engineer units to the forward troops warned them not to tamper with any strings seen in the area, which it was thought would be attached to mines. Such advice was answered by one Argyll with the remark that he already had his equipment and mess tins hanging from strings in his dug-out, which he thought had been generously left behind by the previous tenants.

The Argylls stayed in the area but orders were passed to other units to be ready to carry out the pursuit stage of Montgomery's plan. Suddenly, after all the days and nights of hopeless struggle and little movement, it seemed at last as if Panzerarmee had had enough. A spirit of confidence suddenly swept through Eighth Army. Through the gap that had been created the first British armour had begun to seep; soon it would pour, and later it would flood across the open and unmined desert. On that day it was less the opposition of the enemy that retarded the British deployment than the congestion of thousands of men and trucks still thronging the rear areas or confined within the minefield gaps.

Frederick Jackson, formerly of the 7th Motorized Brigade, on the miserable elevation that was the Tel el Aqaqir, looked from a slit trench on the western side of the ridge and marvelled. 'The tanks — there seemed to be thousands of them — looked like a whole fleet of little boats on the sea. Miles away, to the left of me, there was a great dark cloud where there was a great "stonk" going on. There were little shining specks dodging about. I could see flashes where there were guns firing.' Jackson was watching the opening stages of the armoured clash as the leading elements of the 7th Armoured Division charged into action against the Italian XX Corps. Beneath the huge dust cloud, thickened and darkened by smoke from burning tanks, bombarded by the furious artillery and fired at by the Sherman tanks, the under-gunned and under-armoured tanks of the Ariete Division were being torn apart. The slaughter of the Ariete was in train.

'Half left of me', Jackson recalled, 'was another group of our tanks. They passed below me and to my right, and kept getting lost to sight as the lines of them crossed over low hills and then passed into dead ground.' It was the armoured regiments of the 1st Division moving forward.

Montgomery, in his command caravan, had been well aware of the course of the battle. All the enemy's messages — Rommel's sitrep to the OKW, Hitler's reply and Panzerarmee commander's restatement of the serious situation in which his forces were placed, all had been intercepted, decoded and laid out for Montgomery to read. The British wireless intercept service had also laid on the Eighth Army commander's table the texts of conversations that had passed between the headquarters of Axis formations, so that he knew precisely the positions, intentions and moves of the German and Italian units facing him. With all this information to hand, Montgomery had appreciated that the time was ripe, and in the evening of 3 November issued the orders that, for him, closed the Battle of El Alamein. He knew his men. He knew that his armour, exhausted by constant combat though its men were, depleted by losses though its regiments were, nevertheless still had strength enough to go on and win. His orders loosed them.

The opening moves of this, the last stage of the battle, were those made by the regiments of the 1st Armoured Division. On the night of 3/4 November, its units lay laagered east of the Rahman track and somewhat south-east of Tel el Aqaqir. The order came for it to move out and, with the 2nd Armoured Brigade in the van, the division struck north-westwards towards Kharagh, the first bound in the advance upon the Afrika Korps base at El Daba. Contesting the division's advance with strong and well-placed panzer rearguards were the few remaining tanks of the 21st Panzer Division, the survivors of the great tank struggles of 2 and 3 November.

While the 1st Armoured Division was struggling forward in the face of small but fierce defensive actions, the 7th Armoured Division had passed along the left flank of 1st Armoured and had struck out on its own drive. On the left flank of the 'Desert Rats' was the New Zealand lorry-borne brigade, which began a long drive westward with their open flank guarded by a South African armoured car unit. Montgomery's strategy was a 'left hook' — not with a clenched fist to punch the enemy, but with open fingers with which to grasp him. While the 1st Armoured Division aimed at El Daba, the 10th was set towards Galal, where it would form a barrier across the coast road, and the 7th Armoured Division and the New Zealand Brigade were to head westwards, after which they would come up out of the desert behind the escarpment at Fuka. It had been planned that the whole attacking force of three armoured and two infantry divisions would begin to move shortly after first light, but there were too many units and too many men trying to struggle through the narrow minefield gaps. The first units, including the 22nd Armoured Brigade, were unobstructed and so moved off on time, roaring into the desert unsupported, relying upon themselves to bring the advance forward. But behind the fighting echelons delay piled upon delay. Armoured brigades were separated from parent divisions, and the confusion of congestion lasted for the greater part of the day. Fog over the battlefield also played its part in halting the deployment of the armoured armada, and units went either piecemeal into 'the blue' or waited for hours until their components had arrived and their strength had been concentrated. 'In the gaps there was terrible confusion, with every type of vehicle scrabbling for position. The whole carefully worked out traffic control broke down', Sergeant Meedham of the provost remembered. 'I have never seen such a hopeless mess. It was just as well that Stukas didn't come over. They would have had a field day.'

The trigh was more than a foot deep in dust. Every vehicle came enshrouded in a canopy of it. Everybody was caked in the stuff, with only eyes and lips prominent: eyes shone through the dust mask, and lips were unnaturally red, contrasting with the grey pallor of the face. The congestion of traffic in the minefields lasted all day, but enough British armour got through to carry out the Eighth Army commander's plan. The 7th Armoured Division encountered the Ariete Division, the principal unit of the Italian XX Corps and destroyed it; the shattered survivors pulled back, joining in the now general retreat of Panzerarmee from the battlefield.

Meanwhile, the dust cloud that Corporal Jackson had seen from his slit trench on Tel el Aqaqir, and which marked the crushing of XX Corps, had also been observed by von Thoma, the commander of the Afrika Korps. Alarmed by what he was seeing, and with an old soldier's instinct for battle situations, he guessed what was happening and advised Rommel. But the Supreme Commander would not accept that a crisis was developing on his right wing, although he did concede that British armoured cars — not tanks — might have broken through. So far as Rommel was aware, the Ariete was still in position, together with the bulk of XX Corps.

Von Thoma was deeply concerned about his Afrika Korps armour and, when he received a signal at 07.55 hours that about 150 British tanks were swinging north-west from Tel el Aqaqir, he immediately radioed that he would stay with the troops in the front-line and that he would be with the battle group. Later he was to signal that the tank attack had been halted at 09.45 hours, but because his messages were not all coming through his Chief of Staff went forward to Tel el Manpara. Here, the Korps commander was in his command tank at the junction of the 15th and 21st Panzer Divisions, but he was forward of the boundary between the two units and with his battle group almost surrounded by British tanks. The battle group was under heavy fire and the Korps commander could not be contacted. General Bayerlein (the Chief of Staff who witnessed the battle) wrote a dramatic account of a dust-covered battlefield and the tall, dignified figure of von Thoma standing alone by his burning panzer, upright in the shellfire. The story is taken up by Trooper Lindsay of the 10th (PWO) Hussars: 'I was a member of the IC (Internal Communications) section of the regiment. This was made up of seven Dingo scout cars under the command of Captain Grant Singer, and it was our task to carry our reconnaissance ahead of the regiment's tank squadrons.

'The Dingo was a low-profiled scout car — a standing man could look over the top of one. They were very fast, with a top speed of 70mph in forward gear and 60 in reverse. There was no fixed armament, but each of the two-man crew had personal arms, and each Dingo carried a Bren gun. My car commander was Captain Singer, the finest officer I ever served under. Early in the morning of the 4th, we were told to move forward of the regiment to act as OP and to observe the movements of a number of German tanks, which were known to be behind a crest some 800 yards to our front. The German vehicles were on the reverse slope, and every so often one or more of them would drive forward to a hull-down position and would fire off a few rounds. Captain Singer would then indicate these targets to the regiment, and our tanks would bombard the position. Our shooting was quite good because we could see black smoke rising from behind the ridge, evidence that some of the panzers were on fire.

'Heat haze in the desert, even in November, was enough to distort vision, and this is perhaps the reason why the captain and I did not see a large, immobile shape about 200 yards in front of us. For all I know it may have been camouflaged as well. Anyway, neither of us saw that it was a Panzer III until there was a sudden flash, followed immediately by a crashing explosion. A 50mm armour-piercing shell had torn through one side of our Dingo and had passed out through the other side. The solid shot had passed between Captain Singer's head and mine, without injuring either of us. I reversed the Dingo very quickly, swung her in a tight circle and then raced back to "B" Squadron headquarters tank. Captain Singer pointed out to the squadron commander where the panzer was positioned, and our tanks opened fire upon it. The enemy machine began to burn, and when the dust from the bombardment had cleared a hand could be seen waving a white cloth. A single figure appeared. The remainder of the crew must have been killed. "B" Squadron commander ordered the captain and me to go forward in our Dingo and to bring in the prisoner.

'We drove towards the upright figure, and I could see that he was holding his pistol upside down, that is by the barrel, and that he had a white handkerchief in his left hand. Before we got out of the Dingo the captain said to me, "Take your personal arms, just in case." We walked together towards the tall man who was standing between us and the burning German tank. I could see that there were rank badges on his lapels and on his shoulder straps. He had a very large pair of binoculars around his neck. The German walked forward, then stopped, saluted Captain Singer and handed over his pistol. Both officers then shook hands. Von Thoma introduced himself in English, took his field glasses from around his neck and hung them around mine. We then walked back to the Dingo. The general would not ride inside our vehicle nor on top of it. Finally, he sat on a small tool box, about 8 inches deep, which was fitted at the front of the Dingo. The general sat on that little ledge and we drove him back, firstly to squadron, then to regiment and farther and farther back until we reached the salt flats where Eighth Army TAC HQ was located. Ritter von Thoma dismounted from his narrow, metal seat, saluted Montgomery and then ducked under the fly sheet outside Monty's caravan. Captain Singer and I then returned to the battle.'

17.

VICTORY IN THE DESERT

Volume IV of the British official history of the Second World War in the Mediterranean and the Middle East states, 'The Battle of El Alamein may be said to have ended at dawn on 4th November, with the enemy breaking away and the British setting out to catch him.' Be that as it may, there was still a great deal of fighting to be undertaken. El Alamein was not an end but a beginning: it did not conclude the war in Africa, rather did it set in train the series of events that led to an Allied victory in that continent. For many in Eighth Army, the day was the usual slogging round. For others there was excitement at the prospect of the chase — joy in the knowledge that, after days of pounding, without seemingly any movement, Panzerarmee was at last pulling back. Who knew where its retreat would end? There were to be on that day of 4 November, as well as during succeeding days and weeks, land battles of startling ferocity. But never again, with the exception of a few local offensives in Tunisia, would the Axis forces regain the military initiative.

4 and 5 November are a jumble of impressions, a kaleidoscope of drama, humour, death and movement. The 'Jocks' of the Highland Division who found crates of champagne in some German stores thought little of this 'German whisky'. The ordinary soldiers of the British Army, not allowed anything stronger than beer, were astonished at the lavish supplies of alcohol available to the German troops. In many British units, however, the days after the break-through were ones of short commons and hard living. Battle supplies for the front were the important consideration, and convoys of lorries laden with petrol and ammunition were given priority passage through the bewildering congestion of vehicles that waited impatiently for their chance to move westwards. Unit ration or water trucks had a low priority, and there were inevitably shortages of many kinds among the fighting troops. Men who had lived on their nerves for weeks, who had managed to continue fighting without rest or sleep, did this on a diet of cigarettes and tea. Suddenly there were no more cigarettes coming up and very little water either. The enemy suffered no such restriction. It was clear that the Axis quartermasters had thrown open their stores for, as J. Carbines, formerly of the Queen's, recalled, 'We had no cigarettes and no water. The prisoners we took had cigarettes and vino.' German soldiers came in carrying a bewildering variety of food and drink — bread, Danish butter, fresh fruit, wine and cognac.

With or without adequate supplies there were still battles to be fought, and in one short, sharp action a number of Italian armoured fighting vehicles that had survived both 'Lightfoot' and 'Supercharge' were destroyed. The Italian column of armour was driving westwards in the afternoon of the 4th, unaware that the coast road on which it was travelling had been cut. British armoured regiments, which had crossed the desolate plain leading towards Galal station — a plain covered with burning tanks and guns — halted and faced east. When the Italian tanks appeared, a destructive fire was brought down upon them. The under-gunned and under-armoured machines were blown apart. More than twenty of the survivors of the Ariete and Littorio Divisions were 'killed' that hot afternoon near Galal station.

It was not everywhere an unqualified success story. Down in the south, the Ramcke paratroops, without transport, force-marched across the desert to the coast road, intercepted a British convoy and used the captured trucks to escape and rejoin the Panzerarmee. Ramcke's meeting with those who had abandoned his unit was said to have been stormy. His was not the only unit left to its own fate. The shortage of lorries and fuel in the Axis forces meant that there was inadequate transport to move all the men, machines and guns. Rommel had to make a decision: which units should be preserved to fight another day, and which left behind to face captivity? Inevitably, it was chiefly the Italian infantry formations that were left, as well as those German ones (like Ramcke) that had been considered to be too distant to be reached and saved.

The desert in the days after the Battle at El Alamein was filled with milling mobs of men waiting to surrender, and with columns tramping stolidly toward the tarmac road where British transport would convey them to camps along the Canal and the Great Bitter Lake. Such sights produced among the men of Eighth Army the belief that this was it. The battle had been fought and won, and some enthusiastic soldiers remembered that this day, 5 November, would have been filled with fireworks and noise had they been in 'Blighty', so they were determined to have their own Guy Fawkes Day by firing off German signal rockets in all directions. It was all over. At the very least, they would not be going back this time. It was goodbye to the Sweet Melody and the Pam Pam, goodby to the Birka and to Sister Street. Very few of the Eighth Army would ever seen Cairo or Alexandria again.

The rising confidence of the men on the ground and of their commanders infected the politicians at home, and this then spread to the people of the United Kingdom. Mrs. Lilian Bell thought back to the days when, as a young evacuee in the west of England, the news spread of the barrage, the battle and the victory. She recalled a line in a school play, 'The finest sight in all the world; the Union Jack flying over Benghazi.' El Alamein was a battle important enough to be remembered by a young girl. Nor is she alone; it was the opinion of many British civilians who lived through those days that the victory in the desert marked the turn of the tide. The church bells that had been silenced by the threat of invasion two dark years before, now rang out to proclaim the desert victory. Almost without exception those whose memories fill these pages consider, as do civilians like Mrs. Bell and her contemporaries, that Operations 'Lightfoot' and 'Supercharge' changed the course of the War. Until then, British victories had been short-lived: the Battle of El Alamein produced a victory from which there was no looking back.

There are those who will point out that from 1941 only the European Eastern Front had significance. The desert war, they will say, was an irrelevance. They can quote figures to show that all the forces that served in Libya and in Egypt did not amount in numbers to those of a single German army group fighting in Russia. Mere numbers are not significant. What was important was that an army, largely native British and Imperial, had taken on and defeated a German force. The Army had proved on land, as the RAF had proved in the skies of Britain in 1940, and as the Royal Navy had continually proved on the seas, that its units could take on and defeat the Germans, whose reputation as masters of the military art had for so long put their opponents in awe.

Then there are some who will claim that Panzerarmee was not beaten at El Alamein, but that it was merely pushed back by the British into the jaws of an Allied trap. Others will claim that it was a battle of attrition, and that the side that could continually pour new material into the fight must inevitably win. The ability to bring to a given point at a given time the superiority in numbers and material that will produce victory is nothing but concentration of effort, a sound military principle. In the global struggle that was the Second World War, the battlefield of El Alamein was the place at which the British Empire concentrated its effort — and won. That is the test of the battle — who won.

It is irrelevant whether Operation 'Lightfoot' was a slogging match fought by the British without finesse; nor is it of consequence whether it was a battle of attrition and that victory for Montgomery was guaranteed by the masses of material at his disposal. These things are irrelevant. It was a victory that was needed and it was victory that Eighth Army gained — the first *permanent* land victory in the desert. And it had been gained at the cost of acceptable casualties. British losses were about 2,400 killed, 9,000 wounded and about 3,000 missing, from the army whose strength was about 195,000 men.

El Alamein was the first of a chain of victories, and it was one that gave hope to the people of Britain. It was their victory and theirs alone. That is why it was important to the British people then and why the memory of it is still relished today. It is not mere sentimentality, but a realization that Operation 'Lightfoot' marked the end of Great Britain's independent military role. Since then, she has been a partner, an ally but never the senior partner, nor the principal ally. But then, at El Alamein, the might of the British Empire covered the desert. Two generations have been born since 1942, and the children of those generations can have no conception of the pride of Empire, which time has not diminished.

Across those four decades which separate us in time from the battle in the desert, the memory of 'the blue', the joy of the desert and the comradeship that was found there is still strong. As a result of Britain's closer links with Europe, that comradeship is no longer restricted to just the soldiers of the British Army, for the unorganized international freemasonry of fighting men maintains a comradeship that binds those who fought. Now many former enemy soldiers come as honoured guests to British reunions to tell what life was like on the other side of no man's land. Asked why former Afrika Korps soldiers were made so welcome at one regimental reunion, an old soldier retorted, 'Well, it wouldn't have been the same without them, would it?' I don't suppose it would.

Forty years ago the men whose story this is were young and, for the greater part, unworldly. The fortunes of war sent them to North Africa and cast them into an alien and hostile environment in which death or mutilation were frightening companions. How do they now view their part in the desert war? Nostalgia can soften or erase completely the most painful memories. But it cannot be the amnesia of nostalgia alone that is responsible for the theme of great contentment which runs through the accounts of many old soldiers. J. W. Harris, in the 7th Armoured Division's Engineers, recalls that despite a natural apprehension about the imminent battle he would, upon reflection, not have missed it for the world. This same feeling is shared by C. J. Adams of the 11th Hussars, who recalled that there were some good days, mostly the opposite, but that he was glad to have experienced them all. There is also the recurring theme of comradeship experienced to a degree in the desert that was never to be recaptured in Europe. R. Ager of the Royal Tank Regiment made that point, and this feeling was confirmed by Alexander McDonal, who described the feelings as humanity at its best and added, 'I miss and think of those days.'

There is, of course, the other side of the coin: the death of a family in the United Kingdom as a result of air raids, the loss of a beloved parent and an application for compassionate leave being turned down by the contemptuous refusal, 'mere senility does not constitute grounds for compassionate leave.' The applicant's mother was 49 years of age.

There were those who hated and feared the desert, the flies, the sand and the locals. One former soldier described Cairo as a paradise inhabited by the scum of the earth. The judgement was not unique, even though the choice of words was. The mystery of the desert places took a hold on many, and a number of former soldiers appreciated why the prophets of old went out into the empty wastes. 'There is a beauty in the desert', reflected W. Hall, formerly of the Royal Corps of Signals. 'In the quiet one could sit and look and be at peace with everything. I felt at home there.'

The last word on the desert campaigns — the suffering, the waste of men and material, the beauty and the misery, the euphoria and the depression, the whole tragedy which was enacted four decades ago — all that is encapsulated in the words of A. P. McLane who, having expressed the bitterness of his feelings, so far as he could recall them, finished with the quotation, 'But now I am proud to wear the Africa Star.' Long may he and his like enjoy that pride.

GLOSSARY

AFV: Armoured fighting vehicle
AP: Anti-personnel; armour-piercing
Bint: Girl or woman
Bivvy: Bivouac
Blighty: England; home
Bobby: British policeman
Brew-up: Make tea; catch fire
Bully: Corned beef
CB: Confined to barracks; counter-battery
CCS: Casualty clearing station
Char wallah: Person who gives tea to troops
CLY: County of London Yeomanry
Compo: Army box of hard rations
CRA: Commander Royal Artillery
CSM: Company Sergeant-Major
Desert rose: Lavatory; silicate rock eroded by wind and sand to form an attractive shape
DF: Defensive fire
EFI: see NAAFI/EFI
ENSA: Entertainments National Service Association
Dhoby: To wash
Digger: An Australian
Div: Division, divisional
EPI: Egyptian Pattern Mark I mine
FAP: Forward aid post
FDL: Forward defence line (or zone)
Fellahin: Arab peasants
Field traces: Tracings on semi-transparent paper to mark mine-fields or defensive positions
FOO: Forward Observation Officer
FUP: Form-up position
'going': The condition of a surface such as a road or field
GPO: General Post Office
Griff: Information (essentially Army term)
Groppi's: A café in Cairo; an elegant establishment, air-conditioned and spotlessly clean. It served chiefly pastries, strawberries and cream and marvellous ice cream. It was also a popular meeting place. Although other ranks were not forbidden, their presence was not encouraged
HE: High explosive
IC: Internal communications
Intelligence: The skill in collecting scraps of information about the enemy and his military plans and the fitting of these together to anticipate his future moves. At the highest level of command the British had 'Ultra' (which see), but at tactical level relied upon the Y Service of intercepted wireless messages. It must be understood that in the vast distances of the Western Desert the only means of communication was by wireless. The disadvantage of wireless was that the messages could be picked up by the enemy. The British Army relied to a very great extent upon Palestinian Jews as operators. These men were refugees from Hitler's Germany and were knowledgeable about the German Army and its slang. On the German side the most skilled unit of the German 'Y Dienst' was a Captain Seebohm, whose incredible speed in passing back information often gave the Germans a tactical advantage during the fighting. In order to deprive Rommel of his 'ears', Seebohm's unit was attacked and destroyed. It was located near the Tel el Eisa and a

commando operation was undertaken by men of the Australian
2/48th Battalion. Seebohm died of
wounds. Among the pieces of information gathered from this raid was
the realization that British wireless
procedures were sources of Intelligence information to the
Germans. These were tightened up
to such an extent that the
Germans were never able to build
up an accurate picture of British
intentions. Another piece of
information was that the Axis had
broken the American diplomatic
code and that all the messages
which the American military
attaché in Cairo had been passing
to Washington on British
strengths, plans and intentions
were known to the Germans and
Italians. Thus, while the British
had 'Ultra' the Axis had the 'Black
Code'. Aerial reconnaissance photographs were also a source of information and it was to deceive the
officers of the German aerial photo-
graphic interpretation units that
the Eighth Army launched its
great deception plan Operation
'Bertram'.
Jerry: A German
Jock: A Scot
KD: Khaki drill
Kip: Sleep
Kiwi: A native of New Zealand
Konner: Food
KRRC: King's Royal Rifle Corps
LOB: Left-out-of-battle
M & V: Meat and vegetable or
  Machonachies stew
Marsh: An area of 'boxes' linked by
  dense concentrations of mines
Milton; Antiseptic
MP: Military Police
NAAFI/EFI: Navy, Army and Air
  Force Institutes/Expeditionary
  Forces Institute, which provided
  canteens, shops, etc., for British
  military personnel
OKH: Oberkommando der Heeres
OP: Observation post

PAD: Passive air defence
PBI: Poor bloody infantry
Plebs: Plebians
Pox: Syphilis
Pukka gen: Reliable information
QM: Quartermaster
RAP: Regimental aid post
RASC: Royal Army Service Corps
RE: Royal Engineers
Recce: Reconnaissance
Redcap: A military policeman
RSM: Regimental Sergeant-Major
RTR: Royal Tank Regiment
RTUd: Returned to unit
Sally Army: Salvation Army
Sapper: A private of the Royal
  Engineers
Shufti: The Army version of the
  Arabic verb 'to look'. Arabic
  replaced Hindustani as the source
  of words with which British
  soldiers enriched their conversa-
  tions or with which they made
  contact with the native populations
  of the Middle East. Thus the
  Hindustani verb 'dekho', meaning
  'to look' and used by generations
  of soldiers, was replaced by the
  Arabic 'shufti'. I have removed all
  the Arabic words that were in
  common currency and that were
  included in letters or interviews,
  except for 'shufti' and 'bint', which
  are now almost accepted in
  vernacular English. Among the
  words which were in use in the
  post-War Army were the expres-
  sions for 'I don't care' ('ala keefik');
  'It doesn't matter' ('Malish') and
  'very good' ('kwois katcer').
SIB: Special Investigation Bureau
  (Army crime detection unit)
Sitrep: Situation report
SIW: Self-inflicted wound
SP: Self-propelled
(On) stag: On guard
Stonk: Bombard
Swaddies: Soldiers
TAC HQ: Tactical Headquarters
Tiffin: Cold lunch
Tommy gun: Thompson machine-
  gun

'Ultra': The abbreviation for 'Ultra Secret', the highest Intelligence designation. In the context of this book, 'Ultra' refers to the messages received from Bletchley Park Intelligence Centre, known as the Government Code and Cypher School. Before the outbreak of the Second World War, the Allied Intelligence organization had obtained a German cypher device known as 'Enigma', and by crypto-analysis had used it to read the messages which passed between German headquarters. Thus, when Montgomery was planning Operation 'Lightfoot', he was able to know the strength of his enemy and details such as the dates and routes on which the Axis convoys were sailing. To hide the existence of 'Ultra', British Intelligence let it be known that top secret informa-tion was coming to them from highly placed Italian sources. 'Ultra' was less useful once battle had been joined. Its greatest use was in the planning and prepara-tion stages of a battle. On the battlefield, wireless intercepts were the most fruitful source of informa-tion.

Wallah: A person

Wren Writer: The Women's Royal Naval Service was popularly known as the Wrens. They replaced men in a great number of duties, one of which was that of clerk. A writer could be any sort of clerk, thus a 'Wren writer' was a female clerk in the Royal Navy.

W/T: Wireless telegraphy

CHRONOLOGY

1939

3 September   Great Britain declares war on Germany.

1940

10 June   Italy declares war on the United Kingdom.

11 August   Italian troops attack in British Somaliland.

15 August   British troops begin to evacuate Somaliland.

19 August   The British evacuation of Somaliland is completed.

13 September   The Italian Army crosses the frontier with Egypt and occupies Sollum.

17 September   Sidi Barrani is captured by the Italians.

12 November   The German Supreme Command issues Instruction No. 18, requesting that a force be raised to support the Italians in North Africa for the purpose of an attack upon Egypt.

6 December   The British Western Desert Force moves out to open a counteroffensive against the Italians

9 December   The British offensive opens at 07.15 hours.

11 December   The British recapture Sidi Barrani.

17 December   The British counteroffensive recaptures Sollum.

23 December   A head-count of prisoners shows that 35,949 Italians have been taken since the opening of the British offensive.

1941

5 January   General Berganzoli surrenders the town of Bardia.

22 January   The Australian Division enters Tobruk.

29 January   British troops re-enter Somaliland.

30 January   Derna falls to the British.

4 February   British 7th Armoured Division leaves Mechili to cut off the retreating Italians beyond Benghazi.

25 February   Italian Somaliland is occupied by the British.

27 February   The first patrols of the German Afrika Korps clash with the British.

12 March   A parade in Tripoli of the newly arrived units of the Afrika Korps.

24 March   The Afrika Korps attacks and captures El Agheila.

31 March   The Germans strike at Mersah Brega.

3 April   Benghazi is captured by the Germans.

5 April   Addis Ababa, capital of Ethiopia, is captured from the Italians.

6 April   German forces invade Yugoslavia and Greece.

7 April   Derna falls to the Axis troops.

10 April   The British Army withdraws on Tobruk.

11 April	German panzer forces cut the Tobruk—El Adem road. Two thousand British soldiers are taken prisoner, including three generals.
13 April	Tobruk is encircled and Bardia captured.
14 April	The German attacks on Tobruk are repulsed.
27 April	Part of the Afrika Korps thrusts across the Libyan—Egyptian frontier and captures Halfaya Pass.
28 April	Sollum falls to German troops.
15 May	General Wavell opens Operation 'Brevity', a limited campaign to gain jumping-off positions for a future and larger offensive.
16 May	The Duke of Aosta's forces surrender in Ethiopia. Rommel throws in a counterattack against the British.
27 May	German panzer forces drive the British out of the Halfaya Pass
15 June	Wavell's major offensive, Operation 'Battleaxe', opens.
22 June	The German Army invades Russia.
1 July	Wavell is replaced by General Sir Claude Auchinleck.
17 November	British commandos, led by Lieutenant-Colonel Keyes, raid what is believed to be Rommel's headquarters.
18 November	A new British offensive, Operation 'Crusader', opens.
19 November	Sidi Rezegh is captured by the Eighth Army.
20 November	Fighting continues around Sidi Rezegh.
21 November	The British garrison of Tobruk makes a sortie to link up with the forces in the Sidi Rezegh area.
22 November	The 21st Panzer Division attacks the British armour.
23 November	The German armour, now massed, defeats the piecemeal British tank attacks. New Zealand troops occupy Bardia.
24 November	Rommel flings a column over the Egyptian frontier.
26 November	General Cunningham, commanding Eighth Army, is replaced by Ritchie. The British Tobruk force captures Duda and links up with the infantry force taking part in Operation 'Crusader'.
29 November	Von Ravenstein is taken prisoner.
30 November	During the day, severe German attacks are launched against the British corridor between Sidi Rezegh and Tobruk.
6 December	There is heavy fighting south of Sidi Rezegh, which lasts until 8 December.
13 December	Rommel's counterattack comes in and opens a five-day offensive battle.
17 December	The German effort fails and the German troops begin to withdraw from Gazala.
19 December	The Eighth Army recaptures Derna and Mechili.
23 December	Barce is recaptured by the British.
24 December	Benghazi falls to the Eighth Army.

1942

2 January	Bardia is recaptured.
5 January	The Eighth Army's attack opens on Halfaya Pass.
6 January	Rommel's offensive against Eighth Army opens from a jump-off point at Agedabia.
8 January	The Eighth Army drives back Rommel from Agedabia.

CHRONOLOGY

12 January	The British take Sollum.
17 January	The Eighth Army recaptures Halfaya Pass.
21 January	Rommel's offensive re-opens at El Agheila.
23 January	The Afrika Korps recaptures Agedabia.
4 February	The Axis troops retake Derna.
14 February	After a two-week pause, Rommel renews his offensive.
26 May	The third German offensive opens with an attack against the Gazala position.
2 June	The siege of Bir Hakim at the southern end of the Gazala position opens. Rommel begins to gap the British minefields. General Crüwell, commander of the Afrika Korps, is shot down and captured.
3 June	General Ritchie's counterattack fails. The British 150th Brigade is overrun.
10 June	The Free French holding Bir Hakim are ordered to withdraw.
12 June	The tank battle in the 'Knightsbridge' area opens.
13 June	The 'Knightsbridge' battle continues.
14 June	The Eighth Army begins a fighting withdrawal from Gazala.
16 June	The Axis troops attack at Sidi Rezegh.
17 June	The British Eighth Army withdraws to the Egyptian frontier.
18 June	The Afrika Korps opens its attacks upon Tobruk.
20 June	The German attack continues upon Tobruk.
21 June	Tobruk falls. Bardia is captured.
24 June	The Panzerarmee advances into Egypt.
25 June	Auchinleck takes command of Eighth Army.
27 June	The Germans battle for Mersah Matruh.
28 June	Mersah Matruh is captured.
1 July	The Panzerarmee reaches El Alamein.
2 July	The First Battle of El Alamein begins.
3 July	Rommel breaks off the battle.
4 July	The Eighth Army's counterattacks go in along the Ruweisat Ridge.
10 July	The Australians capture the Tel el Eisa from the Italians.
23 July	Mussolini visits North Africa.
26 July	The British attacks are held by the Germans and flung back.
18 August	General Alexander to take over as Commander-in-Chief, Middle East. General Montgomery takes up his post as commander of Eighth Army.
31 August	The Battle of Alam el Halfa opens.
3 September	The New Zealand Division mounts a drive in the Alam el Halfa sector to cut the German lines of communication.
7 September	The attack fails and Montgomery stops the battle: the Second Battle of El Alamein.
1 October	A limited offensive is opened by the British in the Deir el Munassib sector.
23 October	After an opening bombardment, the infantry corps of Eighth Army go into the attack. The armour of X Corps begins to move forward.
24 October	A reorganization and tidying up of the battle situation is put in hand in the area of XXX Corps. In XIII Corps sector

	the offensive makes little headway. The armour has still not gone forward.
25 October	Operations in the southern sector of the British line (XIII Corps) are halted. The Germans launch panzer counter-attacks. An attack by 10th Armoured Division to capture the Wishka Ridge fails. Field Marshal Rommel returns to Africa from sick leave.
26 October	Air operations against the Panzerarmee.
27 October	Torpedo-carrying aircraft from an RAF squadron attack and sink the tankers bringing fuel to the Panzerarmee. The British attack 'Snipe' position. Montgomery produces a new plan, Operation 'Supercharge'.
30 October	Australian attacks in the north of the line begin to 'crumble' the Germans.
2 November	The infantry go in for Operation 'Supercharge'.
3 November	The 9th Armoured Brigade carries out its sacrificial attack.
3 November	The Battle of Aqaqir Ridge. The 1st Armoured Division beats off the panzer counter-thrust. In reply to Rommel's telegram on the need to withdraw from the El Alamein positions, Hitler orders the Panzerarmee to stand fast and fight. Rommel cancels the orders to withdraw.
4 November	Rommel orders the withdrawal to take place, as it is clear that Eighth Army has outflanked him. General von Thoma, commanding Afrika Korps, is captured. The Panzerarmee begins to withdraw from the El Alamein battlefield.
8 November	Operation 'Torch' opens. Allied troops land in French North Africa.

1943

12 May	The last organized resistance by Axis troops on the continent of Africa ceases.

SELECT BIBLIOGRAPHY

Published works: British
Barnett, C. *The Desert Generals*. Kimber, London, 1960
Beddington, William R. *A History of the Queen's Bays (the 2nd Dragoon Guards), 1929–1945*. Warren, Winchester, 1954
Braddock, David W. *The Campaigns in Egypt and Libya, 1940–1942*. Gale and Polden, Aldershot, 1964
British Troops Egypt *Official Handbook for British Troops in Egypt, Cyprus, Palestine and the Sudan*. BTE, 1936
Clay, Ewart W. *The Path of the 50th: The Story of the 50th (Northumbrian) Division in the Second World War, 1939–1945*. Gale and Polden, Aldershot, 1950
Collier, R. *The War in the Desert*. Time-Life International, London, 1978
Connell, J. *Auchinleck: A Biography of Field Marshal Sir Claude Auchinleck*. Cassell, London, 1959
Crawford, R. *I Was An Eighth Army Soldier*. Gollancz, London, 1944
Crisp, R. *Brazen Chariots: An Account of Tank Warfare in the Western Desert, November–December 1941*. Muller, London, 1959
Duncan, William E. and others (eds.) *The Royal Artillery Commemoration Book, 1939–1945*. Bell, London, 1950
Eighth Army HQ. *Intelligence Summaries 344–417* (incomplete). Eighth Army, Cairo, 1942
Freyer, W. *The Military Water Problem in the Northern Egyptian Desert, 1940–1943*
Graham, A. *The Sharpshooters at War: The 3rd, 4th and the 3rd/4th County of London Yeomanry, 1939–1945*. Sharpshooters Regimental Association, London, 1964
Horrocks, Sir B. *A Full Life*. Collins, London, 1960
Jacob, A. *A Traveller's War: A Journey to the Wars in Africa, India and Russia*. Collins, London, 1944
Johnson, R. F. *Regimental Fire: The Honourable Artillery Company in World War Two, 1939–1945*. HAC, London, 1958
Liddell Hart, Sir B. (ed.) *The Tanks*. 2 vols. Cassell, London, 1959
Lucas, J. *Panzer Army Africa*. Macdonald and Janes, London, 1977
Macksey, K. *Rommel: Battles and Campaigns*. Arms and Armour Press, London, 1979
Majdalany, F. *The Battle of El Alamein*. Weidenfeld and Nicolson, London, 1965
Montgomery, Bernard L. *Alamein and the Desert War*. London, 1967
Moorehead, A. *The Desert War: The North African Campaign, 1940–1943*. Hamish Hamilton, London, 1965
Naval Intelligence, Directorate of *A Handbook of Libya*. Admiralty, London, 1937

Packenham Walsh, R. P. *History of the Corps of Royal Engineers.* vol 8: 1938—1948. Institution of Royal Engineers, Chatham, 1958
Phillips, Cecil E. L. *Alamein.* Heinemann, London, 1962
Playfair, I.S.O. and others. *History of the Second World War: The Mediterranean and the Middle East.* HMSO, London, 1954
Rainier, P. *Pipeline to Battle: An Engineer's Adventures with the Eighth Army.* Heinemann, London, 1944
Salmond, James B. *The History of 51st Highland Division, 1939—1945.* Blackwood, Edinburgh, 1953
Thomas, Evan W. *An Ambulance in Africa.* Appleton, New York, 1943
War Office. *Military Report on the North-Western Desert of Egypt.* War Office, London, 1937

Published works: Australian
Argent, Jack N. L. ('Silver John'). *Target Tank: The History of the 2/3rd Australian Anti-Tank Regiment, 9th Division, A.I.F.* Paramatta, Cumberland, 1957
Combe, Gilchrist and Ligerwood *2/48th Australian Infantry Battalion.* 2/48th AIF Club, Adelaide, 1972
Goodhart, D. *The History of the 2/7th Australian Field Regiment.* Rigby, Adelaide, 1952
Laffin, J. *Middle East Journey.* Angus and Robertson, Sydney, 1958
Masel, P. *The 2/28th: The Story of a Famous Battalion of the 9th Australian Division.* 2/28th Battalion and 24th Anti-Tank Comrades Association, Perth, 1961
Maughan, B. *Australians in the War: Tobruk and El Alamein.* Australian War Memorial, Canberra, 1966
Serle, R. P. (ed.) *2/24th Australian Infantry Battalion of the 9th Australian Division: A History.* Jacarawa, Brisbane, 1963

Published works: German
Büschleb, H. *Feldherren und Panzer im Wüstenkrieg: Die Herbstschlacht 'Crusader' im Vorfeld von Tobruk, 1941.* Die Wehrmacht im Kampf Series, Bd. XL. Kurt Vowinckel Verlag, Neckargemünd, 1972
Carell, D. *Die Wüstenfüchsee.* English-language edition: *The Foxes of the Desert*, Macdonald and Janes, London, 1960
Esebeck, Hans. Gert von. *Helden der Wüste.* Verlag der Heimbücherei, Berlin, 1943
Theil, E. *Rommels verheitzte Armee.* Fritz Molden, Vienna, 1979

Published works: Indian
Prasad, N. (ed.) *The Indian Armed Forces in the Second World War: The North African Campaign.* Longman, 1956
Stevens, Lieutenant-Colonel G. R. *Fourth Indian Division.* McLaren, Toronto, 1948

Published works: Italian
Faldella, E. *L'Italia e la Seconda Guerra Mondiale.* Edito Service, Geneva, 1970
Maravigna, R. *Come Abbiamo Perduto la Guerra in Africa.* Tosi, Rome, 1949
Ministero della Difesa *La Seconda Contraoffensiva Italo-tedesco in Africa settentrionale: Agedabia a El Alamein.* Ministero della Difesa, Rome, 1949

Published works: New Zealand
Burdon, Randal M. *24 Battalion.* Department of Internal Affairs, Wellington, 1953
Cody, Joseph F. *21 Battalion.* Department of Internal Affairs, Wellington, 1953
— *28th (Maori) Battalion.* Department of Internal Affairs, Wellington, 1956
Henderson, J. *22nd Battalion.* Department of Internal Affairs, Wellington, 1958
Kay, Robin L. *27th Machine-Gun Battalion.* Department of Internal Affairs, Wellington, 1958
New Zealand, Department of Internal Affairs. *Documents relating to New Zealand participation in the Second World War, 1939—45.* 3 vols. Wellington, 1949
— *New Zealand in the Second World War, 1939—45, episodes and studies.* 2 vols. Wellington, 1948—54
Norton, Frazer D. *26 Battalion.* Department of Internal Affairs, Wellington, 1952
Puttick, Sir E. *25th Battalion.* Department of Internal Affairs, Wellington, 1960
Ross, Angus. *23 Battalion.* Department of Internal Affairs, Wellington, 1959

Published works: South African
Bernstein, B. L. *The Tide Turned at El Alamein: Impressions of the Desert War with the South African Division and the Eighth Army, June 1941—January 1943.* Central News, Johannesburg, 1944
Martin, A. C. *The Durban Light Infantry.* Vol. 2: 1854—1960. HQ Board of the Regiment, Durban, 1969
Orpen, N. *Gunners of the Cape.* CFA Regimental Committee, Cape Town
Simpkins, A. *The Rand Light Infantry.* Howard Thomas, Cape Town, 1965

Other published sources:
Regimental magazines of the Regular Army units mentioned in the text

Unpublished sources: British
44th Division. 'Attack: The Fighting 44th' (manuscript)
War Diaries of the 50th Infantry Division, 51st (Highland) Division, 1st Armoured Division, and 10th Armoured Division
Personal diaries, accounts of battle, letters, interviews and correspondence with old soldiers

Unpublished sources: German
War Diaries of Deutsches Afrika Korps, Deutsch-Italienisch Panzerarmee, 15 Panzer Division, 21 Panzer Division, 90 (Leichte) Afrika Division and 164 (Leichte) Afrika Division

INDEX

1. INDEX OF MILITARY FORMATIONS AND UNITS

Allied Corps

X, 26, 108, 115, 138, 139, 144, 145, 147, 149, 196, 204, 213, 225, 226, 231, 245, 246, 248; planned role in 'Lightfoot', 122, 129; and 'deception' plan ('Bertram'), 125; order of battle for 'Lightfoot', 136—138

XIII, 109, 116, 139, 142, 164, 176, 179, 194, 196—201, 204, 206, 234, 247; planned role in 'Lightfoot', 122, 129; and 'deception' plan ('Bertram'), 124, 125; order of battle for 'Lightfoot', 133—136

XXX, 31, 136, 138, 139, 147, 158, 164, 176, 194, 196, 197, 201—206, 215, 216, 225, 227, 234, 247; re-inforcement of, 108—109; method of minefield gapping employed by, 115—116; planned role in 'Light-foot', 122, 129; and 'deception' plan ('Bertram'), 124; order of battle for 'Lightfoot', 130—133

Military Police, Corps of, 60, 142, 144

Pioneer Corps, 115, 145, 155, 228, 229, 230

Royal Army Medical Corps, 66

Royal Army Service Corps, 40, 55, 56, 145

Royal Corps of Signals, 66, 95, 105, 136

Royal Electrical and Mechanical Engineers, Corps of, 94

Royal Engineers, Corps of, 81; maps produced by, 14; minelaying activities of, 35; role and training of, 113—120 *passim*; activities in 'Lightfoot', 143—144, 157, 160, 185, 186, 194, 197, 199, 203. Units men-tioned: 2/7th Field Company, 157;

7th Field Squadron, 213; 21st Field Squadron, 143, 150, 198

Allied Divisions

1st Armoured, 26, 36, 37, 116, 158, 195, 196, 202, 204, 213, 214, 243, 244; proposed role in 'Lightfoot', 136; composition of, 137; ops on 24 Oct., 181—184; relieved by 10th Armoured Division, 223; role in 'Supercharge', 233, 235, 238, 239; reasons for late arrival, 245; on Aqaqir Ridge, 248, 249, 253, 254

7th Armoured, 24, 116, 129, 133, 136, 137, 196; at Alam el Halfa, 43, 44, 46; composition, 134; ops in 'Lightfoot', 198; is withdrawn, 201, 225; on Aqaqir Ridge, 246, 248, 251, 253, 254

8th Armoured, 126, 136

10th Armoured, 116, 135, 191, 214, 245; proposed role in 'Lightfoot', 136, 184; composition, 137; ops on 24 Oct., 184—187, 195, 196, 202, 203; withdrawn from line, 204; relieves 1st Armoured Division (27/28 Oct), 223; on Aqaqir Ridge, 254

44th Home Counties, 133, 134, 137, 144, 176, 193, 197, 198, 225, 246; at Alam el Halfa, 43, 135; misfortune of, 135; proposed role in 'Light-foot', 136

50th Tyne Tees, 23, 29, 32, 53, 103, 104, 133; tasks in 'Lightfoot', 134, 135, 201; in 'Supercharge', 225, 234

51st Highland, 30, 141, 145, 149, 150, 181, 189, 191, 194, 195, 213, 214, 215, 233, 234; task in 'Light-foot', 131; position before 'Light-

2. GENERAL INDEX